This Other Eden

This Other Eden

Seven Great Gardens
and Three Hundred Years
of English History

ANDREA WULF

and

EMMA GIEBEN-GAMAL

LITTLE BROWN

LITTLE, BROWN

First published in Great Britain in October 2005 by Little, Brown

A CIP catalogue record for this book
is available from the British Library.

ISBN 0 316 72580 3

Typeset in Fournier by
Palimpsest Book Production Limited
Polmont, Stirlingshire

Printed and bound in Italy

Little, Brown
An imprint of
Time Warner Book Group UK
Brettenham House
Lancaster Place
London WC2E 7EN

www.twbg.co.uk

For Linnéa and Leila

Contents

Enclosed garden. *Le Roman de la Rose*. Illumination in a medieval manuscript, *c.*1487–97

Introduction

'My dear sir,' said Mr Milestone, 'accord me your permission to wave the wand of enchantment over your grounds. The rocks shall be blown up, the trees shall be cut down, the wilderness and all its goats shall vanish like mist. Pagodas and Chinese bridges, gravel walks and shrubberies, bowling-greens, canals, and clumps of larch, shall rise upon its ruins. One age, sir, has brought to light the treasures of ancient learning; a second has penetrated into the depths of metaphysics; a third has brought to perfection the science of astronomy; but it was reserved for the exclusive genius of the present times, to invent the noble art of picturesque gardening, which has given, as it were, a new tint to the complexion of nature, and a new outline to the physiognomy of the universe!'

As an observer of contemporary culture and politics, the vitriolic essayist and poet Thomas Love Peacock liked to mock the fads and fashions that preoccupied the English gentry and middle classes of his time. Mr Milestone, a landscape gardener 'of first celebrity' is one of several memorable characters that he brings together in his satirical novel *Headlong Hall*, published in 1816. Like many of his contemporaries, Squire Headlong wants to 'improve' his gardens, and Mr Milestone is the man he believes can help him. An assiduous self-promoter, Milestone assures his host that with some 'shaving and polishing' he could transform the 'mere wilderness . . . [and] plantations of nettles' before them into the most fashionable garden in the country. Under no circumstances, he explains, should nature be left to her own devices. Not all the guests gathered at the squire's country house agree and so a heated discussion ensues about natural beauty and the extent to which man should intervene in it.

This scene could have been witnessed at many a small country estate in the early nineteenth century, when the middle classes were gripped by garden mania: books and journals about horticulture along with guides to England's gardens and landscapes filled their bookshelves; nurseries and seed merchants enjoyed a thriving trade; tourists travelled the country to assess the 'capabilities' of the gardens on their carefully planned itineraries: the ability to judge a landscape 'correctly' was seen as a sign of refinement. *Headlong Hall*'s critique is at its most caustic when Mr Milestone suggests that gardening will contribute as much to man's understanding of the universe as philosophy and science do. Peacock may have exaggerated the passions of his protagonists, but he nonetheless captured the essence of what had driven generations of estate owners and gardeners who had wrestled with new technologies, risked their lives – or those of their employees – to collect flora from all corners of the globe, and bankrupted themselves in pursuit of their grand designs. For them the garden was not only a place of beauty, pleasure and relaxation but also a stage on which to demonstrate one's intellectual prowess, one's taste and one's understanding of politics, art and science.

It is this idea that drives *This Other Eden*. As the motivations of our visionary garden-makers are uncovered, a picture emerges in which garden design and the themes that have shaped England's past are inextricably linked. Thus, history is imprinted on Capability Brown's rolling lawns, on the baroque fountains of Hampton Court and on the glasshouses at Chatsworth. At the heart of this phenomenon is the changing relationship between man and the natural world, for there have been few other spheres of human endeavour that have so consistently reflected the extent to which man has sought to control his environment. We see how the conquering of oceans, Newtonian physics and even the steam-engine played a significant role in these great English gardens. Indeed, all the garden-makers encountered in this book have shaped nature according to the ideas and possibilities of their age; whether by moving huge quantities of earth to make terraces or lakes; carving massive rocks into cascades and grottoes; using natural springs to create or divert rivers and canals; constructing gravity-defying fountains that reached unprecedented heights; or transplanting a twelve-ton palm from Surrey to Derbyshire.

To tell this story we have chosen seven country-house gardens, each of which was created at a pivotal point in English history. All were built at a time of political, cultural and social flux, and each heralded a new era in garden design. Unlike many other art forms, gardens are often collaborative ventures between patrons and professionals, in which personalities become indelibly stamped on the earth. It is through the eyes of these individuals and through their relationships with each other and the outside world that we discover how horticulture, history, ambition and – in some cases – sheer genius came together to create the gardens that still capture our imagination today.

Our story begins in the early seventeenth century when garden-making had become one of the most important public manifestations of an individual's power, wealth and taste. Until the reign of Henry VIII, gardens had been enjoyed as private sanctuaries by religious orders and a handful of wealthy courtiers and their monarchs. Hidden behind high walls, their design and the plants that grew in them were dominated by religious symbolism. Offering protection from the untamed landscape beyond, whose forests were believed to harbour wild animals and mythical beasts, these little havens spoke clearly of man's sense of vulnerability in relation to his environment.

With Henry, and then his daughter Elizabeth, the role of the English garden changed: it became a part of court pomp and performance. Elizabeth, in particular, expected her courtiers to show their loyalty by entertaining her, on her annual 'progresses', at their country estates, and a key part in the spectacle with which to impress the queen was increasingly played by the garden. It was still enclosed and divided into 'garden rooms', each preserving that feeling of intimacy; but no longer quite the private, secluded playground enjoyed by earlier generations, it now became the stage for masques and parties.

Meanwhile, in Italy, gardens were undergoing a transformation. Inspired by the Italian poet Petrarch, who in the early fourteenth century had climbed to the top of a mountain with the revolutionary idea of admiring the view, the men of the Renaissance saw the landscape as something to be embraced rather than feared. Looking back to a classical tradition, they rediscovered Pliny, who in the first century AD had described his gardens and outdoor living as part of cultivated life. The first to turn this tradition into practice was the architect Donato Bramante, who designed walks, terraces and steps to link the Pope's Villa Belvedere to the Vatican, and thereby succeeded in reconnecting the garden to the surrounding landscape. With wonderful views of the countryside around it, the Belvedere provided a blueprint for the magnificent Italian hilltop villas of the mid-sixteenth century. It was the ideas underlying such buildings that foreign artists and designers brought with them from the continent and that would influence gardens in England during the Jacobean period. Now English men and women dared to look over the garden wall into a world that was waiting to be discovered.

In 1607 Robert Cecil, the most powerful man behind the English throne, began to transform an old rambling palace and its walled garden into one of the most desirable estates in the country. Breaking with tradition, he sculpted tiered terraces into the landscape, which permitted unrivalled views over the country-side beyond, then cut a wide avenue stretching from his newly built house to the edge of the encircling park. Thus he linked his garden to its surroundings – an audacious move that set the course of garden design in England for the next three hundred years. Cecil was acutely attuned to the times he lived in, and his garden at Hatfield reflected it. England's mercantile power was reaching out to distant continents, and increasing numbers of foreign artists and craftsmen were introducing fashions from abroad. Cecil was one of the first to take advantage of the cultural rapprochement, employing the French engineer and designer Salomon de Caus to construct magical waterworks, harnessing the latest technologies to create cascades of water, like the ones de Caus had seen in Italian Renaissance gardens. Together with his gardener John Tradescant, Cecil also brought the horticultural treasures of the emerging Empire to his garden in

Hertfordshire. So Hatfield came to symbolise the discovery of nature and of a world beyond the English Channel, proclaiming man's urge to embrace a broader horizon.

Eighty years later, in 1688, William of Orange had no sooner arrived in England than he asked to meet Isaac Newton, who the previous year had published his *Principia Mathematica* – the *Mathematical Principles of Natural Philosophy* – setting out among other ideas his theory of universal gravitation and the laws of motion. William's gardens at Hampton Court would reflect this revolutionary idea that the natural world could be understood via mathematical laws. He commissioned Christopher Wren, one of the best mathematical minds and the most famous architect in England, and Daniel Marot, a leading French designer who was also a 'very ingenious Mathematician', to design them. Scientific thinking allied with art would demonstrate man's control over nature: Wren drew up a carefully calculated grid in which symmetry ruled, and Marot mapped out intricate scrolling designs which would be transferred to the parterres with new surveying instruments. Two gardener-nurserymen would implement these ideas: George London and Henry Wise, who traded on their royal commission to make their London-based nursery the largest in Europe. Suppliers of plants in their thousands to the aristocracy, they set a fashion at Hampton Court that would transform many of England's grand gardens. One of William's great achievements was to blur the boundary between garden and countryside even more successfully than Cecil had at Hatfield – his workmen installed, instead of perimeter walls, the finest decorative railings, that allowed in light and a distant view.

But it was at Stowe, in Buckinghamshire, that nature, for the first time, was allowed to enter the garden. Thirty years after William and Mary embarked on Hampton Court, Viscount Cobham and his designer Charles Bridgeman enclosed the garden with a virtually invisible barrier: a ha-ha. This permitted unobstructed views into the park and fields beyond without sacrificing security. Where William had emulated Versailles' opulence, Cobham aligned himself with the writers, artists and designers of his time who advocated a new simplicity. In gardening this translated into a reaction against French pomp, which these arbiters of taste saw in the stiff topiary and swirling arabesques of the baroque parterres at Hampton Court. Cobham and other innovative garden enthusiasts, such as his neighbour at nearby Rousham in Oxfordshire and the Prince of Wales at Carlton House in London, now left their trees unpruned and their grass unmown. 'All gardening is landscape painting', the poet Alexander Pope declared in 1734, 'like a landscape hung up', and so Cobham created a scene of bucolic tranquillity when he enclosed within his pleasure grounds a patch of pastureland and set cows and sheep to graze there.

For decades Stowe remained at the vanguard of fashion. In a period when the polite classes aspired to live by codes of behaviour based on classical ideals of civic duty and virtue, Cobham was the first to use his garden as a vehicle to convey these ideals, along with a sense of his own taste and his political beliefs. His temples and monuments told a story of virtue and vice, of 'patriotism' and corruption – much of the invective was directed against George II and his first minister Robert Walpole. But though nature was invited into the garden at Stowe, it was still an idealised and manicured version. The desire to experience nature in all its rawness would not reach its peak until the late eighteenth century, when Britain was at war with France and those who could afford to toured the country. These 'tourists', as they were first called in the 1780s, traversed the British Isles in search of a sense of nationhood in the rugged and untamed corners that were to be found in Wales and the Lake District. Here was a landscape, untainted by foreign influence, that revealed what they felt to be the true spirit of Britain: her strength and sublimity.

Thus at Hawkstone Park in Shropshire, a landscape that generations of gardeners would have regarded as intimidating and ugly became one of the most popular gardens in the country in the 1780s. Exploiting the unique geography of his estate, Richard Hill presented the tourist with four rugged hills, a medieval ruin, labyrinthine tunnels hewn into the rocks, and precarious bridges spanning breathtaking crevasses – like scenes depicted in the popular Gothic novels of the day. Inspired by Edmund Burke's writings on the sublime, people now wanted to experience awe and encounter '[a] sort of delightful horror', instead of 'reading' a garden intellectually. Hill invited his visitors to feel the force of nature rather than to rationalise and dissect it.

Within thirty years, fashions were changing yet again. No longer wanting cliffs, ravines and blasted trees in the garden, the genteel middle classes sought to celebrate the agricultural landscape – including those who worked the land. Far less grand, and incorporating tracts of farmland, gardens such as Abbot Upcher's at Sheringham in Norfolk reflected the squirearchy's urge to express their benevolence. Not content simply to turn his estate into a pretty picture, Upcher brought his cornfields to life with toiling labourers and sowed barley in front of his drawing-room window, incorporating the working life of his estate into the garden. In contrast to earlier generations of garden owners, Upcher valued moderation and domesticity. The man he chose to realise his ideas was Humphry Repton, the most sought-after landscape designer of the day, who had already designed some three hundred gardens. Many of Repton's clients were, like Upcher, minor gentry or from the rising middle classes. With their modest, picturesque estates they too would leave their mark on the English landscape.

In the late 1820s, ten years after Upcher embraced agriculture and its imagery, Joseph Paxton, gardener to the 6th Duke of Devonshire, welcomed the Industrial Revolution into a garden in the Peak District. Utilising the technology and inventions that powered the factories, Paxton mass-produced nature in the artificial climate he devised in his hothouses at Chatsworth. As well as propagating his own plants, he received batches of rare species from the Indian subcontinent sent by the Duke's personal plant-hunter; others he bought from London nurseries – almost fifty were now trading – and from local nurseries in Derbyshire and neighbouring counties. By 1840, when Paxton finished the Great Conservatory – the largest glass building of its time – Chatsworth had become a Mecca for horticulturists and gardeners. Paxton had filled the hothouses with hundreds of orchids, palms, dwarf bananas and other rarities. Where Viscount Cobham at Stowe and Richard Hill at Hawkstone Park had celebrated the 'genius of the place', the Duke of Devonshire now worshipped the genius of his gardener's manipulation of nature – Charles Darwin said of Chatsworth: 'Art beats nature altogether there'. As factories spewed out cotton and steel, so Paxton produced plants by the thousand to fill his hothouses and the flowerbeds with garish colours.

This industrial-scale production of bedding plants with which Paxton and others had wrought their spectacular effects would appal a future generation of garden designers. One of these was Gertrude Jekyll, who looked back to an earlier gardening tradition. Like others at the turn of the twentieth century, she and her colleague, the architect Edwin Lutyens, combined formal architectural layouts with more naturalistic planting styles. Jekyll set flowers in irregular drifts and in the nooks and crannies of walls, so that nature seemed to reclaim the manmade structures, creating the perfect balance between the two. An accomplished painter and embroiderer, she aimed to 'use plants [so] that they shall form beautiful pictures'. Jekyll and Lutyens' masterpiece was Hestercombe in Somerset – now considered to be the epitome of the English garden. Characterised by its walled enclosures, old English plants, geometric flowerbeds and pergolas, it evoked an era of timeless aristocratic stability.

The reality, however, was rather different. The power of the nobility was declining; many of the great country houses were being sold off; and the Liberal government, determined to curtail the power of established interests, was beginning to implement ambitious social reforms. The garden at Hestercombe appeared to have been there for centuries, impervious to change; but unlike the grand Jacobean pleasure grounds that had proclaimed the power and privilege of an elite, Jekyll and Lutyens' work conserved a mere image, one of a golden age of great estates that was now drawing to a close.

The people who owned and made these seven gardens bring the stories in this book to life. Working together for years and in some cases decades, they left for posterity a unique expression of their skill and endeavour. Most of the patrons offered more than just a salary – they encouraged their gardeners and enabled them to develop their talents; many of them influenced and inspired each other. Robert Cecil financed John Tradescant's search for rare plants from around the world, helping to launch the career of the most influential plantsman of the age. Some, such as Abbot Upcher of Sheringham, knew what message they wanted their gardens to convey, but relied entirely on their designers' expertise and taste; while others such as Viscount Cobham at Stowe collaborated so closely with friends and professionals that it is often impossible to distinguish their individual contributions. The most inspired of these partnerships was that of Joseph Paxton and the Duke of Devonshire at Chatsworth. Their letters and diaries give us a unique insight into their relationship: we see it evolve from one of employer and employee into a partnership of equals, from servitude to friendship, based on mutual interests and affection.

Just as each designer and owner was influenced by the concerns of their times, so these are mirrored in their gardens. Thus, a broad avenue radiating out into the countryside proclaims a king's confidence and power; the transformation of a graceful sweep of lawn into a patch of farmland suggests fear of social unrest. Similarly the creation of the ha-ha, which allowed unkempt nature back into the garden, signalled the first step towards an open landscape as a symbol of liberty. A walk over rugged terrain could inspire a sense of nationhood; an exotic plant testified to England's emerging Empire – and later, when mass-produced in a steam-heated hothouse, to the march of industrialisation.

Taken together our seven gardens tell more than just a story of botany and horticulture, of idiosyncratic display and technological advance. They also show how gardens have established a hold on the English imagination; how, as barometers of social change, they reflect the manners, ideas and culture of a nation.

I

In Pursuit of Pleasure: Hatfield House

'My Lords gardener . . . showed me . . . above all, the gardens,
such as I have never saw in all my life; nor so good flowers,
nor so great gooseberries, as big as nutmegs.'

Samuel Pepys on Hatfield, 22 July 1661

'God Almighty first planted a garden. And indeed it is the
purest of human pleasures. It is the greatest refreshment to the
spirits of man; without which, buildings and palaces are but
gross handiworks.'

Francis Bacon, *Of Gardens*, 1625

Any of the numerous aristocrats who visited the palace and garden at Theobalds
in Hertfordshire in the summer of 1606 would have been impressed by its size
and splendour. Even King James I had never seen anything more extravagant
than this palace belonging to his most trusted adviser Sir Robert Cecil.* Three
storeys high, it was built around five courtyards, and the many windows in its
quarter-mile-long façade glittered magically when the sun caught them. Inside,
during the night, a cunning device moved a mechanical sun along the ceiling

*During his lifetime Sir Robert Cecil's titles changed several times: he was made Baron Cecil
of Essendon in 1603, Viscount Cranborne in 1604 and Earl of Salisbury in 1605. To avoid
confusion, he remains Sir Robert Cecil throughout the chapter.

of the Great Chamber, illuminating artificial stars. This 'sky' was supported by twelve 'trees' each with real bark, leaves and birds' nests – so authentic that birds flew in from the garden. It was as if nature could be shaped according to man's wishes.

Outside, a more geometric artificiality had been imposed on the garden. Visitors could circumnavigate the seven-acre pleasure garden along the moat that surrounded it, or explore the two miles of paths that gave access to the nine square 'compartments' into which the garden was divided – each seventy feet square and enclosed by clipped hedges. Here heraldic statues, Roman sculptures and delicate flowers declared the owner's taste, his knowledge and his allegiance to the king. Occasionally visitors would step on the hidden stopcocks that set off ingenious 'water jokes', instantly drenching them. Ships equipped with sails, cannons and flags gave life to the fountains, into which the water gushed from the mouths of serpents. Only a few guests might have seen similar devices in the Renaissance gardens of Italy. As the contemporary writer Ben Jonson put it, Theobalds was 'built to envious show'.

Eight years earlier, at the age of forty-three, Cecil had inherited the house from his father Lord Burghley. Now he was Master of the Court of Wards and Secretary of State: the first was a lucrative position, giving him control over

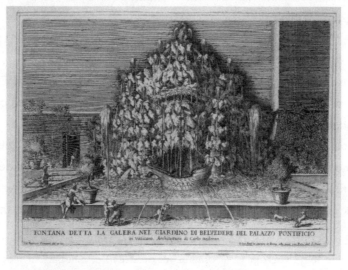

Visitors getting soaked by water jets in an Italian Renaissance garden

Robert Cecil, 1st Earl of Salisbury, *c.* 1608

the income of wealthy minors, and the latter placed him at the heart of political decision-making. In short, he was the most influential man behind the English throne, controlling both foreign and domestic policy, heading his own secret service and enjoying the ear of the king. Yet Cecil was a lonely and introverted man – the two most important people in his life, his father and his wife, had died a decade before. Nevertheless, despite his friends' concern that he would end up 'a surly, sharp sour plum' and misanthropic 'melancholy mole', he took no heed, immersing himself in politics and gaining a reputation as the most Machiavellian of all King James's courtiers.

His scheming and political machinations provoked scorn which was intensified by his physical disabilities. His back was bent, supporting his head at a crooked angle, and his splay foot hindered his movements. Although dressed in the most exquisite bejewelled clothes, his twisted figure was regarded as a sign of the devil, a symbol of sin and wickedness. In an age that celebrated beauty, it was easy for his rivals to use his disability against him. They would turn away in disgust – 'it was unwholesome to meet a man in the morning which has a wry neck, a crooked back or a splay foot'; this 'dissembling smooth-faced dwarf' to their mind had a body shaped like a spider's back. Even the king could not resist, addressing his letters to 'pygmy' and 'beagle'. The scheming hunchback was a stock-in-trade of writers: Samuel Daniel, a former court poet, employed no subtlety in casting Cecil as the treacherous dwarf Craterus in his tragedy *Philotas*, while Shakespeare's *Richard III*, with its evil hunchbacked protagonist, was regularly reprinted during Cecil's lifetime. Everybody understood these allusions.

Cecil, though, did not despair. He was ambitious and 'a courtier from his cradle'; few were better equipped than he for the power-play of court life. His father Lord Burghley had been Elizabeth I's chief minister and had 'nourished [Cecil] with the milk of policy'. Already as a young man Robert had been his father's accomplice in the espionage that had cost Mary Stuart her head. Later, in 1601, anticipating Elizabeth's death he had begun a secret correspondence with Mary's son, James VI of Scotland. This move had been a cardinal betrayal of the queen; though old and childless, she did not want to be reminded of her mortality, nor did she like the idea that James, the son of her old adversary, might wear the English crown. But Cecil achieved the impossible – without losing the trust of the dying Elizabeth, he had helped James to become King of England.

The court was the forum for politics and debate, as well as for receiving royal favours. Having watched his father for so many years, Cecil knew he had to make liberal use of his family connections, his wit and political finesse, as well as purveying flattery and royal entertainment, in order that James would grant him titles, estates and the power to collect taxes. Any diminution of his powers would be both personally humiliating and financially damaging. Given that courtiers were elevated – or not – according to the monarch's whim, it was important to indulge the flamboyant and temperamental James. If they entertained him in splendour, he would be more inclined to bestow royal favours.

Leaving behind his lean years as King of Scotland, since his accession to the English throne in spring 1603, the spendthrift James had enjoyed the wealth of England and its courtiers. Beauty and pleasure were his obsessions, perhaps in reaction to the brutality of his upbringing – his father had been murdered, his mother, Mary Queen of Scots, executed, and as a boy he had been imprisoned and kidnapped by the quarrelling Scottish nobles. He spent much of his time hunting and drinking, and his court was described as 'a nursery of lust and intemperance'. Unlike Elizabeth, who had busied herself with the day-to-day business of government, James was more interested in reflecting on the art of statecraft – he wrote the political treatise *The True Love of Free Monarchies* in 1598 – as well as indulging in 'a lethargy of pleasure', as an Italian visitor reported back to the Doge of Venice in 1603. He and his wife, Queen Anne, welcomed to their court international artists, poets and musicians, thereby opening court life to continental fashion. The years of parsimony were over, and for the first time in five decades royal patronage thrived again.

Despite their different temperaments, Elizabeth and James both expected to be entertained and flattered. As a young man Cecil had watched in awe as his father had beguiled the queen at Theobalds, constantly enlarging and redecorating the house and gardens until it became a royal palace in all but name. When James's brother-in-law, the King of Denmark, arrived in England in the summer of 1606, Cecil grasped the opportunity to show James his respect and his generosity by organising for his pleasure a theatrical event. Little did he know how much it would change his life.

Cecil set the date, 25 July, planning a great feast that would last for several days and include hunting and a court masque. To ensure the quality of this lavish entertainment he recruited the finest artists in England, including Ben Jonson to write the lyrics, and Inigo Jones to design elaborate costumes and stage sets following the latest in Italian architecture. Music would be supplied by his own musicians, who were already leading the fashion for new stringed instruments. Food would be heaped high, and his guests would leave with sumptuous gifts. Though this would cost him a fortune, Cecil had little option. Since most of his income comprised the gratuities from his official positions in government, his future depended upon the king. Planning to spend in excess of £1100 on these festivities, at a time when a wealthy yeoman could live comfortably on a yearly income of £300, Cecil must have been fairly sure that this investment would be repaid.

From the moment of James's arrival, it was clear that Cecil had surpassed himself. At the gates stood a full-sized oak tree to which his workmen had attached thousands of green taffeta leaves, written on each of which was the word 'WELCOME'. Under the tree stood the musical ensemble, ready to serenade the royal visitors. The next five days were filled with hunting and hawking, as well as lavish meals washed down with vast amounts of alcohol – which would have pleased one of the guests, the King of Denmark, who had the reputation of being a voracious drinker. Cecil had spent half his budget – more than £550 – on food and drink, but the pièce de résistance was his carefully devised masque.

Symbolising wisdom, wealth and plenty, the *Entertainment of the Two Kings* was set in Solomon's temple in honour of James, who liked to style himself as the biblical figure. The ladies-in-waiting and other courtiers had been practising their verses for weeks, but now after several days of feasting they were quite incapacitated. Cecil's friend Sir John Harington observed that the men 'had women and indeed wine too, of such plenty, as would have astonished each sober beholder'. The masque began with the offering of delicate jellies, wine, cakes and exotic spices to the royal guests. The lady playing the Queen of Sheba made her way drunkenly towards the canopy where James sat with the Danish king. Misjudging her steps, both she and her presents fell into the latter's lap. Intoxicated himself, the king did not mind – on the contrary, he 'humbled himself before her' and after much confusion was carried to bed. The other noble actors, in their stupor, fared no better. The character Hope tried to remember her lines, but, failing in the effort, ran out of the room in shame; Faith remained, but she too was hopelessly lost. Charity came with gifts, but bluntly told the king that she had nothing for him that he did not have already. Peace 'rudely made war with her olive branch', while both Hope and Faith were now 'sick and spewing' – the ladies had abandoned their modesty and were 'seen to roll about in intoxication'. Not a single guest, including the royal ones, was sober. Even those who had never before been known to succumb to alcohol were observed to 'follow the fashion, and wallow in beastly delights'. Harington, who observed the scene in despair, saw here the work of the devil, who wanted that 'every man should blow up himself, by wild riot, excess, and devastation of time and temperance'. The sobriety and frugality of the Elizabethan court was but a distant memory.

Although James was famous for his debauchery, Cecil must have been horrified that his festivities had turned into an orgy. But he need not have worried on the king's account – he was thoroughly enjoying himself. And as a permanent reminder of the event he asked Cecil to give him the palace and garden. Even compared to the demands of Elizabeth, who would ask her courtiers to enlarge, sometimes rebuild, their houses when she visited them on her annual progress across the country,* James's request was extravagant. Yet, as King of England, he could ask for anything – which left Cecil with two alternatives: to keep his house and risk the king's displeasure and his career, or hand it over. He therefore offered Theobalds to the king.† This, of course, left Cecil with a further problem – in future, where would he stage his parties?

In exchange for Theobalds, Cecil received the old royal palace at Hatfield in Hertfordshire as well as sixteen manor houses. On 14 April 1607, five weeks before officially handing his home over to King James, he 'borrowed one day's retreat from London' to go and inspect his new estate at Hatfield. With him went three other courtiers who had taken the day off to accompany him: Shakespeare's patron, Lord Southampton; Lord Worcester, the Master of the Horse; and the Lord Chamberlain, the Earl of Suffolk. The four men must have realised how difficult it would be to turn the old building into a palace fit for royal guests. Built in the late fifteenth century as a bishop's palace, it was dark and rambling. After the Reformation, Henry VIII had used it as a nursery for his children, but had made no improvements. Made entirely of red brick, and lacking any fashionable elements such as carved stone balustrades, columns or large windows, it was outdated and to the contemporary eye it left much to be desired. '[U]pon what part of ground should I place my habitation?' Cecil asked his friends. Certainly, it was not grand enough for the purposes of a Secretary of State.

Compared to the pleasure grounds at Theobalds, the garden at Hatfield, small and compact, was not very promising, either. A thick brick wall

---

*Being frugal, as well as wanting to avoid the plague in London, Elizabeth had set off every summer on a tour of her realm with her entourage of 1500 courtiers and servants, 400 carts, and 2400 packhorses and mules, staying for varying lengths of time at the country houses of her courtiers.

†Theobalds would be destroyed during the Civil War.

surrounded both palace and garden. Divided into modest squares and rectangles it contained an orchard, a walled privy garden and some grassed courtyards. Two square knot gardens were the ornamental focus. One featured swirling shapes, probably cut into the turf, forming a fleur-de-lis in each corner, while the other was planted in a geometrical pattern possibly consisting of fragrant plants and herbs. The traditional plants for knot gardens included evergreen hyssop, with narrow dark-green leaves and bluish anise-scented flowers whose natural bushiness was perfect for the purpose. With it grew germander, a low-growing herb, clipped as a hedge. Its broad, oak-like leaves and small rose-coloured flowers gave the patterns substance. Lilac flowering thyme, fragrant purple lavender and lemon balm would also have been used, and all were grown for medicinal purposes and as food. Planted in ribbons, the herbs created intricate shapes, and the spaces left between them were often filled with coloured earth.

Knot gardens like these were the legacy of an era stretching back to the late Middle Ages, when simpler versions had been used to express religious sentiments.* Often divided into quarters, they had symbolised, for instance, the four rivers flowing out of Eden as described in the Book of Genesis, and God's four corners of the earth in which stood four angels in charge of the winds. Plants, too, had held particular meanings: the lily stood for the purity of the Virgin Mary, and the triple lobes of the strawberry leaf alluded to the Trinity. Later, during Henry VIII's reign, these Christian allegories had been eclipsed by heraldry, so that the red rose, which had once denoted the blood of martyrs, became the emblem of the House of Tudor. Turf benches and places of sacred contemplation gave way to coats of arms, heraldic beasts and figurative topiary. By the second half of the sixteenth century the beds' simple geometric patterns had become more intricate and were often planted in sinuous lines, each continually turning and interweaving with itself. The more complex the pattern, the more it was admired.

---

*Many garden historians claim that knot gardens had played an important role in medieval gardens, but recent research suggests that they only became fashionable in Tudor times. Medieval gardens did, though, feature square ornamental beds in which flowers and herbs were grown for medicinal and symbolic purposes, but not in interlacing designs.

When Cecil gazed for the first time at the garden at Hatfield, he could not have failed to register its shortcomings. The knots were simple, and the whole place was devoid of fashionable continental influences such as fountains, canals or ponds – unlike Theobalds, packed as it was with French features such as the ornamental canal, classical statues and garden pavilions, as conceived by Lord Burghley. Having visited France, Burghley had brought home with him books by the famous French architect Philibert de l'Orme and engravings by Jacques Androuet du Cerceau, which recorded the great houses and gardens of France as well as depicting elevations of garden buildings and fountains. Theobalds, stretching out over a plain, had been the ideal place to use these French ideas to best advantage. The traditionally defensive moat had been transformed into a decorative waterscape, and the flat land had lent itself to the creation of huge ornamental beds much like those at Fontainebleau and the Château d'Anet in northern France.

Château d'Anet designed by Philibert de l'Orme, 1548–54

So Hatfield had nothing of Theobalds' splendour; but it provided Cecil with the opportunity to shape a house and garden according to the latest fashions that were just then percolating in from Italy. In an age of personal rule, when the character of a monarch still determined much of the political and cultural life of a nation, James's accession radically changed England's art and architecture. Breaking with the frugality and insularity of Elizabeth's rule, James's patronage and the truce that he and Cecil established with Spain in 1604 ushered in artists, craftsmen and ideas from the continent, as well as enabling more aristocrats to travel to Italy and return with paintings and sculpture. Seventy years after Elizabeth's father had broken with the Catholic Church, Britain was once again receptive to Italian influences.

Cecil had long been fascinated by Italian art and architecture – his library, for example, was stocked with classical works such as Euclid's mathematical theories and Vitruvius's architectural treatises. Though he had never travelled there himself, he had seen engravings of the spectacular hilltop Renaissance gardens at the Villa d'Este in Tivoli and the Villa Pratolino north-east of Florence, and had probably talked about them with Thomas Wilson, his chief financial controller who was also an Italian scholar. In addition, contacts with the growing Italian community in England kept him informed of Italian fashions, and Sir Henry Wotton, the English ambassador in Venice, sent paintings for Cecil and 'some things about the subject of architecture'.

It was just as garden mania was reaching a new peak that Cecil embarked on his garden at Hatfield, and in doing so he was perfectly in tune with the changing function of the country estate. The medieval nobleman's house had been the centre of local power, the forum for the community and a stage for the aristocracy, whereas the gardens had been a private sphere enclosed within high walls – an earthly paradise or *pairidaeza*, the ancient Persian word for an enclosure. But during Elizabeth's reign, as power had shifted from the manor house to the court in London, the courtiers' country palaces had begun to look outwards in order to impress royalty on their annual progress. Stretching out and wrapping round the house like a dazzling cloak, gardens became a sign of the owner's wealth and position in the court hierarchy. James had further encouraged this trend by urging his nobles to spend more time in the country, writing verses to bring the point home: 'The country is your Orb and proper sphere,' went one line.

So it was Cecil's intention to transform his new estate into the most fashionable he could devise. The old palace, he decided, must go. Leaving only the wing containing the banqueting hall, which would be used as additional lodg-ings for the king's entourage, he now planned a new house to stand at the grounds' highest point, just a few dozen yards away. As the house would over-look the estate he would introduce descending terraces and cascading water in the Italian Renaissance style. Nobody had attempted such a garden in England before.* At Hatfield, nature had sculpted the land perfectly for Cecil's ambitions.

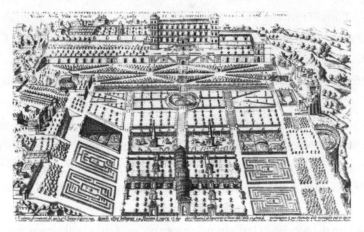

Descending terraces at the Villa d'Este at Tivoli, 1573

Three months after Cecil took possession of his new estate in the summer of 1607, Mountain Jennings, his gardener at Theobalds, rode to Hatfield to survey the grounds. Cecil had instructed him to set out a 'plot' for a substantially enlarged and altered garden. Jennings had already been to Lyveden in Northamptonshire, the home of Cecil's old acquaintance Sir Thomas Tresham, in order to see the celebrated water garden and moated orchard, where Cecil had wanted Jennings to 'pick some such observations as may enable him to spend my money to better purpose'. The large garden, enclosed by a moat, formed a square island with two round 'mounts' in the corners. Paths spiralled up to their peaks, from where Jennings would have been able to observe the whole area; on the other side of the island, opposite the two mounts, was a raised terrace with two smaller, pyramid-shaped, hillocks.

*Only his brother, Thomas Cecil, had devised something similar when he introduced sloping terraces for the approach at Wimbledon House, though not in his garden.

Perhaps it was surprising that, as a jailer of papists, Cecil was friends with the staunchly Catholic Tresham, who from time to time over the past fifteen years had been imprisoned in the Tower of London; but it seemed that the love of gardens transcended the fissures caused by faith and politics. Also, Tresham had been helped by Cecil in the past, and so not only did he welcome his gardener, but as a small gesture of gratitude his wife later sent fruit trees for Hatfield from their orchard: '[T]hanks are no requital for your many favours,' Lady Tresham wrote in 1609.

During the five months after the first inspection of Hatfield, Cecil had many discussions with his trusted advisers, made careful calculations about the scope of the project and visited his future home several times.* Finally, in late autumn 1607, work began with the clearing of the site. During the next few months the labourers dug the foundations, prepared the bricks and the stone, and set up the wooden scaffolding. The gardeners kept well away from this busy, muddy building site, concentrating instead on planting trees in the park, but in March and April the following year the workmen pulled down the old chapel and parts of the old palace to make way for the new gardens.

While the work at Hatfield was progressing fast, Cecil's career was scaling new heights. In May 1608, on the death of the incumbent, James awarded him the post of Lord Treasurer – the most lucrative office in England – thereby adding to Cecil's command the control over England's finances. Never before had one courtier held so much power. To express his elevated status, Cecil decided to make Hatfield even more palatial, and quickly ordered changes to the plans. For a start, the site for the new chapel had to be altered and, more drastically, Cecil instructed his workmen to pull down two load-bearing walls that had just been erected – despite already being fifty-eight feet long and over twenty feet high – probably to make way for new extensions. As the building took shape, its size began to tax even Cecil's bulging coffers. His financial adviser, worrying that expenses were outstripping revenues, told him that if he carried on in this way,

---

*Cecil went there on 14 March, 14 April, 2 August and 14 September 1607. Unless otherwise stated, his visits and the chronology of the making of the gardens at Hatfield are based on R. T. Gunton's unpublished compilation of related bills, accounts and letters, and Lawrence Stone's article, 'The Building of Hatfield House', in *Architectural Journal*, vol. 112 (1956), pp. 111–13.

'by this proportion your LP [Lordship] shall Continually increase your debts'. To save himself from financial ruin, Cecil would have to find some additional income.

Throughout his lifetime, widespread governmental corruption was taken for granted, in part because official positions were notoriously badly paid. Bribes, gifts and gratuities were in fact the main sources of income for most courtiers, and with his impressive portfolio of posts Cecil was in a prime position to receive them. Since it was he who dictated England's foreign policy, navigating her role within the delicate balance of power in Europe, he received bribes from foreign governments – the Spanish ambassador had told the Spanish king, Philip III, in January 1606, that Cecil was 'the one that manages everything here, without whom no one plays a role'. For much of the previous three decades England, France and the Netherlands had been at war with Spain. Slowly, the conflict was being replaced by an unsettled peace. First, in 1598, France and Spain had signed a treaty, leaving England and the Netherlands as allies. At the same time the two halves of the German territories of the Holy Roman Empire, split by the Reformation into Catholic and Protestant, each sought international allies who succeeded only in deepening religious division in Europe still further. In June 1603, two months after his accession, James brought an end to England's naval hostilities against Spain, living up to his motto *Beati Pacifici*, 'Blessed are the peacemakers'. The cards of allegiance were being reshuffled and Cecil, as the conduit for these negotiations, was being courted by all sides and accepting an unprecedented number of bribes. During the Spanish peace negotiation he received a pension of more than £1000 from Spain, while the Dutch, in fear of losing England as an ally against Spain, gave him £10,000. The Spanish king, aware of Cecil's double-dealing, now offered £12,500 to keep 'this little man . . . less hostile'. Cecil had no qualms in accepting such a sum, which effectively covered one-third of the costs of what would be the most expensive building project of its age. So throughout the summer of 1608 the building work at Hatfield could continue – after all, he was providing for the king's future entertainment.

Part of Cecil's vision for Hatfield was the creation of a large unified landscape, in which terraces would fall away from the house towards an enormous park stocked with deer, like the Italian Renaissance estates he so admired. He would turn the arable land into a space for leisure and sport, most certainly with the king's passion for hunting in mind. By leaving his land untilled, Cecil would display his wealth: contemporary accounts bemoaned this extravagance, complaining that such a park was a 'vain commodity which brings no manner of gain or profit to the owner'. But Cecil did not care – his park was to be enjoyed on foot or on horseback. Hunting was, after all, the sport of the aristocracy, another way of imposing their power over nature, and Cecil's profit would be the king's admiration.

Unlike Tudor and Elizabethan gardens, where the deer park had been treated as a separate unit within the estate, often connected to a hunting lodge rather than to the main house, Cecil's garden and park were to be part of a whole. To connect house, garden and park he devised a scheme anticipating a fashion that would take hold of English gardens some fifty years later: avenues cutting through the estate on an axis. Departing from the paths and walks that traditionally zigzagged through English estates, Cecil was again inspired by continental trends: in Italy, avenues had long been used to align the different parts of a garden into one vista. The arrangement of drives, balustrades and steps at the Villa Lante and Villa Medici, for example, had created the unified landscapes that Cecil so admired. In England, only Sir Francis Willoughby at Wollaton Hall in Nottinghamshire had connected the garden with the house, in the 1580s, when he designed them to relate to each other symmetrically.

When in 1609 Cecil's workforce began to build the long drive that led straight from the walled courtyards in front of the house into the park, their remit was to extend the vista from the house and garden far into the distance – so far, in fact, that more than fifty years later a French tourist admired the avenue for 'mak[ing] you lose your sight'. For the first time in England, the separate components of a garden, from the formal plots near the house to the outlying deer park, were linked through a grand avenue that created prospects radiating out into the countryside beyond.

The execution of this plan, however, proved difficult because much of the land that Cecil wanted to turn into his great park belonged to the people of the village of Hatfield, who had worked its unfenced strips for centuries. To

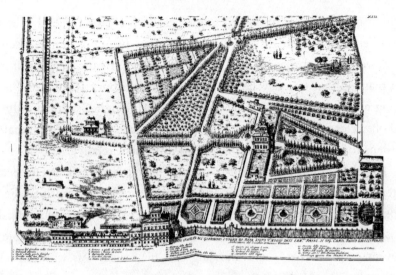

Avenues in an Italian Renaissance garden

fence in, hedge and ditch the land for the park, Cecil needed to buy out these farmers, who knew that their lowly place in the social hierarchy left them with little option but to accede to his wishes. So they meekly obliged, just as Cecil had had to comply with the king's demand for Theobalds. In April 1608 one tenant, Sir Henry Butler, wrote to Cecil: 'Since I see you now determined to make you a seat at Hatfield, and my little manor there lying so near you and environed with the demesnes of your manor of Hatfield, I must confess it is fitter for you than for me.' To the great resentment of the local people, Cecil also fenced in half of the forest, which they had used for centuries to gather firewood. For many years they remembered Cecil 'Not [as] Robin Goodfellow nor Robin Hood/ but Robin th'encloser of Hatfield Wood'. By enclosing the common land – the forests and the fields – Cecil forced his vision upon the landscape and upon the established rural community, changing the face of the countryside around Hatfield for ever.

In the summer of 1608, while the locals were being informed of their landlord's enclosure plans, Cecil continued to be besieged by people wanting to use him to better their own position. One of those to approach him was his cousin, the philosopher Francis Bacon, who, the year before, after decades of obsequiousness had been promoted to the post of Solicitor-General. The relationship between the cousins was difficult. Despite being his junior, Cecil was much more powerful than Bacon, but in the true spirit of Jacobean intrigue Bacon planned that one day he would 'succeed Salisbury [Cecil], and amuse the King and Prince with pastime and glory'. Although Cecil had only ever placed obstacles in Bacon's path, the latter now hoped to use their mutual love of gardens to become more 'pryvie' to his influential relative.

To celebrate his new-found status and to impress Cecil, Bacon decided to extend the garden of his home at Gorhambury in Hertfordshire. Feeling confident of his horticultural expertise – a few years later he would publish *Of Gardens*, which became one of the most influential treatises on the subject in the seventeenth century – and knowing that his cousin was working on the pleasure grounds at Hatfield, Bacon instructed his workmen to make the garden at Gorhambury 'handsome' for the impending visit of Cecil's secretary. He planned a 'plott to be made of my poole', which would become a four-acre water garden with islands, mounts, banqueting houses and arbours. He could not wait, he wrote, 'to speak of them to my L. of Salisbury'. Although many of Bacon's garden features would be copied at Hatfield, Cecil never offered a helping hand to his cousin, who had to wait until after Cecil's death before rising through the court hierarchy. Eventually he took his revenge by writing *Of Deformity*, which held that disabilities were a sign of a person's inner depravity and alluded to Cecil as a prime example.

While Bacon continued in his attempts to advance himself, Cecil was forging ahead with his plans for Hatfield. By spring 1609 the fencing and planting in the park were well under way, the house was progressing – the builders had finished the first floor and were starting on the walls of the second – and the main outline of the garden was taking shape. Divided into two parts, each garden had distinct functions. The one to the west, situated between the new building and the remaining wing of the old palace, was smaller and more intimate than the one to the east – the grand showpiece that would be sculpted into three terraces descending towards the river.

The design of the garden mirrored the layout of the house, which was built in a U-shape; the two strokes of the U constituted the east and west wings.

Unlike the houses that had been built to accommodate the unmarried Queen Elizabeth, Hatfield needed two sets of state apartments – one for the king and one for his wife. Accordingly, the entire first floor of the east wing was to be occupied by James, while the queen would stay in the west wing. From his rooms the king would be able to admire the larger formal plots with raised and balustraded walks, which would lead down from the house to the water terrace that Cecil had planned as the centrepiece of the East Garden. The queen would look out on to the West Garden, with its elaborate knot gardens now being laid out by the gardeners.

The new knot gardens were cut out of turf and edged with bands of carnations – Cecil's favourite flowers. Using squares and circles and the harmonious proportions that these shapes provided, fashionable knot gardens were based on the same principles as Italian Renaissance architecture. The theories of Euclid and Plato's ideas of universal forms had elevated geometry into a vehicle for understanding and ordering the world. The shapes emerging in Cecil's garden mirrored this, as well as combining the English love of turf with the continental obsession for large ornamental displays. Here Cecil was probably also influenced by the work of the Dutchman Jan Vredeman de Vries, whose pattern-book was first published in 1583 and then reprinted in an

Ornamental garden design by Jan Vredeman de Vries, 1583

expanded edition in about 1600. Unlike traditional Tudor knots which were planted with low-growing herbs and flowers, de Vries's illustrations depicted elegant geometrical patterns cut into grass — a style that would soon dominate English gardens.

Progress was so rapid that Cecil made the twenty-mile trip on horseback from London three times in the space of a few weeks to inspect the work. There he found labourers pounding the old bricks from the demolished palace to a fine red powder, which garden hands then used to make paths, while others were mowing the new grass walks. Yet others were moving tons of earth to the West Garden to complete a large mount projecting from the terrace. In this Cecil was perpetuating a feature that had first appeared in medieval gardens, where mounts had been used as a vantage point for peering over the high cloister walls of monasteries. Mounts had remained popular in the walled Tudor gardens for the same reasons; Henry VIII, for instance, used over 250,000 bricks to build an enormous elevation overlooking the entire garden at Hampton Court. Since then the fashion had persisted, perhaps because the nobility liked nothing better than to admire their property unfolding below them. Over time mounts had become ever more elaborate, featuring spiralling walks such as Lord Tresham's at Lyveden, or the 'Venusberg' at Theobalds. In Italy some designers

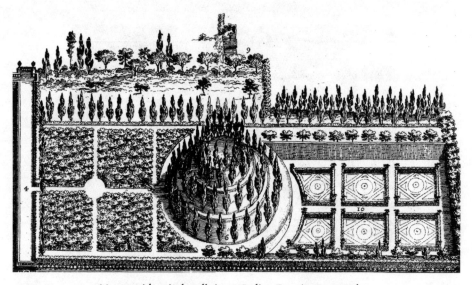

Mount with spiral walk in an Italian Renaissance garden

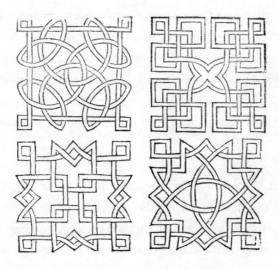

Designs for knot gardens by Didymus Mountain, 1577

had turned their love for playful waterworks into water-spouting mounts, such as the famous Mount Parnassus at the Villa Pratolino.

The prospects from Hatfield's mount would be unlike any other garden's in England: in one great panoramic sweep Cecil could show off his knot gardens and ornamental planting schemes, his new park and the landscape beyond it. Seduced by the impact of the scene, he set two stone buildings in the corners of the East Garden, which served as additional viewing platforms (they were later raised by six feet to increase the field of vision even further). As the mount was nearing completion, the gardeners were finishing off the intricate knots and 'laying the grass quarters in celleres [colours]' – filling the gaps between the precisely cut grass with coloured gravel or earth to highlight the patterns. Contemporary 'recipes' instructed that the yellow should be achieved with clay, white with coarse chalk, black with charcoal and red with pulverised bricks. The designs for knots were often drawn from books, the most influential being Thomas Hill's *The Profitable Art of Gardening*, published in 1568 and reprinted in 1577 as *The Gardeners Labyrinth* under the pseudonym Didymus Mountain. The book had been dedicated to his father, so Cecil most certainly owned a copy. Designed to be seen from above, the linearity and two-dimensionality of the knot gardens mirrored the aesthetic of the era. The same patterns were applied to all kinds of surfaces: tapestries, embroidery, woodwork, carpets, book-binding, clothing and even to food, such as marzipan knots as desserts. In time, not one corner of Hatfield would be left unembellished: Cecil would leave no surface plain, either in the garden or inside the house. Nothing that could be carved, painted, gilded, embroidered or otherwise ornamented was excluded: balustrades and pediments, ceilings and walls, fireplaces and tapestries, panelling and staircases.

While the West Garden was prepared for its first summer, Cecil invited the royal family to the opening of another of his building projects – the Britain Burse. A parade of elegant shops along the Strand in London, it was England's first luxury shopping mall and traded only in the finest goods, such as perfumes, books and Chinese porcelain. In April 1609 Cecil welcomed his guests under a shop sign that read, 'All other places give for money, here all is given for love'. Inside he had assembled exotic curiosities, mechanical toys, and scientific tools, which were offered to the king during a masque set in a shop specially designed for the performance.

With building works going on in London, at Hatfield and at his other estate, Cranborne Manor in Dorset, the state of Cecil's finances was becoming increasingly parlous – he was already burdened with huge debts, but now they were exacerbated by the expense of presents and entertainment for the royal family. The king, who had himself been generous with gifts since his accession, was in similar trouble, his personal debts amounting to nearly £600,000. Having to juggle both his own finances and those of the king, Cecil had followed Harington's advice 'to make money of anything fit to be sold'. He had imposed import duties on more than fourteen hundred goods and had tried to curtail the royal expenses by persuading James to cut down on his gifts to courtiers. In July 1608 Cecil had introduced the new Book of Rates which substantially increased taxes, and in November that year James had publicly announced that he would reduce the gifts of land that he was accustomed to make to favoured courtiers.

Now it was time to cut his own expenditure, and so Cecil sent his surveyor to Hatfield 'about estimating what might be saved in the building'. By 25 May 1609 the architect, Robert Lyming, had compiled a list of what savings could be made: these ranged from simplifying the ornamentation – such as doing away with the stone lions and columns – to leaving the kitchen court-yard unpaved. Three days later Thomas Wilson, his adviser and chief finan-cial controller, made the even more radical suggestion of abolishing the terrace scheme in the East Garden that included ten pavilions and their balustrades, which had been designed to line the parterres and steps. So the building work came to a standstill, and labourers were sent home while everyone waited for Cecil to come to a decision. Lyming knew what a difficult client Cecil could be – during the previous months he had become increasingly irritated by his mercu-rial character; and many of the workmen knew only too well that designs 'may bee changed and alltered at my lords pleasure'. The hedges, for example, could not be set, Lyming complained later to Wilson, 'unless I understand my Lord's mind', while Wilson had always to 'dispute' any new suggestion with Cecil. Unable to delegate control, it took Cecil six weeks and three more visits to Hatfield before he would give the go-ahead, on 28 July, for the slimmed-down building scheme.

Three months later he regretted his parsimony, and all the changes were cancelled. Lyming, pleased with his employer's volte-face, promised that the house 'will be as strong & substantial as any work in England, or else my Lord put me to prison all the days of my life'; and as if to counterbalance his earlier frugality, Cecil decided to spend even more. This time he sent for Inigo Jones, then a young masque designer, to supply 'drawings of some architecture', and on 30 October Jones and Wilson rode to Hatfield, spending two days surveying the building site and plans. The first to recognise Inigo Jones's talent as an architect, Cecil gave employment to the man who a few years later would trigger a craze in England for classical Italian buildings. Unlike many architects of the period, he had studied in Italy and incorporated this first-hand experience into his designs for Hatfield. Applying his attention to the south façade and the clock tower, Jones changed the designs yet again. For the first time, he had been given the chance to prove that he was not just a designer in *papier-mâché* but a serious architect.

Cecil also reinstated the terraced scheme of the East Garden, and throughout the winter of 1609 the labourers continued the 'digging, carting &

carrying of earth' so as to raise the walks and construct the different levels. They built the hundreds of yards of coped and pencilled walls dividing the various sections – as a last gesture of frugal housekeeping these were made of 'stones & flints of the ruins of the old building'. The fencing of the park was also completed; Cecil happily accepted 'gifts' from friends and ingratiating courtiers – trees, plants, wild boars and deer as 'a sufficient complement to furnish . . . a park'.

Despite the considerable progress, the workload of his former Theobalds gardener Mountain Jennings was still enormous; work had only just begun on the East Garden, while the completed parts already required a lot of maintenance. As Jennings did not live on site, the daily organisation of the ever increasing work-force was becoming too complex. In September Cecil thought he had found a head gardener to oversee the work, but then received the news that the man could not take up 'his continual Residence at Hatfield' because he was too old. Instead, he offered to look after Cecil's garden in London and sent a drawing for a plot, but this still left Cecil in need of someone for Hatfield.

Then in January 1610, with the employment of John Tradescant, the problem seemed to have been solved. Coming from an inauspicious background, Tradescant had already worked for country squires and was known to John Gerard, who had been Cecil's father's gardener at Theobalds. His credentials

John Tradescant the Elder

must have been good because Cecil granted him a yearly salary of £50, four times that of a garden hand at Hatfield, as well as lodgings on the estate.

When Tradescant arrived with his young family, Hatfield was abuzz with labourers toing and froing with wheelbarrows, carting off old bricks from the demolished palace to the new terraces in order to build the walls and garden pavilions. By now the house had reached its full height, the roofers had finished their work, and more than thirty masons were carving the stone for the south façade. From the raised terraces, the belvederes or the mount, Tradescant could view the park in all its vast splendour. And he would immediately have recognised the garden's uniqueness: rather than looking inward, the long vistas united the ornamental pleasure grounds with the park, embraced the countryside and reached out to the world. The sculpted terraces, radiating drives and intricate knot gardens expressed the power of man to tame nature. Forgotten were the intimate enclosures of medieval times that suggested a fear of nature, and the separate enclosed garden rooms of the Elizabethan garden. Here, in front of John Tradescant, unfolded the garden that would shape his career. As with Inigo Jones, Cecil had chosen a man who would become the best in his field – the most famous plant collector of his time, admired by kings, courtiers and scholars alike. And it was at Hatfield that this passion began, inspired by Cecil's own fascination with the bizarre and outlandish.

Ever since the foundation of the East India Company in 1600, Cecil had regularly ordered curious 'toys' from India and China, as well as exotic animals such as monkeys, a 'bird of Arabia' and a tame parrot that drank red wine. The merchants of the East India Company had come late to the race for the globe – the Spanish, Portuguese and Dutch were already controlling the trade routes to the Far East – but by 1610, when Tradescant moved to Hatfield, they were catching up. To Cecil and his gardener's delight they also imported novel plants from the new colonies. The arrival of each vessel was keenly awaited by men such as Tradescant and Cecil, anxious to see these wonders of the world for the first time and to grow them in English soil.

During the first months of his employment, however, Tradescant concentrated on more mundane tasks, such as settling his wife and three-year-old son into the gardener's lodge and organising the kitchen garden. When the house was finished, the household would need a constant supply of vegetables and fruit for its kitchen, so Tradescant bought seeds, herbs and compost and set his men to work. Even at the building stage the cooks needed provisions for the workmen, as well as for Cecil who sometimes stayed at the parsonage, which had been repaired and altered at his request and at a cost of £400.

Cecil, at this time, was on the brink of exhaustion, feeling particularly burdened by the effects of James's excessive spending habits. The royal coffers were empty, and the situation was not helped by the assassination in May of the French king, Henry IV, leaving the French Crown in the hands of a minor and dashing all hopes that the French debt of £400,000 to the English Crown might be called in. At the beginning of the year Cecil had requested from Parliament an unprecedented peacetime subsidy of £600,000 to pay off the king's debts. In what would be called the Great Contract, he also asked for a guaranteed annual income of £200,000 for James's 'ordinary needs'. In return James would give up or reform feudal rights such as wardships and import duties.*

Unlike an absolute monarch, the king needed Parliament when it came to raising money – only it could vote to increase taxation and for extra funds. It in turn needed him, because he had the power to call and dissolve Parliament. In this interdependent relationship both parties exploited their leverage as much as possible, Parliament refusing to pay such sums as James requested while James threatened adjournment. Caught between the two, Cecil had to summon all his diplomatic skills in the greatest test of his career. He had to find a compromise that would grant James enough money without upsetting Parliament too much. After a long bargaining tussle lasting several weeks, the MPs offered first an annual payment of £100,000, then increased it to £180,000, but insisted on the abolition of wardships rather than their reform.† In return the king

---

*If a landowner died before his heir had reached the legal age to inherit the estate, the Crown became – for the time being – the owner. The Court of Wards, of which Cecil was the head, would then sell (and keep the profit for the royal purse) the temporary rights to the estate to someone else, who could then exploit the land and tenants if he wished. By the time the minor came of age to take possession of his land, the estate was often run down or even ruined.
†Cecil had suggested reforming the wardships thus far: a minor's estate could be sold only at a fixed price to a family member.

pressed for £240,000, but was eventually placated by the Commons' offer of an additional £20,000. The request to write off the £600,000, however, was steadfastly ignored. Since Parliament was prorogued on 23 July, the final contract had to wait until late autumn, after the summer recess. When Cecil arrived at Hatfield on the 28th he was worn out by the months of negotiations.

As Cecil contemplated his gardens, three years after the planting of the first trees, it must have been a relief to find refuge here from his life as a public figure. In London the king could summon him at any time and courtiers were constantly knocking at his door. With his privacy rarely respected and the increasing pomp of aristocratic life, Cecil was not alone in appreciating the respite offered by more intimate surroundings. The occasional withdrawal into seclusion became an important part of many courtiers' way of life. To accommodate this need at Hatfield, Cecil had ordered two sets of apartments: the dazzling formal state rooms, and smaller, simpler private quarters. Outside, the gardens followed the same pattern: a sumptuous area for state entertainment in the East Garden, then more intimate spaces, such as garden pavilions, which served as secret retreats. In addition, Cecil had given instructions for 'two little square buildings' to be set in the wall of the South Court, as well as two more for the West Garden, each fourteen feet high and twenty-four feet square. Often called banqueting houses, they were places for solace and more intimate socialising.

Every garden enthusiast built them; Lord Tresham had a banqueting house at Lyveden based on the shape of a cross, thereby testifying to his faith; Bacon's at Gorhambury was of two storeys and surrounded by water; and Cecil's father-in-law Lord Cobham had a retreat at Cobham Hall in Kent that was sixteen feet up in a tree, with branches spread out as platforms and accessible via a spiral staircase also made of branches. Garden writers recommended that these pavilions be placed 'at some remote angle of your garden: For the more remote it is from your house, the more private will you be from the frequent disturbances of your family and acquaintances'. Here a handful of guests could enjoy a 'banquet' – an intimate dessert course after dinner consisting of 'conceited dishes . . . with pretty and curious secrets'. Cakes, marzipan, 'artificial cinnamon sticks' and meringues would be served with spiced wines, and often presented on ornamented plates made of sugar.

This desire for intimacy was reflected not only in garden architecture but also in literature and art. The sonnet became popular, in particular Shakespeare's first collection, published in 1609. Whispered into a lover's ear or hidden in the secret compartments of writing-boxes or in the folds of dresses, these 'poems of love' became an essential element of the wooing that took place in dusky corners at court. In painting, miniature portraits held a similar cachet: small enough to be worn, they were personal tokens of love. Courtiers and friends also exchanged them as symbols of private allegiance. Compared to formal oil paintings, which displayed the public persona of the sitter, the miniature was an intimate depiction of character – Robert Cecil employed only the most famous portraitist, Nicholas Hilliard, who had popularised the art form at the end of the previous century.

Sonnets, miniatures and banqueting houses also reflected the lascivious undertone of aristocratic life. The sexual aspect of banquets and the adulterous use of garden houses featured frequently in the literature of the time. Both Ben Jonson and Thomas Middleton wrote of 'banquets in corners'; and the countess in John Marston's *The Insatiate Countess* desired 'to stirre up appetite to Venus banquet'. Had Cecil been building his banqueting houses for such a purpose, few would have been surprised; his doctor had diagnosed a liver sickness that 'kindles and nourishes concupiscence', which gained him the reputation of philanderer. Gossips spoke of his 'unparallel lust and hunting after strange flesh'.

At Hatfield Cecil probably also intended to use these little lodges for plotting, like the 'conveyance' that was planned for the main house 'whereby messengers may be sent . . . without any apparent note' to others in the building. Banqueting houses, separated from the comings and goings of the main house, were the perfect cover for Cecil's scheming and spying. Whether intended for lovers or for political confidants, he had them designed, like so much else, in the latest Italian Renaissance fashion. Though none of Cecil's garden buildings survives, his architect Robert Lyming designed one for Blickling Hall in Norfolk only a few years later, of which the drawing still exists. Since the house at Blickling was closely modelled on Hatfield, it is likely that the banqueting houses were too. Lyming's drawing shows a building with a triangular pedi-

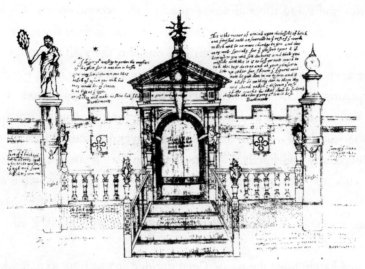

Robert Lyming's Banqueting House at Blickling Hall in Norfolk

ment, cornices and a frieze. Balustrades lined the steps and veranda, carved figures posed on pedestals, and a stone 'fire ball' adorned the apex of the roof – features also to be found in Hatfield's garden buildings.

Cecil's private time at Hatfield did not last long. For years he had been involved in negotiations with the main European powers – Spain, France and the Netherlands – and he now invited the French and Dutch ambassadors to join him at Hatfield. Treaties had been signed between Spain and England, as well as between Spain and the Netherlands, but the French feared that Spain might break the peace with the Dutch, and in February 1610 the French ambassador had proposed a pact between France, England and the Netherlands to defend the Dutch against Spain. The ambassador also hoped that this move would 'take away all jealousies and coldness' between England and France. Negotiations had been dragging on, and Cecil had tried – unsuccessfully – to retrieve some of the money that England had loaned to France and the Netherlands. So it seemed a good moment to bring everybody involved together at Hatfield. Cecil arrived there on 6 August, two days before the French and Dutch ambassadors were expected, so as to ensure his first party at Hatfield would go according to plan.

The house was not yet finished, but the builders had almost completed the exterior walls and the stairs now reached the second storey. Cecil could not yet accommodate guests at Hatfield and so had invited them for the day. In the garden, the terraces had been laid out and the visitors could venture down the avenues into the park. For the feast, Cecil threw open the doors of the banqueting hall of the old palace. The labourers had clipped the knot gardens and strewn herb and flower cuttings among the rushes on the floor, so that the fragrance of thyme, hyssop and lavender wafted around the old walls to mask any bad smells. Fish, meat and poultry were delivered from the village, while the storerooms were stocked up with plenty of wine and ale. Tradescant's kitchen garden provided artichokes, cabbages, spinach, asparagus, rosemary, lettuce, radishes, tarragon, rocket, parsley, carrots and onions.

Immediately after the party, Cecil decided it was time to embark on the waterworks. As soon as the illustrious guests had left, work began on the Dell, the lowest part of the East Garden across which a natural river ran. The first months were spent straightening it: just as babies used to be swaddled to straighten their legs, so with buttresses and walls the labourers forced the river into a perfect line.

With the water features under way, Cecil and Tradescant sat down in October 1610 to decide which plants to buy for the rest of the garden. Tradescant recommended that they be ordered from Brussels, which was then a hub of the horticultural trade. He had a good contact there through whom he had procured seeds and flowers before: one William Trumbull. As a British diplomat, Trumbull would be able to act as Cecil's plant agent. Tradescant wrote to him: '[I]t hathe plessed my Lord tresorur to give me enterteynment and he Spake to me to know wheare the Rarest thing wear'. He enclosed a long shopping list that included lilies, irises, crocuses, roses and clematis as well as vines – 'bothe Cuttings and Roots and all other Sorts whatsoever he can furnishe me withe, for my Lord maketh a Vinyard'.

Tradescant had no sense of smell,* but this unfortunate disability was outweighed by his exceptional botanical expertise, not unlike Cecil's use of his political skill to compensate for his crooked back. Immune to the seductive

*He mentions his disability in his Russian travel journal in 1618 (Leith-Ross 1998, p.63).

scents of honeysuckle or jasmine, Tradescant favoured rare plants over the sweet-smelling, and so he ordered from Trumbull 'What other Sorts he knowethe that be Strange', 'any strang sorts of any seede that is Rare', and anything new. The new and unusual included the crocus-like *Colchicum byzantinum*, introduced from Asia only a few years earlier; the cherry laurel which originated in eastern Europe; St Bruno's lily with its large white trumpet-shaped flowers, and the delicate sky-blue *Brimeura amethystina*, also called the Spanish hyacinth. In addition, he asked Trumbull to send the 'greatest quantities' of the more common plants and trees.

Before the arrival of foreign plants, soft colours had dominated English gardens. The native blossoms such as honeysuckles, dianthus, harebells and foxglove came mainly in subtle yellows, creamy whites, pale pinks, light blues and soft purples; oranges and reds were rare, and came in soft shades such as that of the scarlet pimpernel. Tradescant, though, favoured showy varieties, and he bought double-flowered forms of purple *Hepatica nobilis*, which in England was only available as a single variety; voluptuous red *Ranunculus asiaticus; Pulsatilla vernalis*, whose petals and leaves were covered in silvery hair; several multi-headed varieties of narcissi; martagon lilies with their flamboyantly sculpted petals, striped and patterned flowers such as 'specled' anemones, as well as specimens with serrated leaves and two-layered blooms. As long as they looked novel – even deformed – and were brightly coloured, they were desirable. To ensure safety during their long journey, Tradescant gave Trumbull meticulous instructions on how to pack the delicate plants: '[T]he flower Roots they may be put into a Basket or a Box withe Dri mose or dri Sand, sealed uppe'.

While Tradescant was busy ordering plants, on 16 October, after the summer recess, Cecil hurried back to London to reopen negotiations with Parliament over the Great Contract. James was becoming increasingly impatient, but had retreated to his hunting lodge, leaving Cecil to deal with the problem. Although the king had reduced the lump sum he was requesting to £500,000, Cecil had few further concessions to offer Parliament, and on 7 November MPs rejected the king's demands. To pay off his debts and to grant him an annual income would mean that they would lose their hold over him, as he would have even fewer reasons to call regular Parliaments. Although everyone sensed a spirit of opposition in the Commons, the king blamed Cecil alone for the failure of the deal. Hurried meetings with MPs followed, but neither side was willing to compromise. Parliamentarians accused the king of squandering public money, while James was irritated by Cecil's 'strange discourses' in the House of Commons. When he wrote to Cecil on 6 December 1610, because 'I rather write than speak it unto you', it was clear that Cecil's position was becoming precarious. Being himself £53,000 in debt, he needed more than the annual £6000 revenue from his estates. The trouble was that all his other income – from taxes, the secret service and from bribes – came from his official posts, which in turn were dependent on the king's favours.

On 7 December James wrote in fury to the Privy Council, accusing them of tossing his demands about like 'tennis balls amongst them', making him ill and straining his purse. At the same time heated letters flew between him and Cecil: James lamenting, then complaining; Cecil explaining and soothing, but to little avail. Desperate to win back the king's favour, two days later Cecil went to see the queen, possibly in the hope of winning her support. But by the 31st James had had enough, and dissolved Parliament. He still needed the money, though, and if Cecil was to stay in power he had to find it from somewhere. So he began to revalue the gold coinage, called in the Dutch debts and sold titles – £1095 bought a baronetcy, for instance. Slowly the empty coffers began to fill up again. Still set on ingratiating himself with the queen, Cecil entertained her in March 1611 at his London house and plied her with presents, such as richly embroidered green velvet hangings that had cost him over £1000.

Playing on the king's love of lavish entertainment, Cecil now invited him to Hatfield. He had planned a splendid dinner, as a foretaste of what the great house would be able to offer his royal guest on future occasions. Although he would not be able to accommodate him and his entourage overnight, as the house was as yet unfinished, he wanted the garden to be immaculate. But it still lacked the lively sound and movement of the water features that were so much a part of contemporary Italian gardens – the 'thousand . . . effects of water' at the Villa Lante, the crystal cascades of the Pratolino, or the Villa d'Este's sinuous canal that gushed down beside the steps. So, again to impress the king, he commissioned the Dutchman Simon Sturtivant to create a complicated hydraulic system that would power the extensive waterworks in the East Garden – presumably Cecil thought no Englishman was up to it. When Sturtivant arrived at Hatfield to measure the gardens one morning in late January 1611, he encountered England at its worst – rainy, grey and cold. For three days he worked in the garden, calculating the layout of the pipework that would be needed for the water displays. The water would have to be carried more than a mile, from the springs in the Conduit Grove to the East Garden, where Sturtivant planned a new river and fountains. As Cecil was expecting the king on 5 July, Sturtivant, with the assistance of Mountain Jennings, had less than six months to complete the earth-moving, pipe-laying, installation and ornamentation.

To fund his stunning *mise-en-scène* for the royal delectation Cecil continued to exploit the tug-of-war in Europe. Making use of his international connections, when the import of Caen stone from France was stopped he sent Thomas Wilson to see the French ambassador, who quickly obliged. It was not the only good turn the French did Cecil: in February 1611, the French ambassador's wife stocked up on political favours by sending thirty thousand vines from France. Planted to the north-east, almost a mile from the house, the rectangular vineyard was intended primarily as an extravagant showpiece. It was laid out in the fashionable geometrical manner with turf walks and beds hedged with sweetbriar. Concerned about the tending of his treasure, Cecil also asked the gardener, who worked for his brother Thomas Cecil, to come down to Hatfield to discuss different ways of planting the vines. Even thirty years later, the diarist and horticulturist John Evelyn thought that 'the most considerable rarity besides the house [was] . . . the garden & vineyard'.

In addition to these political 'gifts', Cecil acquired many other plants. Some were bought from English gardeners who traded in plants on a small scale as a profitable sideline, and others came from garden enthusiasts who swapped seeds, bulbs and saplings – an important network, as nurseries were as yet barely established in England. In the Netherlands and France, on the other hand, they were much more widespread and offered a greater selection of plants. Consequently, many garden owners in England turned to their agents on the continent to source the best available there. One of these was Robert Cecil, who bought many fruit trees from 'beyond seas', '500 mulberries' from France,

400 sycamores 'out of the lowe Contryes', '12 Rare Ripe Chery trees, 6 flem-
mish Chery treese . . . 34 Quince treese' and 70 walnut trees from Flanders.
Anticipating the fashion for Dutch lime, which was soon to become the most
popular avenue tree in England, Cecil also ordered four hundred lime trees
from the Netherlands. Together with the hundreds of elms, walnuts and
sycamores they would line the new avenues, some of which were forty feet
wide.

In May 1611 Cecil travelled to Hatfield to oversee progress. Until then
he had mainly come for day trips, but now he stayed for five days, ordering
yet more changes and improvements. An industrious scene met the visitor's eye:
women working away on hands and knees at the elaborate knot gardens, digging
weeds out of the gravel paths and flowerbeds with blunt knives; garden hands
cutting the grass with scythes; others placing pots of brightly coloured plants
on the terraces and at the corners of the knots. Keeping a close eye on everything, Tradescant made sure that his special plants were situated at the centre
so that the king would not be able to miss them.

Meanwhile, workmen were levelling the lower terrace of the East Garden
and turfing the paths on the new island in the river below. The carpenter was
making the doors and gates for the garden walls, and, following Cecil's instructions, some of the newly planted hedges were being removed. The South Avenue
was now completed, and the section of the North Avenue nearest the house
was being lowered by the removal of what would amount to two thousand
barrow-loads of earth to the North Court. Using almost two miles of fencing,
more parts of the park were enclosed and several crosswalks completed.
Progress at the waterworks was less straightforward, as Mountain Jennings was
struggling not only with the river but also with Cecil's fickle temperament.
First he was ordered to take the gravel out of one river because it 'hyndereth
the passage of the water', then he had to make a new stream crossing one of
the terraces 'run more shallow, which will be more handsom'. On 1 July, with
just four days to go before the king's visit, Jennings was still battling with nature,
having been forced to alter 'a rocke twice in the east garden'. In the house
workmen were still laying down the matting and hanging the tapestries – the
main rooms, at least, would look sumptuous.

When on the appointed day James arrived, for the first time since he had lost Theobalds Cecil was able to entertain his king royally outside London. The cooks had spent days preparing the dishes – altogether Cecil spent £200 on food and drink, double what he had spent per day on the infamous party at Theobalds five years earlier. The house with its altered South Porch was almost completed, the scaffolding removed and the balustrades fixed on the roof. It had taken an unprecedentedly short time to construct – in only four years Cecil had built one of the most outstanding houses in the country, its gardens already rivalling the greatest estates. The party was a success. Cecil kept his various posts, and was able to finance the remaining work at Hatfield.

By September 1611 the house was fully furnished and ready to be occupied. Cecil, though, once again changed his mind about the waterworks. Having recently seen 'Mount Parnassus' in Queen Anne's new garden at Somerset House in London, he had decided that Sturtivant and Jennings's endeavour had been futile. The centrepiece of the queen's garden was a huge rugged rock set in a large pool, peopled with elegant statues holding vessels from which gushed streams of water. Herbs and other flowering plants grew in the crannies, and inside was a huge grotto covered in fossils and shells.

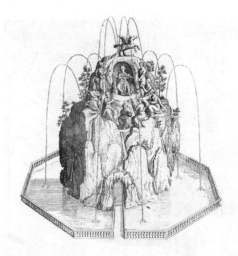

Mount Parnassus. Salomon de Caus's rock fountain. This design is almost identical to the one he built for Queen Anne at Somerset House

Thirty feet high and eighty in diameter, the queen's Mount Parnassus surpassed the original at the Pratolino by far.

The designer of the masterpiece at Somerset House was Salomon de Caus, England's latest import from the continent. He had travelled extensively through Italy and had seen the water pergola and statues at the Pratolino, the Fountain of Lights at the Villa Lante and the waterworks at the Villa d'Este. Having studied how murky ponds could be turned into liquid crystal, how millions of drops of water could create sparkling cascades and how to devise rainbows as the finishing touch to these spectacles, de Caus had arrived in England in 1609 to replicate them in the queen's garden. Cecil wanted to buy de Caus's discerning eye and his miraculous inventions.

Speaking statues, rotating fountains, grottoes and giant figures, all motorised by ingenious hydraulic mechanisms and solar energy, brought Italian gardens alive – and de Caus knew their secrets. One of his systems focused sunrays through lenses, so as to heat up water, which then passed through pipes to drive the fountains and statues. He made mechanical birds chirp and had statues move around their pools while playing trumpets to tunes he had composed. These musical automata were his speciality – some of which were

Solar-powered fountain by Salomon de Caus

powered by expanding water forcing air through organ pipes. To manipulate nature in this way, de Caus deployed a combination of water pressure and suction, pulleys, counterweights and cogwheels. His aim was fantastical entertainment. The great chasm that would divide science from the occult did not yet exist – scientists still experimented with alchemy, for instance, and creations such as de Caus's hydraulic Greek gods demonstrated the still active alliance between science and mythology during the Renaissance.

In hiring de Caus, Cecil was in illustrious company: the queen had also persuaded her son, the Prince of Wales, to use the Frenchman's talents. By employing their favoured craftsman, Cecil could be sure that the theatrical devices he presented at Hatfield would be a success with his royal masters. Although John Dacombe, one of his financial advisers, warned him towards the end of the year, 'I beseech your Lordship to forbear buildings', Cecil went ahead, commissioning de Caus and ordering the destruction of Simon Sturtivant's devices. Poor Thomas Wilson was still doing the accounts for Sturtivant's hydraulic system when he had to tell the workmen to down tools. Although the pipes had been laid and the trenches covered in the Conduit Grove, construction in the East Garden now came to a halt.

Tormented by toothache and a cold, finance man Wilson accompanied de Caus on his visit to Hatfield in late November 1611. Reporting back to Cecil that 'every journey brings new designs', he sounded more than a little wearied by the idea of yet more construction work in the East Garden. Nevertheless, he gave his master a full report of de Caus's suggestions. A little drawing in the margin of Wilson's letter gave Cecil an idea of what the Frenchman was planning: and the design was even grander than that de Caus had constructed for the queen. Taking advantage of Cecil's three descending terraces in the stately East Garden, he suggested a system of fountains, one of which would be shaped like a rock, probably similar to Queen Anne's at Somerset House. A great new cistern (in the left-hand corner of Wilson's sketch) alongside the upper terrace would be connected by underground pipes to the first fountain, placed in the centre of the highest terrace. This fountain would feed two more (on the middle terrace, nos. 2 and 3) and these in turn would feed the main fountain (no. 4) situated in the centre of the lowest terrace. Three of the fountains would sit in square pools, of which the lowest would encompass the entire terrace. Below this, on the island situated in the Dell, de Caus designed a 'force', or pump, housed in a mill-like building that would supply water for two more fountains sited there (not in the sketch).

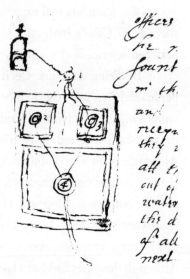

Salomon de Caus's waterworks at Hatfield,
sketched on the margins of a letter written by
Thomas Wilson in November 1611

A few days after his visit to Hatfield, de Caus supplied Cecil with models of his designs, and work began. The cisterns built earlier by Sturtivant were declared useless and de Caus ordered that they be dismantled, unless Cecil would 'like to have the great open cistern in the garden to put fish into, to be ready upon all occasions'. Starting afresh, the bricklayers built new structures to house the new cisterns. Following de Caus's instructions, the engineers and plumbers devised a complicated pipe system that would provide enough water for the fountains as well as for watering the parterre. Pumps forced the water, supplied by springs in the Conduit Grove and from the river, to the cistern, where it was stored, then piped to the other fountains. The architect Robert Lyming drew up some new designs for the plots around the fountains; the plumbers laid the pipes in the East Garden and as far as the mount in the West Garden, where de Caus was presumably also planning a fountain. By the end of 1611 Cecil had already spent well over £1000 on his water project, and more was to follow.

Work was also continuing on the diamond-shaped island in the Dell at the bottom of the terraces, which was set in a square parterre. Bisecting it was the river that the workmen had straightened with walls during the previous winter and around the parterre ran a canal. Diagonal tree-lined walks divided the island into triangular garden plots, and like Francis Bacon's water garden at Gorhambury it had a banqueting house in the middle. There were two fountains in the river, and a few garden buildings fringed the parterre: a pavilion set in an orchard; a mill housing the pump; another pavilion on a mount with a grotto underneath, and opposite this a tower-like structure. Fifty years later visitors still admired the beauty 'of a small river, which . . . forms compartments of a large parterre, and rises and secretly loses itself in a hundred places'.

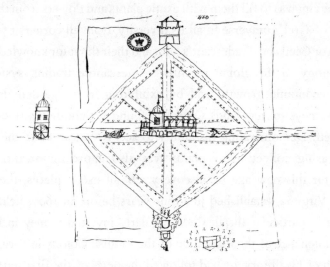

Drawing of the island in the Dell in the East Garden at Hatfield, with the banqueting house in the middle and the other buildings on the edges

Hundreds of yards of stone needed to be carved and laid for the steps leading from one terrace to another. As Cecil wanted more garden structures, the carpenters built 'four pretty slight arbours in the west garden' as well as 'ten or twelve arbours . . . in the east garden'. Bridges were now erected 'for the passage over the waterworkes', and the gardeners planted hedges on the island in the Dell. With Cecil harrying everybody, the workmen promised that they would be finished by Easter. Mountain Jennings may well have been wondering whether he would ever complete his little river in the East Garden, which by now he had changed countless times. His latest effort featured a rock decorated with cast metal leaves, snakes and fishes, out of which water flowed. His men had spent weeks digging out a zigzag-shaped canal, like the one at Thomas Cecil's lodge near Burghley House, which Robert Cecil and Lyming had admired earlier that year. But when the river was finished, Lyming reported to Cecil that it was 'not pleasing to the eye', and poor Jennings had to alter it yet again.

Having commissioned de Caus, Cecil had also discussed more planting schemes with Tradescant. Vases and stone 'cups' for displaying the plant specimens had been carved, painted and set up on the balustrades and pedestals, and now the aim was to fill them with exotic plants and flowers from the colonies. The glory of God's universe in all its diversity, from all corners of the world, would mirror Cecil and Tradescant's faith and their thirst for knowledge. Botany bore testimony to the global reach of a mercantile trading system and to England's economic growth, and by exhibiting in his garden the fruits of perilous journeys to new lands Cecil had found yet another way of aggrandising himself. Demonstrating his ability to access vast areas of the world, his ever increasing collection of plants was also, more importantly, a visual metaphor for this new age of discovery. Of all exotic places, the American colony of Virginia, established just four years before in 1607, held Cecil and Tradescant in particular thrall. Cecil regularly invested money in his 'adventure of maintenance of the Plantation of the English Colony in Virginia'. From the warmth of his library, he had followed the news of the first settlers as they gradually turned what had been little more than a swamp into a fortified trading post. Indeed, Tradescant too became so fascinated with it that a few years later he invested £12, almost a quarter of his yearly income from Hatfield, in the Virginia Company, and his son would later travel there three times to collect specimens. Virginia became a window into the strange world from where Cecil and Tradescant would procure plants never before seen in England.

Unlike the explorers of the fifteenth and sixteenth centuries who had tried to find the original Garden of Eden, people in the next century were taken with an idea even more audacious. If God had created nature, they reasoned, then he was present in everything he had made, and the more things they assembled the more evidence they would possess of God's ingenuity. To fill the garden at Hatfield with as many plant varieties as possible would be to display God's abundance. The ever expanding world of Robert Cecil's day made the re-creation of the botanical entirety of Eden a continual challenge. In building this horticultural paradise, Tradescant presented nature as a book that man might read like the Bible. He understood the world in the same way as Johannes Kepler, the brilliant German mathematician and astronomer, who had described it as 'the very Book of Nature in which God as Creator has revealed and depicted His being and His Will with Man in a wordless tract'. Furthermore, the successful nurturing of foreign plants accustomed to different temperatures, soils and humidity was proof that the gardener, or patron, controlled nature: and to the extent that he could re-create a place where flowers and fruit would grow all year round, a 'perpetual spring' – a notion intrinsically linked with paradise. Twenty years earlier Edmund Spenser, in *The Faerie Queene*, had evoked the vision of both continual spring and continual harvest in the Garden of Adonis:

> No needs there Gardiner to set, or sow,
> To plant or prune: for of their owne accord
> All things, as they created were, doe grow.

If only Tradescant could gather enough plants from other parts of the world that flowered at different times, he could create what Francis Bacon would describe fourteen years later as a garden 'for all the Moneths in the Yeare'.

Although John Tradescant had worked at Hatfield for less than two years, Cecil already admired his gardening genius so much that he had had his portrait depicted on the newel of the Grand Staircase, amid carvings of the flowers and fruits he had introduced into the gardens. Now gilded and painted, the staircase was the magnificent centrepiece of Hatfield House. Cecil trusted Tradescant's expertise enough to send him to the continent to scour the nurseries there for yet more plants.

Equipped with letters of introduction, money and spare clothes in his 'cloake bag', Tradescant departed for Ramsgate, Kent, in September 1611 to board ship. At Ramsgate the gardener's excitement was temporarily blunted 'by contrary wind', which delayed him by four days. When he finally arrived in the Netherlands, he went first to the nurseries at Middelburg and Rotterdam, choosing the best plants available. Since it was autumn he was able to judge the fruits, as well as assess which trees could be easily uprooted for shipping home. In Delft he bought many varieties of quince, cherry, apple and pear trees; in Leiden, 'Roots of flowers' which were 'strang and rare'; in Haarlem eight hundred tulips, and in Antwerp five hundred more. In Haarlem he also succeeded in obtaining two specimens of the coveted arbor-vitae (*Thuja occidentalis*), the first conifers to have arrived in Europe, in the sixteenth century, from North America. He filled his caskets with as many varieties of 'gilliflowers' (carnations) as he could find, then added roses and multi-headed narcissi. Later he found anemones, much sought after because they flowered in many different colours, often striped and variegated, while the chequered petals of fritillaries would complement the garden's patterns and colours. In Brussels he must have been pleased to receive plants from the 'archedukes gardner Called Peere' – he knew that they were of the best quality because he had already ordered flowers and vines from him through Trumbull in 1610.

Then he was off to Paris, where he acquired such tender plants as figs, oleanders, orange trees and myrtles, hoping they would survive the journey to Hatfield and the climate when they got there. Filling yet more boxes, he bought a cherry tree – which would bear his name until the nineteenth century – and flowers like the fiery orange *Lilium pomponium*, crimson roses and the bright-yellow Spanish broom with its spiky blossom. At the same time he purchased a 'packet of books 6 in number', and could not resist adding some curiosities, among which were 'on Chest of Shells with eyght boxes of Shells', 'a great buffells horn' and an 'artyfyshall byrd'.

There were many gardens and other attractions for Tradescant to admire during his journey. The garden of the Prince of Orange at The Hague was famous for its covered walks. The encyclopaedic collection of plants in the university physic garden at Leiden must have excited his quest for new species, but was perhaps outshone by the spectacular objects and rarities at the local anatomy school. Near Brussels he saw a three-acre field full of 'Chardon' artichokes, a sort that English gardeners had failed to cultivate. As well as furnishing so many acquisitions and filling his head with new ideas and plans, the trip provided him with the opportunity to meet other enthusiasts. In Paris he contacted the French king's head gardener, from whom he received 'many Rare Shrubs', marking the beginning of a good relationship during which the two men exchanged horticultural treasures for years. Later, when Tradescant was back in England, the Frenchman sent seedlings from Canada that had been brought back by French explorers, and Tradescant reciprocated with plants from the new English colony of Virginia. Grafting plants and collecting seeds to despatch to colleagues and friends was something that Tradescant would do for the rest of his life.

While his head gardener was thus occupied in Europe, life in England was becoming increasingly difficult for Cecil himself. His career as chief minister had been irreparably damaged by the collapse of the Great Contract almost a year before. James continued to blame him personally for this fiscal disaster, and Cecil feared that he would not be able to retain his powerful position for much longer. But burdened as he was with his own huge debts, he could not afford to be cut off by James. Then, in December that year, Cecil collapsed with fever and rheumatism. The best doctors were summoned, and they prescribed a frightening regime of remedies ranging from purging clysters (seventeenth-century colonic irrigation) and pills to induce vomiting, to 'destructively explosive laxatives'. With little hope left, courtiers and government officials wrote to each other, preparing for Cecil's imminent death: '[I]t is on all hands concluded that his Lordship must shortly leave this world,' declared one. When Tradescant returned in January 1612 he immediately busied himself, nurturing all his newly acquired treasures, overseeing the planting, watering and weeding. If there was still some hope for Cecil, it was important that he see his garden at its best – the most colourful, the most splendid, in the country.

Cecil was resilient, and he surprised everyone by recovering. From now on he would be surrounded by the country's most reputable physicians. He was 'somewhat thinner than usually', wrote his close friend the Earl of Shrewsbury on the 23rd. Still weak, he needed to rest, and what better place to do that than at Hatfield? So everyone set to work, anxious to finish Cecil's biggest and most important building project in anticipation of his arrival. Tradescant made sure that the latest batch of plants were adjusting to their new environment, and loads of earth were moved for planting trees in the park. Bridges were built at the river so that Cecil could cross over to his island, more fences were erected and fresh gravel scattered on the walks. But, relapsing in February before he could leave London, Cecil was unable to enjoy his garden as planned. He was suffering from a tumour – probably cancerous – of the liver, as well as from piles, indigestion, fever and swollen legs, and had to take to his bed once more. More doctors were called in, and the clyster ordeal began again. Stuck in London, unable to get to Hatfield where he might have drawn comfort from viewing the progress of his garden, he benefited in one way at least from his relapse. With Cecil ill, government business was seriously interrupted, and James realised the incalculable worth of his minister's advice. In March 1612, waiting for Cecil's recovery, the king refused to make any political decisions.

Meanwhile, Tradescant and his team of gardeners at Hatfield continued their work. Now fully furnished, the house was ablaze with bright colour and gilt. Everything had been painted: ceilings, fireplaces, windows and panelling. Cecil's bed was decorated with flowers, birds and figures. The frieze in the king's bedchamber glowed red and gold, the fireplace in the chapel was black and gold, and the pendant above the staircase shone white and green. A sculpture of the king had been painted to look like copper, while the organ was resplendent in gold. Fifty-four gilded stone lions gazed over the garden from the roof, and the spring sun slanted in through one of the first stained-glass windows since the Reformation, illuminating the chapel in brilliant colour.

In a race against Cecil's failing health, Tradescant and his men set up seats and railings along the river, completed the planting of the ornamental scheme in the East Garden and trimmed the hedges. The carpenter put the finishing touches to the banqueting houses and swans were shipped in from Cecil's house in London. The chests of shells that Tradescant had bought in Rouen were emptied on to the bed of the stream, where together with coloured pebbles they gleamed and glittered from beneath the water's surface. The gates, balustrades, railings and seats were lavishly painted and gilded. The twenty-four stone lions lining the steps in the East Garden were each painted with Cecil's coat of arms. Mirroring the interior of the house, the garden was a symphony of colour and gilding. Finally, on 5 May 1612, de Caus's fountain was finished. A huge rock and a monumental figure painted to resemble copper were set in an imposing marble basin, forming the centrepiece of the garden.

At last, the house was ready to be lived in and the garden in bloom. It was time for the master to return. But already by the end of April, Robert Cecil's condition had worsened and his physicians recommended the waters at Bath. For the arduous hundred-mile journey on roads bedevilled with holes, mud and stones, twenty-three pounds of down was stuffed into the bedding in the coach to lessen his pain. When he arrived in Bath five days later, he was exhausted. Once there, he was hoisted into the waters on a specially constructed padded chair suspended from a pulley. Cecil wrote to his son William that he was immersing himself in the waters no 'higher than the navel. I am already warmed from that part downward.' Hopes were raised that he would be revived by the treatments. When 'blue & livid spots' appeared on his body, he was treated for scurvy. The Earl of Shrewsbury sent 'scorbute grass' from the Peak District to relieve his discomfort. Organising twenty people to scour the Derbyshire hills, Shrewsbury had asked them 'to gather so much of thereof as can be put into a basket made to carry behind one on a horse', and then made sure that a fresh consignment was sent to Bath every four or five days. His wife the countess recommended the 'quintessence of honey' as the best medicine for Cecil, whose ulcerous open sores, combined with his bad breath – the symptoms of scurvy – were later described as 'filthy froth'. Spending an enormous £1500 on his little army of physicians, quacks and apothecaries, Cecil believed wholeheartedly in their healing powers. But it was too late: when his friends and his son arrived with a diamond ring from King James as a token of his affection, Cecil's strength was failing fast. They decided it was time to take him home.

Cecil died one week short of his forty-ninth birthday, surrounded by friends and doctors, on 24 May 1612, at a friend's house in Marlborough on his way home. He would never see his finished house and garden, hear the water gushing from the fountains or stroll down the immaculate walks. He would never receive a secret visitor in one of his banqueting houses, or climb the mount to admire his 'Book of Nature'. When Cecil's coffin arrived at Hatfield, it was Tradescant's last sad task to prepare the gardens for his master's funeral. He ordered a new scythe, 'for mowing of the courts and east garden against the funeral'. Rushes were mixed with fragrant cuttings from the knot gardens and strewn in the chapel.

Against his wishes, Cecil's funeral was a lavish affair. The tomb that would eventually be placed in Hatfield's parish church was not yet finished, but Cecil's son and heir William, now 2nd Earl of Salisbury, insisted on commemorating his father appropriately. The occasion cost him almost £2000, £800 being spent on special mourning 'cloaks' for all the guests and £300 on food alone, ensuring that the man who had surrounded himself with beauty and splendour was buried in similar style. Hatfield House and garden, though, were never used as Cecil had intended. Lacking his father's political clout, William played no significant role at court, and so Hatfield slipped from centre stage, no longer the place from which England would be ruled.

2

Subjugating Nature: Hampton Court

'If I have seen further, it is by standing upon the shoulders
of giants'.

Isaac Newton to Robert Hooke, 5 February 1676

'Gard'ning took up a great part of his Time, in which he was
not only a Delighter, but likewise a great Judge'

Stephen Switzer on William III, 1718

On 5 November 1688, William of Orange, ruler of the Netherlands and self-
proclaimed protector of Protestantism, landed near Torbay on the south coast
of England with an armada of fifty warships and fifteen thousand troops.
Billowing triumphantly from the mastheads were great banners emblazoned
with the words 'For Religion and Liberty', and his motto *'Je Maintiendrai'* ('I
will uphold'). England was gripped in a religious and constitutional crisis that
brought back terrible memories of the Civil War forty years earlier, and William
had been invited by a group of Whig parliamentarians known as the 'Immortal
Seven' to restore faith and order. James II, the reigning king, had dissolved
Parliament and reinstated Catholics in both the government and the army, giving

The gardens of Versailles in 1710. Note the cross-shaped Grand
Canal in the middle and the radiating avenues and 'compartments'

cause for concern that 'the King may suspend all the laws on the kingdom'.*
At least as significant, the queen had given the king a Catholic heir – after
fifteen barren years – making England's future as a Protestant nation uncertain. William was considered a suitable saviour because, as the grandson of
Charles I and the husband of Mary, eldest daughter of James II and his first
wife Anne Hyde, his Stuart pedigree was impeccable. In addition, he was a
committed Protestant who had fought for sixteen years against France's
territorial ambitions, to prevent Europe from falling under a Catholic tyranny.

*The opinion of the Seven Bishops' Council, who opposed James's Declaration of Indulgence
which permitted liberty of worship (Hill, 2002, p. 237).

As his career had been ruled by this passionate opposition to Louis XIV, William for his part had accepted the invitation of the 'Immortal Seven' in order to avert any possibility of an Anglo-French Catholic alliance and eventually to enlist the English army in his campaign against the French king.

Louis was the embodiment of absolutism, ruling in line with his famous credo, '*L'état, c'est moi*' ('I am the state'). The self-styled Sun King's most famous symbol was the Palace of Versailles, its garden celebrated for its elaborate fountains in their large pools and its intricately patterned terraces adorned with statues. Stretching over many acres, it contained mazes, geometrically planted groves and countless garden buildings; its most potent sign of Louis's rule was the cross-shaped Grand Canal, representing both his faith and his mercantile prowess – according to its designer André Le Nôtre, it was large enough to accommodate Mediterranean trading ships. Just as the long avenues stretched for miles into the distance, so did Louis's power radiate from Versailles into the rest of France and beyond. William, at thirty-eight, was a very different kind of ruler: as Stadtholder of the United Dutch Provinces, he shared his power with the representative assemblies of each province and their municipal delegates.

Within a month of William's arrival at Torbay, James II had fled to France and England was in William's hands. On 13 February 1689, in the great Banqueting Hall at Whitehall, William and Mary, ten years after their wedding, were pronounced king and queen – the first 'double bottomed monarchy', as Bishop Gilbert Burnet would call it in his *History of My Own Time* (1724–34). The royal couple looked an odd pair, with Mary towering four inches above her husband. While she was elegant and beautiful, he was neither handsome nor charming – though his piercing eyes and his courage were much admired. Although they stood, during the ceremony, under a painting by Rubens celebrating the divine right of English kings, William and Mary were the first monarchs not to claim that their authority was bestowed by God. It was from Parliament that they accepted the crown, and as the Declaration of Rights was read to them they agreed to limit their powers to those of a constitutional monarchy. The relationship between Parliament and monarch was thereby changed irreversibly: the umbilical cord joining God and ruler had been cut,

William of Orange, 1677   Queen Mary II, *c.* 1690

and the principles of parliamentary supremacy were established. The intellectual justification was provided by John Locke's *Second Treatise on Government*,
published the same year. At the core of his theory was the fundamental shift
of the people's status from subject to citizen, in which divine right was replaced
by a social contract between them and those who governed them.

After the ceremony, William and Mary made their home at Whitehall, the
rambling palace around which English court life radiated. But soon the courtiers,
vying for royal favours as was their habit, were complaining that 'the gaiety and
the diversions of . . . court [had] disappeared'. Finding it difficult to warm to
their garrulous triviality, the king 'observed the errors of too much talking, more
than those of too cold a silence'. He preferred the battlefield where he 'was all
fire', priding himself on his fearlessness rather than on his manners or fashion
sense. In contrast to his noblemen with their long curly hair and luxuriant silks,
he dressed in the plainest clothes and eschewed wigs. Even his close friends said
that he lacked charisma, and that he 'gave too much occasion to a general disgust'.
Mary, by contrast, showed 'great vivacity and cheerfulness', but because she was
unhappy at Whitehall, brought little playfulness to the court. Compared to the

intimate Dutch court with its clean and orderly rooms, Whitehall was dark and dank. It was also very public, eyes following the couple wherever they went, and, as she revealed in her memoirs, Mary hated this 'noisy world full of vanity'. Moreover, the thick smoky air exacerbated William's asthma, adding a wheeze to his foreign drawl. Not even outside the palace walls could he ease his discomfort, London being, in John Evelyn's words, 'so filled with the fuliginous steam of the sea-coal, that hardly could one see across the streets'.

Hampton Court. The old east front and the canal at
the time of Charles II

Ten days after they had been pronounced king and queen, William and Mary visited Hampton Court, a few hours' ride from London on the banks of the River Thames.* Now, as King of England, William must have wanted a royal seat befitting his new status. Although – or maybe because – they were only constitutional monarchs, William and Mary felt the need for a palace such as Versailles that radiated power, to compensate for their personal lack of it. Not having been a principal royal seat for more than a hundred years and

---

*Unless otherwise stated, the dates of William and Mary's visits to Hampton Court and William's campaigns in the Netherlands are based on the unpublished manuscript 'William and Mary Chronology' held at the Curatorial Office, Hampton Court, compiled by G. D. Heath from public records, letters and accounts.

consisting now of only a scattering of Tudor buildings, Hampton Court's glory days were long gone. By contrast, the gardens included some then fashionable elements added by Charles II in the 1660s, such as an extensive semicircular plot edged with lime trees, from which stretched an avenue and a canal. To the south of the palace in the Privy Garden was a mount with a spiral path and a formal parterre. Divided into four grass squares with fountains and statues in the corners, it was laid out in what Samuel Pepys had called thirty years earlier 'the present fashion of gardens, to make them plain'.

Mary's first reaction was to declare the whole place 'badly neglected'. Compared to other grand gardens in England, such as Badminton in Gloucestershire and Longleat in Wiltshire, which had French-style parterres with elaborate arabesque patterns, Hampton Court was too plain by far. Walking through the grounds, the new English monarch and his queen saw all too well that although the basics were in place, compared to the work of art that was Versailles it was a mere sketch waiting to be realised.

William and Mary were united in their love of gardens. In Holland they had followed the latest horticultural fashions, not least because William's physician had advised him to take up gardening for its therapeutic value. They had spent many hours in their gardens, discussing improvements and working with some of the world's best plantsmen. On the point of leaving for England they had been involved in constructing what was to be their hunting seat at Het Loo in the heart of the Netherlands, north of Arnhem, later famous for its water features and intricate gravel-and-box parterres.

Hating Whitehall so much, the royal couple rushed to transform Hampton Court. Only two days after their first visit, on 25 February, they invited Christopher Wren to discuss their plans for what Mary called 'a proper improvement'. Wren, who had been Surveyor-General of the King's Works for both Charles II and James II, may have been surprised – even relieved – to be approached for this new commission. For although he had held the most prestigious architectural post in the country, the fifty-six-year-old architect was a Tory and a favourite of the previous regime. William might well have chosen to employ a Dutch architect – because he still mistrusted the English – or a Whig in gratitude for their support of his invasion. Perhaps, in commissioning an English architect, William was simply being diplomatic, given that his subjects may still have been suspicious of their foreign king. Or perhaps Wren's talents and professionalism, his rebuilding of fifty-one City churches and of St Paul's Cathedral after the Great Fire in 1666, made him the obvious choice.

Whatever the reasoning, only one week after Wren's visit, on 2 March 1689, the bed of state was moved to Hampton Court and newsletters announced that 'Sir Christopher Wren hath received orders to beautify and add some new building to that fabric'. At the same time orders were despatched to courtiers and foreign ministers to 'reapaire unto Hampton Court' because William and Mary had decided to stay there in temporary lodgings until the winter, rather than wait for the alterations to be completed. Ten days later, the court began to prepare for the move. One day at the end of March, fourteen shiploads of goods and furniture made their way up the Thames from Whitehall, followed a day later by the royal couple. Far removed from Westminster, the hub of political activity, Hampton Court would afford them, William and Mary hoped, a more private life. It was the least accessible of all the royal palaces, and courtiers complained that it took them five hours to get there, but Mary confessed in her diary: '[M]y heart is not made for a kingdom and my inclination leads me to a retired quiet life.'

In April, a little more than a month after William and Mary had first seen Hampton Court, an account for the rebuilding of the palace and gardens was opened. Wren was still estimating the cost of his ambitious plan – which involved no less than the demolition of all the Tudor buildings except Henry VIII's banqueting hall, and the creation of an entirely new palace surrounded by a new garden. As a celebrated astronomer, accomplished mathematician and anatomist, he approached architecture as a natural philosopher would rather than as a draughtsman who would be content just to copy the continental baroque style then in vogue. Versailles, with its gilded ornamentation and its 'little Knacks', as Wren called the fussy ornaments that littered every surface, did not meet with his approval. Fashions should not interfere with architecture, he had declared, because 'Building certainly ought to have the Attribute of eternal, and therefore the only Thing uncapable of new Fashions.'

Searching for lasting beauty, Wren looked to the harmonious proportions and mathematical laws that underpinned nature. These he found in the buildings of antiquity, in their columns, their symmetry and their calculated dimensions – the square and the circle were for him the perfect shapes. He had no time for Gothic arches or the 'Works of Filigrand [filigree]' (intricate ornamental metal-work). Like the architects of the Renaissance, Wren tried to present an ideal image of nature – one inspired by the world but improved by the mind – where geometry and the classical laws of proportion prevailed. Free from superfluous decoration, Wren's Hampton Court would be a monument to his restrained elegance. In the garden he employed the same approach, but here he retained the existing master-plan along with the canal and the avenue to the east of the palace created for Charles II, which was to form the central axis of the new design. He perfected the geometry by adding another avenue, stretching to the north into Bushy Park. The palace would stand where the avenues intersected, and around it Wren divided the garden into a grid of semicircles and squares. Each plot and decorative element in the garden would form, or be framed by, a geometric shape, the whole arranged in such a way that all vistas radiated from the palace into the distance.

Once Wren's plans had been approved, the royal couple had to appoint a team to deal with the details of the garden and implement the scheme. For the post of Superintendent of the Gardens, William chose his best friend of twenty-five years and political confidant, Hans Willem Bentinck – a man as passionate about gardens as the king himself. One of Holland's most significant garden-makers, Bentinck was already overseeing the building work at Het Loo, and was the owner of a huge exotic plant collection. His own garden at Zorgvliet in the Netherlands was admired for its elaborate parterres with their swirling patterns in box and gravel, as well as for its sophisticated greenhouse. Bentinck had advised the king on his invasion of England; his reward was this new post, and the title Earl of Portland.

As Portland's deputy William employed one George London, who had worked for several years for Henry Compton, Bishop of London – the proud owner of more than a thousand exotic plants and one of the 'Immortal Seven'. After studying gardens in Holland and France, George London had introduced French-style parterres into England, making him the ideal candidate to realise a project whose ambition was to rival the gardens of Versailles. During the previous eight years, he had worked on some of the finest gardens in the country, such as those of Longleat in Wiltshire and Burghley House in Lincolnshire; only six months earlier he had signed a contract to build a parterre, 245 feet by 187, at Chatsworth in Derbyshire. In addition to his annual salary of £200 as Deputy Superintendent, London would also profit by supplying plants from his own nursery at Brompton Park – at over one hundred acres, it was the largest in Europe and delivered flowers, shrubs and trees to aristocratic gardens. The diarist and horticultural writer John Evelyn singled the business out as the most impressive in Europe, admiring the rare plants in particular, and London and his business partners' methods of cultivation. By 1705 the Brompton Park Nursery contained nearly ten million flowering plants, shrubs and trees and was worth 'perhaps as much as all the Nurseries of *France* put together'. To his gardening credentials should be added the fact that London was also a Protestant – who had proved his loyalty, moreover, by escorting and protecting Princess Anne, Mary's sister, during the invasion.

Another member of the Hampton Court team was the distinguished architect William Talman, who was respected in Whig circles and had many influential patrons, including Portland, who most probably recommended him. Talman was also a close friend of George London – they had worked together at Chatsworth where he remodelled the south front of the house. At Hampton Court Talman was appointed Comptroller, responsible for the finances of the project, with a salary of £140 a year, well below Wren's, who as Surveyor-General earned nearly £400. An ambitious and competitive man, the forty-nine-year-old Talman hoped that he would eventually be able to oust Wren, whose position he coveted. But for now he had to bide his time.

With the four principal players in place – Wren as architect, Portland as Superintendent, London as his deputy and Talman as Comptroller – foremen were now appointed for each garden section, and work on the great project began.[*] In May, after Wren had handed in his estimate for the building costs,

---

[*] Unless otherwise stated, the chronology of the making of the garden at Hampton Court is based on the monthly Office of the Works accounts at the National Archives.

the old Privy Garden was fenced off to become the main store yard, as Charles II's grassy patterns disappeared under piles of timber, stone and all the other materials needed to build a palace. Workshops were set up for the carpenters, bricklayers and masons, and there was also one with a table for Wren or his assistant, one for a forge, and one for George London, who liked to supervise his workmen closely. At Longleat, for instance, he and his business partners from the Brompton Park Nursery had stayed alternate months to oversee the execution of the designs. At Hampton Court his work would become so intensive and time-consuming that, like Wren, he would eventually move into lodgings on the estate.

While the men set up the workshops, William was preparing for war. Two months earlier, James II had landed in Ireland – backed by an army provided by Louis XIV – intending to recapture his kingdom. William was threatened on two fronts, since the French were also making territorial gains in a campaign in Europe that aimed to establish Louis as 'universal monarch' over one great Catholic state. William persuaded the English Parliament that its religious freedom and national autonomy depended on its joining in a crusade against Louis, and on 6 May 1689, during a Privy Council meeting at Hampton Court, he declared war 'against the French King'. Negotiations were concluded for a powerful coalition with the Netherlands, Austria, Brandenburg and Spain – the Grand Alliance, as it was known – and confident in his allies, William prepared his army for war.

As pro-war pamphleteering intensified in the coffee-houses of London, Mary occupied herself with the less momentous pursuit of gardening: she 'lost no time . . . either measuring, directing or ordering'. 'In Gardens, especially Exotics, she was particularly skilled', and yearned for the collection of plants that she had been forced to leave behind in the Netherlands. One month after their move to Hampton Court, she had asked for an estimate for the erection of three hothouses, having already chosen a south-facing plot next to the Privy Garden. At the end of the garden was a Tudor building known as the Water or Thames Gallery that Wren's men were converting into a pleasure house to which she could withdraw. On the other side of the palace, George London's team began the planting of the chestnut trees that would create the avenue that

Wren had designed to run from the north front of the palace out into Bushy Park.

Seen against the tumultuous events unfolding in Ireland and Europe, William and Mary's preoccupation with their garden plans might seem inconsequential, even irresponsible; but they played a key part in William's strategy to cast himself in the image of powerful monarch. For although his constitutional position may have been the antithesis of Louis', he wanted to emulate his regal grandeur. By the summer of 1689, when John Evelyn visited William on business, he could already admire the building works and 'spacious Garden with fountaines [which] was beginning in the Park at the head of the Canale'. Word had spread that William was engaged on a massive project. But while garden enthusiasts might endorse it, Parliament – who had to pay for it – was far from pleased. Although the king resented the limits placed on his powers and on his expenditure, he was aware that 'the entertaining so soon on so expensive a building . . . spread a universal discontent in the city of London', and so he reluctantly bowed to Parliament's pressure and asked Wren to revise the scheme. By conceding, he hoped to retain Parliament's support for the war with France. And he was not the only monarch short of cash: like William, Louis had had to sacrifice, at least for the moment, his plans for further embellishments at Versailles. Between 1688 and 1690 the French king reduced his annual expenses there by more than 90 per cent, as well as ordering that all his solid silver furniture be melted down to alleviate his country's financial situation.

The changes that Wren suggested limited the rebuilding of Hampton Court to the state apartments and left the rest of the Tudor palace intact. In the garden, he scaled down the avenue that George London had already begun at the Bushy Park end. Although his budget was limited, Wren's new plan was marked by ingenuity. Instead of recommending a fashionable white stone façade like the one at Versailles which would have been expensive, Portland stone being in short supply because of the war, he based his design on red brick, so redolent of the Dutch architecture familiar to William and Mary. Portland stone provided, instead, the architectural trimmings, creating variety in colour as well as in detail but lacking the fussiness of the French baroque. Wren did, however, incorporate some of Versailles' stylistic elements, such as the unbroken skyline, which would make this new side of the palace appear as one monumental unity when viewed from a distance. William was pleased: '[F]or good Proportion, State and Convenience, jointly, were not paralleled by any Palace in Europe,' he declared.

But though they compromised on the design of the house, William and Mary were unwilling substantially to change their plans for the gardens. William knew he could not hope to match the scale of Louis', as the Thames limited the southern expansion, but he could surpass it in variety by the inclusion of a myriad small details and intricate planting patterns, both so lacking at Versailles. The result was that, far from reducing their spending, between April 1689 and March 1691 they lavished £25,000 on the gardens – half of what they had allocated for the palace.

The king's preoccupation with Hampton Court was interrupted by the news that James had set himself up as king in Dublin. Impatient with the ineptitude of his army and frustrated by the failure of his generals to deliver military gains, on 27 June 1689 William ordered more than 25,000 men and almost 4500 horses to be shipped to Ireland. The royal couple now found themselves constantly rushing between the palace and Westminster, but despite the seriousness of the political wrangling they continued to oversee the works. Some days they were so determined to return that they would consume the first course of dinner at Whitehall, to finish it at Hampton Court. The current most pressing concern in the garden was to choose the right design for the semicircular plot allocated to what was to be the Fountain Garden to the east of the palace.

Once again, the king and queen themselves 'ordered everything that was done', now calling for Daniel Marot, who had designed their garden at Het Loo. As a Huguenot, along with tens of thousands of other French Protestants he had fled France in 1685 following Louis's repeal of the Edict of Nantes, which had removed the civil rights of Protestants. One of the best French designers, Marot was an all-rounder – an accomplished engraver, ceramicist, interior decorator and garden designer – but he was not a practical gardener. Laying out a garden was generally considered to require, as well as artistic ability, scientific skills such as surveying and geometry, and it was Marot's aptitude as a 'very ingenious Mathematician' that fitted him for mapping out the complex geometrical schemes. By August, he had produced a drawing for an elaborate parterre, to be three times the width of the east façade and stretching over two hundred yards eastwards from the palace towards the canal, called the Long Water. Unlike the terraces of earlier gardens, where separate plots or knot gardens had been laid out like a sequence of outdoor rooms, this parterre unified a whole terrace in one large sweep of swirling arabesques and stylised ornaments. William and Mary instructed George London to begin work on it immediately.

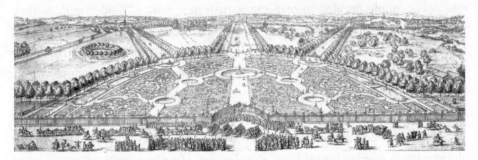

Daniel Marot's design for the Fountain Garden at Hampton Court

His first task was to order the new 'mathematical instruments' that would allow him to transfer the paper drawing on to the ground itself. Instruments such as the graphometer, which transposed actual landscape on to maps, had been improved in the mid-seventeenth century, and they could also be used in reverse to turn garden plans into gardens. Bisecting the large semicircle of the parterre was a gravel path running down to the Long Water. Each of the two quarter-circles was further divided into four elaborate plots. William had asked for as many fountains as possible, and so Marot had placed a huge pool and a fountain at the centre of the design as well as dotting twelve smaller ones along the parterre. Over three thousand yards of piping would be needed to convey the water from the conduit in Bushy Park.

The work would be expensive – over £1500 just for the lead and solder – but fountains had been the crowning glory of his gardens in Holland, and more than any other feature they were regarded as an unequivocal symbol of man's power to subjugate nature. Though Versailles had more fountains and larger parterres, Marot's design would be the grandest and most complex in England. Throughout the summer of 1689 Hampton Court buzzed with the sounds of hundreds of labourers at work. In June, they dug the foundations for the new building and made 'trenches and . . . ditches for draining the park in wet weather and laying new turf'. Others, meanwhile, worked on bringing water to the Long Canal, while more men were occupied with carting loads of rubbish out of the gardens. Fences and sheds continued to go up and in Mary's pleasure house, workmen were lathing and plastering the rooms. Having abandoned Wren's initial plan to build a new entrance to the palace's north façade, the royal couple decided to turn the garden here into a 'Wilderness', as they had at Het Loo. It was a popular garden feature of which Versailles boasted seventeen, but by allocating nine acres for it William and Mary made sure that the one at Hampton Court would outshine all others in England.

Despite its name, a wilderness was the opposite of 'wild' or 'unruly' – paradoxically, it was an enclosed plot planned on geometrical lines. On entering it, the visitor would encounter both straight and gently curving gravel paths lined with precisely clipped hornbeam hedges. Here and there the corridors of hornbeam would open on to square or circular 'rooms', also enclosed by hedges, and often adorned with fountains and statues. The Wilderness was designed as a counterbalance to the untamed nature that people had feared in medieval times. Its mathematical orderliness represented what was believed to be God's 'first' nature: the land of Eden before the fall of man. It mirrored the link between science and religion that shaped the thinking of educated people at this time.

William, in particular, was interested in these new ideas. He disliked the mystical aspects of religion as much as the quasi-magical and ceremonial aspects of kingship. Believing in scientific enquiry, he was not averse to breaking with tradition, for instance, by refusing to 'touch for the king's evil' – the ceremony whereby, it was believed, by touching a sufferer the monarch could heal scrofula. Dismissively, the afflicted were turned away: 'It is a silly superstition . . . give the poor creatures some money, and let them go.' In fact, so fascinated was William by the new scientific theories that just two days after he had arrived in England he had called for Isaac Newton, who had published *Principia Mathematica* in 1687. It was this publication that cemented the profound shift in man's understanding of God. Newton demonstrated that the natural world was governed by a set of laws that were, in principle, accessible to the human mind. Overturning the image of God as an arbitrary power whose workings were forever mysterious, he argued that God was bound by his own rules. Consequently, the divine creator was no longer regarded as some sort of magician, but more as a clock-maker, as it were, whose works obeyed universal laws. Through the emerging scientific disciplines of mathematics, astronomy and chemistry, man would be able to reveal the operation of God's engineering. Thus, just as nature followed its own order and mathematical principles underpinned the shaping of the garden, so, it was believed, God's hand was revealed.

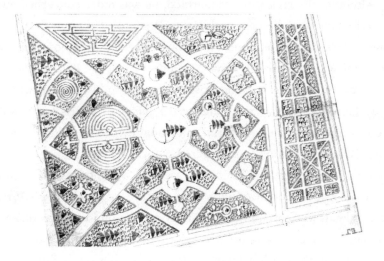

The Wilderness at Hampton Court, *c.* 1710–14

With the building work well under way, in mid-October 1689 the royal couple along with thirty or more carriages of goods decamped for the winter to Holland House in London. Their dislike of Whitehall was so strong that they had asked Wren to build Kensington Palace as an alternative London residence. In order to oversee the work there, they had temporarily leased Holland House nearby. As at Hampton Court, Mary would walk with Wren over the building site, 'impatient' to see all the changes taking place and spending hours 'examining and surveying the Drawings, Contrivances, and whole Progress of the *Works*'. Then, on 7 November, shortly after she had left the Kensington site, a part of the roof collapsed, tearing down walls and destroying floors, as well as killing one workman and injuring several more. Five weeks later, a similar accident happened at Hampton Court: the central section over the new south range gave way, this time killing at least two workmen and injuring eleven. Although accidents were a regular occurrence on building sites, several deaths in so short a time was unusual. Wren was 'troubled' and Mary immediately blamed herself. Having felt 'unsettled' at Holland House – probably because the lodgings were only temporary – she wrote to William, that this 'made me go often to Kensington to hasten the Worckmen': the two accidents, she was sure, were a sign of God's anger, and she felt 'truly humbled'.

Although the king too was alarmed, he was more concerned about the structural damage to the new building at Hampton Court than about God's revenge. Work was halted, and on 20 December he ordered a survey and a report from Wren. William Talman, Comptroller at the Palace, was quick to use the accident to undermine his boss by slandering his workmanship. A row blew up between the two men, and on 10 January reports from both were read out to the king. Despite Wren's personal evidence, William insisted on hearing Talman's opinion, and ordered a formal inquiry. Three days later, Wren and Talman met at Whitehall in front of a committee. Having chosen as witnesses two contractors who were already in dispute with Wren over money, Talman was certain of their support. The building was unsound and cracks had appeared before the accident, they stated. Wren was furious. He declared one of them a 'madman', pointing out that the building had withstood a hurricane that had swept through England just two days earlier. He was supported by the Master Carpenter of the Works, who explained that only a few hairline cracks had appeared and that he himself would guarantee the structural integrity of the building. But Talman continued his attack, claiming that the cracks were so many and so large 'that one may putt his finger in'.

The dispute escalated. 'Pray let 6 be chosen by me, and 6 by you to judge the matter,' Talman demanded. But the Committee had seen enough; they knew that Talman and Wren would never agree because 'one part will say one thing th'other another'. So the two architects and their witnesses were dismissed, and the committee sent three independent judges to Hampton Court to see for themselves. The king, needless to say, was impatient for the work to be resumed, and the three experts were given only forty-eight hours to read the reports, survey the site and decide if the building was sound. The verdict went in Wren's favour, and work recommenced immediately.

While the row between Talman and Wren rumbled on, an event of greater consequence for both William and the country had been unfurling at Westminster: the Declaration of Rights had been formalised as a bill by Parliament. Over the previous months William had watched its progress through the legislature, and although he hated to see the royal prerogative limited, he had conceded in order to keep Parliament loyal. If he wanted to pursue his plans against Louis XIV in Europe, he would need a standing army, which was feasible only with the consent of Parliament.

At Hampton Court preparations for the Fountain Garden were coming on apace, and Talman – having failed to oust Wren – focused on his duties as Comptroller. George London had ordered the best English turf – the envy of continental gardeners – as well as caseloads of dwarf box and other plants to fill the parterre. With the materials ready, Marot's drawings finished and Talman's careful eye focused on the budget, London instructed his gardeners to plant low box hedges in the two sections closest to the palace and lay turf in the remaining six. The box-and-turf parterres, patterned with interlaced arabesques and plumes set against a background of coloured earth and gravel, soon filled the whole semicircle fronting the east façade. Framing each section were narrow raised beds edged with dwarf box and planted with flowers and shrubs of varying heights. In the intricacy of the scheme as it came to life, could clearly be seen the mathematical skill of Marot; once finished, the Fountain Garden would complement Wren's east façade, which would reveal its own geometrical exactitude. With each of its many trees, plants, and turfed areas precisely positioned, the parterres conveyed a powerful message of nature perfected. The Fountain Garden was beginning to blossom. Meanwhile the workmen were still laying pipes and soldering joints, intent on finishing the pools and fountains.

In preparation for the arrival of Mary's plant collection from Holland, London now turned his attention to her flowerbeds next to the Privy Garden. The Queen must have been impatient to see these completed, so as to find solace there when William was away on campaign. She did not see much of him even when he was at home, as he preferred to spend time with his male friends, drinking and playing cards, or out hunting. Mary longed to please him, as evidenced by her diary entries and correspondence. In a letter of 1684 she expressed a lament that would become a frequent theme in her life: 'The Prince is gone . . . so yet I am now alone here[,] when he comes back is uncertain for which I am sure you will pity me.' Feeling lonely in England, she wrote: 'I found myself here very much neglected, little respected, censured by all, commended by none.' For consolation, she turned to gardening and God.

On her return to England just over a year earlier, this daughter of James II had been shocked 'to see so little devotion in a people', and had supported a reformation of manners whether in church services or in literature. Gardening was seen as a righteous endeavour, a pious occupation; John Evelyn had argued in the 1650s that 'Gardens operat upon humane spirits towards virtue and sanctity' and 'prepare them for converse with good Angels'. To Mary, horticulture was a way of paying homage to the creator of this earthly paradise. Influenced by Dutch Calvinism, she would also have interpreted ordered gardens and cultivated land as signs of a well managed soul. Dutch gardening united piety with classical humanism, rediscovered during the Renaissance, and focused on the need for both pleasure and profit. Thus gardening was an occupation that kept Mary busy, as well as fulfilling her desire to please God.

By early spring 1690 the hothouses were completed, and Mary's plants arrived from the Netherlands accompanied by her Dutch gardener Cornelius van Vliet – at last she would be reunited with her precious collection. But not quite yet. Mary had left Hampton Court in October to spend the winter in

London and would not return until late May. On 2 March van Vliet finished cataloguing the four hundred plants,* which were now established in their new homes. These hothouses, the first to have both front and roof entirely glazed, were unlike anything seen before in England. Each was fifty-five feet long with fourteen doors for easy access, and their sloping roofs rested on a brick back wall. Four coal-fired stoves, housed in a shed behind the wall, provided heat. Small coal-filled wagons could be wheeled to the parts where additional heat was required, then back into the shed when the fire became smoky or went out.† Throughout the seventeenth century botanists had been trying to re-create the temperatures of the natural habitats of their exotics, and had worked for decades on the assumption that heat was the only criterion; but even in the most sophisticated hothouses plants frequently died in the smoky atmosphere. Once again the Netherlands was at the forefront of innovation: instead of relying just on heat, the Dutch bathed their plants in sunlight. To ensure that her hothouse would be as efficient as possible, Mary had brought her own carpenter from the Netherlands, and she also asked van Vliet to remain in London just to look after the hothouses, for his experience was unrivalled in England.

With the completion of the hothouses, the gardeners could now provide Mary with cut flowers all the year round, and were already experimenting with exotic fruits such as pineapples, bananas and cashews. Mary was only happy when surrounded by flowers; in Honselaarsdijk, the main royal residence in the Netherlands, she had received at all seasons two or three bouquets of cut flowers every week – in winter, most certainly from her hothouses. Now, in England, it was George London who filled her home with colour and scent.

---

*Van Vliet, also a botanist, was one of several gardeners that Mary brought over from the Netherlands.

†Both Mary's innovative glasshouses and William's 'Water sucking engines' for his fountains reflected the deepened interest in technology as well as the prevailing spirit of enquiry. Mechanical innovations, chemical discoveries, astronomical observations – these and more were being brought into play in an effort to understand the world and harness nature for man's progress. New scientific applications and inventions were being demonstrated at the Royal Society, where Newton had first impressed his fellow scientists with his portable telescope; Robert Boyle's air pump had shown that air was needed for combustion; and Edmond Halley was experimenting with diving bells in order to salvage the gold treasure locked in sunken ships.

Even before Mary had had a chance to see her treasures herself, Charles Hatton, a well-known garden enthusiast, together with 'some of my old botanick acquaintances', had visited Hampton Court in April 1690 to admire the 'famous collection' of '400 rare Indian plants which were never seen in England'. They had also been keen to see the hothouses which, they thought, were 'much better contrived and built than any other in England'. The owner of one of England's best exotic collections, the Duchess of Beaufort, sent a servant to write a full report, which he duly did, including all the necessary details regarding dimensions and construction.

While the Privy Garden remained buried under numerous builders' sheds and materials, Mary's garden was undergoing a transformation. By March 1690, George London's men had replaced the fences separating her south-facing beds from the Privy Garden with a high wall, so as to restrict the view from one to the other and create a clear demarcation between the pleasure garden and the plant collection. Her garden comprised three rectangular plots, one of which was given over to a mass of different flowering plants to demonstrate the diversity of her collection, and another to nothing but auriculas, which had recently eclipsed tulips as the most fashionable flower. Like tulips, their multicoloured blooms came in an abundance of varieties, with flame-like streaks, double stripes, coloured fringes – almost as many variations as could be imagined. Mary had them planted in pots and placed in neat rows on tiered beds so that she could admire and inspect them in detail. The third plot, sunken, with broad steps leading down to it on all four sides, provided centre stage for the House of Orange's citrus collection, in all its potent symbolism.

Mary was now obliged to find a new botanist to oversee the flower collection, as van Vliet wished to 'transfer himself & family into Holland', but when William and a new army of fifteen thousand men left for Ireland in June that year, she was once again diverted from her garden and felt alone 'in my own country'. While William marched valiantly towards his encounter with James, she moaned that her husband had left her stranded, as head of state and with all the accompanying duties. She had no desire to dirty her hands with politics, believing it wrong that 'women should meddle in government'. Irritated at having to stay in London, she wrote to a friend: '[D]uring the absence of the King I have not had time to take care of the building.' Her letters to William were peppered with garden and building details – the smell of paint in his closet, the scaffolding, the furnishings and the lack of money. Writing late at night, she always found time to update her husband on the renovations, but sometimes left news about political developments and events at court till the next day. On 24 June she complained to William that the Portland stone had not arrived because the 'French are in the Channel, and at present are between Portland and us'; there could be no doubt that Mary saw affairs of state through the prism of her building works.

Mary may have been disgruntled, but William was in his element. On 1 July 1690, with the River Boyne between his army and James's, he was to be seen parading before his men, rousing them for the confrontation ahead. Radiating confidence, he was watched from a distance by his opponents, who could see his Star of the Garter glistening in the sunlight. Battle was soon engaged, and before long the king was wounded in the arm; but confident in his invincibility, he continued to ride up and down the front line urging on his men. His Dutch guards now waded across the river to meet James's army, the water up to their armpits. The artillery was so heavy that it took sixteen horses to move it. As the English surged forward, the Irish troops fled, followed soon after by James himself. Having turned his back on his own men, James didn't stop until he reached the house of a loyal subject in Dublin. When he complained that the Irish had deserted the battlefield, he was told: 'If they have, Sire . . . your Majesty seems to have won the race.' The battle of the Boyne was William's first step in his attempt to gain control over Ireland. James had failed to win back his throne; and Louis XIV, at least for now, had had to give up any hopes of invading England.

Two and a half months later, on 10 September, William returned from Ireland and went straight to Hampton Court, where Mary 'found him . . . in perfect health'. Such was her joy that she lacked 'words to express it'. She was impatient to hand over 'all the troublesome business' and to show her husband the progress that had been made at the palace. The Water Gallery, which now featured elaborate plaster ceilings and a bathroom with running hot and cold water, was nearly completed. The new building was steadily taking shape and Mary recorded that her 'husband was satisfied and told me he was much pleased with my behaviour'.

During the next months the royal couple visited Hampton Court almost fortnightly, spending whole days there. William was preparing to leave for the Netherlands for the first time since his accession to the English throne. Although the fight for control over Ireland was not yet won, he was confident enough to leave it to his generals, at last feeling able to turn his mind to his Dutch duties and the war on the continent. In early 1691 he departed for Flanders, where he would assume command of the allied armies rallying against Louis. Once again having royal duties to perform as well as her gardens to supervise, Mary felt uncertain of her ministers' loyalties, writing: '[T]he king and I were less loved . . . we had many enemies, but no friends', and characterising those around her as exhibiting a 'general peevishness and silliness . . . each seeking only their own advantage'. But while the affairs of state were a source of anxiety, the progress of the garden brought pleasure, of course. As a reward for his men's hard work, in May 1691 George London organised a 'gardener's feast' for which the carpenters made eight trestles and twenty-four boards to serve as dining tables.

On 19 October that year William returned from the continent, where his territorial ambitions had been thwarted when the Flemish town of Mons had surrendered to Louis's army. Five days after his return, the king and queen went to Hampton Court, where the carpenters had made special walkways so that they could inspect every detail. They saw immediately how much the Privy Garden had changed: it had been widened in line with Wren's new south façade, and a new wall separated it from the Fountain Garden. Against the wall the workmen had built a raised grass bank to form a narrow terrace mirroring the one along the west wall, where they had made an 'arbour with fir rails and oaken posts and circular ribs'. They had pulled down the old banqueting house on the mount just a few dozen yards from the Water Gallery, as well as three nearby towers. In the Fountain Garden the east façade had finally reached its full height, and Marot's designs, 'figures like lace-patterns', were being admired for their skill and intricacy.

Within a month of William's return, London handed in his invoice for the first phase of the work. He had delivered to Hampton Court – most probably from his Brompton Park Nursery – elms, cypresses, box and other plants, as well as seeds, at a cost of just under £2000; tools such as wheelbarrows, 'waterbarrows', tubs and iron hoops accounted for £1000-plus; then gravel, manure and sand, as well as baskets, wire, pots and turf, for another £2200. All this together with tiles, lead, pipes, iron- and brasswork, glass and gold leaf, amounted to a total of almost £13,000.

In November, the last of the sheds were dismantled and the rubbish moved out of the Privy Garden. With the basic structure of the latter complete, it was time to plant the ornamental parterre that would fill the space between the two raised grass banks. But before the work had started in earnest, the hunt for a Queen's Botanist was brought to a conclusion.

During the previous year many well qualified candidates had been suggested for the prestigious position which included extending and cataloguing the queen's collection. Eventually, friends of the king and queen recommended Dr Leonard Plukenet, who had trained as a physician but had since become a notable botanist, socialising within the inner circle of English horticulturists at the Botanical Club which met every Friday evening at the Temple Coffee House in London. His referee was Henry Compton, George London's previous employer and one of the great plant collectors of the day. By the end of 1691 Plukenet had been awarded the position, at a salary of £200 per annum, the same as the esteemed London.

Mary continued to collect plants, receiving many from specialists in Holland, from her own garden in Honselaarsdijk and from trading companies around the world. The hunt for exotics for Hampton Court had begun in 1690 when the Earl of Portland in his position as Superintendent of the Gardens obtained a permit for the importation of two boxes of seeds and seedlings, four boxes of flowering plants and six more of seeds and saplings from Barbados. Now on Plukenet's advice Mary sent a 'gardener to go to Virginia to make a collection of foreign plants', at a cost of £234. Two more were despatched to the Canary Islands on a similar mission. Like John Tradescant's collection of eighty years earlier, Mary's exotics would proclaim the mercantile prowess of both England and the Netherlands. For, as Princess of Orange she was able to procure bulbs, seeds and plants from a network of well travelled Dutch merchants. So important were her plants to her that even on campaigns William would give leave to a lieutenant to collect specimens from gardens in Holland. The king also paid more than four thousand guilders for one of the best plant collections in the Low Countries. When this latest batch arrived at Hampton Court in October 1692, Plukenet seized on many of the specimens as subjects for his new illustrated book, which would contain almost three thousand plants categorised into families according to a new scientific system. No longer collected simply for their singularity or curiosity, as Tradescant had done, plants were now analysed and catalogued – an endeavour encouraged by the Royal Society, which had been founded thirty years earlier with the purpose of making 'faithful *Records*, of all the Works of *Nature*, or *Art*'. In parallel with this trend and with the advent of new printing technologies, increasing numbers of horti-cultural books were appearing. In Britain alone, over one hundred new titles were published in the seventeenth century – at least eighty of them after 1650 – compared to just nineteen in the sixteenth century.

This new empirical approach excluded traditional beliefs such as the significance of the cycles of the moon in relation to planting, or the use of chickens' blood as compost. Instead of relying on superstition or on received wisdom, botanists now observed and systematised their collections as well as disseminating their new-found knowledge via specialist books. Works such as John Evelyn's *Sylva* (1664) and Moses Cook's *The Manner of Raising, Ordering and Improving Forest-Trees* (1676) were based on the authors' own observations rather than rehashing age-old traditions. A year before Plukenet became the Queen's Botanist, Nehemiah Grew, the first plant anatomist, had described in his *Anatomy of Plants* (1682) the different parts of plants and their functions; he recognised, for instance, that the the stamen is a plant's male reproductive organ. In the same year the naturalist John Ray published his first classifica-tion system, based on live and dried specimens: '[W]e have wholly omitted . . . Hieroglyphics, Emblems, Morals, Fables, Presages', and present only 'what properly relates to . . . Natural History,' he wrote. Like other fields of scientific inquiry, though, horticulture continued to place God at the centre of the universe, as the creator of nature, with the gardener as his steward. Cook declared that it was God's intention that men 'should take care of those [plants] which are tender, lest they be lost'.

By the summer of 1693 the main features of Hampton Court's garden were in place: Mary's plant collection was thriving; according to a catalogue of 'Foreigne plants raised from seeds att Hampton Court' of 1692, the gardeners had already begun to propagate seeds from the exotics, the citrus trees had been pruned into perfect spheres, and the turf of the Privy Garden parterre had been cut into scroll shapes and coloured earth put in between. George London had completed Marot's parterre in the Fountain Garden with three hundred and four yews shaped into obelisks and twenty-four globe-shaped silver hollies. Beyond the parterre, workmen had lengthened the Long Water to three-quarters of a mile and planted 2176 lime trees in the avenues joining the Fountain Garden to the park east of the palace. Limes had been chosen for their height – reaching up to 130 feet when full grown – speedy growth and naturally tapering lines. London had used earth-moving 'engines' to transplant mature trees from other parts of the park, which Daniel Defoe would later admire in his *Tour through the Whole Island of Great Britain*. What the estate could not provide London would have supplied from the Brompton Park Nursery, which sold semi-mature trees, thereby providing height and definition to the layout from the outset.

The impression the lengthened avenues gave was one of sunbeams radiating out from the garden into the countryside, conveying a sense of power and ownership; they appeared infinite – a concept that stood at the fissure between the Church and science. For most of the sixteenth century, it had been generally accepted that the universe was finite, with the earth at its centre and God presiding over all. Then, in 1584, the astronomer Giordano Bruno had disputed this in his *On the Infinite Universe and Worlds*, and as a consequence had been burned as a heretic. By the mid-seventeenth century Galileo had popularised the same idea, but later renounced his views because they were still in conflict with the Church. Nonetheless the notion of infinity seeped into the work of artists such as Claude Lorrain, who painted scenes in which the vanishing-point blurred so as to suggest boundlessness. Similarly, gardeners such as André Le Nôtre experimented with avenues that disappeared at the horizon, again creating the illusion of infinity. Only when Newton published *Principia Mathematica* in 1687 were the observations of astronomy reconciled with the demands of theology. According to Newton, an infinite universe did not contradict the existence of God, but on the contrary celebrated his eternity. The garden at Hampton Court, therefore, expressed not only William's confidence as monarch, but also his belief in both God and cosmic infinity.

With the major works completed, in mid-summer 1693 Portland drew up maintenance contracts with the gardeners. Three head gardeners – all Dutch – looked after the Privy Garden, the Wilderness and the hothouses. Others were employed to roll the grass, remove the wormcasts and rake the gravel: altogether there were eighty men and women (who were responsible for weeding) – including one mole-catcher – employed to keep the garden immaculate. Some features – the fountains, for instance – still needed improvement, but William and Mary's gardens were well on their way to rivalling any in Europe. The tall trees and paths formed a neat grid; order was enunciated and the intellect satisfied via the harmonious proportions and such details as the classical statues. The murmur and glint of water, the sweet scent of the orange trees and the elegant scroll designs executed in the perfect English grass satisfied the senses. The gardens of Louis XIV may have been magnificent, but the Anglo-Dutch appeal of Hampton Court was its mix of grandeur with finesse. Where Versailles was criticised for its monotony and its claustrophobic massing of trees, Hampton Court excelled in its diversity and expansiveness, the unmistakable reflection of an outward-looking confidence.

But William appeared to be losing his war in Europe. In 1693 he suffered a string of military disasters and had to concede more territory to Louis. Then, the French extended their dominance further by capturing an Anglo-Turkish fleet of merchant ships on its way to Smyrna in Turkey in July. There was trouble at home too, as William's trusted Secretary of State, the Earl of Nottingham, was forced to resign and the king's popularity was at an all-time low. Taxes had been raised for the war, but they alone could not cover the government's debt. The royal coffers were gradually emptying, and William was offended by his ministers' resentment: 'Let the Queen rule you, she is English, she understands what you want, I don't,' he seethed. By mid-1694, though, his position was looking a little healthier. The Bank of England, founded that April, was able partially to alleviate his financial problem: financiers could now invest their money relatively safely, and in return the government would receive long-term low-interest credit. Access to secure funds gave William the edge over Louis. For a long time the Sun King had drained France's economy to finance his wars, but without a national bank Louis was now crippled by war debts, and large parts of the population were starving. By contrast, William, now fired by his new cash flow, immediately set off for the continent to engage with the French yet again. In September 1694 he recaptured the territory he had lost the year before.

William returned triumphant to England in November, only to be confronted by a Parliament demanding that he accept the Triennial Act, which would withdraw his right to summon and dismiss Parliament, and replace it with three-yearly elections. Previous monarchs had dissolved Parliaments at will, often letting many years elapse before summoning them again. This now changed: William would have to deal with regular Parliaments. Having already blocked the bill, thereby provoking fierce protest, William was cornered. 'The commons [used me] like a dog,' he spat.

With his pride bruised, he returned to Hampton Court. Mary had recently spent many hours in the now finished rooms of the Water Gallery which Daniel Marot had designed in blue and white, including the curtains, furniture, picture frames – even down to the delftware vases for Mary's cut flowers. For the first time since she had left Holland, the queen had been enjoying her domestic life. Two months earlier, in September, she had asked Wren to design a bridge between the Water Gallery* and the Privy Garden in order to give her private

*Nicholas Hawksmoor, Wren's draughtsman and later a celebrated architect in his own right, provided the queen with three drawings for this bridge.

access to her beloved flowers. But before the workmen could fulfil her wish, Mary fell dangerously ill. By mid-December her health was steadily deteriorating, and she was transported to her state bedroom at Kensington Palace so as to be nearer William at Westminster. When the king arrived at her bedside, the physicians told him that Mary had contracted smallpox, the disease that had killed both of his parents. Distraught, he insisted that a camp-bed be made up for him next to hers, so he could be beside her night and day. The cloying air of the sickroom made him cough, and each night he would weep, convinced 'he was now going to be the most miserable creature on earth'. On Christmas Day Mary felt better. But it was a short reprieve; two days later the thirty-two-year-old queen died. Bells rang through the city announcing her death, while William shut himself in his chambers. In exile in France, Mary's unforgiving father James forbade his court to mourn the daughter who he felt had betrayed him and had robbed him and his son of the English throne.

William took a lock of Mary's hair for solace. He had the mirrors, walls and pictures covered with black cloth, and the court shrouded in darkness. Nearly two months passed before the public was admitted to the Banqueting House at Whitehall, queuing for hours in the freezing snow to see their embalmed queen. Although Mary had asked for a modest funeral, her request had been disregarded: the full cost was £100,000, the most expensive that century. At the state funeral on 5 March 1695, the sermon of the Archbishop of Canterbury, Thomas Tenison, commemorated the joy Mary had found in her gardens: 'How reasonable were her very Diversions; such as *Building* and Gardening, and contriving, and improving, and adorning, and adjusting every thing thereunto belonging.'

After Mary's death, William stayed mainly at Kensington Palace. The gardens at Hampton Court remained frozen at the point Mary had left them; he found himself unable to reconsider the plans the two of them had devised together. This gave George London time to embark on other lucrative projects; having worked for the monarchy, he was much in demand. He was called back to Chatsworth where he had created one of the largest parterres in the north of England a few years earlier. For this commission he and his partner at the Brompton Park Nursery,

Henry Wise, received £500, in addition to the profit they made from selling vast quantities of trees and plants to Chatsworth's owner, the Duke of Devonshire. London now began what would become an annual tour of the country in order to give advice and 'directions' at the gardens of his clients. Seemingly tireless, he rode sixty miles every day for six weeks visiting the country seats of northern England, then repeated the feat in the west of the country. At Chatsworth he was collaborating once again with William Talman, who, like London, spent a large part of his working life on the road. While based at Hampton Court, he had averaged 150 days a year in the saddle. Remaining the king's Comptroller, Talman must have enjoyed the architectural commission at Chatsworth, allowing him as it did the authority that Wren had refused him in the past.

Over the next months the king slowly adapted to life without Mary, but he would still frequently burst into tears, and was able to forget his sorrow only when on the battlefield or drinking with his closest friends. In the late summer of 1695, eight months after Mary's death, he achieved his greatest military victory, crushing the French army and taking the strategic town of Namur in Flanders. At last William had something to celebrate: he had won not only a major battle, but the hearts of the English people. Nationalistic poems and ballads could be heard in towns and villages across England. But the fighting had not ended, and two more years were to pass before William and his allies were finally able to force Louis to sign a peace treaty, on 20 September 1697, at Ryswick in the Netherlands. Having to return most of the territory he had seized during the previous twenty years, Louis, for the first time, was obliged publicly to recognise William as the King of England.

Even the French court quietly acknowledged that William was Europe's most formidable military leader. Resplendent in his glory, he returned to England in November 1697. To his disbelief, Parliament still refused to grant him sufficient money to maintain his standing army and his elite regiment of Dutch guards, thereby seriously limiting his martial ambitions. In January 1698 he complained bitterly to his old friend Anthony Heinsius, the Grand Pensionary of Holland:[*] 'You cannot form an idea of [the] indifference with which all

---

*With William away in England, Anthony Heinsius was the most powerful man in Holland as President and chief administrative minister of the Dutch Republic.

foreign affairs are now considered. People here only busy themselves about a fanciful liberty.' To maintain the balance of power in Europe, William tried for a diplomatic resolution to the remaining international problems. Though the victories of the previous year had brought a temporary peace, he now wanted to reach an agreement with Louis regarding the division of the Spanish Empire, should the heirless King Carlos II of Spain die. Having already successfully negotiated the Treaty of Ryswick, William decided to send his old friend Bentinck, the Earl of Portland, to France as his ambassador. Fluent in the language and accustomed to the rigid French court etiquette, he was the ideal candidate to broker a partition treaty.

Despite this being one of the most important moments of William's political career, he insisted that Portland also inspect the French gardens, taking George London with him. Three years after Mary's death, William had regained his enthusiasm for their gardening projects. Writing almost daily, Portland informed him about every conversation he had with Louis or his officials. 'Be at Versailles as often as you can', William reminded him, because winning the French king's confidence was of the utmost importance for the negotiations; but also – 'visit the gardens . . . which you know I am very fond of.' So Portland and London, despite the cold weather, set off to see the Sun King's famous pleasure grounds. Versailles looked 'dead and dirty', Portland reported back, not neat like Hampton Court; the fountains were not switched on, and though the orange trees were of a good size, in shape they weren't a patch on William's. What surprised both Portland and London most was the total lack of flowering plants. Whoever had told William that Louis's parterres bloomed at all seasons had been quite wrong, Portland told the king – 'I have not seen a single one, not even a snowdrop.'

William was impatient for news, and while Portland's letters made their way to London the king wrote to his ambassador that he should stay another six weeks in Paris so as to continue with the diplomacy, but also 'to make excursions and see the finest places' and, of course, their gardens. At the end of March William received news that the King of Spain was seriously ill. If he died now, before a partition treaty was signed, the balance of power would swing in Louis' favour and war would be inevitable. William had 'never been more vexed and melancholy', he wrote to Portland. Louis, meanwhile, was feeling confident. His ambassador reported: 'The King of England is very far from being master here' because, he noted with satisfaction, all his decisions had to be made 'in concert with the nation'.

Portland had found it difficult to establish cordial relations with Louis, until one evening in late April at Versailles when the king offered him a tour of the candlelit garden. Walking along the gravel paths, 'conversing cheerfully' and admiring the parterres and fountains, they discussed 'all kinds of subjects'. Portland's diplomatic efforts were finally beginning to pay off, and one month later William was able to send a draft peace treaty to his advisers in Holland. The treaty was finally signed by both rulers in October 1698.

Preparing for his journey home, Portland nonetheless found time to visit yet more gardens – all designed by Le Nôtre, the genius behind Versailles. First he went to Fontainebleau, where he especially liked the many avenues into the park, ideal if one wanted to 'follow the hounds'; then he took in the gardens at Vaux-le-Vicomte, which had first brought Le Nôtre to Louis's attention and which Portland described as 'beautiful'. His greatest honour was Louis's invitation to join him at Marly, the French king's retreat not far from Versailles. This was the only garden still undergoing major changes: Louis had decided in late 1697 to celebrate the end of the war with a monumental cascade, now under construction. Louis, well aware that Portland would report every detail to William, insisted that the ambassador should wait until early June before visiting, 'when all the fountains will be finished'. Portland was so impressed with what he saw that he tried to recruit Le Nôtre for Hampton Court. The gardener, well into his eighties, declined – he was too old, he said, to visit King William's palace. Nonetheless, Portland persuaded him to prepare plans for the royal garden at Windsor, and it was agreed that his nephew, also a gardener, would come to England in his place.

On 3 January 1699, a few months after Portland and London's return, the king ordered his team to finish the palace and garden. Shortly afterwards, an

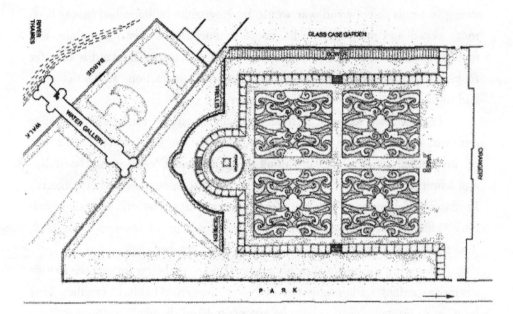

The Privy Garden in 1695 before Mary's Water Gallery, hothouses
and the mount were demolished

estimate for just over £10,000 was submitted by Talman, most certainly in consultation with his friend London. In February Talman and London were joined by a new member of the team: Henry Wise. As London's partner at the Brompton Park Nursery Wise had probably already had some involvement in the work at Hampton Court, but now he submitted an estimate in his own right for £6638 for the planting of trees and the making of avenues, as well as for gravelling in Bushy Park. In March William gave the order to proceed with the avenue in the park that London had been forced to abandon a decade earlier, as well as asking for a new piping system for the fountains – probably inspired by London and Portland's observations in France. Wise now took over the planting of new trees as well as the maintenance of the existing scheme. While this provided an additional income for the Brompton Park Nursery, consolidating its monopoly on the provision of plants, it also freed London from his daily business in the capital to travel the country to oversee their other projects.

On 22 April 1699 William visited Hampton Court for the first time in four years. The king had also asked for estimates for the completion of the state apartments and on 28 April Wren presented his costings. Two weeks later, on 12 May, Talman seized the opportunity to try and elbow Wren out. Presenting his own plan, he undercut Wren's estimate by £1300* and imposed his own deadline – something Wren had avoided doing because much of his time was still being consumed by his work on St Paul's Cathedral. William lost no time in accepting Talman's estimate. The next day he met the Comptroller at Hampton Court to discuss the details. Though Wren still held the post of Surveyor-General, Talman had finally succeeded in usurping his superior. His position was further cemented when, that same month, Portland resigned as Superintendent of the Royal Gardens. Portland had enjoyed the king's friendship and confidence since they were young men, but now William left him in no doubt that the handsome young Earl of Albemarle had replaced him in his affections. Portland had threatened to go once before, but now he left the king's service for good. For the time being his position remained empty, with Talman in control of the gardens.† An army of designers and labourers leapt into action. Hundreds of yards of pipe were laid in the Fountain Garden, and tons of materials were unloaded from Thames barges into the park. Determined to make an impression, Talman ordered large amounts of Portland stone for Hampton Court, yet again undermining and annoying Wren, who was having trouble procuring it for St Paul's.

While William was away on his annual trip to the Netherlands that summer, four hundred men were doing their utmost to get the house completed for his return. He was kept up to date with progress by the obsequious Talman, who in September informed him that the state rooms were almost finished. 'I have made use of my time,' he reported smugly. Knowing that William was interested in every last detail, Talman explained at length that he had replaced

---

*Wren's estimate was for £6800, Talman's for £5500.

†Portland was replaced more than a year later in July 1700, but his successor, Lord Ranelagh, had to deal with a much broader range of duties, and Talman remained in charge.

the old locksmith with the 'most ingenious man in Europe'. The 'difference between the two men in their art', he said, '[was] as between Vulcan and Venus'.

He reported that the garden too was coming along well – Henry Wise was putting the finishing touches to the great approach to the palace through Bushy Park. Having widened it to a hundred feet,* his men were now laying some thirty thousand cubic yards of gravel. About six hundred yards away from the palace entrance (one-third of the way down the avenue) they had excavated a five-foot-deep hole, four hundred feet in diameter, in readiness for a new fountain. That done, they laid more than three thousand square yards of turf around the basin. Adding 732 lime and chestnut trees to the 1243 that London had already planted ten years earlier, Wise now planted four lines of trees along either side of the avenue, leading up to the fountain's basin, round it and beyond – something never done before in England. The bill was more than £4000. The king's enthusiasm for grand avenues encouraged many of his courtiers to follow suit at their own estates, further boosting the Brompton Park Nursery. Daniel Defoe observed that 'the King began with the gardens at Hampton-Court . . . and the gentlemen follow'd every where, with such a gusto that the alteration is indeed wonderful thro' the whole kingdom'.

On his return to England in October, William immediately rushed to Hampton Court, where he was so pleased with the progress that he decided to 'to lye' there. All he needed now was an estimate from Talman for the cost of making the palace habitable. The prospect of yet more work must have come as a relief to the quarrelsome Comptroller; he had just lost the prestigious commission to build Castle Howard for the Earl of Carlisle. Outraged by the earl's decision and by the meagre payment for his drawings, Talman was even prepared to sue him, but for now he concentrated on pleasing the king. And the opportunities were plenty, since William visited Hampton Court more than thirty times over the next seven months, often staying several days.

At last in April 1700, the king moved into his state apartments, where he stayed for ten weeks. Particularly interested in improving the power of the

---

*The central causeway was sixty feet, extended by another twenty feet on each side.

fountains, he had called in a *jet d'eau* specialist, insisting on watching him as he worked. To William's disappointment, his waterworks had turned out less powerful than he had envisaged, so the engineer with a team of assistants was ordered to work both day and night, repeatedly filling the cisterns, then testing the fountains. Louis XIV fared no better with his fountains at Versailles. They were so inefficient that his engineers had to whistle to the garden boys to switch on the water whenever they saw the king coming within sight of them. One visitor remarked with a sneer that they worked only two or three times a year, while the 'remainder of the time . . . one only meets . . . half filled basins, stagnant and ill smelling'. Determined that his fountains would not suffer the same fate, William demanded that the engineer return regularly so as to bring 'the water more plentifully to Hampton Court'. The following year he agreed with London to maintain the system for an annual £200.

During William's first long stay at his new palace, work began on the installation of the statues for the fountains and the parterre. The two most striking were the *Borghese Warrior* which had formerly stood in St James's Park, and the statue of Hercules uprooted from Whitehall. The classical statues expressed William's achievements allegorically in metal and stone, telling stories of power, victory and virtue. The Greek hero Hercules had succeeded in retrieving the golden apples of the Hesperides (oranges) by holding the heavens on his shoulders while the Titan Atlas fetched them for him. The figure was thus intended to endow William's family name, Orange, with a superhuman strength.

Having put the final touches to the more public part of the gardens, William now turned his full attention to the Privy Garden. More than five years had passed since Mary's death, and he was at last willing to accept that her Water Gallery would have to go if he wanted to extend the garden. In July 1700 he sent instructions from Holland to demolish it, and as a gesture of good housekeeping he entreated his workers 'to preserve many of ye materialls' of the old building. In its place Talman was to build a new banqueting house. So workmen began to dismantle the Gallery, carting away thousands of loads of rubble and storing away stones, metalwork and other materials for future use.

Four months later, affairs of state were again absorbing William's attentions. Now it seemed that his diplomatic efforts of the past few years had come to nothing. In November the Spanish king died, and to William's 'utmost mortification', he wrote to Pensionary Heinsius, Louis ignored their partition treaty, accepting Carlos II's will: he had left his entire Spanish territories to Louis' grandson, thus tightening the French grip on Europe. William denounced Louis' actions as 'shameful', writing to his officials in the Netherlands: 'England and the Republic [the Netherlands] are in the utmost danger of being totally lost or ruined.' Parliament, however, was hesitant about challenging the Sun King.

International upheaval did not prevent William from pursuing his plans for the gardens whenever he could. There were now over five hundred workmen, many of them engaged in the Privy Garden where, under Henry Wise's instructions, they were digging out the former mount garden so as to lower it by several feet, improving the view over the River Thames. With shovels and pickaxes, buckets and wheelbarrows, they removed more than 10,000 cubic yards of earth. But despite their efforts, William was still not happy with his view over the Privy Garden towards the river, and called Wise back in early spring 1701 to announce that the height was not satisfactory. To ensure that his work would not be wasted again, this time Wise built platforms so as to get an idea of the view if the area were to be lowered by another eight feet. William must have approved, because Wise ordered his men to remove another 13,700 cubic yards.

Throughout this time William was spending at least two days a week at Hampton Court. In March 1701 he was presented with a wooden model of a hothouse, constructed with a view to replacing the three in Mary's flower garden, and a new design for the Privy Garden. To enable the king to see how these changes would affect the prospect across the river, the workmen erected temporary iron railings and screens at the bottom of the Privy Garden. The twelve ornamental panels were designed by Jean Tijou, the only man in the country thought to be able to create sufficiently delicate decoration, with its stylised flowers, out of wrought iron. The Frenchman had covered his screens with regal symbols such as fleurs-de-lis, thistles, roses and the royal monogram.

Placed on a low wall with alternate panels of plainer railings, the screens stood about eight feet high and, while separating the end of the Privy Garden from the landscape beyond, their intricate scrollwork, painted light grey and gold, created – visually – only the haziest of barriers. Whereas in earlier years thick brick walls had seemed the obvious means of keeping out the world, Tijou's railings, reflected the confident mood of the time: the natural world, far from being excluded, was there to be explored and classified. But even with the railings in place, William remained indecisive. Work came to a halt, although the workmen did nightshifts guarding the expensive new ironwork. Thieves were not the only problem: in early June, the locksmith had to be called to make '4 new stays to rivett into Mr Tyous pillars to hinder the people from pissing att the end of the rails of the Privy garden'.

Jean Tijou's design for the iron gates at Hampton Court

On 12 June 1701 the Act of Settlement was passed. This was a significant moment for William. It established the succession to the English Crown, but also limited the monarch's powers. Under the new law, he could not leave England without Parliament's consent; moreover, no foreigner, his Dutch friends and advisers included, could hold office, nor were they allowed to receive land from the Crown. Only four days later, as if in defiance of the new limitations to his power, William approved the various new designs that he had seen as models.* Having already spent well in excess of £20,000 on the last phase of his grand project, in addition to the £65,000 that the making and maintaining of the garden had cost between 1689 and 1699, he was now about to spend even more.† Although the turf that Wise had laid a few weeks before had barely begun to grow, the gardeners were instructed to dig up the Privy Garden and start all over again.

Two weeks later on 30 June, William left England, as he did every year, for Holland, and so the work on the Privy Garden could continue without interference. The labourers dismantled Tijou's screens, and new sheds were set up in preparation for more work. Henry Wise dug up all the plants in the Privy Garden, transferring them to another part of the estate for storage, while the masons removed the statues and the fountain stonework. Then, with the removal of more than 20,000 cubic yards of earth, the main part of the garden was lowered by another two and a half feet, so that it was now lower than the terrace in front of the palace. The view down the garden from the king's private rooms was improved immeasurably. In August, work began on a new basin and fountain and a month later the plumber was called in to fit new pipes.

At about this time came the news that Mary's father James II had died. For a moment it seemed that the long saga of James's claim to the throne had finally ended. Then, Louis XIV announced that James's son was the true king of England and war seemed unavoidable. At last the sympathy of the English people swung towards William. Having anticipated Louis' betrayal – he had already broken the Partition Treaty the previous year – William had secured a

---

*'New makeing ye Privey Garden, according to a Modell that his Majestye Last Ordered and Concluded on ye 16 June 1701', estimate of Henry Wise, 5 July 1701 (TNA T1/75 f.6).
†Talman's bill of 19 December 1699 was for £10,864 (TNA T1/67 f.98). Henry Wise had additionally handed in bills for more than £12,000 (TNA Work 5/51 ff.530, 542, 550; and Ibid. 5/52 f.575v). The total expenditure on all royal gardens from 1 May 1689 to 25 March 1696 was £83,000, of which more than three-quarters was spent on the gardens at Hampton Court (TNA AO 1/2482/298); total expenditure on Hampton Court from 12 March 1698 to 12 December 1699 was nearly £5000 (Ibid.).

second Grand Alliance a week before James's death, reuniting the old allies against the French king, once more in preparation for war.

When William came back from the continent in early November 1701, Wise had just finished the new parterre in the Privy Garden. Each of its two levels comprised two large squares on which he had laid almost 8000 square yards of turf, cut from the common nearby and delivered in three-foot by fourteen-inch sections. Showing off the excellence of the English grass, Wise had created scroll patterns in the style of Daniel Marot. Raised flowerbeds enclosed with box ran ribbon-like along the edges of the grass, and between the grass patterns and the beds Wise had inserted bands of sand known as 'alleys', highlighting the lines of the design.

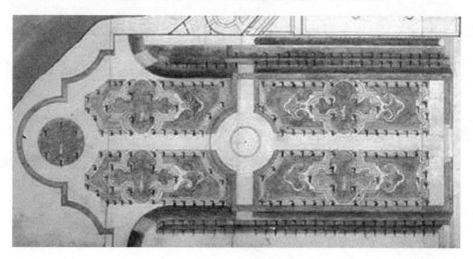

The final layout of the Privy Garden, *c.* 1710–13

The backbone of the garden was created by 160 mature clipped ever-greens – among them, round-headed hollies, as well as eight-foot pyramid yews and hollies, supplied by the Brompton Park Nursery – situated along the flower borders around the four quarters of the parterre. The planting followed a regular pattern: in between the topiary trees the gardeners had placed four tall plants – lilacs, for instance, with their fragrant blossom – plus honeysuckle and standard roses. Interspersing these were single low shrubs such as lavender and

Detail of the Great Parterre at Longleat in Wiltshire. The ribbon-like flowerbeds in the parterre at Hampton Court would have been planted in much the same way

Juniperus sabina creating a continuous wave of colour and height.* Many of the shrubs were compact and hardy – the juniper, for example, was admired for its dense needle-like foliage, which provided an evergreen backdrop to the flowers at the outside edges of the beds.

Changed twice a year, these annuals and bulbs gave colour, texture and variety to the garden. A year earlier Wise had supplied and planted twenty-four thousand bulbs and 'fibrous root flowers' for Marot's parterre borders in the Fountain Garden, and it is likely that he chose similar specimens such as several sorts of tulips, crocuses, hyacinths, polyanthus, snowdrops and irises for the Privy Garden. In these long, narrow flower borders he would probably also have used lilies, delicate hepaticas with their heart-shaped leaves, and brightly coloured lychnis, all planted as individual specimens rather than in large ground-covering clumps. Tall, dense clusters of snapdragons and the pompom flowers of chrysanthemums would also have featured, bringing softness to the strict geometrical lines. Many flowers favoured by John Tradescant, such as *Fritillaria imperialis* – the stately crown imperial – and martagon lilies,

*Wise reused these plants from his first design – he had supplied them in spring 1701 (his bill for 12 February to 24 April 1701).

and the sculptural blossoms of amaranthus, continued to be popular. In addition to those from the Brompton Park Nursery, many plants were grown from seed in the kitchen garden at Hampton Court, where the gardeners also propagated snapdragons, sweet williams, tall valerians and ground-covering periwinkles. Mary's flower garden most certainly produced auriculas and peonies with their voluptuous blooms. In the summer, rounding off the design, orange trees snug in their white tubs with green iron hoops would be sited in prominent places, as a reminder of the garden's patron. By the beginning of 1702 Wise had finished in the Privy Garden, and William could admire his masterpiece every Friday when he came for the weekend from Kensington Palace. From his rooms he had a fine view of the immaculately patterned parterre, the clipped evergreens and the little round lawn by the river with its central statue. All that remained was to install Jean Tijou's ornamental railings and screens.

In January and early February the workmen prepared the low walls that would hold the ironwork at the bottom of the Privy Garden and at the head of the canal in the Fountain Garden. William was there waiting to see the railings unpacked and fixed. With his health improving, he decided on 20 February to go for a ride. Somewhere in the park his horse stumbled on a molehill and threw him off, breaking his collar-bone. As news of his fall spread, embittered Jacobites raised their glasses to the 'little gentleman in the velvet coat'. Twelve days later William suddenly deteriorated, and over the next few days his temperature soared. 'I am drawing towards my end,' he said, hot with fever. Shortly after eight the next morning, on 8 March 1702, at the age of fifty-one, he died. Under his shirt lay Mary's ring and the lock of hair he had taken at her death, tied with a black ribbon.

Despite his recent rise in public opinion, William's death caused little sorrow. His funeral took place at midnight on 12 April at Westminster Abbey, and was so inconspicuous that Bishop Burnet complained it was 'scarce decent'. If William had foreseen this, he probably wouldn't have cared: his concern had always been his standing as defender of liberty and Protestantism in Europe, and as military ruler. Even his enemies could not begrudge him this. He had dragged England into the heart of European affairs, and now she was emerging as a major player. His other passion, his love of gardens, had resulted in the grandest garden in England, one that epitomised the height of baroque design. Outshining Versailles in elegance and detail though not in scale, it symbolised the bold aspiration of a king who believed he could conquer nature just as he had conquered England and saved Europe from a Catholic despot.

3

Nature to Advantage Dressed: Stowe

'A man might make a pretty Landscape of his own possessions.'
Joseph Addison, *Spectator*, 25 June 1712

'He leaped the fence, and saw that all nature was a garden.'
Horace Walpole, *The History of the Modern Taste in Gardening*, 1771

'No, no, hang him, he has no taste.'
William Congreve, 'Double-Dealer', 1694

Standing before his grand stucco-fronted house, which he was in the process of enlarging and improving, Sir Richard Temple, Viscount Cobham, surveyed his garden stretching down a gentle hill and across twenty-eight acres to the south and west of his family seat, Stowe, in Buckinghamshire. Immediately in front of him was a formal parterre with sculptures, fountains and pools, from which a long, wide avenue led down to an octagonal lake, three hundred feet by four hundred, at the south end of the garden. To the east of the avenue the garden terminated abruptly at an old approach road, but to the west groves could be seen with pathways snaking their way through them. About halfway down the avenue the trees gave way to a clearing of fine, smooth grass through which a canal ran, and opposite, on the western edge of the garden, stood one of the many monuments that punctuated the grounds. Singled out by visitors as 'delight-full', the Rotunda was a round, open temple, its tapering columns supporting a domed roof with a small sphere on the top. Presiding over the temple from her stone plinth in the middle was a gilded copy of the Venus de Medici, goddess of love and patroness of gardening. Designed with meticulous reference to the work of Vitruvius, the celebrated first-century BC Roman architect whose theories of proportion had been revived by Renaissance designers, the Rotunda at Stowe was one of the first truly classical garden buildings in England. As such it testified to Viscount Cobham's refined taste, for it demonstrated his understanding of the classical arts – a necessary prerequisite for any aspiring person of culture.

By 1724 Viscount Cobham had achieved much of what he had strived for as a young man: he was wealthy, influential and respected by the ruling political and cultural elite. Almost fifty years old, the handsome and debonair Cobham could look back on a successful career in the army which had won him military honours and earned him a peerage with, in 1718, a seat in the House of Lords. He was the friend of dukes and men of letters, and his home was one of the most fashionable in the country. However, Cobham had not been born into the highest echelons of the nobility. His great-grandfather had been a wealthy farmer and had bought a baronetcy from James I in a straight-forward commercial transaction – part of Robert Cecil's moneymaking schemes in the early seventeenth century. Though the family retained its minor title, subsequent generations of the Temples had squandered much of the fortune, and so when Cobham inherited the small estate of Stowe in his early twenties, he found himself burdened with debts.

Having chosen a career in the army, he had risen quickly through the ranks, making his reputation fighting with William III at the decisive battle of Namur in 1695, then with the Duke of Marlborough in the War of the Spanish Succession.* Described by Jonathan Swift as the 'greatest Whig in the army',

---

*The War of the Spanish Succession began in reaction to Louis XIV's rescinding of the parti-tion treaty with England after Carlos II of Spain died, and his recognition of James II's son, the 'Old Pretender', as the King of England and Scotland. In May 1702, the Grand Alliance (which William III had joined in September 1701) declared war on France.

Cobham was dedicated to the principles of the Glorious Revolution – to maintain the liberty of England, the supremacy of Parliament and the constitutional monarchy – all sentiments that helped to bring him to the attention of the German-speaking Elector of Hanover, who had been made George I of Great Britain and Ireland in 1714. The king was distrustful of the Tories, many of whom he suspected of supporting the Jacobites, who opposed his accession and defended the claim to the throne of James Edward Stuart, the 'Old Pretender' – the son of James II. But to loyal Whigs like Cobham he was happy to grant titles – which boosted their party's position in Parliament.

Richard Temple, Viscount Cobham, *c.* 1740

Cobham's goal was to create a powerful new dynasty, but though his military career had brought some financial rewards it was through his marriage in 1715 to Anne Halsey, a brewery heiress with a fortune of £20,000, that he would finance his desire to create a family seat that would reflect his ambitions. From then on, as his friend the dramatist and architect John Vanbrugh observed, Cobham was 'much entertain'd with (besides his Wife) the Improvements of his House and Gardens, in which he Spends all he has to Spare'. Preparing for all eventualities, he had also altered his father's settlement. This had laid out that Stowe would go to a distant and impoverished cousin if Cobham's marriage remained childless. In the event that this might be the case, he bought out the relative for £7000 and chose as his heir his nephew Richard Grenville, the eldest son of his second sister.

But money, a title and a settled lineage were not enough to distinguish him from the rising urban class of merchants, bankers and financiers who were trying with some success to push their way into the upper levels of society by buying country estates of their own. Having married one of their daughters, Cobham needed all the more urgently to set himself apart from the nouveaux riches. To do this he had to demonstrate a refined sense of taste; this, he and his contemporaries believed, was the defining characteristic of the cultivated. Central to it was the ability to appreciate beauty, which depended on an under-standing of 'proper culture' – classical literature, art and architecture. Since only a small proportion of the population had access to this, taste became, inevitably, a socially divisive tool; as Joseph Addison had aptly remarked in 1712 in the *Spectator*, 'A Man of Polite Imagination is let into a great Many Pleasures that the Vulgar are not capable of receiving.'

By the mid-1720s Cobham had spent a decade transforming his house and garden, though it had been during the last five years that the most dramatic changes had been made.* Without his wife's fortune, no such transformation would have been possible, but the task was not without its difficulties: while he wanted to demonstrate his wealth, he had to avoid at all costs any accusation of vulgarity. To help him in this and to create a garden that would display his refinement, Cobham had taken advice from his friends, many of whom ranked among England's leading writers and artists. As a member of the Kit-Cat Club, the most influential literary coterie of the eighteenth century, Cobham was also at the hub of enlightened thinking. Here he had met writers such as Joseph Addison and Richard Steele, editors of the *Tatler*, the *Spectator* and the *Guardian*, journals of news, letters and essays. Declaring themselves the 'Censor of Great Britain', they promoted a reformation of manners and morals. Frivolous consumption, opulence, flamboyant displays of wealth and vanity were all dismissed as vulgar and symptomatic of a character susceptible to vice.

*Unless otherwise indicated, the chronology of the making of Stowe is based on the *Stowe Gardens Survey*, prepared by Land Use Consultants for the National Trust, 1992, articles in the *Stoic*, contemporary letters and diary extracts and various maps of the garden.

Advocating a new simplicity in behaviour and appearance, these thinkers rejected baroque ostentation in architecture and garden design, especially the French-inspired formal gardens with their neat topiary and enormous patterned parterres.

As a young man Cobham had spent 'six nights in seven' drinking in London's coffee-houses, discussing politics and culture with these men. And having listened carefully, he had been the first to take these new ideas out into his garden. He was helped in this endeavour by Vanbrugh who, like Cobham, had been a member of the Kit-Cat Club and an army man. The most sought-after Whig architect of his time and well informed about the classical revival, Vanbrugh had been commissioned to alter the old house that Cobham's father had built in 1680 and to design the garden's monuments. Charles Bridgeman was responsible for the layout and the planting, and together with Vanbrugh, he had decided on the positioning of the temples, statues and pavilions. Having begun his career as assistant to Henry Wise, William III's gardener at Hampton Court, Bridgeman had already worked at Blenheim in Oxfordshire which Vanbrugh had designed to commemorate the Duke of Marlborough's victories in Flanders. Bridgeman had worked for Cobham since 1714 and had fast become one of the most innovative garden designers of his time as he rolled out a scheme at Stowe that parted from the old rules of symmetry. It had been

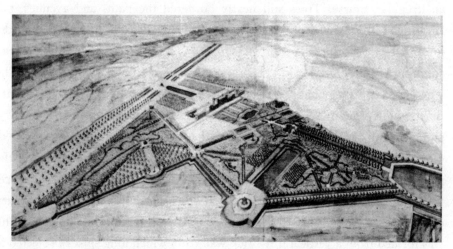

Bird's-eye view of Stowe garden by Charles Bridgeman, *c.* 1719. The plan shows the first stage of improvements at Stowe, such as the zigzagging ha-ha, the Octagonal Lake, canals and the groves with snaking paths

five years since Cobham had first approved Bridgeman's drawing for the revolutionary new design and now the work was almost finished.

Bridgeman's most challenging task had been to extend the garden to the south and west of the house where the limitations of the site posed a particular problem. The old approach road to the east of the avenue that led down to the Octagonal Lake prevented eastward expansion, while to the west the ground was marshy in places, and in others, heavy with clay. Given such terrain, it was impossible to achieve the regular lines in the layout and planting that had for so long been fashionable. But he would not be deterred. If symmetry was out of the question, he would let the natural conditions lead his design. So he had extended the garden into those areas that he could reclaim, creating a boundary to the west that zigzagged around the good land, while skirting around the unusable.

Lopsided this layout might have been, but it was revolutionary, for it defied the notion of symmetry that had ruled the design of gardens such as Hatfield and Hampton Court – and still did, spawning huge parterres, long, straight avenues and geometrically laid out plantations. The groves that Bridgeman had designed for the west part of the garden also defied convention; for instead of being laid out on linear grids like those at Hampton Court or Versailles, the paths that wove their way between and through them followed an irregular course. Trees still neatly bordered the paths and avenues, but Bridgeman had stopped pruning them into artificial shapes, thus softening the linear effect. 'Nothing is more irregular in the whole,' Lord Perceval, an admiring visitor, observed in 1724, and 'nothing more regular in the parts'. The winding paths left Cobham's guests disoriented and surprised: 'You think twenty times you have no more to see, and of a sudden you find yourself in some new garden or walk as finish'd and adorn'd as that you left,' Perceval had exclaimed.

The most radical feature, though, skirting the western boundary of the garden, was the ha-ha. This garden feature, somewhat menacing in appearance, was reminiscent of the stockade ditches Cobham had seen during his military campaigns. Its outer, grassed edge sloped gently upwards, while its inner bank was formed from a vertical turf-brick wall from which long spikes projected at regular intervals. Although the ha-ha served the same purpose as a wall, separating the garden from the countryside beyond in order to prevent intrusion,

Vanbrugh's Pyramid and view from the north-west corner of the garden, looking across the ha-ha to the pasture of Home Park, *c*.1733. Here Bridgeman's juxtaposition of art and nature becomes clear as the straight avenues are softened by the unpruned trees.

it did not obstruct the view because it was at ground level. During the winter of 1726 Bridgeman went further, extending the ha-ha so that it no longer simply marked the boundary between the garden and the outside world, but enclosed a part of the pastureland – called Home Park – within the garden. This was Bridgeman's answer to Addison's question, 'Why may not a Whole Estate be thrown into a kind of garden?' Enclosed plots and parterres had dominated the scene for centuries, but Cobham had finally liberated the English garden from its brick corset. He had introduced what Horace Walpole, the first English garden historian, hailed as 'the capital stroke, the leading step to all that has followed'. It was one step further in the rapprochement between man and nature that had begun in the early seventeenth century when Robert Cecil had created tiered terraces at Hatfield that allowed him to look over the walls of the garden out into the countryside; while Tijou's decorative railings at Hampton Court had extended the idea further by creating a pleasantly diffused view of the parkland beyond the garden.

The idea behind the ha-ha originated in the book *La Théorie et la pratique du jardinage* (1709) by the French garden theorist Antoine-Joseph Dézallier d'Argenville, translated into English in 1712 as *The Theory and Practice of Gardening*. The strange invention was originally called an 'Ah, Ah' – the French, when they first saw it, had exclaimed 'Ah! Ah!' in surprise. This device had been recommended by Dézallier in order to create vistas that stretched beyond the perimeter walls. He had proposed that small sections of the wall might be opened up rather like doorways, while protecting the garden from intruders with a short ditch on one side. Seizing on the notion of an unfettered view, English garden writers had taken up the new concept. Stephen Switzer, for instance, who like Bridgeman had worked under Henry Wise, insisted in 1715 that 'all the adjacent Country [should] be laid open to View, and that the Eye should not be bounded by high Walls'.*

In 1724 Cobham had effectively retired to Stowe. Although he was still a

A ha-ha

member of his regiment and had his seat in the House of Lords, he was neither politically nor militarily active. The object of his attention now was his garden, and it seemed as if his passion for horticulture was paying off. Word had spread that Stowe, and especially its 'improvements', were worth seeing. Indeed, so

*There was one previous example of a ha-ha in England before Bridgeman built his at Stowe; on a much smaller scale, it was constructed by a French gardener, Guillaume Beaumont, at Levens Hall in Cumbria in the 1690s.

many arrived, particularly in the summer months, that the inn – described as 'scurvy' by one visitor – that Cobham had built to accommodate the estate's foremen and artisans, was now being used by sightseers. So keen were they to see the garden that they were willing to put up with beds full of 'fleas and gnats'. Lord Perceval remarked: '[T]o erect so many Summer houses, Temples, Pillars, Piramids and Statues . . . would drain the richest purse, and I doubt not,' he added acidly, 'but much of his wife's great fortune has been sunk in it', but he still praised Cobham's designs because '[w]e all know how chargeable it is to make a garden with taste; to make one of a sudden is more so.' Not content that his home had already been proclaimed the 'finest seat in England', Cobham continued to enlarge and embellish. Vanbrugh died in 1726, obliging him to find a new architect to design more monuments. But since it was the garden that people most wanted to see, it was to this that he increasingly turned his attention. By the end of the 1720s, a new water feature, the Eleven-Acre Lake, had been dug west of the Octagonal Lake, with a cascade tumbling over rocks between the two, and Bridgeman was overseeing the extension of another ha-ha around the new southern perimeter.

It was now widely held that the Viscount had put together a garden 'with great taste'. High praise – but even more welcome were the compliments he received from Alexander Pope, the most admired poet of the time. Visiting Stowe almost every summer, on his 'rambles' from 'Garden to Garden', Pope held that Stowe outshone all others, enjoying it each time 'with fresh Satisfaction'. 'If any thing under Paradise could set me beyond all Earthly cogitations,' he wrote to a friend in the summer of 1731, 'Stowe might do it.' He and Cobham would pass tranquil days, walking in the garden, talking and admiring the latest additions. His growth restricted by a childhood illness – he was only four feet six inches tall – Pope impressed people with his eloquent choice of words and his beautiful voice. As a satirist of the day-to-day affairs of fashionable London life he made an entertaining guest.* And although he was a Catholic and a Tory, he and Cobham enjoyed each other's company.

---

*Pope was the first writer in England to make a comfortable living from his profession.

Like Cobham, Pope was passionate about gardening and had spent much time creating his own at Twickenham, just outside London. Teased by his friend, the poet and playwright John Gay, that he 'talk'd only as a Gardiner', Pope admitted 'My gardens improve more than my writings.' In 1731, Pope publicly praised Cobham's taste in a poem, part of a series called *Moral Essays*, in which he reflects on contemporary moral values. Presenting garden design and architecture as an expression of taste, he offers Stowe and Lord Burlington's estate at Chiswick as outstanding models. 'A man,' Pope later wrote to a friend, 'not only shews his Taste but his Virtue, in the choice of . . . Ornaments': if opulence and pomp were thought to be vulgar, modesty and restraint were seen as worthy.

To many, however, including Cobham and his circle, the reign of George II, begun in 1727, was marred by a decline in morals and manners. In this, the country's rulers were seen as especially culpable. The king's first minister Robert Walpole's predilection for luxury – not least the rich clothes and jewellery with which he festooned his large, ungainly body – provoked ridicule. But more seriously, both he and the king were accused of indulging in debauchery and bribery. Walpole's close relationship with Queen Caroline, who, it was rumoured, had so much influence on her husband that she was said to speak to Walpole 'through the King's mouth', was also subject to lewd speculation, while the king had caused a scandal when he pardoned a convicted rapist. In fact, depravity seemed to cling to the royal court: George II's promiscuity was legendary, and his wife's confidant Lord Hervey was lampooned for his effeminacy. In his *Epistle to Dr Arbuthnot* (1734) Pope wrote of Hervey: 'Fop at the Toilet, Flatt'rer at the Board/ Now trips a Lady, and now struts a Lord.'

But for now Cobham was loyal to the king and to Walpole – he had dutifully erected several monuments in his garden that demonstrated his allegiance to the House of Hanover. He was also keen, though, to present himself as a man aware of the pitfalls of vice, hoping thereby to circumvent any possibility of being accused of vulgarity. The monuments that Vanbrugh had erected at Stowe had already aligned Cobham with those classical values that underpinned the professed codes of conduct of the time. But, rather than make a series of isolated statements, he now wanted to link the monuments in the grounds west of the house into a moral essay.

The notion that a garden structure or ornament represented the owner's religious, political or philosophical beliefs, or some universal absolute, wasn't new. In medieval gardens, for instance, water had symbolised the fount of life; the Tudors had emphasised loyalty to their king with heraldic displays, and William III had used sculptures of Greek heroes such as Hercules to represent his own bravery. Cobham, however, planned something rather different: he wanted to create a whole narrative, which would unfold as the visitor passed from one monument to the next along a planned route through the garden. Most of the temples and other buildings had been built randomly over the course of the previous fifteen years, but now they had to be assembled into one story on the pitfalls of vice.

The man commissioned to supervise the changes that would have to be made to the interior of these buildings, and who would design two more, was William Kent. He had already worked in the main house, when Cobham asked him in the early 1730s to devise his 'garden of vice'. As a young man, Kent had travelled and studied in Italy for ten years with the intention of becoming a painter, and he was deeply interested in Italian architecture, gardens and art. Known as 'Signor' or 'Kentino', he adopted Italian mannerisms, dropped Italian phrases and referred to himself as 'Guglielmo'. Returning to England, he had been patronised and influenced by the 'Apollo of arts', Lord Burlington, whom he had met on the continent. It had been Burlington with his passion for Palladian architecture who had persuaded him to switch from painting to architecture. Now Kent combined his talents, introducing classical painting into interior decoration. He was also Master Carpenter to the royal family. Bridgeman, who had himself been made 'the Kings Gardner' a few years previously, had met him at the Board of Works. Bridgeman may well have recommended him to Cobham, but Pope too knew Kent through Lord Burlington, so it may well have been he who advised Cobham of the young architect-designer's talents.

By 1732, a year after the publication of Pope's poem praising Cobham, the didactic tour of the 'garden of vice' was nearly finished. Taking its inspiration from classical myths and popular pastoral dramas, it told tales of frustrated love, infidelity, celibacy and licentiousness. Visitors would start at the Octagonal Lake at the southern end of the garden, first encountering 'unrequited love' in the Lake Pavilions, which stood like sentries at the southern border of the garden. Then they walked along the boundary, skirting the new Eleven-Acre Lake until they reached the south-west corner. Here they entered Kent's newly built Temple of Venus, a semicircular Palladian villa consisting of a central pedimented block connected by arcaded passages to two smaller pavilions. It was furnished with busts of the adulteresses Cleopatra and Faustina, and the licentious emperor Nero. A naked Venus languished on the ceiling, and the walls were embellished with explicit murals of the beautiful young Hellinore from Edmund Spenser's *Faerie Queene*, abandoning her senile husband Malbecco to frolic with satyrs. As the story went, Malbecco, having seen his unfaithful wife cavorting, went mad with jealousy and fled to a cave – not unlike the Hermitage that Kent had sited nearby. Like many popular paintings of the time, teeming with coquettish nymphs and bare-breasted women flirting with their admirers, the images portrayed in the temple were not considered lewd. The point of these promiscuous figures, that adorned the walls of the other temples in this part of the garden, was to warn of the perils of desire and the consequences of succumbing to self-indulgence.

Later that year another of Cobham's nephews, the poet Gilbert West, published a poem called 'Stowe' which described the new tour through the garden and the meaning of the various buildings. Anyone who read it could be sure of interpreting all the lessons correctly. In effect, the poem became the first guidebook to Stowe. West must have whetted many a potential visitor's curiosity with his descriptions of scenes such as the 'Mysterious Orgies' depicting the revels of Bacchus: a 'jolly figure on the Cieling reels', West informed his readers, was none other than the local vicar. No doubt with the approval of Cobham, who had little time for religion, West described how the vicar pursued a young girl with lustful thoughts after seeing her on a swing, exposing her 'mysterious Charms'. Bursting out from behind a thicket, he had chased her to a grotto where 'The fierce Pursuer seiz'd the helpless Fair'. From then on the grotto was known as the Randibus after the vicar, Conway Rand.

With the Western Garden finished, Cobham turned his attention to extending the boundaries on the east side. Here he would create what became known as the Elysian Fields. Until now he had been reluctant to demolish the village of Stowe that was situated there, along with the old road to Buckingham, but now his gardening fervour prevailed; he relocated the village to another part of the estate and built a new approach road to the house.

Two years earlier, in 1730, he had shown his old army friend Lord Cathcart some designs for this part of the garden. In response to the drawings, and having surveyed the proposed site, Cathcart had remarked: 'What is left to do in my opinion will be the most noble of all.' The design for the Elysian Fields, with its meandering rivers, undulating lawns, unpruned trees and winding pathways would be the culmination of Bridgeman's career – and the springboard for Kent's reputation as a landscape architect. It marked the total departure from formality, geometry, straight lines; once executed, it would make real what many writers and garden owners had long desired instead of the fastidious planting schemes and layouts that had held sway for well over a century. It would also mean, as the engraver and antiquary George Vertue observed,

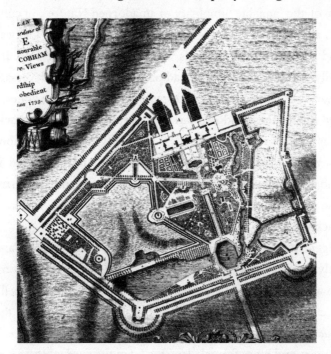

Detail from Bridgeman's plan of Stowe Garden, 1739. The Elysian Fields, with a river running through, are to the east of the central avenue

that 'no nobleman['s] Gardens were thought to be of Tastes unless Mr Kent had disposd or planted [them]'.

The ideas that Bridgeman and Kent drew on had been forming for several decades. As early as 1624 Henry Wotton, poet and ambassador to James I in Venice, had recommended that just as 'Fabriques [buildings] should be regular, so Gardens should be irregular, or at least cast into a very wilde Regularitie'. In a similar vein the essayist Sir William Temple, a relative of Cobham's, had, in 1685, drawn attention to the Chinese fondness for 'forms wholly irregular', and in the mid-seventeenth century the poet Andrew Marvell had dismissed enclosed gardens as 'A dead and standing pool of air'. 'Art is onely Natures ape . . . therefore let our Workman . . . contrive rather how to apply to it the best shape that will agree with the nature of the Place,' John Evelyn had pronounced, articulating the mantra that Cobham and his contemporaries would later adopt.

Already in 1712 Addison had condemned the 'Marks of scissors upon every Plant and Bush' in an article in the *Spectator*, while the following year Pope wrote of the 'amiable Simplicity of unadorned Nature', in contrast to the 'Monstrous attempts' to cut trees and bushes into the 'most awkward Figures of Men and Animals'. Although this was an aesthetic judgement, it also had a determinedly political intent. Pope had particularly criticised Versailles, as had the 3rd Earl of Shaftesbury, an esteemed Whig philosopher, who had pronounced the neatness and regularity of baroque gardens a 'mockery'. Both men disliked such formality. Versailles, especially, with its allusions to Louis XIV, epitomised what the Whigs stood against: the tyrannical rule of an absolute monarch. Instead of forcing patterns, shapes and structures upon the garden, one should make use of what nature had provided. Liberty was to be allowed back in.

Bridgeman was in tune with their ideas, as was Cobham, and followed them closely. A voracious reader who made good use of his patrons' libraries, Bridgeman would have read the relevant books and pamphlets as well as keeping abreast of current thinking with such publications as the *Tatler*, the *Spectator* and the *Guardian*. Although never one to let nature run wild, he had slowly eradicated more and more formal elements from the garden. Pope was so struck by what he saw at Stowe that he instructed his readers to 'Consult the Genius of the Place' and 'follow Sense', just as Cobham and his team had done. It was Bridgeman's use of the lie of the land that Pope so admired:

> In all, let Nature never be forgot.
> But treat the Goddess like a modest fair,
> Nor over-dress, nor leave her wholly bare;
> Let not each beauty ev'ry where be spy'd,
> Where half the skill is decently to hide.
> He gains all points, who pleasingly confounds,
> Surprizes, varies, and conceal the Bounds.

Bridgeman, however, took offence at the lines 'The vast parterres a thousand hands shall make/Lo! Bridgman comes, and floats them with a lake.' Pope, chagrined, replaced the designer's name with Cobham's – Bridgeman, 'not having the taste to see a compliment', did not deserve it, he concluded.

Bridgeman and Kent's design for the Elysian Fields took further what Bridgeman had done earlier elsewhere. The two new rivers that they were plannning, for instance, would exemplify the direction in which garden fashions had been moving over the previous couple of decades. Bridgeman's earliest water features were two canals and the Octagonal Lake – all of which still celebrated the straight line. When he had constructed the Eleven-Acre Lake, only four years previously, he had already abandoned symmetry: though they were still straight, each side of the lake was of a different length. Furthermore, as well as the cascade he had created between the lakes, he had built a causeway with three ruined arches, thereby introducing an element of ruggedness into the scene. Continuing this relaxation of formality, the new rivers that would run the length of the eastern part of the garden – the Elysian Fields – were designed so that their manmade origins should be undetectable. There would be no hard outlines or sharp angles. Their sinuous shape would recreate what Cobham and his friends would perceive as a natural river. No one was better placed than Bridgeman to realise such a project: he had just finished work on the Serpentine, for the 'Diversion of the Royal Family', in Hyde Park in London. But by the end of 1732, his health, which had been failing for some time, declined rapidly and it became clear that he would have to cede control of the gardens to Kent. Before he retired he commissioned a set of drawings to commemorate his work at Stowe. In February 1733, Jacques Rigaud, a Frenchman famous for his illustrations of the royal palaces of France, came to England – 'at the request of Bridgeman', George Vertue tells us – and headed for Stowe to make his preparatory sketches.

Meanwhile, a political furore was erupting in London, which would profoundly influence the design of the Elysian Fields. At the centre of it was Robert Walpole and his controversial excise scheme, which catapulted Cobham, after years of political inactivity, into the fray. Walpole wanted to introduce taxes on wine and tobacco, but many feared it would lead to a wide-ranging excise on all kinds of items. If approved, the scheme would give revenue officers extensive powers of inspection of warehouses and other properties, in order to investigate tax liabilities and fraud. This was seen as an infringement of the basic Whig belief in the right to privacy and protection of one's possessions. Tories and Whigs alike feared that the creation of an army of collectors – who could potentially be bribed – would lead to even more corruption than Walpole was already credited with. Such was the hostility that one Londoner commented: 'The rising tempest of an excise makes a furious roar in this town.'

Walpole won a sizeable majority for his Excise Bill in the Commons, but when it became obvious that a large number of lords, including Cobham, would vote against the government, on 11 April 1733 he dropped the bill. Yet for many days afterwards, effigies of Walpole were burned in the streets, and supporters of the bill complained in the House of Commons that they were 'menaced, insulted, and assaulted' by the mob. To take revenge on those Whig peers who had humiliated him, Walpole advised the king to dismiss seven of them from office. Cobham was stripped of his regimental post, in June that year. This caused something of a scandal, as it had been a personal reward from the former king for Cobham's bravery on the battlefield.

This show of vindictiveness galvanised opposition, leading many prominent Whigs to disavow their loyalty to the government. Walpole was highly regarded for his political skills. He was a brilliant orator, had a fine grasp of finance, and fought to promote international peace. But for years his governing style had provoked dissent, even in his own party, as he controlled both Parliament and king and became the sole conduit for all applications for royal favours and political positions. With such an exclusive hold on the reins of power, he was the first English politician to be habitually referred to as 'prime minister'. Cobham had remained loyal to the government for years, but his dismissal from his regiment was more than he could tolerate, and along with other prominent Whigs he rose in opposition to Walpole. The incident took its toll on Cobham's nerves and he confessed to feeling 'out of order'. But his friends rallied round him, and Pope now wrote his 'Epistle to Cobham' as a public demonstration of his high regard.

> And you; Brave COBHAM! to the latest breath,
> Shall feel your Ruling Passion strong in death:
> Such in those moments as in all the past;
> 'Oh, save my Country, Heav'n!' shall be your last.

In response to the draft that he received that November, Cobham replied: 'Tho I have not enough modesty not to be pleasd with your extraordinary compliment I have wit enough to know how little I deserve it'; he felt honoured to have received 'a publick testimony of your esteem'. In January 1734 Cobham and other opposition members founded the 'Liberty or Rumpsteak Club' in honour of their dismissal from the 'Royal Rump'. One month later they proposed a motion to force the king to reveal who had advised him to cashier Cobham and the Duke of Boulton* and to state 'what crimes were alleged against them'. Though it would be humiliating for the king, these MPs insisted that 'the removal of those two noble lords is looked on to be a wrong step' – the 'wicked person' who ordered it should be 'pointed out to the world'.

As friends and relatives gathered at Stowe, Cobham began to groom his heir Richard Grenville and his other twelve nephews for their role in a caucus of opposition to Walpole – all under thirty, they were known as the 'Cobham

---

*Boulton lost his regimental post along with Cobham.

Cubs' or 'Boy Patriots'.* As his marriage had remained childless, Cobham had spent years preparing Grenville for public life, as the head of the dynasty he he was so determined to found. Grenville's mother, unlike Cobham's oldest sister, had complied with his wishes and married into a wealthy family, and so the young man would be rich in his own right. The Grenvilles' estate, Wotton, was near Stowe, so it would be easy to join the two estates after Cobham's death. Grenville was a tall, ungainly boy, later nicknamed 'Squire Gawky', who had become Cobham's charge when his father had died a few years previously. Since then, the Viscount had ensured that Grenville finished his classical education. One vital element of this was a Grand Tour through Europe, visiting in particular the great architectural and archaeological sites of Italy. This had long been considered essential for architects and painters as well as young aristocrats, who often travelled abroad with their tutors to complete their education. By the 1730s it had become a rite of passage for any self-respecting gentleman, in order to cultivate the good taste that familiarity with Renaissance art and culture was thought to bring about. After four years on the continent Grenville was back, and in 1734 Cobham decided he was ready to enter Parliament. Through his uncle's influence, Grenville won the Buckingham seat at the election that year, and duly entered the House of Commons.

Many of Cobham's nephews became MPs at some stage in their lives. The active political nucleus of the coterie, though, consisted of Richard Grenville, George Lyttelton and William Pitt. Pitt was not a nephew, but had befriended Grenville and Lyttelton at Eton and would become part of the family when he married Grenville's sister. A few years previously Cobham had helped Pitt to a commission in his regiment, and he was always welcome at Stowe.

All through the summer of 1734, while his workmen were implementing the designs for the Elysian Fields, Cobham was in 'excellent spirits' and taking pleasure in entertaining his guests who, as always, flocked there in large numbers. '[P]erfect in the Pleasing Art', as his friend the playwright William Congreve

---

*The Whig factions who opposed Walpole during the 1730s and 40s were known as the 'Patriots', the inference being that the government was neglecting the national interest. The Boy Patriots constituted the 'junior wing'.

had described him, Cobham was such a good host that on one occasion 'two coachfuls' of visitors who had planned only to dine at Stowe ended up staying three days. '[I]t is enchanted ground', one visitor explained, 'and not in people's power to leave when they please.' Among the many guests were Pope, the poet James Thomson and the Cubs. The days were spent enjoying the grounds, and in the evenings there was music, gardening talk and literary exchanges, as 'Pope diverted us by translating Horace'.

The pleasant soirées also served a more serious purpose. Cobham's plan was to make the Elysian Fields a manifesto spelling out his opposition to Walpole. This he would achieve by means of temples and statues, the whole design inspired by an allegory on honour and virtue set in an ideal garden, written by Joseph Addison in 1710. Published in the *Tatler*, Addison's essay had described a garden that featured a temple of virtue dedicated to heroes and philosophers; a temple of honour to which men who had promoted 'the good of their country' could retire; and in stark contrast, a crumbling temple of vanity 'filled with hypocrites, pedants, free-thinkers, and prating politicians'. In Addison's vision, those who walked through this garden and appreciated what they found there, did so in the 'service of mankind'. Cobham wanted to translate this allegorical landscape into a real one – one that would contrast his own virtues and those of his like-minded friends with the corruption and degeneracy that were widely held to characterise Walpole's rule.* In the context of the whole garden, this 'garden of virtue' would also complement the west part, where Kent had made 'vice' the overriding theme. As the visitor passed through the gates of Stowe, he had to make a choice: to turn either west or east, towards 'vice' or towards 'virtue'.

Cobham's friends and contemporaries were fascinated by these moral quandaries. Addison's translation, in 1709, of the allegory 'The Choice of Hercules', for instance, still resonated. Published '[F]or the benefit of the youth of Great Britain', it told of the Greek god who had to decide between two beautiful women, one of whom embodied virtue, the other pleasure. A contemporary of Addison's, the Earl of Shaftesbury, had also written a treatise on *The*

---

*And to show his displeasure at George II's complicity, Cobham also moved the statue of the king to a less prominent position.

Judgement of Hercules and commissioned a painting on the subject. As men of the early Enlightenment, they focused on meaning beyond the material world: the choice was between instant gratification and vanity on the one hand, and modesty, honour and 'immortal reputation' on the other. And it was in this spirit that Kent began his buildings for the Elysian Fields, the paradise where immortal heroes found their resting-place.

A year later, in the summer of 1735, Cobham's friends were back at Stowe; and Cobham, as always, was the perfect host. Lady Suffolk, the king's former mistress, was particularly charmed. 'Lord Cobham,' she told a friend, 'says I am the best looking woman of thirty that he ever saw' (she was in fact forty-seven). His nephews came, and amused themselves playing cricket; Pope stayed for three weeks, and William Pitt for four months. Earlier that year, in April, Richard Grenville, George Lyttelton and William Pitt had all moved to the opposition and had given their maiden speeches in the House of Commons. With this gesture Lyttelton had jeopardised his relationship with his father, who was a staunch court Whig and loyal to Walpole. But Cobham's magnetism had consolidated the young man's inherent political sympathies, and he had acted in the full knowledge, the *Old Whig* newspaper claimed, that he might thereby exclude himself from his father's will.

Absent from Stowe was William Kent, who was busy in London working on commissions for the royal family – for the Prince of Wales at Carlton House and for the queen at Kensington Gardens. Because of his poor health, Kent preferred to meet his patrons in London, and he rarely inspected his sites in the country more than once a year. Equipped with drawings that he supplied them with, the foremen at Stowe were largely able to execute his designs, but for the planting and the siting of monuments they needed Kent's on-the-spot directions. They would 'rough levell' the ground according to the plans, then wait for him to give the precise instructions on one of his rare visits. At Rousham in Oxfordshire, one of Kent's most admired projects, the letters of the steward and gardener reveal how much depended on the designer's decisions. 'Nothing further shall be done, till fresh Instructions from Mr Kent come down,' wrote the steward William White, but then when Kent, as so often, wasn't there to

The Elysian Fields with the Temple of British Worthies, Thomas Rowlandson, 1805

consult, the gardener, John MacClary, would grow desperate: '[I]f Mr Kent don't come soon I must turn off half my men,' he wrote to the owner. Kent seems to have enjoyed being courted and cajoled; it was to be hoped that 'Mr Kent can be persuaded to come', said one who was concerned by his absence. Here at Stowe, despite Kent's tardiness, the first monument had been installed on the Elysian Fields: the Temple of British Worthies, on the east bank of the Worthies River.

This building was Cobham's answer to Addison's temple of honour, its design inspired by the Rotunda of Ancients at the Renaissance Villa Brenzone near Lake Garda in Italy. The workmen had carved sixteen niches into the two wings of the semicircular structure, ready to house a pantheon of English heroes – men of ideas and men (plus one woman) of action: Pope, financier and philanthropist Thomas Gresham, architect Inigo Jones, Milton, Shakespeare, Locke, Newton, Francis Bacon, King Alfred, the Black Prince, Queen Elizabeth, William III, Walter Ralegh, Francis Drake, the parliamentarian John Hampden and Sir John Barnard, merchant and politician. Of these only Pope and Barnard were contemporaries.

Although the choice of men of ideas was uncontroversial, Cobham's selection of men of action was decidedly partisan in its patriotic fervour, as he looked back to the heroes of British liberty and strong leadership in an intentional contrast with the corruption and weak foreign policies for which Walpole's government was so condemned by the opposition Whigs. There could be no mistaking the contemporary significance of the inscriptions above the busts, either. Elizabeth had 'destroy'd the power, that threaten'd to oppress the liberties of Europe'; Ralegh had risen 'against the ambitions of Spain'; William III had 'preserv'd the liberty, and religion of Great Britain', and Drake had 'carried into unknown seas . . . [the] glory of the English name'. King Alfred, 'the founder of the English constitution', had 'established juries, crush'd corruption, guarded liberty' – here the allusion, by contrasting with the failings of the current king, could not fail to be understood. The Black Prince, on the other hand – the 'delight of England', who was praised for his modesty even at the 'height of glory' – personified the Prince of Wales, in whom Cobham and other opposition Whigs now placed their hopes. It had been Cobham, his nephews and friends who had come up with the subjects for the busts, and their inscriptions – which, unlike all the others in the garden, were written in English rather than Latin. As a postscript to this propaganda exercise, Cobham could not resist adding a touch of humour in the inscription he chose for the back of the temple – a few words in memory of 'Signor Fido', his dog.

The landscape in which the Temple of British Worthies was set was also complete now, as were the two rivers, made from an old diverted mill stream. The bed of the Alder River, to the north, was laid with black sand to make it appear melancholic. It would eventually be shaded by a dense canopy of alder and chestnut trees, in order to accentuate the light and uplifting atmosphere of the Worthies River below, which ran by soft grass banks edged with different shrubs in shades of light green. No elaborately patterned turf, no lacy arabesques, no garish gravel on walkways, no evergreens topiarised out of all recognition were to be found in this part of the gardens. Admittedly, it had all been manicured and staged like a theatre set, but in an apparently natural way – there was no trace of the gardeners' shears anywhere. 'There is a new taste in gardening just arisen,' an acquaintance of Kent wrote to the Earl of Carlisle, 'after Mr Kent's notion of gardening, viz., to lay them out, and work without even level or line.' Kent's methods achieved 'the appearance of beautiful nature' of which, his acquaintance noted, 'one would imagine art had no part in the finishing'. This was the scenery that would later inspire Horace Walpole to declare that Kent had 'leaped the fence, and saw that all nature was a garden'.

The River Alder, J. C. Nattes, 1805

Irregular clusters of trees and shrubs lined the meandering walks, revealing, then obscuring, views. Though no nursery bills have survived for this period at Stowe to indicate the numbers and kinds of plants he bought, Kent's other gardens reveal details of his planting schemes. At Carlton House for the Prince of Wales, for example, he ordered during the same period fourteen thousand trees and shrubs for a site of only nine acres (less than a quarter of the new area at Stowe), of which two thousand were flowering plants such as fragrant lilacs and jasmines, honeysuckles, roses, bright-yellow Spanish brooms and bladder sennas. Nurserymen also delivered some American exotics, which were admired for their fiery autumn foliage and brilliant winter berries. There were tulip trees – which John Tradescant junior had introduced from America – as well as scarlet oaks, Virginian black walnut and sumacs. These were all still rarities, as was the *Catalpa bignonioides* – commonly known as the Indian bean tree – which had arrived in England only thirteen years previously. A few years later at Rousham, which shares with Stowe many design features, Kent planted evergreens along the paths, and among them, roses, lilacs, honeysuckles and other shrubs, all intertwining with each other in a seemingly natural way. 'Here,' the gardener John MacClary wrote in admiration, 'you think the laurel produces a Rose, the Holly a Syringa, the Yew a Lilac, and the sweet Honeysuckle is peeping out from under every Leafe'. Instead of the erect hedges that lined the Wilderness at Hampton Court, these shrubberies rose gradually, low-growing plants in front and the highest at the back, giving the scene a fluid feel. The wide petticoats of passing women would brush against the flowering shrubs that bordered the pathways, releasing the gentle fragrances.

It is very likely that Kent planted the same specimens at Stowe, interspersing them with the trees and shrubs Cobham had raised on the estate. Though there is no evidence of how Cobham procured the trees for the Elysian Fields, he probably also, as before, relied on local gardeners and foresters. For Bridgeman's designs in the Western Garden, for example, he purchased 5750 privets and maples from the local suppliers, as well as almost 20,000 other saplings from the forester of a nearby village. Trees such as chestnuts and beech had been sown some years ago by Bridgeman's men in a corner of Home Park in order to provide a constant supply for the ongoing improvements, and it's likely that Kent was now using some of these. The estate had provided Bridgeman with several thousand mature horse chestnuts for the avenues, and Kent probably continued his predecessor's habit. Friends and relatives would also have offered specimens from their stocks. Provincial nurseries were now proliferating and stocking a good selection, so other plants would have been bought from them. In addition to being cheaper than London-based nurseries, their proximity to Stowe made the transport of the fragile goods less hazardous. Cobham's head gardener went regularly to Paradise Garden in Oxford for trees; we know that he bought elms, horse chestnuts, firs and limes there for Stowe.

As with the monuments, the gardeners had to await Kent's instructions for the planting scheme, so some delay always had to be allowed for. Kent had no qualms about uprooting recently planted specimens if their position failed to please him. At Rousham, MacClary lost so many trees in this way that in the end he didn't dare make his own decisions. He wrote to his employer: 'I don't know [where] to plant but very few trees without being in danger of having them removd again'; he would wait 'till Mr Kent comes down and tells me', he insisted.

The following year, 1736, the workmen started on the next building, the Temple of Ancient Virtue on the other bank of the Worthies River opposite the Temple of British Worthies. Cobham's theme here was the ancient principle of civic virtue – that a good citizen should take an active part in public affairs. Again, it was via ancient heroes that he illustrated his views on contemporary politics. The temple would house statues of the poet Homer, the philosopher Socrates, the lawyer Lycurgus and the general Epaminondas – the pillars of society about whom Addison had written in his essay. In the inscriptions above the niches in which the life-sized figures would stand, Epaminondas would be praised for bringing liberty and empire to the Republic of Thebes; Lycurgus for establishing laws that brought liberty and fought corruption; Socrates for putting philosophy at the service of society; Homer for being the 'Herald of Virtue'. The temple itself was of a domed, circular design, with sixteen columns. It was based on the ancient Temple of Vesta at Tivoli, which Kent had seen when he was in Italy. Situated on a mound at the top of the gently rising riverbank, it commanded a spectacular view of the Temple of British Worthies on the opposite side. The two temples stood as if in conversation with each other, the British heroes, reflected in the water separating them, seeming to look up at their ancient forefathers. It 'abounds with lasting Beauties; it is really placed in a sort of Paradise,' the novelist Samuel Richardson wrote of the new building in 1742.

By the time the temple was finished, Kent was no longer working for Cobham. His health had deteriorated and he had become increasingly busy with his clients in London. His withdrawal from Stowe may also have been triggered by a conflict of interests between two of his patrons. Queen Caroline, for whom he was redesigning the royal gardens at Kensington Palace, was at this time in dispute with her son, the Prince of Wales, who was on friendly terms with the Cobham Cubs. She may well not have liked her designer working on what was becoming the horticultural and ideological heartland of the Whig opposition. Indeed, that year, Cobham was expecting a visit from the prince. Having fallen out with his parents, he was now banned from court. Recently,

Pitt – described as 'a very pretty young speaker, one the Prince is particular to' – as well as Grenville and Lyttelton had all given speeches in the Commons warmly praising the prince while indirectly criticising the king. As a warning to them all, Walpole promptly stripped Pitt of his commission in Cobham's old regiment. But the Boy Patriots were not cowed. Spurred on by Cobham – who was believed to be their 'chief promoter' – the Cubs demanded in February 1737 that the king increase the prince's annual allowance to £100,000 – a clear indicator of their allegiances. In return, the prince made Pitt the Groom of the Bedchamber when he set up his own court in autumn that year. Pitt, as one contemporary observed, was now 'perpetually with the Prince, and at present in the first rank of his favour', while Lyttelton became the prince's Secretary – an appointment that could only be seen as confirmation that the heir to the throne was aligning himself with the opposition. As if to underline this shift, the prince, a keen gardening enthusiast himself, used the same iconography at Carlton House as Cobham had at Stowe – and thus conveyed the same message to the prime minister and the king by displaying busts of King Alfred and the Black Prince.

The third temple in Cobham's political essay, the Temple of Modern Virtue, represented Addison's temple of vanity. To symbolise his disgust at the state of contemporary politics and society Cobham had built it as a 'ruin' and set it amidst rampant uncut grass, in vivid contrast to the flawless classical architecture of the Temple of Ancient Virtue on its neatly mown mound. In a final insult to the prime minister, Cobham instructed his workmen to erect a solitary headless figure in contemporary dress amidst the ruin's fallen stones; it didn't take a huge leap of the imagination for Cobham's guests to see the figure as Walpole.

　　Work on the Elysian Fields was almost at an end. Even before the renovations and additions were all in place, the gardens had been 'esteemed the finest of their kind in England', in which 'beautifull Nature' was 'improved by happy Art'. Pope's delight in them was unabated; in the summer of 1739 he wrote to a friend: 'I am every hour in [the garden], but dinner & night, and every hour Envying myself the delight of it.'

*

The Temple of Modern Virtue was to be Cobham's last direct attack on Walpole. Maybe his friend Pope, too, was questioning the effectiveness of satire. He had just published the *Epilogue to the Satires*, a caustic poem that accused the government of 'insuperable corruption and depravity of manners', but now he wrote that he would henceforth refrain from more 'ineffectual' protest. Perhaps, for his part, Cobham felt that his Elysian Fields made a sufficiently eloquent statement. In both conversation and letters, though, his criticism remained fierce; on 18 August 1739 he wrote to his friend the Earl of Stair about 'the folly and wickedness of our minister', adding wryly 'nothing but supernatural intervention can help us'. His hopes were now pinned on his nephews, who were rising to prominence. Ever more active at Westminster, in spring 1739 the leading Cubs attacked Walpole's foreign policy towards Spain which they – and many others – believed to be too lenient. Spanish naval aggression against British merchant ships was gruesomely illustrated when a ship's captain called Robert Jenkins appeared in the Commons holding a jar that contained his pickled ear – cut off, he claimed, by a Spaniard. Walpole, as so often, argued for a diplomatic solution, while Lyttelton's opinion was that 'we should go into war against Spain'.* Pitt also spoke on the issue – 'very well, but very abusively'.

Cobham must have been pleased to see his young protégés at the hub of political affairs. He, though, was now more than ever content to focus his energies on his garden – and at this particular moment on a new section to the east of the Elysian Fields, called Hawkwell Field.

While Cobham had been developing the Elysian Fields at Stowe, Philip Southcote, as part of his garden at Wooburn in Surrey, had laid out an ornamental farm combining cattle and arable land with garden buildings, winding paths and shrubberies. Having long enjoyed his position at the vanguard of English gardening fashion, Cobham would have been aware that the so-called

---

*The War of Jenkins' Ear, ostensibly triggered by the incident described here, was in fact caused by Britain's attempt to break Spain's monopoly of trade with South America. The conflict began in 1739, when Walpole reluctantly declared war on Spain, and soon merged into the more momentous War of the Austrian Succession (1740–8).

Pastoral scene by Claude Lorrain, 1673

ferme ornée was attracting praise from gardening enthusiasts,* and he responded to the challenge by creating his own. So in Hawkwell Field he now made a pasture enclosed by an ornamental walk. Though he stopped short of incorporating a working farm into the area, the inclusion of pasture land in his garden represented another step in the blurring of the boundary between garden and countryside. For although the unpruned trees and shaded paths in the Elysian Fields brought the mythical landscapes of classical paintings alive, Cobham now wanted to create an even more naturalistic scene: an Arcadia, an earthly paradise of rustic simplicity.

This celebration, in the garden, of a pastoral idyll mirrored the work of painters and writers influenced by classical poetry who had hailed agricultural life as a model of virtuous living. Painters such as Claude Lorrain and Nicolas Poussin had depicted beautiful landscapes populated with shepherds, cattle and temples; and more recently Alexander Pope, envisaging men working with nature rather

*Stephen Switzer suggested this combination of utility and pleasure in a garden in *The Nobleman, Gentleman, and Gardener's Recreation* (1715), and first coined the term 'ornamental farm' in the *Practical Husbandman* (1733).

than dominating it, had drawn on the verses of Virgil and Homer (whom he translated) in his own work. The vision was that of a harmonious community in which
landowners accepted their civic responsibilities, ruling paternalistically over their
labourers and tenants while cultivating their estates in such a way as to balance
beauty with use, pleasure with profit. As such, ornamental farms came to symbolise
an idealised society in which the labourer happily toiled in the fields and the land
yielded stability and contentment as well as income for all.

Cobham and Southcote were not alone in their enthusiasm for the *ferme
ornée*. Bridgeman had already made a 'pretty paddock' at Rousham, where he
and Kent had again worked together. Separated from the garden by a ha-ha, it
was stocked with 'two fine Cows, two Black Sows, a Bore, and a Jack Ass', as
gardener John MacClary noted. Even before work began on Hawkwell Field,
Cobham already had a pasture: the tract of grazing land that Bridgeman had
enclosed with the ha-ha, back in the 1720s, in the west part of the garden.
Visitors had marvelled then at the 'gadding Heifers' below as they paused to
look down from the raised walks that skirted it. But this time Cobham wanted
to take the experience a step further: he wanted his visitors actually to walk
through Hawkwell Field. Bridgeman had already laid out some paths and
enclosed Hawkwell Field with a ha-ha some years previously, so now all the
workmen had to do was to complete the remaining landscaping (probably from
plans left by Kent). With Kent no longer around, Cobham had to rely on head
gardener William Love to implement the designs. Though Love had been at
Stowe for thirteen years and was familiar with Kent's style of working, it seems
that during this period he had a somewhat uneasy relationship with his employer.
For when Cobham sought to replace him a few years later, he specified someone
'free from the vanity and conceit which had rendered his former assistants disinclined to alterations which he had determined upon'.

For the time being, though, Love would oversee the planting at
Hawkwell Field. But Cobham needed a new architect to design the buildings
for this part of the garden, and his choice fell on James Gibbs, who had already
worked for a while at Stowe in the late 1720s after the death of Vanbrugh.
Now in his mid-fifties, the portly Gibbs was considered to be among the best
in his profession. The first British architect to receive professional training

abroad, he had been awarded one of the most prestigious ecclesiastical commissions of the age – the rebuilding of the parish church of St Martin-in-the-Fields in London. Other major commissions included St Bartholomew's Hospital in London (begun in 1730), a new wing for King's College, Cambridge, and, later, the Radcliffe Library at Oxford. He had come to Cobham's attention in the first place as Pope's architect at Twickenham, and through Bridgeman with whom he had regularly collaborated on other commissions.* Like Bridgeman he was a member of the prestigious St Luke's Club of Artists, described by George Vertue as one of the 'Tip top Clubbs of all, for men of the highest Character in Arts & Gentlemen Lovers of Art'. In fact, Gibbs and Bridgeman were good friends, enjoying intellectual conversations about the arts – Gibbs was also respected for his books on architecture – as well as drunken evenings at the tavern. On one occasion the patron for whom they were both working, hearing that they had made their fellow drinkers and landlord 'terribly scar'd', had felt it necessary to send horses to collect them. As a Catholic with Jacobite sympathies – demonstrated by his friendship with Lord Mar, who had led the Jacobite rebellion in 1715, and the patronage he had received from him – Gibbs was certainly not Cobham's ideal candidate. But the recommendations of his friends and his skill as an architect had persuaded the ardent Whig to employ him a decade before, and he had not been disappointed. So Cobham invited him back again.

Having already created a parable on the dangers of vice in the Western Garden and celebrated virtuous men in the Elysian Fields, Cobham now asked Gibbs to add a sequel to the moral tale by introducing to Hawkwell Field the theme of liberty and friendship, thereby making manifest his own favourite themes. On 20 March 1739 Gibbs received ten guineas for his first design. Paid by the drawing rather than with a retainer, he was not expected to oversee the building work, which was the responsibility of William Love as head gardener and clerk of works. Gibbs's first building at Hawkwell Field was the Temple of Friendship, to be situated at the south-east tip of the new area. The central block

*For example, Wimpole Hall in Cambridgeshire, Kedleston Hall in Derbyshire, Tring Park and Sacombe Park in Hertfordshire in the early and mid-1720s.

would be square and built of stone, with a pyramidal roof topped with a small cupola, and two side-rooms with arched porticoes. Also equipped with a kitchen and a cellar, unlike the other temples at Stowe it would have a practical function, serving as a private retreat where Cobham could entertain his guests – like the banqueting houses of the previous century. Inside, busts of Cobham, his political friends and the Prince of Wales were to adorn the walls.

Personal connections were the key to gaining and retaining influence within the patronage system – politics, art and literature all functioned on the basis of who one knew. But friendships of a closer kind were also important to Cobham. As boys he and his contemporaries would have been taught the tenets of classical philosophers such as Cicero, who believed that moral strength derived from properly maintained friendships, and Cobham's appreciation of his friends was to be found everywhere in the garden. A pyramid in the Western Garden was dedicated to Vanbrugh; an entrance pavilion had been fitted out as a home for one of his old army colleagues; in the Temple of British Worthies was a bust of Pope; and in memory of one of his closest friends William Congreve, who had died ten years earlier, Cobham had erected a monument in the form of a pyramid with a monkey astride it looking into a mirror – playfully embodying the aphorism that 'art is the ape of nature'. At the Temple of Friendship, celebrating friends united in their political beliefs, the theme would take on a decidedly patriotic tone. Inside would be murals of Britannia holding aloft the 'Glory of her Annals' – the reigns of Elizabeth I and Edward III. The reign of George II would be conspicuous by its absence.

In 1741, as the Temple of Friendship was nearing completion, the carpenter John Smallbones and his team began work on the Temple of Liberty – also called the Gothic Temple – situated at the east edge of Hawkwell Field. Once again Cobham wanted to express his patriotism,* but instead of drawing

*The word 'patriotism' was coined in 1726 (in Nathan Bailey's *Universal Etymological Dictionary*), although the meaning behind it was not new. It denoted a civic virtue in which citizens had to place their public duty before their own self-interest – something the Boy Patriots prided themselves in. Their political opponents, however, would have been more inclined to describe their 'patriotism' as self-serving. Indeed, during the Hanoverian period the term was often used pejoratively. Dr Johnson's definition of a patriot in his dictionary (1755) as 'a factious disturber of government' reflects this.

The Gothic Temple, 1805

parallels with classical architecture, this time he adopted the Gothic style, to celebrate the roots of liberty in England's own history: 'a real Whig', as Viscount Molesworth had noted in 1721, should always uphold 'the true *Gothick Constitution*'. Later described as 'half Church half Tower', the temple was triangular and built of dark red-gold ironstone, with crenellated turrets and pointed arched windows with tracery and stained glass. The design was inspired by medieval buildings such as Westminster Abbey and King's College Chapel at Cambridge.

The temple mirrored the beliefs held by many of those who opposed the king, his first minister and their policies. The younger generation, the Boy Patriots, presented themselves as the defenders of Britain's long heritage of liberty, which they feared was being eroded by what they considered to be Walpole's corruption of power and weak foreign policy. Although in 1739 he had finally declared war against Spain, his reluctance to act sooner was still held against him. In February 1741, both Pitt and Lyttelton spoke in the Commons in support of a motion 'for the Removal of Sir Robert Walpole'. They were unsuccessful. It would take another year for Walpole's majority to crumble and for him to resign. Others would then rebuild the administration, but leaving Pitt, Grenville and Lyttelton still in opposition.

Tories and dissident Whigs, united as they were in their hostility to government, took up the theme of patriotism. Walpole's erstwhile Tory rival and Pope's friend, the vitriolic writer Viscount Bolingbroke, had already published his views on England's struggle for liberty in the 1730s in his *Remarks on the History of England*. Though Whigs and Tories used history for their own ends, most believed that the roots of Parliament could be traced back to the *witenagemot*, or Anglo-Saxon assembly, considered the birthplace of liberty and democratic principles. In this widespread upsurge of national feeling, King Alfred came to be regarded as the benevolent law-giver and defender against foreign invasions – above all, a potent symbol of strength and endurance. To Cobham and his friends, the Prince of Wales was Alfred's modern-day embodiment. Although the Gothic style postdated Alfred's reign by some two hundred years, it was nonetheless associated with the Anglo-Saxon king and became assimilated into the English vernacular. To further reinforce this symbolism at Stowe, Cobham dedicated the Gothic Temple 'To the Liberty of our Ancestors', and surrounded it with unruly grass and trees that were left unpruned so as to evoke the image of a free nation. As if the message was still not clear enough, visitors would read above the door '*Je rends grâce aux Dieux de n'estre pas Romain*' – 'I thank the gods that I am not a Roman' – spelling out the belief that England, not Rome, was the home of liberty. Like Lyttelton's 'Temple of Justice' in his *Letters from a Persian in England to His Friend at Isapahan*, a fictionalised account of England's morals and manners published in 1735, Cobham's Temple of Liberty was an 'Old Gothic Pile', and revered as such. As one of the earliest buildings of this sort in England, it helped spur the Gothic Revival that would come to dominate English architecture for many decades.

The theme of liberty continued in Hawkwell Field with the covered Palladian Bridge. It provided shelter, as one visitor remarked, if 'a Sudden Shower interrupts your Walk'. In June 1742, while the Temple of Liberty was still under construction, the 'magnificent bridge' with its arches, colonnaded arcade and more patriotic murals, was completed. Inside were depicted Walter Ralegh holding a map of Virginia, and Britannia receiving the world's harvest. The bridge straddled a new river that came from the Octagonal Lake and crossed Hawkwell Field from west to east, extending the drive around the east edge of the garden so that guests could enjoy the tour from the comfort of a carriage. The side of the bridge facing the garden was open, giving a view over Hawkwell Field – the other side was enclosed, to prevent visitors getting a glimpse of the untended terrain beyond. Although Cobham liked to think of himself as embracing the whole landscape, the version of nature that he promoted at Stowe was a carefully controlled one. The vistas on to the surrounding estate conformed to a specific ideal – any grubby farms and dreary workers' cottages were kept well out of sight.

About this time, Cobham had begun to look for a new director of operations. He had received years of loyal service from a handful of men, but few of them now remained. First William Love, his head gardener of more than fifteen years, had left. Shortly afterwards his steward William Roberts, a 'great favourite' of Cobham's, had hanged himself. The man had been so upset by the conviction of a local deer poacher that he had spoken out against the assize judge. Cobham had reprimanded him for his outburst and Roberts, according to a neighbour, was so 'vex'd' about it that 'he made away with himself'. Roberts was quickly replaced, but in April 1742, when Cobham's attorney started to query irregularities in the accounts, the new steward disappeared together with a large sum of money. Months passed, and they were no nearer solving the case. In November and December, four advertisements in the *Northampton Mercury* offering a reward of ten guineas for information that would lead the authorities 'to apprehend' the fugitive, were also unsuccessful. He was never found.

Amidst the disruption, Cobham had to find a new head gardener – a position he was very particular about: he wanted a man 'who could continue with him at Stowe, able to converse instructively on his favourite pursuit'. The young man who arrived at Stowe one day in 1741, after Love had left, to take up the new position would prove to be Cobham's best investment yet. In Lancelot Brown he had found a gardener both intelligent and enthusiastic, and willing to try out new ideas. Despite being born into an ordinary yeoman farming family in Northumberland, Brown had attended school until the age of sixteen. Unusual as this was, it had prompted rumours that he was the illegitimate son of his mother's employer, the local squire, who had also given him his first gardening job in 1732. After seven years Brown had moved south, taking up a position at Kiddington Hall on the Oxfordshire–Buckinghamshire border thirty miles from Stowe. It was at this point that he came to the attention of Cobham, who probably heard about him from one of his nurserymen. Although Brown was only in his mid-twenties, Cobham immediately put him in charge of nearly forty men, at the same salary as Love – £25 a year plus £9 in board.

Soon after he took up the post of head gardener, Brown also became effectively the clerk of works, responsible for dealing with the accounts, taking on the contractors, buying in the materials and supervising the masons and carpenters. Although the atmosphere when he first started at Stowe must have been uneasy, given the suicide of one steward and the absconding of the other, Brown's affable character and his perceptiveness must have helped him navigate these early months, earning him the esteem of both his patron and his colleagues.

One of his first tasks was to fell Bridgeman's neat rows of beeches at the north front of the house and to soften the straight lines of the avenues. The accounts of 1743 record twelve men 'filling up tree holes where the large lime trees were taken out', as well as Brown's removal of the formal grass parterre and basin with its fountain below the south façade. This involved employing dozens of men throughout winter 1743 and spring 1744, and digging up and disposing of 'unmeasurable' amounts of earth. Brown's aim was to replace Bridgeman's design with a lawn sweeping gently down towards the head of the avenue that led to the Octagonal Lake at the south edge of the garden. This lawn would mark the culmination of Cobham's gradual shift towards the 'new taste' for the natural look, which had spread so rapidly across the country that one commentator wrote: 'One large room, a Serpentine River and a Wood are become the absolute Necessities of Life, without which a gentleman of the smallest fortune thinks he makes no Figure in the country.' Brown had grown up as this trend took hold and as a member of a younger generation he felt no attachment to the old formal style. He embraced the new approach wholeheartedly, and his efforts were so well appreciated that Richard Grenville asked if he could borrow his uncle's gardener for his own garden at Wotton.

The end of May 1744 saw the completion of the vast expanse of lawn at the south front. All that remained to be done was to tidy up the paths where the gravel had been 'abused by ye carting'. With the onset of summer, work slowed and visitors began to arrive.

Cobham's friend and fellow Patriot, James Thomson, who had written the poem 'Rule Britannia' celebrating Britain's strength and freedom, was so taken with the maturing garden that in the new and expanded edition of his poem *The Seasons* published that year, he had added some lines celebrating the beauties of Stowe:

> Or is this gloom too much? Then lead, ye powers
> That o'er the garden and the rural seat
> Preside, which shining through the cheerful land
> In countless numbers bless'd Britannia sees,
> Oh lead me to the wide-extended walks,
> The fair majestic paradise of Stowe!

Although customary in Italy, in England there were scarcely any guide-books to places of interest. The few exceptions included Wilton in Wiltshire (1731) and Houghton Hall in Norfolk (1743), where it was possible to buy, at considerable cost, leather-bound catalogues of the art collections held there, aimed at rich dilettantes. For the last decade, the gardens at Stowe had been well enough publicised by Cobham's nephew Gilbert West's poem 'Stowe', and by Samuel Richardson's description of them in the third edition of Defoe's *Tour through the Whole Island of Great Britain*, published in 1742. Now, in 1744, the first guidebook to Stowe was available.* Written by a local 'writing master', one Benton Seeley, it gave a 'plain Account . . . a simple, regular Relation of every Thing' that visitors would encounter (including an explanation of the inscriptions and the names of the buildings) as they made their way along the prescribed route. It was so popular that an enlarged edition appeared within a year, to be followed by others during the next decade.

Once the summer guests had left, Brown got down to work again. As

---

*The cost of the original edition is not known, but the 1756 edition sold for sixpence. The version with a plan cost one shilling and the one that included views of the garden, five shillings.

usual, Cobham was spending the winter in London, so he was free to turn the garden into a building site – there was no one to be disturbed by muddy paths, piles of earth and workmen felling trees and digging holes. Winter was the most active period; labour was cheaper because villagers were expected to accept a reduced daily rate, from tenpence down to eightpence, as they couldn't work on the fields. This winter, Brown married Bridget Waye – at the parish church of Stowe, the only vestige of the village that Cobham had destroyed to make space for the Elysian Fields, and now well hidden by trees so that it would not spoil the view of the garden.

Meanwhile in London, Cobham, at sixty-nine and retired from active politics, made what would be his last big political gesture, but now he followed the Cubs rather than lead them. Appalled that Britain was paying Hanoverian troops to fight in the War of the Austrian Succession, William Pitt – speaking, according to Grenville, 'like ten thousand angels' – had already in 1742 declared the king's beloved Hanover a 'despicable electorate' and accused the government of 'squander[ing] the public money'. George II, fearing that France would use the war as an excuse to invade Hanover, supported the conflict. Thus Britain and the Netherlands were now allied with Austria in her battle against Bavaria and her allies over the succession to the Habsburg Empire. The Cobham Cubs, though, felt that the king was ignoring British interests, as the war drained both the Exchequer and military resources. In 1744, two years after Walpole's resignation, Cobham helped to negotiate what became known as the 'broad-bottomed' administration, led by Henry Pelham and of which Lyttelton was a prominent member as Lord Treasurer. This coalition of many factions would go some way towards reunifying the Whigs.

In the summer of 1745 England was threatened again, when the Young Pretender Charles Edward – grandson of James II and the last of the Stuarts – landed in Scotland to claim the throne of Great Britain. Marching south with an army of Jacobite supporters, by December he had reached the Midlands. Cobham's concern was that a Catholic Stuart would endanger the constitutional monarchy and the power of Parliament, as well as sparking nationwide unrest. As a precaution, he instructed his nephew to remove all the plate from the house.

Although the invasion was quashed, the crisis had unsettled Cobham and his Whig colleagues.

Cobham's plans for a new extension to the north of the Elysian and Hawkwell Fields went ahead all the same. The trees were to be planted in clumps, their branches left unpruned in imitation of nature and as a symbol of political freedom at a time when England's liberty was seen to be threatened. After numerous conversations on the subject, he and Brown had agreed on the creation of a 'natural' scene that would surpass all others, although art would again be allowed to temper nature. So Brown began shaping the land. With spades, pick-axes and wheelbarrows his men removed 23,500 cubic yards of earth over the next two years, excavating a deep valley that ran eastwards in a broad sweep from the top of the Elysian Fields. Brown planned a long, narrow lake here; he would make use of the natural springs at one end of the valley. At the same time his workmen were digging out an oval bowl at

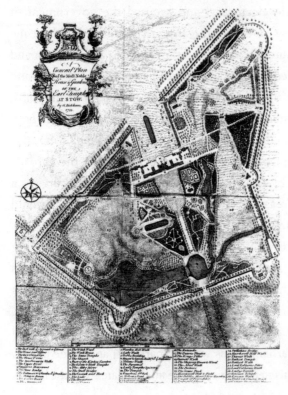

Plan of Stowe garden, 1753. The Grecian Valley is to the north-east of the house, north of Hawkwell Field, and the Elysian Fields, which are to the east of the central avenue.

the opposite side so as to create a grass amphitheatre five hundred feet in circumference.

Cobham asked Brown to keep him informed of progress while he was in London. He had always involved himself in every aspect of the garden – from conceiving the ideas underpinning it, to devising inscriptions, to keeping an eagle eye on such details as the quality of the tools his workmen used: he thought nothing of going with Bridgeman, on one occasion, to inspect an iron roller before he bought it. Writing in February 1747, Brown defended himself for not having completed work on the new area. The reason, he insisted, was that Cobham 'gave me no absolute Orders to finish it'. He would not dare proceed without exact instructions and reassured Cobham: '[A]s to finishing the head of the oval I never formed any other idea on it than what your lordship gave me'. He suggested that they should have a 'summer's talk and tryels' before finalising the plans, and stake out in advance the positions of the trees, temples and statues.

Just as Addison's essay had been an inspiration for the Elysian Fields, it was Cobham's friend James Thomson's long patriotic poem *Liberty*, written in the mid-1730s, that provided the intellectual blueprint for Brown's new valley. As Thomson traced the progress of liberty through history in his poem, so did Cobham in his garden: an obelisk in the Octagonal Lake represented ancient Egypt; the Roman temples commemorated the victories of the Republic; the Gothic Temple of Liberty celebrated England as the crucible of freedom; and now a Grecian temple would preside over Brown's creation to be named the Grecian Valley.

At first the Grecian Temple posed a problem, as both Brown and Richard Grenville, Cobham's heir designate, who took a keen interest in Brown's work at Stowe, had ideas for the design. Grenville considered himself a connoisseur and amateur antiquarian of some distinction; and as Cobham grew frailer he had increasingly given his nephew a bigger say in the decision-making. Brown, for his part, had developed a good practical knowledge of architecture by supervising the works at Stowe. Both men submitted a drawing. Cobham, although in his seventies and ill, was unwilling to hand over completely. 'That thin, decayed carcase of his contains a spirit that is surprising', a friend had remarked a few years earlier, but by now Cobham had become cantankerous enough for Grenville's wife to nickname Stowe 'the house of Discord'. In the end Cobham opted for Brown's design.*

The temple Brown designed was to be larger than any other building in the entire garden. Though Grecian in inspiration, it was not a copy of any particular ancient temple, but would incorporate many classical architectural elements as depicted in pattern-books of the day. Rectangular in outline, it would be distinguished by slender fluted Ionic columns, the top of each ending with the characteristic four scrolls, forming a cushion between the columns and the frieze that ran below the pediment. Now, in 1747, the labourers started on the foundations and Brown began the enormous tree-planting project that would transform the Grecian Valley.

As an avid reader of the books in Cobham's library, Brown had probably used the pattern-books he found there for his design of the temple. But for the landscape he envisaged, he began with the terrain itself. Unlike the classically educated Kent, Brown was inspired less by Arcadian scenes as represented in Italian art and literature than by nature: he wanted to exploit the capabilities of the land – later reflected in his nickname 'Capability Brown'. The Grecian Valley provided him with his first real opportunity to develop his own distinctive style. Surveying the terrain from horseback, he would search for the best example of each landscape element: the ur-form of a river, the perfect cluster of trees, the most elegant rise and fall of the land. His quest for the ideal mirrored Joshua Reynolds' thinking ten years later: that painters should select 'the most beautiful . . . form of nature'.

So Brown took the flat land and sculpted it into a gentle valley, so that it began to look as if the undulating earth could have been shaped by the icy waters of long-forgotten glaciers, or gouged out by centuries of erosion by wind and rain. Along one part of the valley he was working on a river that he planned would snake through the garden, forming what William Hogarth in

*Grenville would commission a painting of himself shown with the plan of the buildings, which has been interpreted as proof that he was the architect. But Grenville modified the Grecian Temple in 1752 and since the portrait was painted in 1760 it probably relates to these modifications.

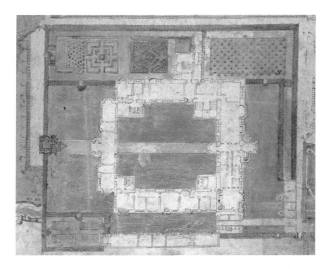

The old palace at Hatfield and its gardens in 1607, before
Robert Cecil demolished most of it. The knot gardens are at the
top, and the orchard is in the right-hand corner. The red line
around the garden is the wall

Striped and double anemones were admired for their
variety by gardeners such as John Tradescant who
bought them for Hatfield from nurseries on the continent

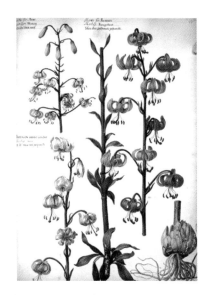

John Tradescant planted *Lilium martagon* at
Hatfield for its sculptural petals

Fritillaria meleagris was prized for its chequered
patterns, and was bought for the garden at
Hatfield by John Tradescant

Hampton Court with the semi-circular Fountain Garden and its radiating avenues in the foreground. The Privy Garden and Mary's flower plots are to the left of the palace. To the right is the Wilderness with its precisely clipped hedges and geometric layout

William and Mary's garden at Het Loo in the Netherlands

A Dutch orangery garden and its hothouse at Brenhelen in Gunterstein in the late seventeenth century. The sloping glass cases at either end of the building are similar to the hothouses Mary had erected at Hampton Court

Auriculars were popular florist flowers in the seventeenth and eighteenth century. One of Mary's flower plots at Hampton Court was dedicated exclusively to them

The Great Parterre at Longleat, in Wiltshire, was designed by
George London and his colleagues at the Brompton Park Nursery.
The planting of the ribbon-like flowerbeds in the Privy Garden at
Hampton Court would have been similar

John Vanbrugh's Rotunda at Stowe with a view to the east across the canal and the groves.
Based on proportions laid out by Vitruvius, the Rotunda was one of the first
classical garden buildings in England

A Conversation of Virtuosi . . . at the King's Arms. In this
painting by Gawen Hamilton (1735), three of Stowe's
designers and architects are depicted. James Gibbs is fifth
from the left, Charles Bridgeman is eighth from the left
and William Kent is the figure on the far right

Two gardeners scything the lawn

At Hawkstone, Neptune's Whim and the windmill opposite it evoke scenes
such as this landscape painted by Jacob van Ruisdael – who was also called
the Dutch Salvator Rosa

Many tourists who visited Hawkstone in Shropshire also went to see the industrial
towns nearby such as Coalbrookdale. Equipped with Edmund Burke's treatise,
A Philosophical Enquiry into the Origin of our Ideas of the Sublime and the Beautiful,
they likened furnaces to volcanoes and mines to natural caves and crevasses – using
the same language for industry as for nature

By the end of the eighteenth century people had become so fascinated by mountains and
rugged landscapes, such as this one painted by Turner in North Wales, that Hawkstone,
with its steep cliffs and ravines, became one of the most popular gardens in the country

his *Analysis of Beauty* (published in 1753) would call 'the line of beauty' – a core characteristic of any good work of art. The grassy riverbanks would be planted with mature trees in order to give a natural look, so that nothing would reveal the river's manmade origin. To create this effect instantaneously, Brown would have to move hundreds of lime and elm trees. Hitherto, this had been achieved by a cumbersome method, used for the previous seventy years, which involved cutting the roots a year in advance, then employing a complicated pulley system to hoist the tree into an upright position and on to a cart. Brown needed to streamline the process, and he came up with a new contraption: a pole with wheels attached to the end of it. This was lashed to the trunk with ropes, then, with the tree attached, it would be levered into a horizontal position, wrenching the roots out of the soil. Finally, horses would pull the tree to its new location. The method was crude in its treatment of the roots, and many trees must have perished, but enough survived to allow Brown to transplant specimens up to thirty-six feet tall.

Some trees he planted in small open groups, and others as dense woodland, so that strolling visitors would be surprised as views revealed themselves, then just as suddenly disappeared. Islands of trees punctuated the valley bottom, while others had been planted in drifts down the slopes in patterns resembling

Tree-moving machine, 1827. This machine is similar to the one Brown used at Stowe

lava flows, their branches entangled or feathered down to the ground. How different from the older parts of the garden this scene was, and Cobham was well aware that Stowe told a story of changing aesthetics. Bridgeman's zigzagging paths, asymmetrical lake and avenues of unpruned trees, so innovatory in their day, such a total departure from the ornate baroque gardens of the previous generation, now seemed outdated and unnatural. Indeed, one visitor dismissed Bridgeman's early designs as 'the worst' part of Stowe. So Cobham instructed Brown to break up and thin out the neat rows of trees dating back to those days. This had the added advantage of providing many mature trees for the Grecian Valley.

While Cobham invested much time and thought in improving Stowe for his own and his many guests' pleasure, he behaved less benevolently towards the people in the neighbouring villages. When two poachers tried to steal deer from his park that year, he revealed himself as an unforgiving and brutal landlord. Taking advantage of the draconian 'Black Act' of 1723, which had been drawn up to protect the property and liberties of the landed classes, he had the two men charged. As Lord Lieutenant of Buckinghamshire he had presided over the local justice system, and he knew full well that they were

The Grecian Valley, 1805

unlikely to receive a fair trial. Local tradition has it that when their wives pleaded for Cobham's forgiveness, he promised to return the men on an appointed day. And he obliged. But it was their corpses that he delivered, and he celebrated his coup by erecting statues of the dead men in the park, a deer slung across their shoulders. No doubt he intended the gesture as a lesson to others.

The following year, 1749, the tree-planting in the Grecian Valley was nearing completion. But the water supply for the new lake was proving unreliable. Despite the absence of water, the rolling green valley that met the visitor's eye was nonetheless perfect in its apparent naturalness. And no knowledge of antiquity was needed to appreciate it, no summoning up of classical myth or Gothic past. Rather, the garden was to be encountered on a sensual level. The visitor could stroll along the paths enjoying the ever-changing moods that Brown had orchestrated. Like a Haydn sonata incorporating different tempos and keys within an overall structure, the Grecian Valley embraced variations on the theme of nature, from grassy open spaces, through mottled shade, to the gloom of the thicket. Richard Grenville was keen to apply this new approach to other parts of the garden, but Cobham remained loyal to the idea that all art, including gardening, should be instructive: '[I]t does not signifie to read unless we know we apply what we read.' Twenty years previously Cobham had carved on Vanbrugh's Pyramid: 'You have played enough, eaten enough and drunk enough/ Now it is time to leave the stage for younger men.' But at seventy-four, despite growing frail, he was not yet prepared to give up control.

Meanwhile, there was more work to be done, and Brown was keen to finish it before his patron's health gave way. Moreover, there was another project in hand: an enormous column, commissioned by the viscountess for her husband. To be built on a hill on the east edge of the Grecian Valley near Hawkwell Field, at 104 feet it would dominate the horizon. A statue of Cobham, dressed as a Roman emperor, was to be placed at the top. Thus, in effigy, he would survey the whole garden and five counties beyond. Brown now put all his energies into building the monument to his patron. But Cobham died on 13 September 1749, just as it was finished. Its inscription read:

> As we cannot live long,
> Let us leave something behind us,
> To show that we have lived.

Cobham had always looked to the future, intending that Stowe would continue to evolve as the status of the family rose. Grenville had been groomed all his life to continue in Cobham's spirit, moving with the times and ready to experiment with new ideas. The two men had disagreed on how far Brown should be allowed to develop his natural style, but on his uncle's death Grenville ordered Brown to soften the contours of the Octagonal and Eleven-Acre Lakes. He abandoned plans for more monuments in the Grecian Valley and began to eradicate the traces of geometric design that still lingered in many parts of the garden.

Cobham's widow was horrified when she heard that Grenville had allowed sheep to graze near the house, telling Brown* that 'she had cry'd all night and never slept a wink . . . if my Lord Cobham cou'd know how Stowe was used how vext he would be'. She went on to moan so much that Grenville's wife Anne wrote to him: '[T]he less we see her and have to do with her the better'.

'Vext' or not, Cobham could not have failed to take pride in what he, his architects and garden designers had achieved during the three decades since he had begun transforming Stowe. The garden now extended over 205 acres. Had Lord Perceval seen it now, he would probably not have recognised the twenty-eight acres he had visited in 1724. The grounds contained over three dozen temples, forty busts, nearly fifty statues, several lakes, many ponds and rivers, and tens of thousands of trees. The ha-ha stretched for almost four miles, making it the longest in England. Having created a princely setting for his house by fashioning one of England's most celebrated gardens, even the king had asked teasingly whether they were 'big enough'. Cobham had fulfilled his dream.

---

*Brown would leave Stowe in November 1750, on amicable terms, to set up his own business, and would go on to become the most fashionable garden designer of his time.

4

All Things Speak a God: Hawkstone Park

'True, all things speak a God; but in the small,
Men trace out him; in great, he seizes Man;
Seizes, and elevates, and raps, and fills.'
                    Edward Young, *Night Thoughts*, 1742–5

'I will not cease from Mental Fight,
Nor shall my sword sleep in my hand
Till we have built Jerusalem
In England's green & pleasant Land.'
                    William Blake, 'Jerusalem', 1804

On 25 July 1774, Dr Samuel Johnson was toiling up a steep and narrow path cut through the red sandstone rocks at Hawkstone Park in Shropshire. For rambling in the countryside he liked to wear a brown jacket and trousers, sturdy boots and a coat with billowing pockets almost large enough to hold the volumes of his famous dictionary. His heavy, square face was framed by an unruly grey wig, and as he went he steadied his large frame on a walking-stick. The poet, playwright, moralist and famous raconteur was more at home in the bustling metropolis than in the countryside. Hawkstone, though, was a detour; he was on his way to Wales, drawn there by a wish to see its rough, barren landscapes.

A century before, such a desire would have been unthinkable; what struck

Hawkstone Park in 1787. At the top of the map is a section of the River Hawk, which William Emes constructed between 1784–6. The L-shaped hill is Terrace Hill with Grotto Hill at the top end. To the left is Red Castle Hill and below it is Elysian Hill. The straight path along Terrace Hill is clearly visible, as are some of the meandering walkways along Grotto Hill.

Johnson as awesome had hitherto been dismissed as 'nothing but hideous, hanging Hills', or what Defoe in his *Tour through the Whole Island of Great Britain* (1724–6) called a 'houling Wilderness'. In the mid-seventeenth century the poet Andrew Marvell had described wild and mountainous landscapes as deformities, 'hook-shoulder'd' and 'ill design'd'; John Evelyn in his diary reported the Alps looking 'as if nature had here swept up the rubbish of the Earth', and in one of his poems the poet John Donne dismissed them as 'warts, and pockholes'. Back then, fearing untamed nature, people had forced their gardens into ordered and manicured landscapes: for example, the geometric flowerbeds in Robert Cecil's sculpted terraces at Hatfield or William and Mary's ornamental parterres at Hampton Court. Dr Johnson's admiration for the rugged scenery of Hawkstone, by contrast, represented the culmination of the slow rapprochement between man and nature over the last fifty years, which had begun with the introduction of seemingly natural forms like meandering rivers or gently rolling pastureland into gardens such as Stowe. Truly wild nature, however, had until recently remained beyond the cultured man's horizon. But now, here at Hawkstone, the rocky outcrops, caverns and windswept boulders were the main attraction.

The roughly hewn steps presented the overweight Johnson with a perilous climb, but when he and his travelling companions arrived at the top of the hill they were rewarded with a view of the stunning rock formations that shaped the garden. Two of these were to the east of a deep glen known as the Grand Valley, while another two enclosed it from the west. The latter were called Elysian Hill and Red Castle Hill, the second boasting a medieval ruin. The two outcrops to the east, Grotto Hill and Terrace Hill, appeared almost like one long continuous ridge bordering the valley, but looking across from Red Castle Hill, one could see a narrow gorge separating them.

Dr Johnson was standing on Terrace Hill, seven hundred feet high and, at three miles, the longest of the four outcrops. Rising abruptly from the valley below and crowned with tall oaks that made it even higher, it dominated the skyline. The shrubs and bushes covering large expanses of the rock gleamed a summer green against the warm hues of the sandstone. To the north, Johnson could see Grotto Hill. Though smaller than the one he was standing on, it was the most prominent natural feature in the park, and its tall firs emphasised its importance in the garden as a whole. Turning to the west, he could see the crumbling ruin on Red Castle Hill and next to it, Elysian Hill, the lowest and least rugged of the four. Together these hills gave Hawkstone its essential character. Between the two ridges, the green lawn of the gently curving Grand Valley accentuated the craggy wilderness that dominated the landscape.

The little group of travellers made their way cautiously towards Grotto Hill. As the teetering paths on the edge of the cliff became ever more treacherous, Dr Johnson felt a 'turbulent pleasure, between fright and admiration'. Once in a while they rested on rough seats positioned at vantage points chiselled out of the rock. Some seemed to have no obvious route of access, but the effort made in order to reach them was handsomely repaid by the view that they afforded over the Shropshire plain towards the Welsh mountains. The final destination was the Grotto, which Johnson and his party now entered through a small opening in the rock. Once their eyes had adjusted to the all-enveloping darkness, they could make out a spacious underground cavern, eighty feet wide, supported by broad pillars giving it the appearance of a petrified forest. As they oriented themselves in the labyrinth of caves, thick, dank air wrapped around them, then dissipated when they opened a small wooden door at the far end, allowing the daylight to burst in. The warmth of the sun invited them to step outside. But now they found themselves on a ledge so high that Johnson's thoughts once again turned to the 'the sublime, the dreadful and the vast'. Below them, the rockface fell several hundred feet, but there at the bottom, only half allaying their fears, was the delicate soft green of the valley. The view was frightening and beautiful in equal measure. But something essential was missing, in Johnson's estimation: 'It wants water,' he decreed; and with this he left the park, setting a challenge that would be taken up ten years later.

Following his father's death in August 1783, nine years after Dr Johnson's visit, the MP Sir Richard Hill inherited Hawkstone and the surrounding estates of over ten thousand acres, making him the largest landowner in the region. He

View from Grotto Hill across the Grand Valley to the ruin on Red Castle Hill

Richard Hill, *c.* 1780

loved Shropshire and its hard-working people, feeling honoured to represent the county in Parliament. Defiantly independent of either political party, he proudly claimed: 'Tories call me Whig, and Whigs a Tory.' During the previous century his family had occupied more and more land, and like many other wealthy estate owners, in order to safeguard his interests, he deemed it best to treat his tenants with a certain paternalism: he was a kind and trustworthy second-generation baronet, rather than a power-grabbing feudal lord. Only two months before his father died, Hill had proudly declared in the House of Commons in June 1783 that 'to feed the hungry and give drink to the thirsty afforded him a singular pleasure'. His friends loved his honesty, humour and goodness, portraying him affectionately as the Sir Roger de Coverley of Shropshire.* Like his fictional counterpart, Hill was an ageing and eccentric bachelor, but he was not a lonely man; on the contrary, he declared himself 'a lover of hospitality' and treasured every minute he spent at Hawkstone in the company of his friends and siblings; his two brothers, both of whom were preachers, and his sister who lived with him at Hawkstone.

*Sir Roger de Coverley was a well-known fictional character. He appeared in a satire written by Richard Steele in the *Spectator* (no. 2, 2 March 1711).

Although he felt more comfortable in the country than in the capital, his parliamentary duties forced him to spend much time in London – over the previous three years he had only occasionally made the thirty-hour coach journey to his father's country seat. Now a large landowner, Richard Hill wielded considerable power in his locality. He was driven by a desire to maintain the old rural order, but the world around him was changing. Britain had just lost the war with America, which entailed the loss not only of thirteen colonies but also of an important source of raw materials such as cotton and a large export market for British goods. This, combined with the costs of war, had brought economic decline. Taxes were high, poverty was rising, and Britain had no ally in Europe. 'Peace at all events, peace upon any terms,' Hill had urged throughout the war. Britain was now a 'tottering nation', he told Parliament, that was not only crippled by debt but 'surrounded by powerful enemies', and for him 'next to peace with heaven, peace with America was to be wished'.

As a country founded on universal male suffrage and liberty, to others America heralded a new era.* Spurred on by her Declaration of Independence of 1776 that claimed all men were equal, people in Britain were becoming increasingly unwilling to accept that the right to vote be limited to those who owned sufficient property, or that to be eligible to stand as an MP a candidate must earn a minimum of £600 a year from his land. At the same time Thomas Paine, one of Britain's most radical thinkers, was calling for elected governments and, in support of the Declaration, America's separation from Britain: his pamphlet 'Common Sense', published that same year, sold 150,000 copies. ''Tis time to part' from the sham of the British constitution, he warned, declaring that 'the monarchy and succession have laid . . . the world in blood and ashes'.

This ferocious political debate was accompanied by considerable social change. Self-made men like Josiah Wedgwood, Matthew Boulton and Richard Arkwright had become affluent from the profits of their factories rather than from inherited wealth. Intellectual enquiry continued to thrive, universities were expanding, and men became rich through their professions. Discoveries and

---

*Even though those of non-European descent were not counted as equal or as eligible to vote.

inventions in geology, electricity and chemistry were transforming British industry. Advances in thermodynamics, for instance, influenced James Watt's invention of the steam engine, while from Joseph Priestley's chemical experiments Wedgwood learned much that was of use in his Staffordshire pottery business. It was an age of industrial progress and radical thought, a world in flux and in which the nobility was beginning to fear for its long-held position in society. Determined to conserve the old order in his own way, Richard Hill defiantly set out to create a garden that would celebrate the values of the old England and his position within it.

The house and grounds that Hill inherited had not changed since Dr Johnson had visited them.[*] Originally built in the late 1690s, the mansion had been altered in the early and mid-eighteenth century when his father Rowland had added an attic storey and the wings. Built in red brick with stone surrounds, the house now also featured classical columns and an Italianate triangular pediment above the main entrance. In the 360-acre park, Rowland Hill had opened up the caves and created a system of paths linking the Grotto with Terrace Hill. Having also purchased the ruin on Red Castle Hill, he had laid the foundation of the garden that his son would convert 'into a sort of paradise', as one friend observed.

In autumn 1783, with typical vigour, the stout, broad-backed Hill set himself immediately to the task of turning his garden into the visual expression of his beliefs. One of his intentions was to include in the design the symbols of an age when the social order was stable and one's position in it fixed. At Hawkstone, the oldest monument to this era was the remains of the thirteenth-century castle at the top of Red Castle Hill, two hundred feet above the Grand Valley. The lower walls were formed out of the rockface, and the battlements were partly obscured by ancient trees growing out of the rocks. Only one of the towers remained, its crumbling walls largely covered by the plants and moss that had made a home there. The grandeur of the ancient edifice testified to a chivalrous and ordered past, rather than to change and revolution. To open up

---

*Unless otherwise referenced, all descriptions of Hawkstone, its follies and people's responses to the landscape are based on the *Hawkstone Survey* of 1787, contemporary guidebooks and numerous visitor accounts.

more vistas, Hill ordered his workmen to cut back some of the gnarled old trees, and to cut peep-holes into the thick tower walls so that visitors could peer through like medieval sentries.

In looking to England's past for a model of national character and social ideals, Hill was in tune with contemporary fashions. By the 1780s many people of all political persuasions shared the view that the medieval age had been one of stability and power and that its decaying castles and cathedrals, as symbols

Red Castle, 1787

of national pride, were to be cherished. However, this heritage was used for a wide variety of purposes and personal agendas: to Lord Cobham of Stowe, it had represented the origins of liberty under King Alfred, while conservatives like Hill used it to legitimise their demands for a fixed social order of a particular kind. The soaring pitched roofs and pointed windows of the Gothic Revival could be put to almost any political purpose, which was one of the reasons for its resurgence.

Seventy years earlier, the Gothic style with its towering proportions had been reviled as the ill-formed product of an uncivilised society – Christopher Wren had called the Goths 'destroyers rather than builders'. But now it had become the visual vocabulary for English nationalism. The first great 'Gothic' castle had been built by the Duke of Argyll in 1745 to assert his power after the decisive defeat of the Jacobite rebellion. Since then, both Tories and Whigs had competed to reclaim the age for themselves. The Tory Sir Roger Newdigate had decorated the interior of his home Arbury Hall in Warwickshire with Gothic tracery, while in 1757 the Whig nephew of Lord Cobham, Sir George Lyttelton, commemorated his love for the medieval by building a ruined castle at his estate at Hagley in Worcestershire. At the same time the Gothic style captured the imagination of the fashionable elite with its decorative luxuriance: some neo-Gothic buildings were mere fashionable ornaments, such as the Ruined Abbey and Gothic Temple at Painshill in Surrey. The chivalrous connotations of the style added to its popularity and when the 'improvements' to the Red Castle were being carried out, there must have been much excitement at Hawkstone as one of the workmen, having cut through the undergrowth, brought his pickaxe down on a mouldering coffin inside which lay a skeleton with an old iron weapon in its hand.

But above all, it was Methodism that dominated Richard Hill's life, and this too he wanted to express in his garden. For decades he had been airing his religious belief in sermons to colliers, writing passionate pamphlets and, to some of his fellow MPs' amusement, spreading the word via his parliamentary speeches which were peppered with quotes from what he referred to as 'that excellent old book called the Bible'. His obsession with religion, though, they believed, 'weakened his character', as the abolitionist William Wilberforce put it some years later, and earned him the nickname 'scriptural Killigrew'.* Since his early twenties Hill had been a member of the Methodist movement. Founded in the 1730s, it had grown rapidly over the previous five decades on the strength of its attacks on the increasingly materialistic Anglican Church. Clergymen were criticised for pursuing natural history, philosophy and poetry instead of their pastoral and other religious duties. Worse still, some frequented taverns, smoked and drank, while others used church funds to live the life of country squires. Hill claimed that the Church of England 'fleece their flocks, & cloth themselves with the wool'. Rather than taxing servants, government should concentrate on these 'idle, non-resident clergy', he thundered during one of his parliamentary tirades in 1782.

*A Killigrew is a crow-like bird.

As well as focusing on the religious and moral laxity of the established Church as they perceived it, Methodists emphasised private revelation. John Wesley, the founder of the movement, decreed it 'a religion of the heart'. For this Methodists attracted a fair amount of ridicule – the philosopher David Hume, for example, regarded all religious enthusiasts, as 'fanatic' madmen. What Methodists wanted to do was to bring man closer to God by stripping away superfluous ritual, while at the same time injecting joy and emotion back into faith. Hill rejected the 'cold manner' of the Church of England liturgy, preferring instead the style of the Methodist lay preachers who addressed large open-air gatherings with a memorable fervour.

At Hawkstone, the overarching theme was the celebration of God as the divine architect of nature. Hill wanted to create a garden of epiphany, inspired by feelings rather than reason, a landscape that would display God's majesty in the natural grandeur of Hawkstone's rugged hills. He would build follies, but of a kind that would symbolise his faith; combined with the landscape this would touch his visitors' emotions, enabling them to feel God's presence. Like John Milton's Eden in *Paradise Lost*, Hawkstone would have 'all trees of noblest kind', 'some irriguous valley', lawns, a lake and 'umbrageous grots and caves'. A cleverly laid out route through this earthly paradise would lead the visitor to the 'rocks, and hills, and fertile vales' that would 'proclaim the hand divine', Hill trumpeted.*

Like many other 'gentlemen improvers' of the time, Hill probably designed the layouts for the new paths and planting schemes himself, then left the execution of his plans in the able hands of his steward, workmen and gardeners – all trusted local men.† Described by his friends as modest, he was perhaps also too frugal to splash out on an expensive landscape designer when, assisted by contemporary garden literature, he could do it himself. He was

*Hill's inscription at the Retreat at Hawkstone Park.
†There is no evidence that Richard Hill employed any professional landscape designers other than William Emes for the lake, since there are no account books or letters regarding the designing of the garden at this period (except one letter from Emes regarding the alterations to the lake). According to the *Hawkstone Survey* (1787), the improvements were 'to infinite credit to the Taste of the Proprietor [Hill]'. The chronology of the making of Hawkstone is based on contemporary guidebooks, visitor accounts, newspaper articles and the *Hawkstone Survey*.

probably familiar with William Mason's four-volume poem *The English Garden*, published between 1772 and 1781, a popular publication that did the rounds of country-house drawing-rooms, instructing its readers on ways of creating gardens in the new style.

The new pathways at Hawkstone would form a prescribed tour: the plans read much like the meandering routes that Mason advocated in *The English Garden*, with carefully positioned vantage points – each should 'present/A different picture, new, and yet the same'. The aim was to 'hide/The view entire', to reveal the garden only slowly, as the visitor wandered along. At Hawkstone, Richard Hill took Mason's game of hide-and-seek to a masterly level, making the landmarks such as the ruin on Grotto Hill visible from multiple viewpoints so that they assumed 'a variety of shapes according to the different situations'. Planting trees and shrubs just as Mason had instructed, Hill contrasted decid-uous hardwoods such as oaks, elms and beeches with evergreens such as larches and firs. Trees in all their variety had always played an important role in the English imagination, and had lent their special presence to English poetry and prose as well as to gardens. Anglo-Saxon runes testify to this, as do the works of Chaucer, Spenser and Shakespeare. In the *hortus conclusus* – the enclosed medieval sanctuaries of monks and the nobility – trees had symbolised the 'tree of life', and later they lined the straight avenues of many celebrated baroque gardens; at Hawkstone, though, they grew 'irregularly . . . exhibiting much wildness'. Hill used trees to frame the different prospects, as well as momen-tarily to obscure other parts of the garden so as to achieve a sense of surprise: 'Admit it partially, and half exclude/And half reveal its graces', Mason had advised.

Winding along the thickly wooded ridge of Terrace Hill, paths would suddenly open out on to glades revealing this view or that, before plunging back into the half-light of the woods where alongside the old spreading pines and oaks Hill had planted young ones. The visitors were led through the park and over the hills on a seemingly circular route. Only a map, which Hill did not supply, would have revealed that the path looped back on itself and retracked sideways, creating a ten-mile circuit out of one that would have been only half the length if straight. The deliberately deceptive experience led visitors to believe that Hawkstone was much larger, and more mysterious, than it actually was.

These 'improvements', however, could not conceal Hawkstone's great flaw: the lack of water. Lofty heights and green valleys, rugged rocks and winding caves Hawkstone had in abundance, but there were no rushing waterfalls or silvery lakes reflecting the sky. Garden writers of the time, such as Thomas Whately in his *Observations on Modern Gardening* (1770) and William Mason, were united in their opinion that water constituted a key element in the new landscape. A visitor to Hawkstone had already in 1748 exclaimed: 'The principal defect is in water.' Hill's father had tried to build a small lake in the Grand Valley, but it had been dismissed by Mrs Thrale, the writer and friend of Dr Johnson, as a 'mean canal which were better away'. So dismal must it have been that Johnson had not even bothered to mention it.

Hill was persuaded: he knew from contemporary books that a gardener should 'show the advantages of a place' and 'correct its faults'; he also knew that his hymn to nature and God would not be complete without the presence of water. The creation of a lake, though, required professional engineering skills, and had Lancelot ('Capability') Brown not died the year before he would have been the obvious choice, famed as he was for his many lakes such as those at Blenheim, Luton Hoo and Petworth. In early 1784 the search for such an expert came to an end, when William Emes, who worked in the style of Brown, introduced himself to Hill. For the last twenty years Emes had been 'improving' estates, mainly in the Midlands and on the Welsh borders, and had earned the reputation as a lake specialist. He had also extended the lake at Holkham Hall in Norfolk by giving it a sinuous shape, and had widened and softened the contours of James Brindley's famous canal at the point where it passed through the Tixall estate in Staffordshire. While Emes's skills were exceptional, the geology of Hawkstone was particularly challenging, as there was no substantial natural water source. A torrential waterfall that gushed down the rocks such as the famous cascade at Hafod in Wales, or a rapid river like the one cutting through the three-hundred-foot limestone cliffs at Piercefield in Monmouthshire, was out of the question.

There was just a small brook to the north of the house, but Emes thought he would be able to dam it so as to produce a long serpentine stretch of water encompassing the northern boundary of the estate.* More than a mile in length and a hundred yards wide, the lake was intended to look like a river, to be seen from the house and all four hills. At the same time it would provide a new viewing-point from which to admire the garden. Furthermore, the excavation of the lake would give employment to the poor of the neighbourhood, which for Hill was a good enough justification for this purely ornamental extravagance. '[T]here can be no happiness in riches,' he always insisted. The provision of work, he told his friends, was the 'first gratification in the great expense'.

Emes left precise instructions and drawings for Hill's workmen, enabling them to start on the huge task while the designer himself was visiting his other clients. To gouge the required hole, twenty feet deep, into the gentle slopes of the garden, Hill employed more than one hundred men over the next three years. Along one of the mile-long sides they built an embankment and along the other, a dam. Every day, except on 'holy' Sundays, Hill's men worked away with pickaxes and shovels to remove the earth and the tons of rocks, carting it all away in a conveyor-belt of buckets and wheelbarrows. After months of heavy labour, their excavations had produced a gaping wound that, without water to fill it, scarred the landscape. Moving on to the next stage, the workmen prepared to make the riverbed waterproof by kneading a mixture of sand and clay into a water-resistant paste. Thick layers of this paste, some more than a foot thick, were applied to the lake's floor – probably with wooden rammers of the kind that were also used in streets for hammering in paving-stones, a technique that James Brindley had invented for his canals.

Emes's long, winding lake was designed to be 'picturesque', an effect that had recently become so desirable that it had infiltrated every aspect of middle- and upper-class life – from gardening to literature, from architecture to interior design. A picturesque landscape combined ruggedness of texture with variety and irregularity; it had been popularised by William Gilpin, vicar, indefatigable traveller and amateur artist, who had spent decades travelling the length and breadth of Britain. During his innumerable tours, he had written

*Emes also designed another lake, of six acres, to the south of the Elysian Hill called the Menagerie Pool. The larger lake would eventually be forty-four acres (*Hawkstone Survey*, 1787).

notebooks that were part travel guide, part instruction manual on how properly to view the countryside. Assisted by drawings, the reader was encouraged to observe the particular landscape from *his* recommended angles and 'stations'. In 1782, a year before improvements started at Hawkstone, Gilpin began to publish his notebooks. Though he never wrote an account of Hawkstone (nor of the rest of the county of Shropshire), he is likely to have visited Hill's garden when he gave two sermons in Shrewsbury at the Humane Society in 1791. By this time, William Emes's lake was finished, bringing Hawkstone in line with Gilpin's ideal romantic landscape: a swathe of land consisting of 'mountains – lakes – broken grounds – wood – rocks – cascades – vallies – and rivers', as well as the obligatory ruin. In fact, Gilpin considered a ruin 'a sacred thing' that complemented the irregularity of the scene and finished it off perfectly.

There was dissent, though, among contemporary writers as to the exact definition of 'the picturesque'. Gilpin, for instance, who was never strong on theory, merely described it as a quality 'capable of being illustrated by painting'. It was not until 1794 when Uvedale Price, a gentleman improver

William Gilpin's 'Composition of Ruins', 1809

himself, published his *Essay on the Picturesque* that a lasting definition would be proposed: the picturesque should be regarded as the category between the beautiful and the sublime. Hawkstone was all three of these: the smooth lawns gave it beauty; the lake and the ruin made it picturesque; and the craggy hills singled it out as one of the very few sublime gardens in the country. Although the search for sublimity in nature was one of the most popular pastimes, virtually no one had attempted to create it in a garden. Where Gilpin's preference for trees, thickets and scattered rocks could be incorporated into the scenery relatively easily, sublime grandeur was restricted to landscapes where nature had provided a hilly terrain, which few gardens offered. A picturesque scene might be variegated and wild, but a sublime one was vast and awesome.

The most influential aesthetic treatise of the time popularising the notion of the sublime was *A Philosophical Enquiry into the Origin of our Ideas of the Sublime and Beautiful*, which had been published in 1757 by one of Richard Hill's House of Commons colleagues, the political philosopher Edmund Burke. Three decades later when Hill was working on Hawkstone, it still dominated the way people thought about nature. Burke had defined the beautiful and the sublime in relation to each other. Beauty was small, smooth, light, delicate and evoked pleasure, whereas the sublime was rugged, vast, dark and gloomy, thereby stimulating thoughts of pain, even terror. The ideal way to experience the two, according to Burke, was in the swift transition of one to the other, which heightened the contrast and increased the effect of each, thus setting astonishment at the pinnacle of feeling. For Burke, astonishment was the most important response to nature, and Hill excelled in producing this reaction to his garden.

The circuit at Hawkstone highlighted Burke's contrast between the sublime and the beautiful. Here, Hill led gently winding paths to the brink of crevasses, juxtaposing the carefree stroll with the danger of the jagged precipice below. The effect was strongest at Grotto Hill, where visitors suddenly emerged from the dark eerie caves on to a rock ledge bathed in sunlight. It was only when their eyes had adjusted that they realised they were standing over a seven-hundred-foot drop, filling their minds with what Burke called 'a sort of delightful horror'. This hyperbole of risk was an essential part of the experience of the sublime. Many a wild landscape, untouched by the hand of man, was capable of producing these 'raw' feelings, but very few gardens could evoke them. In this, Hawkstone was unique.

Burke and Gilpin's work provided the tools with which to evaluate, understand and appreciate nature. However, many of the visitors who now arrived at Hawkstone differed markedly from those who had seen Lord Cobham's gardens at Stowe in the mid-eighteenth century, in that they were of the moneyed middle classes such as manufacturers, tradesmen, bankers and engineers. Touring the great houses and gardens of England had become such a popular leisure activity for those with enough time and money to engage in it that in the 1780s a new word had been coined to describe them: tourists.

This eager generation of landscape tourists wanted to develop and demonstrate their good taste through their choice of places to visit and their appropriate appreciation of the features and views they encountered there: the ability to judge nature, art and architecture was a prerequisite for getting to the top. In seeking to learn this skill they were challenging the long-held view that taste was the purview of the aristocracy, famously advocated by thinkers such as Joseph Addison and the 3rd Earl of Shaftesbury, who had insisted that although taste could be cultivated, it could not be acquired. It was when, in 1757, David Hume wrote in *Of the Standard of Taste* that the judgement and appreciation of these aesthetic 'pleasures' could in fact be 'improved by practice' that the rising middle classes were encouraged to acquire what for centuries had been regarded as exclusive to those of noble birth and wealth. This process was accelerated by the increasing accessibility of culture. On his death, Hans Sloane's enormous collection of fossils, plants, shells, medals and sculpture formed the nucleus of the British Museum which was founded in 1753, and since 1768 the leading painters of the age had exhibited their works at the Royal Academy. Equally, books were more affordable and cheap prints were produced in ever larger runs to meet the growing demand. And so people were keen to read Burke's widely available *Enquiry* and Gilpin's practical instructions, with a view to clarifying for themselves the underlying principles of taste and of the judgement of nature.

As Hawkstone attracted more visitors, Hill commissioned a booklet telling them how to interpret his garden.[*] Having spent many long hours writing proselytising pamphlets with titles such as *A Present to Your Poor Neighbour* and *The Deep Things of God*, Hill welcomed the opportunity to instruct the tourists at Hawkstone. Sold for one shilling, less than the cost of a meal in a London tavern, the guidebook advised them to focus on the 'romantic scenes' that 'would justly come under the denomination of the Sublime'. Like Burke and Gilpin's work, the booklet served an urban audience that longed for 'untamed' nature. During the eighteenth century an increasing proportion of the population had become alienated from the land, and, in reaction, the middle classes now wanted, as never before, to experience nature. Urbanisation had proceeded at an unprecedented pace, and new agricultural techniques had reduced the numbers of farm workers needed. Furthermore, enclosures had transformed the landscape: anything inconvenient to the farmer – boulders, hillocks, trees – disappeared, and the sweeping views across the countryside were now measured by the straight lines of the fences, hedgerows and walls that divided the land into rectangular fields. By the last quarter of the century 70 per cent of the land had been enclosed.[†] And so people became increasingly removed from the daily business of experiencing and cultivating the land. In addition, the permanent stench of sulphur in the iron-producing towns, other pollutants such as the black dust produced by coal-mining and the smell of disease-ridden sewage, were pushing the population towards rediscovering the lost landscape. One result of this was to generate an outpouring of sentimentality, which was catered for by the picturesque and the sublime. By the 1780s, tourists were flocking to the remoter regions of Scotland, England and Wales to experience an environment from which their daily lives had separated them. But how much did the city dweller really want to encounter nature in all its wildness? Hill's garden

[*]Until then only a few famous gardens had become the subject of individual guidebooks, such as Stowe, Blenheim and Wilton. Although the guidebook was not written by Richard Hill, he must have been involved in its production.

[†]During the first half of the eighteenth century 74,000 acres were enclosed; by the end of the second half the figure had risen to 750,000; and by 1810, to over 2 million (Bermingham, 1987, pp. 9–11).

might have looked rough and rugged, but much of it was manmade and carefully orchestrated, staged like a sequence of set designs.

One morning in early spring 1785, however, Hill's carefully crafted view of the ruin on Red Castle Hill was compromised by a 'miserable hut' that a local man had erected during the night. Like the ruin, the hut could be seen from all the park's viewing-points. Philanthropist though he may have been, this was too much for the connoisseurial eye of Richard Hill to contemplate. Had not Gilpin declared, 'The cottage offends. It should be a castle, a bridge, an aqueduct'? Hill liked to think he looked after the well-being of his tenants, and he wanted the local people to enjoy his garden – but not to make their home in it. So he sent a servant to ask the intruder to leave. He refused. Hill then offered him money, in the hope of an amicable solution. But to his great annoyance the man stubbornly rejected his offer, referring to ancient land rights which, he believed, allowed him to set up his hut below the castle. The 'benevolent' Hill was outraged: his father had bought the land forty years earlier, making him the rightful owner. So he sued the man, and on 1 April the predictable verdict was announced in court: the hut had to go. Hill could once again concentrate on improving his garden.

During the previous two years Hill had employed 'a vast number of men' to help construct the lake, thereby providing the 'industrious poor in the neighbourhood' with a means of subsistence. They had excavated and waterproofed the site, and in spring 1786 they finished constructing the high dams. Emes's lake – which everyone now referred to as the 'river' – was complete. Hill ordered his workmen to fill it with water and put the dams to the test. He must have been anxious that the water might just trickle away, as it had when his father had tried something similar – but as the water level rose it became clear that Emes's calculations had been accurate. The dams held and the clay was watertight.

At last Hawkstone had water, but Hill was disappointed with the shape of the lake: it ran in one large curve, looking artificial and lacking the ruggedness and broken outline that Gilpin and Mason had recommended; it certainly did not look like a natural river. Emes was told to go back to the drawing-board. A few weeks later, in May, he sent Hill an estimate for 'lengthening both ends of the River Hawk'. The extra seven hundred yards would cost Hill £362, small change for a man whose annual income was £15,000. The extensions would add another gentle curve to the east and a sickle-shaped bow to the west, each designed to disappear into a little sunken thicket. This trick of perspective would create the impression that the river led into a natural valley, thereby suggesting a more realistic setting – a method Brown had devised and that Emes had often copied. By June a third edition of the guidebook had been published, proudly announcing that half of the river was now filled with water and – as Hill had accepted Emes's suggestions – that it would eventually stretch for two miles.

Another new project was the landscaping of Tower Glen, an area at the south-west end of Terrace Hill, dominated by a tower erected by Hill's father. Hill had opened up a cave in the bay below the tower, to which a narrow path led. The view from the top of the path took in Red Castle, Grotto Hill and the Grand Valley, but as visitors descended the narrow steps towards the cave their field of vision became increasingly restricted. Simultaneously, their attention was drawn to the ruin on Red Castle Hill and to a deep inlet – Tower Glen – at the bottom of Terrace Hill. Filled with trees and shrubs that swayed wildly on windy days, it gave the impression of waves surging back and forth

Tower Glen and the Urn in front of the cave entrance, 1787

on a rough sea. The crude path followed the bowed line of the 'steep dingle', which eventually led to an urn and the entrance to the cave, which was seven feet wide.

When the visitors reached the cave, they were able to read an inscription on the base of the urn telling the story of Hill's long lineage and of his connections with royalty, as well as accounts of grisly battles. The climax of the narrative concerned his Royalist ancestor Rowland Hill. Having abandoned his house during the Civil War for fear of being beheaded by Roundheads, he took refuge in a cave – by implication the very cave in front of which they were now standing. Despite Rowland's best efforts, he had been found and imprisoned with his son in his very own Red Castle; then both were executed. The compelling tale fitted the prevailing mood. It was, however, untrue. The preening Richard Hill had taken the life of his ancestor, which in reality featured neither cave nor castle, and embroidered it so as to make a better story as well as cast himself as the descendant of a grander and braver man.

In summer 1787, Hill's men filled the redesigned lake with water. Its completion was announced in the fourth edition of the guidebook, which was now sold in London and other major British cities. Hawkstone had become a key destination for those in search of the sublime and picturesque, an essential stop on the polite tourist's itinerary, and easily accessible thanks to improved transport and the extended turnpike system. Financed by tolls, local trustees built, maintained and improved the roads, as well as setting up milestones and signposts. And for the first time coach operators published reasonably exact timetables. The coach from London to Shrewsbury cost £1 16s, took thirty hours and ran three times a week. Because Hawkstone was so close to Shrewsbury it became the gateway to the wild landscapes of north Wales.

As the numbers of visitors increased, demand grew for accommodation. So on 9 July 1787, the Hawkstone Inn opened with a celebratory inaugural dinner, under the management of Richard Hill's trusted butler George Naylor.[*]

---

[*]Naylor paid £30 annual rent to Hill (*Hawkstone Survey*, 1787).

The entrance to Hawkstone Park at the inn

Perfectly located, close to the crescent-shaped western end of the new river and not far from the village of Weston, the simple inn was transformed by Naylor during the next year into one of the most admired hotels in the country. Many thought of it as a 'gentleman's seat': its rooms were elegantly furnished, and its grounds included a bowling green that was always alive with 'gay parties'. Some enjoyed themselves so much that during the summer they stayed for weeks on end. On 19 April 1788 Naylor proudly announced in the *Shrewsbury Chronicle* that the inn was now 'fitted up . . . in a genteel manner', and boasted about the good food, brandy and assortment of wines on offer. As the journey time from London to Shrewsbury had just been cut to twenty hours (for an increased fare of £2 5s), the reopening of the inn could not have been better timed.

The visitors streamed in. One of the most attractive features was dinner on the river on the inn's yacht. Such was the demand that Naylor set up a booking system, with price reductions for group bookings: the fee for dining on the boat was reduced from one shilling per person for small parties to sixpence each if the group was larger than ten. By the end of July that year, however, Hill realised that the increasing number of tourists brought unforeseen problems. People were wandering at will through the gardens, disturbing his private guests and his workmen alike. With the arrival of the crowds, the solitary experience of nature and God had become a rare commodity. On 2 August 1788, Hill responded: he gave notice in the *Shrewsbury Chronicle* that not 'all persons indiscriminately have the liberty to ramble about in the pleasure grounds'. He continued: '[N]obody whatever will henceforth be permitted to see the Park at any time without a ticket', which could be acquired at the inn. Only 'proper persons' could enter the park after writing their names on the tickets, which they had to show to the gardener upon entry to the grounds. Intruders would be 'proceeded against and punished as Trespassers'. To cope with the influx Hill also pioneered a visitor-managing system: guides could be hired, dressed as hermits and druids, to conduct people through the park.* This was in contrast to other houses and gardens, where housekeepers or maids showed tourists around. England had its first themed adventure park.

Hill was anxious to control the threat of disorder in his garden, but he did not want to close his gates as others had done. At Wooburn Farm, for example, the Catholic proprietor had felt forced to close his famous *ferme ornée* because – as Horace Walpole reported – 'the savages, who came as connoisseurs, scribbled a thousand brutalities, in the building, upon his religion'. Other owners had been left with damaged furniture. The 1st Duke of Chandos discovered on one occasion that a tourist had broken a precious table in two by 'jumping up backwards to sit upon it'. As a consequence the Duke of Devonshire at Chiswick House and Walpole at Strawberry Hill allowed in only visitors who had obtained a ticket and agreed to abide by a catalogue of rules.† His ticketing system, Hill must have hoped, would provide a level of control over possible damage. People from the neighbourhood were invited to visit on Saturdays and Mondays, while tourists from further afield were allowed in every day except Sunday, because, Hill announced, 'six days are enough for pleasure'. He wanted to put an end to 'that flagrant violation

---

*Exact visitor numbers for Hawkstone do not exist, but one of the most popular houses, Wilton House in Wiltshire (the seat of the Earl of Pembroke), received 2324 in 1776, while 250–300 people a year visited Horace Walpole's Strawberry Hill in Twickenham, near London, in the mid-eighteenth century.

†The 5th Duke of Devonshire had his ticketing system in place in 1781 and was probably the first to do so, but Horace Walpole followed swiftly in 1784.

of the Sabbath' and hoped to 'keep a few ramblers at home and send them to church'.

For the remaining six days of the week he continued to provide entertainment, of which dining on the yacht remained a favourite. A week after the introduction of the new ticket system, Naylor announced in the *Shrewsbury Chronicle* that the yacht now had to be booked several days in advance. This too had been 'improved' with the addition of cannons, whose firing provoked the kind of excitement produced by thunderstorms.* These theatricals were inspired by Edmund Burke, who had declared that the noise of 'raging storms' and 'thunder' created an 'awful sensation in the mind'. The sound of the cannon salvo ricocheted around the Grand Valley, bouncing off the sheer sandstone walls and reverberating in the glades. Eventually the echo, now a sepulchral whisper, returned to the river. Tourists revelling in the sublime effect of the cannons described it as 'that confusion and horrid uproar, which the falling of these stupendous rocks would occasion'.

With the main attractions in place, Hill proudly presented his pleasure grounds to his private guests. Though he was a man of strong personal convictions, his friends were drawn from both political parties; and although a Methodist, he saw no problem in giving a party for senior Anglicans including the Archbishop of Canterbury. What all these people shared, though, was his distrust of revolutionary ideas; they favoured gentler reforms, which would, as Hill explained, 'take the wind out of radicals' sails'.

Among his friends was William Wilberforce, whom Hill was expecting at Hawkstone on 29 August 1789. Though thirty years his junior, Wilberforce enjoyed Hill's wit and humour, referring to his dry jokes as 'Hillisms'. Both men were Evangelists, dedicated to the religious revival and to charitable groups such as the Proclamation Society and the Society for the Relief of the Poor. But above all, what brought the two men together was their disgust for the slave trade. Never achieving the same public profile as Wilberforce, who led the abolition movement, Hill nevertheless fought doggedly for what he believed. Considering the 'horrid traffic in human bodies' unchristian, they were shocked

---

*Visitors had to pay extra for the gunpowder and explosions (*Shrewsbury Chronicle*, 9 August 1788).

by the tens of thousands of slaves who were, as Hill put it, 'plunged into an abyss of wretchedness'. Hill wrote pro-abolition articles in the *Shrewsbury Chronicle* and gave 'his most hearty assent' to Wilberforce's struggles in Parliament because he was sure that God would judge him by his good works – the reason that made him also feed his labourers in hard times, donate money to the infirmary at Shrewsbury and give food to the local prison.* By letting his tenants use the commons on his various estates rather than enclosing them he also lost out on almost £500 annual rent, but, as he wrote in one of his pamphlets, he was sure that 'my death-bed will not shake under me.'

When Wilberforce arrived at Hawkstone, he had just completed a tour of the Wye Valley and was on his way to the new spa in Buxton, Derbyshire, because his doctor had recommended he take the waters. '[M]ost unwilling to plunge into a hurry of a very crowded watering place', though, he was content for a while to savour the solitude of the Hawkstone hills. His host invited Wilberforce to accompany him on a tour of the park – probably in his open carriage. Usually on these occasions Hill was immaculately dressed, his short wig covered by a spotless white hat. He often got his domestic servants, whom he also employed for their musical abilities, to serenade his guests as they floated down Emes's lake in a boat. Then he would usually take them on a 'walk and ramble among the rocks'. Wilberforce was so impressed by Hawkstone's scenery that he vowed to 'retire up into the mountains and come down only on errands of usefulness and love'.

The day after Wilberforce's arrival Hill took his guest to Gredington, some eight miles from Hawkstone, to dine with the owner, Lord Kenyon, the Lord Chief Justice. Talk of penal reform would almost certainly have figured, since the men had been debating the topic throughout the summer, and the discussion was most likely heated, given that Lord Thurlow, the Lord Chancellor, who detested the kind of reforms Wilberforce and Hill advocated, was also present.

The other topic of the day was the French Revolution. Six weeks earlier on 14 July, the symbol of royal authority, the Bastille, had been stormed by the

*The *Shrewsbury Chronicle* is full of accounts of his benevolence in the neighbourhood.

French people. It marked the end of absolute monarchy in France. Many applauded the Declaration of the Rights of Man and Citizen proclaiming freedom of conscience, of property and of the press as 'the most stupendous edifice of liberty'. Josiah Wedgwood, for one, called it the 'wonderful revolution', while Wordsworth saw it as 'human nature seeming born again'; even the prime minister, William Pitt, declared 'free' France a great country. But not everyone agreed: Hill feared that revolution would spread to England, and in 1790 Edmund Burke published his *Reflections on the Revolution in France*, comparing Paris and its revolutionaries to a 'world of monsters'.

Within two years the growing violence in France polarised political opinion in Britain even further. In September 1792 Paris was awash with blood. Fourteen hundred aristocrats had been murdered, their skewered heads lining the roads. The revolution did indeed cast a long shadow over British politics. The brutalities in France, committed in the name of liberty, pressed into opposition those who had formerly supported limited reform. Hill, like many other MPs, was shocked by what he called the 'barbarities' being committed across the Channel, and was fearful that any parliamentary reform in Britain might lead to similar civil unrest. Two months later, his fears were confirmed when the revolutionary government in Paris urged all the nations of Europe to revolt in the name of liberty, promising assistance to anyone who took up the challenge. When in January 1793 the French executed Louis XVI, the British were stunned; Pitt called it 'the foulest and most atrocious act the world has ever seen'; Hill's only consolation, he declared in a speech to Parliament, was that 'the nation [France] . . . which has cast off all dependence on God' would feel the divine vengeance soon. But buoyed up with confidence, on 1 February France declared war on Britain.

With the outbreak of war, travelling to the continent became hazardous, and once again England was isolated from the rest of Europe. Would-be tourists had little option but to tour their own country. Turning inwards at a time of war became for some an act of patriotism, as they set out to discover the nation in nature. Earlier in the century, notions of patriotism had permeated gentle landscapes such as those at Stowe, but the classical temples that adorned the gardens were distinctly foreign. In the wake of the European turmoil, thousands of British tourists now turned away from these Arcadian landscapes and instead sought the true spirit of a strong, proud Britain in the remote and weathered Highlands, the Wye Valley and the Lake District.

The numbers visiting Hawkstone also continued to rise. Many saw it as part of their patriotic journey, others came in search of spirituality, while some sought excitement. But whatever their motive, everyone was impressed by Hawkstone's grandeur. One such visitor was Joseph Salmon, whose aim was to view the scenery with a 'religious eye'. When he arrived on 21 May 1794, the sun was rising above the four hills and a clear blue sky embraced the horizon. Stepping under an arch made of two large whalebones, he began his trek near the Hawkstone Inn, then took a shady path through a little wood that concealed the jagged hills beyond. At the end of the path he found himself at the River Hawk.* In front of him, near the embankment, stood a Dutch-style cottage that Hill had named Neptune's Whim. Behind it was a colossal stone fountain with a statue of the god of the seas, intended to put visitors in mind of Neptune's violent temper and thus remind them of the storms and earthquakes that had formed the wild landscape all around them. Nearby, contrasting with the jagged skyline, Hill had planted a small flower garden dedicated to Neptune's wife Amphitrite. On the other side of the river stood a windmill painted in soft colours, completing the scene and recalling the dramatic landscapes of the Dutch painter Jacob van Ruisdael. Salmon then came upon a secluded mossy alcove shaped by the gnarled roots of trees; known as the Retreat, it was dedicated to sacred contemplation and the eradication of evil and indulgence. Here, Hill had inscribed verses – 'Tell me, dear Stranger, tell me the true, / what sorrow swells thy breast?' – believing that 'contemplation's soothing balm' would give the 'soul relief'. This was certainly Salmon's experience – he wrote later:

> 'Since GOD is Love, Oh! That He may
> All HAWKSTONE Guests inspire;
> And make their Hearts from Day to Day,
> Burn with this *sacred* FIRE.'

*This path connected the Hawkstone Inn to the river and was a recent addition (after 1787) to the park.

Like Hill, Salmon thought that nature was God's silent language – so clear and universal that anyone, regardless of class or education, would understand it. For Salmon, Hawkstone embodied 'god's spiritual kingdom', and as he crossed the valley towards the dark expanse of Grotto Hill he felt 'rapture and devotion'. Hoping to heighten the dramatic effect of the rock formation, Hill had created below it a meadow where lambs played and grazed at the riverbank amidst the golden lustre of wild flowers. Salmon was touched by God's presence, and resolved to immerse himself in solitude as he ascended Grotto Hill.

As well as turning Hawkstone into a visual expression of his beliefs, Hill carried out his Christian duties on a more practical level. Together with his brother he had set up a School of Industry, a popular institution which ensured that the children of the local poor acquired useful skills, learning, as Hill liked to point out, 'to be good and useful servants'. Every July he organised a prize-giving, thus rewarding dutiful pupils while parading his charity. Schooling, of course, also taught children their place: 'Break their wills betimes. Begin this work, before they can run alone,' John Wesley had advised, and so Hill and his siblings, whom Wilberforce described as a 'family of love and peace', continued to produce faithful servants and promote the 'bettering' of society.

When the heavy rains set in during the winter of 1794 and the ensuing floods devastated Shropshire, Hill handed out food to the neighbourhood poor. Although he helped to alleviate the worst of the shortages, the rain left spirits dampened. The severity of the weather, combined with the financial strains of Britain's involvement in the French Revolutionary Wars, plunged the country into depression. As corn prices rocketed, Hill subsidised his tenants' supplies. When the winter turned into one of the coldest of the century – so severe that chamber pots froze under people's beds – Hill instructed his steward to distribute money, beef, bread, hot broth and clothing to the villagers. He also ensured that none of his labourers were dismissed on grounds of age, ill-health or lack of work.

In March, as the poor became hungrier and more desperate, food riots broke out in Cornwall, Sussex and the Midlands; in Portsmouth, Chichester and

Plymouth the situation escalated when the militia, called in to suppress the uprising, joined it. Although the crowds were driven by rising food prices rather than by political motives, the violent mass demonstrations raked up fears of an impending revolution. The French 'Reign of Terror' alarmed Britain's establishment. Despite this, her role in the coalition against France was widely criticised. In a speech to Parliament in December 1794 Hill blamed the riots in Britain on the ongoing war, pointing out that although the French threat would have been difficult to ignore, the consequence of war was certain starvation among the British population, which in turn might lead to revolution. The war, however, continued, despite the mounting protestations, and when the price of wheat doubled between April and July the food riots intensified throughout the country.

When Parliament adjourned for the summer break, Hill returned to Hawkstone in the hope of boosting morale. On a sunny day in early August, long tables were set up in the stable yard for a feast to which almost four hundred of his labourers and their families were invited. The *Shrewsbury Chronicle* of the 7th picked up the story, and reported that for the first time in months they could tuck into beef, mutton, pies and vegetables from the kitchen garden – all washed down with ale. With plenty of food and at least as many prayers, Hill filled the empty stomachs of his workforce and reassured them that God would soon put an end to their hardship. He was not alone in his attempt to counteract civil disobedience in his locality by such paternalistic measures. Two years later Uvedale Price, landowner and tireless promoter of the picturesque, reminded the landed gentry of their duty when he wrote that estate owners should 'increase their attention' to their employees in order to avoid rebellion.

Hill may have been able to avert an uprising in his immediate neighbourhood, but the national picture was bleaker. The poor wheat harvest of 1795 sparked more trouble, and in October a mob stoned King George III's coach as he travelled to Westminster to open Parliament. The people were demanding bread, an end to the war, and Pitt's resignation. In response to the crisis Pitt introduced two bills outlawing almost all reform movements as seditious and treasonable, and suspended habeas corpus, the decree that for five hundred years had protected personal liberty. The Whigs were outraged, declaring Pitt's measures to be in breach of the Bill of Rights of 1689. Mass meetings were held throughout the country, but nothing could prevent the two bills becoming law in December that year. Radicals like Thomas Paine had already fled the country, but now even moderate reformers were forced to either give up their causes or pursue them illicitly. Groups such as the London Corresponding Society, who had fought for universal male suffrage while maintaining 'their abhorrence of tumult and violence', were now criminalised and driven underground by Pitt's laws.

Throughout the winter of 1795 Hill continued to buy food, selling it to his farmers and labourers at a reduced rate. By March the poor families around Hawkstone and in Shrewsbury itself were relying entirely on Hill's largesse: he was now handing out a weekly ration of six tons of flour to over six thousand people. Times may have been hard for his tenants, but the estate owner continued to prosper. Although Hill claimed that he 'would rather live on £100 or even £50 a year than being the possessor of millions', he was one of the few hundred in the country who owned more than ten thousand acres.* Even after he had accounted for the costs of improving his house and garden, personal expenses and good causes, he still had £5000 worth of disposable annual income.

The national crisis did not persuade Hill to halt his building programme. He was determined to declare his family's power in and around Hawkstone. Ten years earlier Hill had built a house for his steward called the Citadel; situated on the perimeter of the estate, it looked like a castle – its design was based on the family crest, thereby branding the landscape as his. Hill now devised the Obelisk. More than one hundred feet high, it was crowned by a sculpture of his ancestor, another Sir Rowland, who had become the first Protestant mayor of London in 1549, and, like Richard, was known for his good deeds. The monument was the tallest building in the park, set at the top of Terrace Hill and towering a grand total of eight hundred feet above the Shropshire plain. Its

---

*When John Bateman published *The Great Landowners of Great Britain and Ireland* in the late nineteenth century, he defined great landowners as those who possessed more than 3000 acres; about the same time the *Spectator* stated that only 710 people owned more than 5000 acres (Bateman, 1971).

slender white shape, intended further to reinforce the Hill family's dominance, could be seen for miles around. To ram the message home, Hill had fixed a plaque at the entrance highlighting his ancestor's 'private virtues ... and munificent spirit, [which] were quite unlimited, and extended, like the prospects before us, East, West, North and South, far surpassing all bounds'. The message appears to have sunk in: one visitor remarked, after reading the inscription, that Hill represented a 'rare instance' of a country gentleman contributing 'to the support and industry of numbers in his neighbourhood'.

Work on the Obelisk took more than a year, and just as the finishing touches were being added in August 1796, Hill received his most distinguished guests, the exiled Stadtholder of the Netherlands and his wife. The Prince of Orange, William V, had fled his country and sought refuge in Britain eighteen months previously, when the French had invaded the Netherlands. At Hawkstone, the royal couple were welcomed in regal style with a large party in the Saloon – the room, two storeys high, was decorated for the occasion with flowers and fruit from the garden. On the walls hung paintings illustrating Hill's allegiance to the House of Orange: *The Siege of Namur* dominated, with its depiction of William III and yet another ancestor, the 'Great Hill', at the decisive defeat of Louis XIV in 1695. Flanking the doorway were lifesize portraits of William and Mary.

A spectacular bunch of grapes, three and a half feet in diameter and weighing nearly sixteen pounds, hung from the Saloon ceiling between two pillars. Hill was proud to present this viticultural triumph, grown in one of Hawkstone's three hothouses. The next day, at eight in the morning, the prince and his wife set off on Hill's 'private tour' through the garden. The pleasure boat picked them up at the Gothic boathouse near the house, then made its way towards the Dutch-style cottage, Neptune's Whim, so that the guests could appreciate the Hawkstone landscape in all its variety.

The still, mild day did not dampen Hill's enthusiasm for demonstrating the sublime effect of a 'thunderstorm'. He had already sent his workmen up Red Castle Hill to ram the gunpowder into the cannons with instructions to ignite them once the boat came in sight. After the cannon concerto, the royal couple and their host made their way to Reynard's Walk, a recently added path on Terrace Hill, midway up from the valley. The perilous narrow path hugged the spiky contours of the west side of the hill, in contrast to the gentle terrace walk above them. On one side they could see just below them the oaks and elms of Tower Glen, entangled in undergrowth, while on the other the escarpment rose sheer above them. Climbing over the intricate knots and webs made by the exposed roots of the ivy-clad oaks, Hill's royal guests declared themselves 'much pleased with the romantic scenes'.

They left Hawkstone to continue their tour, and Hill accompanied them for at least another four weeks, showing them not only other picturesque landscapes but also the industrial enterprises then being set up in Shropshire.* The ironworks and coal-mines with their monstrous, deafening, mechanical forms spewing dark clouds of dust had come to symbolise England's power, and so played a key part in the patriotic tour. The most iconic symbol of industrial progress was the Iron Bridge straddling the Severn Gorge. The first single-span cast-iron bridge in the world, it had opened five years earlier, and had been compared by Wesley to 'the Colossus at Rhodes'. Leaving Ironbridge – the town named after its famous artefact – the royal tour moved on to the newly founded Coalport china factory. It was probably on this occasion that Hill commissioned a dessert service decorated with illustrations of Hawkstone's garden and its follies, which was delivered a year later.

Although the landscape around Ironbridge and Coalport was dominated by industry, tourists used expressions from nature to describe these scenes. One writer likened the smoke of the foundries to 'mist arising from the agitation of a cataract'; the botanist Joseph Banks compared the molten iron flowing from the furnaces to 'rivers of lava running down the sides of a volcano'. Sudden detonations evoked the sublime which, in Burke's opinion, could 'overpower the soul . . . and fill it with terror'; explosions deep in the mines were 'momentary bursts of thunder', exciting 'the idea of the final consumption of things – of nature sinking into universal wreck'. Such scenes and sounds created the same emotions as the sheer cliffs, dark forests and mysterious caverns of a landscape

---

*We cannot be sure that Hill accompanied them on their whole tour but it seems very possible, given that the *Shrewsbury Chronicle* (9 and 23 September 1796) reported that the Prince of Orange was in Cheltenham and that Richard Hill returned from there on the 23rd.

like Hawkstone. Medieval ruin and modern ironworks, the one celebrating the past and the other signposting the future, both symbolised national pride.

In 1798 the French army under the leadership of Napoleon Bonaparte was sweeping across Europe. As British newspapers filled with reports of French threats to invade, the country rallied and public opinion turned in support of the war. Even Richard Hill, who had once opposed it, gave £1200 – more than a tenth of his annual income – for 'the defence of the country', and his servants gave more than £50. In June, Napoleon seized Malta, and in July some thirty thousand French troops landed near Alexandria. The conquest of Egypt would provide a gateway to the Orient and give France the power she wanted over the British trade routes to the East. No part of the world seemed safe from Napoleon's ambitions. Then at a stroke Britain's naval forces, now under the command of Horatio Nelson, destroyed the French fleet at the battle of the Nile, humiliating Napoleon's navy. Although this victory did not end the war, Britain had something to celebrate. When the news of the triumph reached Richard Hill in Hawkstone, he ordered his workmen to light torches at the top of the Obelisk. That night, Hawkstone and the countryside beyond were visible across the Shropshire plain as if 'the sun shone upon them'.

With the French army still at large on the continent, the British stayed at home. Some published their journals as guidebooks for the ever growing number of tourists. Among them was Richard Warner, who arrived at Hawkstone on 27 July 1801. Seeing himself as a connoisseur of nature, he had acquired his taste for the picturesque from William Gilpin whom he had served as curate, and like his mentor he preferred irregularity to 'tiresome uniformity', and landscapes that would 'look well in a picture'. His writing was so persuasive that William Wordsworth had been inspired to visit Tintern Abbey after reading Warner's description of it.

On his arrival at Hawkstone, Warner entered the garden at Neptune's Whim. But he found the lake too regular and obviously manmade, and dismissed the cottage and the windmill opposite as 'childishly artificial'. Quickly leaving this 'old-fashioned family picture in a circular gilded frame', he ventured into the park in the direction of Red Castle, where the rugged hills promised nature that was more authentic. The path led him first into a little wooded glen where he came upon a hut, the centrepiece of a tableau called 'The Scene of Otaheite', which Hill had modelled on drawings of Captain Cook's voyage to Tahiti. Constructed from sticks and reeds, its floors strewn with pebbles, the cottage was furnished with rough seats made of matting. Spears, arrows and tomahawks lay scattered around, as if the inhabitants had only just left. Inside, Hill had placed bones, feathers, shell necklaces and masks; outside was a canoe, and rare South Sea plants grew there. Although it was nearly thirty years since Cook's voyages, the explorer's adventures continued to fascinate. Books recounting his discoveries were still popular, and the British Museum even had a South Sea Room.*

Hawkstone's visitors would immediately have grasped the link between Cook and 'Otaheite'. Actively involved in fuelling this interest, Hill also supported the London Missionary Society, which five years earlier had sent its first representatives to Tahiti to 'introduce the gospel of Christ among the heathen'.

But Warner was again disappointed; he had come to Hawkstone to see nature, not an educational tableau. When he cast an eye beyond it, however, he glimpsed some crude steps cut into the sharply rising rock, and his spirits quickly lifted. Eagerly climbing 'paths skirting precipices', he eventually reached the ruined castle, which he thought truly picturesque. The variety of form and gradation of colour he observed in the broken red sandstone walls streaked with green minerals created the 'most beautiful and solemn combination of rock and wood' imaginable. He was captivated.

Now he crossed the Grand Valley to see, as he emerged from a wood of old beech trees and dark firs, the garden's next grand spectacle – the Grotto, at the top of Grotto Hill. A rough Gothic arch above its entrance made it one of the most prominent features in the garden. Since their introduction into English gardens in the late sixteenth century, grottoes had been a showcase for taste of one kind or another. They had been variously conceived as sites of mystery and sanctuary, as a vehicle for theatrical display, or as a backdrop for

---

*Such books were regularly advertised in local newspapers such as the *Shrewsbury Chronicle* (e.g. July 1786, October 1787, May 1789, May 1790). The South Sea Room at the British Museum had opened in August 1781, and an account of the missionary voyage to Tahiti had been published in 1799.

a shell collection. In the eighteenth century grottoes had often been the product
of their owners' fascination with the classical tradition, joining forces with
temples and statues to convey the idea of a rustic retreat.

Knowing that Hill's Grotto was a natural cavern, Warner was excited by
the thought of what awaited him – like most curious people, he never passed
up an opportunity to peer into a cave, a mine or a tunnel. But, unlike many, he
had been known to crawl on hands and knees, even abseil three hundred feet
in a bucket, in order to reach a dank hole or the bottom of a pit. Just a few
days before, he had gone down a salt mine, where the salt crystals had sparkled
like 'ten thousand diamonds'. So he had no trouble climbing the 'extremely well
managed' walk up Grotto Hill. As he neared the top, the path narrowed into
a long shady cleft, outcrops of rock overhanging at left and right. High above
him, trees formed a canopy blocking out the light. Eventually the path arrived
at the entrance to a subterranean passage. Both this and the little gorge were
recent additions to the garden, Hill's workmen having carted hundreds of loads
of earth, rubble and rocks down the steep slopes to create this dramatic new
entrance. Suddenly plunged into the pitch dark, Warner crept along the hundred
yards of tunnel, groping his way against the cold rock walls that were no more
than two feet apart.

The interior of the Grotto

The dark passageway opened out into the largest grotto he had ever seen: a labyrinth of caves, pillars and narrow tunnels, it epitomised the sublime. Little stained-glass 'windows' in the roof sent down shards of muted rainbow light. This grotto danced to the rhythm of Burke's aesthetic opposites, the sublime and the beautiful. Sublime vastness was supplied by the dimensions – the main cave alone was eighty feet wide – while exquisite smallness was provided by the fossils, the polished shells, the glittering crystals, the iridescent mother-of-pearl and the glowing pink corals, all glimmering and glinting against the rough rock walls in which they were embedded. Warner was stunned by the size of the pillars and the delicacy of the glass and other embellishments. Throughout the century, grottoes had featured shells and crystals, but Hill's grotto was unique because these and the rest of the decoration were set in the crude walls of the caverns instead of in a manmade surface. Other garden owners, such as Charles Hamilton at Painshill, had to resort to artificial grottoes, their exteriors covered with 'irregular' materials such as tufa (a water-washed limestone), their interiors with chips of white minerals. Hill, by contrast, had transformed his natural cave, according to Warner, into the most 'novel, grand, beautiful and extensive' grotto in Europe.

The layout of the Grotto

Warner's next destination was the Hermitage, via Terrace Hill. The path he took was flanked on either side by dense trees. In places brushing the ground, their foliage interwove with the thick undergrowth, a haven for rabbits, birds and foxes. Hawkstone's Hermitage was typical of its time: a little thatched hut hidden beneath trees, it looked similar to the rustic buildings in the pattern-books that filled the libraries of country houses. William Wrighte's *Grotesque Architecture* (1767) and Batty Langley's *Gothic Architecture Improved by Rules and Proportions* (1742) were particularly popular. A feature of fashionable gardens for sixty years, the hermitage invoked pensive withdrawal, rural retreat, and the rejection of worldly goods. Hermitages were inspired by such legends as Diogenes in his barrel and Milton's poem *Il Penseroso*, which called for a 'peaceful hermitage', a simple 'mossy cell' – hence 'Druid Cell' or 'Merlin's Cave' were favoured names. Gardens had always provided places of retreat, such as Cecil's banqueting houses at Hatfield, but now the concept of solitude was more romantic – to the extent that Henry Hoare, the owner of Stourhead in Wiltshire, thought about becoming a hermit himself. Others would withdraw occasionally to read poetry, while Alexander Pope used his retreat to study in, declaring: 'Contemplative life is not only my *scene*, but it is my habit too.'

When Warner entered the dimly lit hut he saw a gaunt man sitting at a small table on which were placed a human skull, a book, a pair of spectacles and an hourglass. The 'man' then rose to his feet and, in a shaky voice, began to recite: 'Memento mori . . .' ('Remember that you will die'). Warner saw through the trick, having noticed that his guide had slipped away and was now operating the automaton. As with his other follies, the significance of Hill's Hermitage was religious: the hourglass and the motto were reminders of man's mortality. Initially, Hill had employed a pauper to inhabit the folly, perhaps inspired by other owners who had recruited resident hermits through newspaper advertisements.* But the job was demanding, requiring them to stay in the hut at all times, remain silent and leave their nails and beards uncut; as a

---

*Apparently, Charles Hamilton at Painshill found his hermit through such an advertisement. Rumours about Hawkstone's hermit were aired in 1830 in *Blackwood's Magazine*, which claimed that the editor of another magazine had worked for fourteen years in that role, wearing a beard made of goat's hair (Sitwell, 1933, pp.49–51).

result they often left after just a few weeks. To avoid this problem, the naturalist Gilbert White persuaded his own brother to play the hermit at his hermitage at Selborne in Hampshire, while Queen Caroline had hers at Richmond Gardens outside London fitted out with a library, and made a rather bookish labourer both hermit and poet laureate.

Hill had found a reliable hermit, but his conscience pricked him: was it right to constrain a fellow man in this way? After a while the opponent of slavery decided to 'withdraw the reality and substitute the figure'. The hermit was replaced by the automaton, which the guide operated from behind the hut like a puppet, while reciting the words. Its raised hand had bloody stumps for two of the fingers, supposedly 'rotten through age', as one visitor reported. Some visitors thought its effect quite powerful – but only on 'women and children', while others were appalled by the 'disgusting and unnatural' display.

The Hermit at Hawkstone, 1787

Disappointed by the more whimsical follies, Warner was wandering the paths when he caught sight of a sign reading 'Pont de Suisse' (the Swiss Bridge). Following it, he found himself climbing a steep track around Terrace Hill. Suddenly cliffs loomed on both sides, and he was approaching a deep cleft. Above him, perilously high, hung a small rustic bridge no wider than a tree trunk, constructed by Hill's workmen from roughly cut oak beams. This vertiginous alpine scene was one of Hawkstone's greatest attractions, and like most people who visited the garden Warner was captivated. Here, Richard Hill was tapping into the obsession for mountains that was gripping many: Dr Johnson had felt the 'horror of solitude', the pious Joseph Salmon had found God in the 'terrace alps'. Others had praised the singularity of Hawkstone's alpine expanses, declaring the effect to be beyond description; and the guidebook claimed that the 'wide chasms . . . strike you with dread'. Artists too revelled in a scenery that fed their imagination. John Robert Cozens, a British artist whose astonishing watercolour drawings changed the perception of mountains, had set the viewer in lonely landscapes amidst sheer rockfaces, thereby offering a new perspective. Like the tourists, many artists travelled the country at this time, sketching and painting their vision of Britain. J. M. W. Turner turned to the sublime Welsh mountainscapes, capturing threatening rocks, barren peaks and deep crevasses against stormy skies.

But nature had come to represent many things to many people, and as

The Swiss Bridge, 1824

Hill celebrated God in the Hawkstone hills, for others such as Wordsworth and Samuel Taylor Coleridge it was in the contemplation of mountains, lakes and storms that they explored their emotions and their individuality. One of their sources of inspiration had been Jean-Jacques Rousseau, whose *Reveries of the Solitary Walker* had been published in 1783, the year Hill inherited Hawkstone. 'I climb the rocks, the hills, I go down into valleys, into woods,' Rousseau had written, 'to withdraw, as much as possible, from the remembrance of man'; despising man's attempt to rationalise the world by classifying and systematising it, he experienced the Swiss mountains on an emotional level. The *Reveries* became the gospel of the Romantics, inspiring them to venture into the countryside and seek refuge in nature, which for them had become the mirror of the soul. The more untouched the scenery, the better, because they despised what civilisation had made of society. Mountains, Wordsworth wrote in rapture, were 'the symbols of Eternity'.[*] A week after Warner's visit to Hawkstone, Coleridge took the obsession to another level when, climbing down Scafell, England's highest mountain, he deliberately put his life in danger. He was hoping to intensify his experience of nature in order to sharpen his emotions. His reckless gesture, described by one modern commentator as Britain's first true rock climb, demonstrated the dramatically new way in which mountains were perceived.

At the root of this passion was Thomas Burnet's *The Sacred Theory of the Earth*, which had been widely read since its publication in 1681. Burnet had been the first to regard mountains as both awesome and exciting. Instead of drawing the blinds in his carriage or blindfolding himself when he travelled through the Alps, as other travellers did, Burnet had been fascinated by the barren scene. Mountains and chasms were the scars of the Great Flood, he declared, seeing God's signature in the skewed and towering forms. The earth, he maintained, used to be like a gigantic unblemished egg – 'no rocks nor Mountains, no hollow Caves, nor gaping Channels, but even and uniform all over'. Only when God's deluge engulfed the planet did the shell break and scatter, its fragments creating the mountains and valleys. According to Burnet

---

[*]Wordsworth crossed the Alps in the summer of 1790.

the Alps, therefore, were a visible symbol of the Fall of Man. God's might had created 'these Heaps of Stone and Rubbish' – the ruins of a broken world.

While Burnet provided the theory, the poet Thomas Gray made the experience real. His account of his alpine journey of 1739 had made him the hero of the Romantic movement, while also changing the focus of the Grand Tour from Rome and Florence to the Alps. As he was being carried on a chair by four porters along the edges of 'monstrous' precipices, Gray's mind turned to thoughts of death; and he became convinced that his experience would turn any atheist into a believer. It was the 'most solemn, the most romantic, and the most astonishing scene' he had ever looked upon, he wrote, and 'pregnant with religion and poetry'. Gray's travelling companion, Horace Walpole, was similarly captivated (the fact that his lapdog was eaten by a wolf did not diminish his enthusiasm). '[P]recipices, mountains, torrents, wolves, rumblings, Salvator Rosa,' he wrote pithily to a friend in England.

The rugged landscapes of the seventeenth-century Italian artist Salvator Rosa were immensely popular at the time. Aristocrats and wealthy gentlemen bought his depictions of the harsh alpine wilderness to satisfy their appetite for mountains. Thanks to cheaper printing technologies, a wider public now had access to reproductions of his oil paintings, and print-sellers could offer engravings of his best works at affordable prices (they could be bought for between two and twelve shillings each). The savage rocks and wind-blasted trees of Rosa's landscapes, peopled by lonely hermits or *banditti*, adorned the drawing-rooms of the middle classes. Ann Radcliffe used the same imagery in her popular Gothic novels, in which heroines languished in ruined castles and crumbling abbeys. Many of Radcliffe's settings could have been depictions of Hill's park, such as this one described in *A Sicilian Romance* (1790): 'rising on the left into bold romantic mountains, and on the right, exhibiting a soft and glowing landscape, whose tranquil beauty formed a striking contrast to the wild sublimity of the opposite craggy heights'. It was in these terms that tourists understood Hawkstone, both recognising the Salvatorean themes and echoing Burnet when they described the hills as having been thrown up 'by some vast effort from the bowels of the earth', or as the 'raging billows of the great deluge'.

*

Landscape by Salvator Rosa

Britain's fortunes had begun to turn. After years blighted by an unstable economy, bad harvests and the war against France, hardship and revolutionary threat were receding: by the end of the summer of 1801, Britain had forced Napoleon's army out of Egypt. On 1 October the French signed the preliminary articles of the Peace of Amiens, setting the terms of the rapprochement between themselves and England. With the international situation seemingly under control, Hill, as so often, found other issues to fuss about. Adam Smith's *Inquiry into the Wealth of Nations*, with its ideas of free commerce, had for a long time been encouraging greedy merchants to push up prices, he claimed. He feared that England was 'kissing the toe of Pope Adam Smith'. Hill believed that landowners contributed more to the well-being and economic progress of the country than people in trade, and he had reminded Parliament years earlier of Robert Walpole's words: that 'trade was like a hog; pluck but a single bristle and he will grunt'; but that 'the landed interest is like a sheep; you may shear him again and again, and still he has a fleece at your service.' But, with time, his concern that landowners would lose their power began to abate, permitting him once again to enjoy his domestic pleasures. He had spent almost twenty years 'improving' his garden, and now it was finished: the follies were built, boats sailed on the lake; above all, Hawkstone was now the wild and sublime landscape he had so ardently striven for. The time had come to rejoice. On 10 October Hill welcomed 'a large company of friends' to an 'elegant' dinner at Hawkstone. The workmen enjoyed roast beef, pies, puddings and home-brewed ale, though not without first having attended church – as they would again the next day – to thank God for the harvest and the achievements of the nation. After dinner his personal guests set off for the tower on Terrace Hill, where they were entertained with tea and patriotic songs – among them, 'Rule Britannia', and 'God Save the King' – played on French horns and clarinets. After tea, the firing of a cannon announced the illumination of the Obelisk. All eyes turned to watch the display, accompanied by more roaring of cannons, which echoed around the landscape in the most 'astonishing manner', the *Shrewsbury Chronicle* commented. Not everything, though, went according to plan. To Hill's disappointment, the wind got up, blowing out the torches at the top of the Obelisk and tearing down the banners at the four sides of the monument displaying the word PEACE. But despite the setback the party went on until nine o'clock, when the guests made their way to the top of Terrace Hill from where they could look down on the house, the Citadel and the inn illuminated below them. The lights flickering against the looming hills must have looked magical.

The following months were a happy interlude for Hill, now sixty-nine. The peace treaty, signed in March 1802, brought him some comfort, as did the return of his nephew and heir, Rowland, who had been fighting against Napoleon's troops in Egypt. To celebrate his safe return and his thirtieth birthday, Hill organised another party. On a warm summer's day on 11 August, a feast was held in the Greenhouse at the south end of the Elysian Hill. Built from roughly hewn stone and half hidden in ivy and honeysuckle, it was embellished on each side of the entrance with orange trees, geraniums, myrtles and other hothouse plants. Hill's sister, Jane, had decorated the inside with flowers and branches of gilded laurel, as a sign of victory and peace. The guests were spoiled with home-grown melons, nectarines, grapes and pineapples – the one fruit that still challenged gardeners – kept cool with fresh ice from Hill's ice-house. Boys and girls from the School of Industry walked two by two past the Greenhouse singing 'Long Live the King', followed, during dinner, by servants playing martial music. The booty that Colonel Hill had brought back from Egypt was displayed in front of the diners: among the spoils was an Arabian horse that had reputedly belonged to one of the Mameluke leaders, the Turkish tribe that had ruled Egypt for centuries before the French invaded and defeated them – what better symbol of Britain's victory?

After dinner, the party crossed the park to find a new attraction awaiting them at Neptune's Whim. Colonel Hill had brought his uncle a present from Egypt: a tent which, like the horse, had also belonged to the Mameluke leader. Hill had set it up at the end of the River Hawk. The brightly embroidered tent added an exotic touch to the rugged English scene. Inside, striking another patriotic note, Hill had hung a picture of a laurel-clad Nelson, hero of the Nile. When the guests arrived, strong coffee brewed in a Turkish silver pot was served in Turkish cups – yet more Egyptian treasure. Then they made their way to the riverbank, where a three-masted sailing boat would pick them up to take them to the house.

Several new flags, featuring the three crosses of the recently united kingdom, billowed in the wind. The United Kingdom of Great Britain and Ireland had come into being on 1 January 1801, after Britain's victory in Ireland. Order had been restored to Hill's world. The country had emerged from years of war, economic hardship and political repression; and, saved by her naval supremacy, she could afford, Hill believed, to be more optimistic about her future. Hill celebrated Britain's power and glory by decorating one of his boats with branches of oak, the wood that was prized as a national symbol having been used to build the nation's fleet. As the band played 'Rule Britannia', the boat sailed past, then, for the last time that night, came the sound of cannon-fire to echo round Hawkstone's glens. Hill's final reminder that God was the divine architect of nature in all its power and glory.

5

A Benevolent Landscape: Sheringham Park

'So manifold, all pleasing in their kind,
All healthful, are the employs of rural life,
Reiterated as the wheel of time
Runs round, still ending, and beginning still.'

William Cowper, *The Task* (1785)

'Whoe'er from Nature takes a view,
Must copy and improve it too.
To heighten every work of art,
Fancy should take an active part:
Thus I (which few I think can boast)
Have made a Landscape of a Post.'

William Combe, *The Tour of Doctor Syntax
in Search of the Picturesque* (1812)

'It wants improvement, Ma'am, beyond any thing. I never saw a place that wanted so much improvement in my life; and it is so forlorn that I do not know what can be done with it.'

. . .

'I must try to do something with it,' said Mr Rushworth, 'but I do not know what. I hope I shall have some good friend to help me.'

. . .

'Your best friend upon such an occasion,' said Miss Bertram, calmly, 'would be Mr Repton, I imagine.'

'That is what I was thinking of. As he has done so well by Smith, I think I had better have him at once. His terms are five guineas a day.'

. . .

After a short interruption, Mr Rushworth began again. 'Smith's place is the admiration of all the country; and it was a mere nothing before Repton took it in hand. I think I shall have Repton.'

. . .

'Smith has not much above a hundred acres altogether in his grounds, which is little enough, and makes it more surprising that the place can have been so improved. Now, at Sotherton, we have a good seven hundred, without reckoning the water meadows; so that I think, if so much could be done at Compton, we need not despair. There have been two or three fine old trees cut down, that grew too near the house, and it opens the prospect amazingly, which makes me think that Repton, or any body of that sort, would certainly have the avenue at Sotherton down.'

. . .

Fanny, who was sitting on the other side of Edmund, exactly opposite Miss Crawford, and who had been attentively listening, now looked at him, and said in a low voice:

'Cut down an avenue! What a pity! Does it not make you think of Cowper? "Ye fallen avenues, once more I mourn your fate unmerited."'

He smiled as he answered, 'I am afraid the avenue stands a bad chance, Fanny.'

Map of Sheringham from Humphry Repton's Red Book, 1812. To the right is Upper Sheringham village and along the road, towards the house, is the farmhouse, which was to be the temporary home of the Upchers. The flower garden is next to the house. Repton also clearly indicated where to cut the approach road through the hill at The Turn

In 1811 Jane Austen decided to draw on the services of Humphry Repton, the most fashionable landscape designer of her generation, not, as one might suspect, to plan a garden, but as promising material for the novel she had just embarked on, *Mansfield Park*. Repton had worked on over three hundred gardens: his name conjured up images of sweeping lawns, meandering walks and picturesque shrubberies. Ridiculing the fashions of her time, Austen would immortalise Repton as the relentless 'improver' of gardens for the rich and frivolous. Like the characters in her novels, her readers were well versed in the subject of gardens and nature, and the search for the picturesque and the improvement of landscapes had become popular pastimes with the middle classes. Austen used these same themes in her novels, often satirising the society that had spawned this gardening craze.

It was between 1811 and 1817, while her novels were being published,

Humphry Repton, 1803

that Repton was engaged on turning the country estate of Sheringham into his 'most favourite work'. The words of Jane Austen with which this chapter opens offer us a prism through which to view his approach to garden design. In July 1811,* as Austen was writing *Mansfield Park*, Repton was on his way to Norfolk in the hope of securing the Sheringham commission. A year short of his sixtieth birthday, he was feeling his age; and since his recent carriage accident he had been confined to a wheelchair – a severe handicap for someone whose profession demanded the mobility and stamina to spend long hours surveying and studying his clients' extensive gardens. After more than two decades as the most sought-after landscape gardener in the country, his career seemed to be faltering. With few other projects on the horizon and very little money, Repton desperately needed a success.

When, in 1788, he had turned his amateur passion for landscape design into a career, he had set himself up as heir to Capability Brown, the man who, from his first significant job at Stowe until his death in 1783, had created a new taste in gardening. Before then, Repton had tried, unsuccessfully, to establish himself first as a merchant, then private secretary, then country gentleman –

*Jane Austen began working on *Mansfield Park* in February 1811, but it was not published until May 1814.

in this last venture he had squandered his annual £600 inheritance on disastrous investments. But following Brown's lead, he was quickly to demonstrate where his talents lay. Using, also, his connections with the upper classes, he soon secured a string of commissions, being employed to impose a 'natural' landscape on estates from Cornwall to Yorkshire. His success was due, in part, to his ability to parlay into money the friendships he had made during his time as a gentleman, never visiting a big house without keeping an eye open for potential business. He would even decline private invitations if they promised no profit, declaring that 'he had seen fine places enough'.

The meeting in Norfolk had been arranged by Repton's son William, who was brokering the sale of Sheringham for its owner, Cook Flower. The signing of the contracts was set for 10 July, and William had invited his father to join his client, as well as the purchaser of the estate, one Abbot Upcher, for a celebratory dinner. The purpose was to wheedle a commission for his father out of the new owner. The prospect must have been enticing. Sheringham's grounds were larger than most of Repton's recent projects: over a thousand acres of rich arable farmland, heath, parkland and tree-clad hills stretching along the Norfolk coast. To the north, the estate was bordered by the North Sea; to the south, the gentle hills formed a sinuous ridge enveloping the great flat expanses of fields and parkland, broken here and there by hillocks.

It was a good time to buy a working estate. The ongoing war with France, which had resumed eight years before, had continued to push corn and wheat prices ever higher, making farming more profitable. Many large farmers and landowners had expanded their cereal production, and were now enjoying considerable affluence. Having inherited a scattering of farms in Sussex and Essex when he was twelve, Upcher now wanted to 'concentrate [his] property as much as possible', and had been looking for a suitable estate. Two months earlier he had offered £50,000 for another, similarly sized, estate in the county, but to his great disappointment the offer had been refused. Since then, he had been edgy and troubled by recurring headaches – which might explain why he was willing to offer £52,500 for Sheringham.*

*Unless otherwise stated, the chronology of the making of Sheringham, as well as Upcher's thoughts and feelings, are based on his journal 'Sherringhamia', 1813–16, Norfolk Record Office

Upcher wanted to set himself up as a country gentleman who worked his land and looked after his tenants, as well as enjoying his private pleasures such as literature and sermons. Despite being twenty-six years old, he still had a chubby-cheeked boyishness about him. Though blighted by delicate health, Upcher was determined to embrace rural life wholeheartedly. His second child had just been born and his wife Charlotte, the daughter of a respected clergyman, was pregnant with their third. He was looking forward to a domestic country existence and was keen to provide 'a virtuous example' as a charitable landlord. Two weeks before meeting Repton, he had seen Sheringham's grounds for the first time and judged them 'romantic'. He was 'cruelly disappointed', though, by the house, which was no more than a large farmhouse. On leaving the estate, making his way along the coast through thick fog, Upcher had been 'quite at a loss what to do' – the grounds were exactly what he had wished for, but the old house was dismal and uninviting. Three days later, after he had seen yet another estate and conferred with friends, he returned, this time convinced that Sheringham was so beautiful and fertile that it would be worth building a new house.

For Repton, Sheringham's attraction was not only pecuniary. His profession allowed him to enjoy 'the society of those to whose notice I could not otherwise have aspired', and in this respect Repton viewed Upcher as the perfect client. To impress him, Repton employed a combination of elegant taste and sycophancy, an approach he had often used to charm rich noblemen and gentry – some thought him 'dazzling', while others remembered him as an 'everlasting talker'. Whatever Repton's strategy with Upcher, it worked: after dinner, the contract was signed. There would now be a lag of sixteen months between the exchange of contracts and Upcher's taking possession of the estate in October 1812.

Not until a year later, in June 1812, did Upcher and Repton meet again – this time at Sheringham – to decide on the improvements to be made to the

---

(also Yaxley 1986) and his diary entries. The original diary is missing, but large sections are transcribed in Pigott, *c.* 1860.

Abbot Upcher   Caroline Upcher, 1814

landscape, the location of the new house, the walks, avenues and planting schemes.* This was Repton's first visit. Nature had already, it seemed, shaped the grounds according to the principles of the latest gardening styles, and he was delighted with what he saw. Unlike Hawkstone, Sheringham radiated a gentle calmness. Where Hawkstone was wild, presenting the visitor with an interesting new feature at every turn, Sheringham was softly contoured and surrounded by farmland. No subject for Salvator Rosa, Sheringham would have looked entirely right in a painting by Gainsborough or Constable, artists to whom the countryside was their muse.

Where Hawkstone's visitors, in search of the sublime, had been yearning for untouched nature, Upcher and his contemporaries longed for a 'rustic idyll'. This feeling for traditional rural life was a direct reaction to the effects of industrialisation in cities and on the rural economy. What only four decades earlier had been hailed as Britain's future was now under attack. Then, only a few critics, such as Rousseau, had bemoaned the fact that factories and the

*Unless otherwise stated, Repton's visit and the conversations between him and Upcher are based on Repton's Red Book for Sheringham which he supplied a month after the visit, and on Upcher's journal and diary.

'infectious vapours of the mines' had replaced 'the lovely image of rural employment'. But others soon followed; the poet William Cowper, for instance, dismissed the stinking towns as places of

> Ambition, avarice, penury incurr'd
> By endless riot, vanity, the lust
> Of pleasure and variety . . .

The agricultural writer Arthur Young asked why people 'quit their healthy clean fields for a region of dirt, stink and noise'. Constable's reaction was to leave his studio for the fields and villages. When he depicted cottagers working the land by traditional methods, he romanticised what he saw, creating a symbol of stability. Though the farm workers and other labourers who peopled his paintings were often no more than ciphers, Constable nevertheless conveyed 'real' landscapes rather than the idealised Arcadia of a Claude Lorrain. Similarly in poetry, Wordsworth described English rural life in his *Lyrical Ballads* in the language of 'humble' men, because, as he explained, that language was more evocative than the stilted talk of the educated.

This urge for simplicity and leaning towards nature penetrated many aspects of early nineteenth-century life – among them, architecture, poetry, gardening, art, literature and fashion. Women, for example, exchanged their boned bodices and hoops for soft, high-waisted muslin dresses that followed the body's natural shape – they even dipped fully dressed into the bath-tub so that their dresses, when dry, would cling. Neither men nor women any longer painted their faces white or used rouge, preferring to show off their natural complexion. It was four decades since the writer Hannah More had mocked the elaborate wig confections of some women she saw at a party: 'Amongst them, on their heads', they wore 'an acre and a half of shrubbery besides slopes, grass plats, tulip beds, clumps of peonies, kitchen gardens and greenhouses'. But all this had changed, and 'to be natural' had become a way of life; so Upcher wore his own hair, and his wife's fell in ringlets around her face. She wore flowing dresses, and transparent shawls revealed her shoulders and arms. And just as flamboyance and pomp in their personal appearance were eschewed, so they

did not want their home to be ostentatious. They aimed for a traditional paternalistic relationship with their tenants, rather than asserting their wealth and
superiority. The quest for simplicity was also fuelled by Upcher's concern for
his outgoings – 'like Hydra's heads, the more you knock off the more spring
up'. Early on, both husband and wife reduced the number of servants and
disposed of their closed carriage and some of the horses.

Their attitude epitomised a new way of incorporating rural elements
into the lifestyle of the landowner. Much had changed since the mid-eighteenth
century, when gentry and aristocrats alike, following the example of Marie-
Antoinette, had played at peasants and milkmaids in their rustic cottages, doing
their own baking and gardening and looking after their animals in what for
them was an amusing re-enactment of pastoral life. Even the middle classes
had entertained in the aristocratic fashion: the naturalist Gilbert White received
guests dressed up as shepherds and shepherdesses at his hermitage at Selborne
in Hampshire in the 1760s. A little later, though, William Gilpin had declared
that a picturesque scene should never include 'milkmaids, ploughmen, reapers
and peasants'. Instead of idealised peasant life, he favoured the wild and
rugged.

By the early nineteenth century attitudes had changed yet again.
Picturesque gardening and the preference for blasted trees and ruins over a neat
and tidy village was increasingly seen as selfish. People such as Repton's friend
Nathaniel Kent, agriculturist and land improver, promoted model cottages,
declaring that it was the 'moral duty' of the landlord to provide 'happiness' for
his labourers. So instead of Gothic follies, Upcher's estate would boast neat
tenant dwellings, and ploughed fields would replace windswept heathland.
Crumbling cottages overgrown with honeysuckle might have given the
landowner aesthetic pleasure, but they did not provide their inhabitants with
adequate living conditions.

This division between the aesthetic and the moral view of landscape
was again captured by Jane Austen, only a few months before Upcher and
Repton met at Sheringham in November 1811, this time in *Sense and
Sensibility*. Marianne, the most impulsive and romantic of the three
Dashwood sisters, is annoyed with the speaker, Edward Ferrars, who, coming

back from a walk, demonstrates his failure to appreciate the picturesqueness of the countryside:

> 'You must not enquire too far, Marianne – remember I have no knowledge in the picturesque, and I shall offend you by my ignorance and want of taste if we come to particulars. I shall call hills steep, which ought to be bold! surfaces strange and uncouth, which ought to be irregular and rugged; and distant objects out of sight, which ought only to be indistinct through the soft medium of a hazy atmosphere. You must be satisfied with such admiration as I can honestly give. I call it a very fine country – the hills are steep, the woods seem full of fine timber, and the valley looks comfortable and snug – with rich meadows and several neat farm-houses scattered here and there. It exactly answers my idea of a fine country, because it unites beauty with utility – and I dare say it is a picturesque one too, because you admire it; I can easily believe it to be full of rocks and promontories, grey moss and brushwood, but these are all lost on me. I know nothing of the picturesque.'
>
> . . .
>
> 'I like a fine prospect, but not on picturesque principles. I do not like crooked, twisted, blasted trees. I admire them much more if they are tall, straight, and flourishing. I do not like ruined, tattered cottages. I am not fond of nettles, or thistles, or heath blossoms. I have more pleasure in a snug farm-house than a watch-tower – and a troop of tidy, happy villagers please me better than the finest banditti in the world.'

Ferrars stood for a new kind of morality that was emerging in England, one that held that a landscape ought to be lived in rather than looked upon. Like Abbot Upcher, he celebrated the union of productivity and beauty, wanting to find happiness in 'domestic comfort and the quiet of private life'. A landscape was not just a 'scene' in a painting, but home to a rural community threatened by irresponsible landlords and industrialisation alike. Despite having been mocked by Austen as a picturesque 'improver', Repton agreed with Upcher that Sheringham's rural life should be part of the grand scheme.

As Repton and Upcher walked through the grounds, the conversation turned to politics and its effects on the estate. During the last twelve months the Luddite riots had been sweeping across the Midlands, Yorkshire and Lancashire. Groups of workers, fearing for their jobs, had raided towns and villages and smashed the manufacturers' new machinery, in protest against the reduction in their wages brought about by such innovation. He was pleased that no manufacturers had settled near Sheringham, Repton told Upcher – they and their employees were altogether 'a different species of animal to the Husbandman, Sailor, or even the Miner'. Only recently he had asked his son William, who lived just fifteen miles from Sheringham: 'How do your weavers go on – have they begun to throw the Meat about the Market instead of throwing their shuttles?' Concerned about the 'portentous' times they were living through, Repton agreed with many of his contemporaries that the country had not seen such disorder 'since the troubled days of Charles the First'. As the government hastened to deploy twelve thousand troops into the riots' heartland – more men than Wellington had at his disposal for the Peninsular War – fear grew that England was descending into chaos. Already the trade embargoes operating between Britain and France were strangling industry and commerce; and that the king, George III, had succumbed to another of his bouts of madness could only exacerbate the crisis. Repton and Upcher, and many like them, 'trembled for the safety of Old England'.

At a time of such national upheaval, few things were secure: food prices, like taxes, had risen, and who knew whether banknotes might not suddenly become valueless? Stability had been further undermined not only by the illness of the king but also by the assassination of the prime minister, Spencer Perceval, in May 1812. Land, on the other hand, meant security for both Repton and Upcher. The enclosures, new drilling and crop rotation systems, as well as the development of larger and more efficient farms, had made landowners even wealthier over the last three decades. That he could bring up his children in the countryside, away from what he called the 'London mob' and the debauchery of city life – where, under the influence of the prince regent, the upper classes led a life of loose morals and gambling – was an added bonus for Upcher. He aspired to lead a virtuous life; only three months earlier he had promised himself that he would be 'tender and faithful' to his family, as well as 'kind and strict'. While metropolitan high society flocked around dandy Beau Brummel, Upcher 'nursed' his children and 'almost devoured' his little boy 'with kisses'. His life centred on his family, on reading, and walking, and on 'delightful evenings' with Charlotte.

Having given much thought to the subject of what Sheringham's landscape should reflect and represent, Repton and Upcher decided that above all it should demonstrate to the local people that the estate once more had a paternalistic landlord. Upcher disliked the display of power, wealth and prestige represented by the vast expanses of lawn that surrounded the great Whig mansions. The gentleman improver Richard Payne Knight, talking of the estates that Brown had laid out, had ridiculed the 'shaven lawns, that far around it creep/ In one eternal undulating sweep' in his poem *The Landscape* (1794), and Brown's unpopulated parks were coming to symbolise the breakdown of village life, associated as they were with absentee landlords. Landowners such as Lord Cobham at Stowe who had removed a whole village in order to extend his garden, were now, at this time of social uprising, regarded as irresponsible. As Oliver Goldsmith put it in 'The Deserted Village':

> . . . The man of wealth and pride
> Takes up a space that many poor supplied;
> Space for his lake, his park's extended bounds.

Having agreed on what the estate should and should not represent, the most important decision to be made during Repton's first visit was where to build the house. The location had to provide privacy without radiating power or separating it too much from the local community. So the two men spent several hours exploring. As the estate was so close to the coast, Upcher was set on a view of the North Sea from his drawing-room, but Repton pointed out that the house would need to be sheltered from the harsh marine climate.

Stationing his carriage as a marker to help Upcher visualise the effect, he proposed that the house be situated in the valley, screened from the winds by the wooded hills but not too far from the village. Upcher, though, dithering as he so often did, remained undecided.

The positioning of the approach was equally important, since it connected the house to its locality as well as presenting the first impression of the estate. The existing approach passed through Upper Sheringham, a village distinguished by its 'miserable huts', 'shoe and stockingless' children and a workhouse that resembled a 'prison'. The symbolic advantage of proximity to the village and the convenience of having blacksmith, carpenter, tradesmen and church all within reach could not be easily dismissed, but in the end were outweighed by the ugliness of the scene. So both men resolved to forsake in this instance Upcher's benevolent resolutions, and opted for a more scenic approach – though exactly where in the grounds it should be, they could not agree upon. Ideally the new driveway would cut through the wooded ridge at the south edge of the estate, but excavating the hillside would be, as Upcher wrote in his diary that evening, 'an inconceivable expense'. At the end of this day of discussion and argument, all that had been decided was that Upcher would keep the old road as a service route – a compromise, in that it would provide the link to the village. With the main issues still unresolved, Upcher spent a restless night in 'much anxiety'.

While Upcher lay ruminating, Repton was probably fast asleep between the crisp bed sheets that he insisted on having changed every day. Enjoying a reputation for being 'never wrong', he was probably confident of resolving the problems once he and his client had spent a few more hours reconnoitring. After all, 'Nature's physician', as his friends called him, was able to 'dictate, and controul' the landscape, no less. Repton's moments of anxiety came usually in the mornings when, as an acquaintance teased, 'he will dolefully repent' of having indulged in the luxury of fresh sheets, despite having so little money – a habit that was a legacy of his former life as a country gentleman.

The following day after breakfast, he and Upcher met Cook Flower at Sheringham – he remained living there until the contracts were completed in

October.* Hearing of their dilemma over the approach road, Flower offered to accompany them on another tour of the grounds. As they climbed the wooded ridge to the south, he pointed out an existing small road which, he suggested, might be the solution to their predicament. Having overlooked it the previous day, Upcher and Repton now followed it until they came to a large bend, where the sheltered spot for the house that Repton had suggested the day before suddenly burst into view. Again he used his carriage to stand in for the mansion. This time, Upcher agreed.

Published only six months after Repton and Upcher had decided on the site for the approach to the house, *Pride and Prejudice* has Jane Austen's heroine Elizabeth Bennet encountering a scene that reads like Repton's proposal materialised:

> The park was very large, and contained great variety of ground. They entered it in one of its lowest points, and drove for some time through a beautiful wood, stretching over a wide extent.
>
> Elizabeth's mind was too full for conversation, but she saw and admired every remarkable spot and point of view. They gradually ascended for half a mile, and then found themselves at the top of a considerable eminence, where the wood ceased, and the eye was instantly caught by Pemberley House, situated on the opposite side of a valley, into which the road with some abruptness wound. It was a large, handsome, stone building, standing well on rising ground, and backed by a ridge of high woody hills . . .
>
> Elizabeth was delighted. She had never seen a place for which nature had done more, or where natural beauty had been so little counteracted by an awkward taste.

Sheltered by a wooded hill to the back, Mr Darcy's house, like Sheringham,

---

*Upcher had signed the agreement with Cook Flower in July 1811 and paid a 10 per cent deposit (£5250) in October 1811; the remaining £47,250 was due on 11 October 1812, when he would move into Sheringham; until then Flower had the right to live there (Agreement between Cook Flower and Abbot Upcher, 10 July 1811, Norfolk Record Office).

was set in a gently variegated park free of extravagance and conspicuous follies. It was approached along a road that slowly ascended through a beautiful forest. Leaving the woods with an abrupt curve, the road revealed the house suddenly, at the highest point in the park. When her sister asks Elizabeth when she fell in love with Darcy, she replies teasingly, 'I must date it from my first seeing his beautiful grounds at Pemberley' – Elizabeth is being playfully ironic here, but Darcy is nonetheless 'the best landlord and master . . . that ever lived'. Darcy's grounds are unpretentious, devoid of any sign of 'improvements' such as serpentine lakes or elaborate temples. And with this he reveals his modesty to his tenants as well as to Elizabeth – an impression Upcher too was sure he would achieve once he had implemented Repton's suggestions. 'Seeing almost immediately the way in which [a place] should be improved' was a talent of Repton's, and one he liked to boast about. Upcher assured him that he would 'never cease to thank him' for his invaluable help. A few days after Repton's first visit, on 23 June, he and Upcher were back at Sheringham. The weather was bad, but despite the gales they drove through the park, stopping at the site for the new entrance, where Repton measured the area for the gatekeeper's lodge and identified the spot where the new drive would meet the main road.

Humphry Repton's drawing of the approach and site
of the house before the improvements (with overlay), 1812

When the storm picked up, Upcher scrambled up the hill like an excited boy to the highest point so as to catch a glimpse of the raging sea below, while Repton, older and still disabled by his accident, slowly followed. Both thought the view 'grand beyond measure'. Then they returned to their chosen site for the house, where Repton 'made several arrangements', perhaps surveying the area, jotting down details, investigating the drainage prospects.

Thus ended the first stage of the consultation. For five days the two men, sometimes accompanied by Charlotte Upcher, had ranged over the estate, exchanging ideas, weighing up alternatives, pondering. Interestingly, they had also visited another of Repton's clients, which had allowed Upcher to see how the landscape designer could sulk when his suggestions were not taken up. In the evening he wrote in his diary: 'Repton [was] hurt at seeing his oaks cut down in the park and his plans which he had given to Mott [the client] so entirely departed from.' Upcher and Repton, in contrast, had grown close enough for Repton to be pleased by their 'intimacy' and 'confidence'; unlike many of his other clients, Upcher was neither a speculative businessman nor a grasping arriviste. Repton despised these nouveaux riches and their gaudy mansions, which he believed were designed on a whim and founded on greed and vanity. It

Humphry Repton's drawing of the approach and proposed house after improvements. Note his self-portrait on the right (without overlay), 1812

annoyed him, snob that he was, that a man was now judged by his income rather than by his lineage and upbringing. He observed with horror the ease with which these men of lower class – according to him, vulgar, avaricious and without taste – could now become gentlemen. To his despair, though, his financial situation forced him to work for them. Upcher, on the other hand, was a man after his own heart who believed in the traditional order of rural society, epitomising the conservative squirearchy of the time that Repton so admired. So he was happy to compliment the young man on having 'the prophetic eye of Taste'.

A few weeks after Repton had left Sheringham, in July 1812, Upcher received the new plans for the house and garden in the form of an elegant book bound in red leather – one of Repton's famous Red Books, three hundred of which he had already produced. They came in slim quarto or large folio format, the most prestigious commissions such as Sheringham being presented in the latter. Over thirty pages, neatly written in copperplate and illustrated with watercolours and drawings, the 'book' captured what Upcher and he had discussed at Sheringham, bringing alive their vision. Repton preferred his books because maps, which other designers such as Capability Brown and William Emes had used, could not adequately convey the breadth of his ideas. As with all his Red Books, Repton had equipped some of the illustrations with his ingenious 'before' and 'after' overlays: by lifting them up, Upcher could see at a glance how the empty valley at Sheringham was going to be transformed into his perfect home. In Repton's drawings hills could be raised, trees could be planted and lakes could be filled without the Upchers or their architect having to leave the warmth of the parlour. In fact, clients often enjoyed the Red Books more as entertaining novelties than as serious designs for the improvement of their homes. Walter Scott likened them to raree-shows, the popular peep-shows in boxes, only without the magnifying glass and the strings, and the painter Joseph Farington stayed up till midnight with friends 'amus[ing] ourselves in looking over Repton's red book'.

However Repton's clients used the Red Books, and even if the plans were not eventually implemented, his drawings captured their aspirations, transforming their ideas into more tangible form. As an accomplished watercolourist,

Repton knew how to present a landscape to its greatest advantage. As conversation pieces, the Red Books would be proudly shown by his clients to their friends, and they in turn might become new customers. Knowing that no one else had come up with such an effective sales tool, Repton even had used one as an advertisement in his bookseller's shop window, to invite subscriptions for his book *Sketches and Hints on Landscape Gardening* (1794). He had also sent a copy to Edmund Burke for his comments, and on another occasion had borrowed one back from a client to show to the king. The elegantly produced books, so much easier to handle than large maps, rarely failed to impress. Repton always pasted his business card prominently inside, thus ensuring that his reputation would spread across the country estates.

As a clever strategist, he would start by identifying his clients' different needs. At Sheringham, having perceived Upcher's modest refinement, he had concentrated on the '*Feasibility*' rather than on the '*Capabilities*' of the place. So apart from digging the foundations for the house, no levelling or other substantial earth-moving activities would be necessary. Most of the work related to the planting scheme: some of the trees at the bottoms of the hills would have to be removed, and others planted so as to hide the domestic–office wing and the stables next to the new house.

The only issue Repton was unsure about was the main façade – Upcher had not been able to make up his mind during their visit to Sheringham. So as to be certain to please his client, he suggested two different elevations, one he thought 'perhaps too plain', the other 'a little richer'. The only garden building he proposed was a round temple with six open arches, to be built at the top of the ridge three-quarters of a mile from the house in the direction of the village. This, Repton insisted, should be a recreational area for the community and for tourists. Were Upcher to allow visitors to picnic at the temple, they in turn would enliven the scene, turning it into a living tableau for the family to enjoy.

This was the first of many suggestions that indicated the ease with which Upcher could use his Red Book as a manual on how to display his paternalism. In the village, Repton pointed out, he should improve the workhouse by removing the boundary walls, as well as making a village green and embellishing it with what Repton called 'that almost forgotten Emblem of rural happiness & festivity', the maypole. In order to keep the villagers content, he further advised, Upcher should open his park once a month and after storms, allowing them to collect fallen branches for their fires. This, it was hoped, would help to improve the relationship between the tenants and their new land-lord, which had been threatened by the enclosure of Sheringham common the previous year. The 'Sheringham Inclosure Act' of 1811 had benefited Upcher by increasing the size of his estate by a quarter, adding '226 acres'. The villagers, by contrast, who had used the common for centuries to gather wood and graze their animals, had been left with only two small allotments. The enclosures also prevented the villagers from killing rabbits and birds on the common as had been their right – this had provoked incidents of poaching, a capital offence elsewhere in the county. To avoid such trouble, Repton suggested that Upcher should organise coursing days on the beach for the villagers. This was Upcher's favourite sport, and unlike hunting, which only involved the landlord and his guests, it would, Repton explained, promote 'a mutual intercourse betwixt the Land Lord, the Tenant, & the Labourer', creating 'the happy medium betwixt Licentious Equality & oppressive Tyranny'.

To manage this relationship, certain strategies would have to be put in place. The keeper would control access to the grounds – tourists would have

Humphry Repton's vision of Upcher and his tenants coursing on the beach, 1812

to sign in at the lodge, villagers would be allowed into the park only under his supervision, and the dates for coursing events and wood-gathering would be dictated by Upcher. In addition, the sheltered location of the house and its distance from the public part of the park would ensure that villagers and family would not encounter each other accidentally. The design of the house would further allow the Upchers to practise their benevolence towards the poor while remaining ensconced. The diagonal sides of the bay windows, which Repton introduced into the drawing- and dining-room, extended the field of vision to left and right, so that the Upchers could see 'the occasional glitter of Distant moving objects' – tourists, villagers and carriages on the new approach road – from the comfort of their chairs.

This time, Upcher was quick to make up his mind. '[Y]ou have presented me with the key,' he told Repton, to unlock the 'casket' in which Sheringham's beauty was concealed. With Repton's help, these hidden treasures had been revealed and now his designs could be implemented. Work was to begin as soon as Upcher took possession a few weeks hence. The money expended on Repton's fees had proved a sound investment, he was sure. For the Red Book Repton had charged around £40, and each visit to Sheringham cost Upcher twenty-five guineas, half of the designer's usual fee, on account of his sentimental policy of giving a 50 per cent discount to his Norfolk clients as this was his home county.*

They [Henry Tilney and his sister Eleanor] were viewing the country with the eyes of persons accustomed to drawing; and decided on its capability of being formed into pictures, with all the eagerness of real taste. Here Catherine was quite lost. She knew nothing of drawing – nothing of taste; and she listened to them

---

*There are no household accounts for Sheringham, so the sum of £40 is deduced from the fee for the Red Book for Uppark, which was of similar size and for which the owners paid £42 in 1814. Repton had a tiered system of charging according to the miles he had to travel: e.g., 70 guineas for trips up to 140 miles from London, 50 guineas for up to 100 miles (except for his Norfolk clients). This was based on a daily rate of 5 guineas, including travelling days and expenses (Repton to William Wyndham, 3 July 1808).

with an attention which brought her little profit, for they talked in phrases which conveyed scarcely any idea to her. The little which she could understand, however, appeared to contradict the very few notions she had entertained on the matter before. It seemed as if a good view were no longer to be taken from the top of a high hill, and that a clear blue sky was no longer a proof of a fine day. She was heartily ashamed of her ignorance.

. . .

In the present instance, she confessed and lamented her want of knowledge; declared that she would give anything in the world to be able to draw; and a lecture on the picturesque immediately followed, in which his [Henry Tilney's] instructions were so clear that she soon began to see beauty in everything admired by him; and her attention was so earnest, that he became perfectly satisfied of her having a great deal of natural taste. He talked of foregrounds, distances, and second distances – side-screens and perspectives – lights and shades; and Catherine was so hopeful a scholar, that when they gained the top of Beechen Cliff, she voluntarily rejected the whole city of Bath, as unworthy to make part of a landscape.

Here in *Northanger Abbey* Jane Austen describes the reactions of the untutored Catherine Morland to the instructions of Henry Tilney, an educated and well-read clergyman, on how to judge a landscape. Like many of his contemporaries, Tilney was familiar with William Gilpin's writings on the picturesque, in which the quality of a landscape depended on how it would look in a painting. Reeling off a catalogue of dogmatic criteria, Tilney reveals his own uncritical approach, which leads Catherine to dismiss the entire city of Bath in her eagerness to please him. In *Sense and Sensibility* Austen's criticism of the picturesque is more explicit, for although passionate about the movement, the heroine Marianne Dashwood reminds the reader that the 'improvement' of landscapes has declined into a shallow exercise – has 'become a mere jargon'.

Doctor Syntax sketching a lake, 1812

When Austen published *Sense and Sensibility* in 1811, the picturesque had fallen out of favour with the educated elite, who now mocked it as simplistic and rather foolhardy. Its widespread popularity had lost the concept its value as an indicator of refinement. Now, just about everything was evaluated by just about everyone according to picturesque principles – even women could be classified as such, as long as they had ringlets and sparkling eyes like Charlotte Upcher. One of the most witty satires was published in 1812 by the poet William Combe and the caricaturist Thomas Rowlandson. In *The Tour of Doctor Syntax in Search of the Picturesque* they modelled their protagonist, a poor schoolmaster cleric who was touring Britain, on tourist *par excellence* William Gilpin. During his pointless journey, Doctor Syntax stumbles from one absurd situation to the next: he makes 'a Landscape of a Post', he falls into a river while admiring a ruin, and is attacked by a bull when sketching. Three decades after Gilpin had made the picturesque popular, it had become the subject of ridicule.

The rise and fall of the picturesque also paralleled Repton's career. In the late 1780s his inspiration had been the fathers of the movement, Gilpin, William Mason and Rousseau's patron the Marquis de Giardin. Back then, Repton would have agreed with Giardin that 'no scene in nature should be attempted till it has first been painted', but only a few years later, by 1794, he had changed his mind. In a public battle of letters, essays and poems between him and the gentlemen improvers Uvedale Price and Richard Payne Knight, Repton insisted that his experience as a professional had taught him that 'convenience' in a garden was more important than achieving picturesque effects. Known as the 'Picturesque Controversy', this became a defining moment in gardening, marking the divide between designs based purely on the aesthetics of painting and those that took utility and function into consideration.[*]

A painting was static, Repton argued, whereas a garden was constantly in motion: the foliage changed colour with the seasons; light and shade depended on the time of day; visitors moved from one viewpoint to another. In addition, Repton was determined to include in his designs practical considerations, such as the owner's social position and the function of the estate within the locality. A gentleman's house should not look like a farm any more than a squire's should pretend to be a palace. Repton included in his gardens details that mirrored the professions and the actual backgrounds of his clients: ruins and ancient trees for aristocrats, vistas overlooking mills and factories for industrialists, rural life in the form of cornfields and cattle for Upcher. With this step Repton turned his back on the picturesque: unlike Payne Knight and Price, he would no longer take taste and aesthetics as his leading principles.

In parallel with Repton's intensifying disavowal of the picturesque, Austen's views move from subtle irony to scepticism, as can been seen in the increasing shallowness of her protagonists who favour the concept. Thus in *Sense and Sensibility*, begun as *Elinor and Marianne* in 1795 at the height of the picturesque craze, Marianne who adores unkempt landscapes is depicted as a lovable if sometimes selfish character; and in *Pride and Prejudice*, written a year later, Elizabeth Bennet only gently mocks the concept when, taking leave of her companions out walking, she says: 'You are charmingly group'd and appear to uncommon advantage. The picturesque would be spoilt by admitting a fourth. Good bye.' In *Northanger Abbey*, Catherine in her aping of Tilney's ideas is

---

[*]The publication that opened this controversy was Payne Knight's *The Landscape, a Didactic Poem Addressed to Uvedale Price*, in April 1794. In response, Repton added a chapter to his forthcoming *Sketches and Hints on Landscape Gardening*, also published in 1794 – late enough to include a reply to Price's *Essays on the Picturesque*, published in May 1794.

William Gilpin's 'Composition of Cows', which was intended to demonstrate that
three cows make a picturesque scene, while four do not. It was this kind of advice that
Austen ridiculed in *Pride and Prejudice*

naïve; but the culmination of Austen's criticism is the frivolous and morally
flawed Mary Crawford in *Mansfield Park*, begun in 1811, who declares that 'had
I a place of my own in the country, I should be most thankful to any Mr Repton
who would undertake it, and give me as much beauty as he could for my money'.
Not having thought through the consequences of making picturesque 'improvements' to an estate, Mary would happily destroy avenues, raze villages and hide
the church from view. She and the others in the book who support Mr
Rushworth's idea of employing Repton are presented as selfish, ignorant and
irresponsible.

By the time Repton came to design Sheringham, he had long since abandoned the pure picturesque. So, where Uvedale Price was still campaigning for broken boulders and thickets to embellish a foreground, Repton was casting a more practical eye. If Upcher and his family wanted to use their garden, they needed gravel paths to walk on rather than Price's dishevelled walkways, which might look pretty in a painting but would tear their clothes and dirty their shoes. Repton had included some fixed 'stations' that would frame certain vistas, such as the bend on the approach road and the prospect on to the temple from the dining-room; but neither he nor his client was interested in turning Sheringham into a tableau. On the contrary, most of the improvements were to be based on practicality combined with a sense of moral duty. Sheringham was designed to reflect its function as a family home and source of income for the Upchers, and so Repton would set the house in a working landscape.

Repton was pleased with his Red Book for Sheringham, certain that Upcher would listen to his advice rather than treat the drawings as a pretty picture book. The fee from Sheringham eased his finances, and his health was improving. In mid-November 1812, he boasted to his son William that he had earned more than £200 in a month on other jobs alone. Four weeks later, though, his hopes for a carefree future were dashed once again when a client went bankrupt owing him £2000, and he was told by 'the walking talking Essex Gazette' – the local gossip – that Abbot Upcher 'had gone mad'. The truth was that Upcher and his family had arrived at Sheringham a month before, but since the work on the mansion had not even begun they had had to move into the rambling old farmhouse. The inconvenience of living in the chaotic assortment of rooms and outbuildings was further exacerbated by the fact that the former owner Cook Flower had not removed all his belongings. Upcher tended to panic when under pressure, but this time it was serious. The national crisis cannot have helped, either: the bad harvest brought little profit for even the best-run estates, and many people were starving. America had recently declared war on Britain, while the fighting with France continued.

Within days of moving in, Upcher, in his anxiety, tried to sell Sheringham.

But the property market was falling, and the only offer he received was 40 per cent less than he had paid, so he refused it. Instead, he told his solicitor to hurry forward the sale of his farms in Sussex – tied up in them was money he desperately needed for his investments at Sheringham. But here too problems halted the transactions. Two days later Upcher collapsed, seized by a 'nervous fever'. When the local doctor proved unable to provide the necessary medical help, Charlotte decided to move her husband and children to London, where she hoped to find better medical facilities. On receiving this news, Repton went instantly to Upcher's doctor in order to hear at first hand to what extent his fees were in peril: if Upcher's health deteriorated further, Sheringham's improvements would have to be cancelled. When the doctor revealed in confidence the diagnosis of 'great depression', Repton feared the worst and began to look for other work. He had in mind the Nelson Trust, which had wanted to purchase an estate with sea views for the recently ennobled Nelson family. Four years earlier Repton had encouraged them to buy Sheringham, but they had demurred because the estate lacked a mansion. Now, he confided in William, he hoped that he might still 'benefit from building the house' if the Trust were to see his exquisite drawings; and if Upcher still wanted to sell the estate.

Quizzing the doctor again, Repton learned that Upcher was only too happy to get rid of Sheringham. So an interview with the Nelson Trust for the following week was speedily arranged and Repton began to prepare his pitch. To his son he sent a letter with a list of questions covering all possible subjects the Trust might raise. William was to find out if the Walpoles, Sheringham's neighbours, would be willing to sell some of their land – just in case the Trust had something bigger in mind. He was also to enquire as to whether Flower could annul the sale so that William, as agent, could sell it again. 'Consider on the Sale of such an estate you ought to have a percentage. Your advice added 2500,' Repton wrote, finishing the letter smugly: '. . . the odd 500 should be yours – ha! Slap.'

Brimming with confidence, Repton had no doubt that his 'most striking views' of Sheringham would convince the Trust to buy the property. But before he could speak to them, Upcher recovered and announced that he would not be selling Sheringham after all. Four weeks later, in January 1813, he returned to Norfolk to 'take very great pleasure in Farming'.

Six months afterwards Humphry Repton and his other son John Adey, also an architect and his father's assistant, arrived at Sheringham to stake out the site for the house and the adjoining plot, which would contain a flower garden. The contrast between this manicured part of the garden and the often rough sea beyond would be one of Sheringham's main attractions: '[N]ear the house, a more artificial neatness is expected & Art may boldly be avowed,' Repton held forth in the Red Book. This use of flowers in the area around the house marked a turning-point in the English landscape garden, for until now temples, lawns and long vistas had predominated. Decades earlier, both Lord Kames in his *Elements of Criticism* (1762) and Horace Walpole in his *History of Modern Taste in Gardening* (1771) had advocated such 'neatness', but few had been influenced by their views, and lawns sweeping down from the house were still fashionable. Although many gardeners had continued to grow flowers – even Capability Brown had designed flowerbeds – they would be situated at some distance from the house.* There were a few exceptions, such as Lady Elizabeth Lee who in 1799 had proudly shown off the flowerbeds below her windows at Hartwell in Buckinghamshire, most of them coming into flower from early to late summer, to coincide with her visitors. Elsewhere, though, the bright blooms of the type that had filled the formal parterres at Hatfield and Hampton Court had been hidden away in secluded corners and shrubberies, invisible from the main viewing-points. Lord Cobham at Stowe had kept his flowers behind high walls and Richard Hill had tucked his away in Amphitrite's Garden next to the Dutch-style cottage he had called Neptune's Whim. Where flowers were allowed to figure they were often relegated to the female sphere, such as Lady Wake's Garden at Courteenhall in Northamptonshire designed by Repton, the shrubbery laid out by Brown called Lady Griffin's Garden at Audley End in Essex, and Marianne's Garden at Hafod in Wales.

*A few of Brown's gardens featured flowering shrubberies, for example at Petworth in West Sussex, Syon House near London and Belhus in Essex. He laid out formal beds at Brocklesby in Lincolnshire, in 1772.

The flowerbeds at Nuneham Courtenay in Oxfordshire

But Repton roundly rejected any subsidiary role for flowers. He now proposed beds below what would be the drawing- and dining-rooms at Sheringham. Even for him this was rather an about-turn: only ten years earlier he had maintained that flowers should always be kept away from the house. Interestingly, the kind of eye-catching display he now approved of was supported by an unlikely ally: Richard Payne Knight, who had persuaded the Earl of Powis to preserve the late seventeenth-century hanging terraces flanking Powis Castle, when William Emes (Hawkstone's lake designer) had proposed blowing them up and replacing them with a sloping lawn.

For the planting schemes at Sheringham, Repton had been influenced by the circular and kidney-shaped beds that dotted the lawn at Nuneham Courtenay in Oxfordshire (although these were still some way from the house and from the landscaped park). The poet William Mason had devised them four decades earlier, and Repton had long admired the dramatic effect of the 'clumps',* created

*In his *Observations on the Theory and Practice of Landscape Gardening* (1803), Repton, in describing the garden at Nuneham, had insisted that flowers should be separated from the rest of the garden. It was since then that he had placed similar flowerbeds near the house at Woburn Abbey in Bedfordshire, and in his proposal for the Brighton Pavilion.

by the different heights of the flowers. Low-growing plants such as box and pinks edged the taller ones, which peaked towards the centre of the bed with sunflowers, hollyhocks and climbers such as staked sweet peas. Bearing a close resemblance to raked seats in an auditorium, this was called 'theatrical' planting. Along the paths of the Elysian Fields at Stowe, William Kent had devised a similarly tiered scheme with evergreen shrubs, but the effect could not have been more different from Repton's beds. Where Kent's intention had been to create a 'natural' look with the subtle shades of different greens, Repton's flowerbeds would give Sheringham the feeling of neatness that for a century had been excluded from the area immediately next to the house.

The designs in the Red Book showed how Repton would emphasise this formality by edging the beds with a low fence, giving the impression that the flowers were growing out of a basket. In France, these *corbeilles* (literally, 'baskets') were a popular way of displaying plants, though Repton simplified their elaborate and often multi-levelled design with a plainer device – the little fence – to separate the lawn from the beds. The idea was to fill them with masses of differently coloured and scented flowering plants – Repton often recommended dwarf roses as the low-growers, and sweet-scented honey-

A basket for a flowerbed designed by Repton's son, John Adey, for Lady Suffield at Blickling Hall in Norfolk, 1823

suckles, lilacs, hollyhocks and other tall flowers for the centre.* Although he
was not an accomplished horticulturist, he loved natural fragrances wafting
into the house – another reason for suggesting roses and jasmines. A plant's
sensual characteristics – its perfume and look – were what appealed to him,
rather than rarity or exotic origin. However, the gales that came in off the sea
posed particular problems when it came to planting flowers at Sheringham. To
overcome them, Repton proposed an 'artificial screen' of trellis construction,
which would shield some of the more delicate shrubs and flowering plants as
well as to provide for the climbers. Unlike the more natural way of growing
flowers at Hartwell and Nuneham, Sheringham's plants would be sculpted over
arches and arbours, similar to the architectural ornaments of seventeenth-
century gardens.

Chiming in with his vision of society, formal planting, Repton said, represented 'the happy medium between the wildness of nature and the stiffness of
art; in the same manner as the English constitution is the happy medium between
the liberty of savages, and the restraint of despotic government'. To him, the
unruliness of sublime landscapes and picturesque gardens symbolised rebellion,
which did not appeal to his increasing conservatism. So he relegated the picturesque to points further and further away from the house, and sought to reflect
a hierarchical society through well ordered planting schemes near the house.
Separated from the rest of the parkland by a fence rather than what he called
the 'deceitful' ha-ha, the flower garden at Sheringham was not meant to look
as if it was part of nature. It was, Repton was not unhappy to admit, an 'artificial object'. Just because he was using 'Natures materials', he explained to
Upcher, did not mean that the garden would have to appear natural – otherwise, 'houses should resemble Caves and hollow Trees, because they are built
of Stone & Timber'.

Two weeks after Repton's visit, in July 1813, the family assembled at the

---

*There are few surviving details about Repton's plant recommendations. In 1809 he wrote to
a Mr Beauparke advising on the use of dwarf roses, honeysuckles, lilacs and laburnums. For
Woburn Abbey (1804) he recommended hydrangea, Portugal laurels and hollyhocks; at Langley
Park in Kent (1790) he suggested honeysuckle and roses for the flowerbeds, and at Cobham
Hall in Kent he planted roses and jasmine along the walls of the house.

site of the house for a little ceremony to inagurate the building work. Upcher's eldest son, three-year-old Henry, laid the first foundation stone, then each member of the family laid a stone in turn, until one-year-old Emma lost her balance and fell into the wet mortar. A few weeks later there was another accident, when the roof of the cellar gave in, but by mid-November the foundations, the cellar and the upper terrace wall had been completed.

With the house in the making, Upcher turned his attention to some of Repton's other suggestions in the Red Book. Having promised to look after the 'poor and needy' in the neighbourhood, Upcher began to improve the estate for his tenants in order to provide clean and neat accommodation – caring for them just as Jane Austen's Emma cared for the poor at Highbury.

> They were now approaching the cottage, and all idle topics were superseded. Emma was very compassionate; and the distresses of the poor were as sure of relief from her personal attention and kindness, her counsel and her patience, as from her purse. She understood their ways, could allow for their ignorance and their temptations, had no romantic expectations of extraordinary virtue from those for whom education had done so little; entered into their troubles with ready sympathy, and always gave her assistance with as much intelligence as good-will. In the present instance, it was sickness and poverty together which she came to visit; and after remaining there as long as she could give comfort or advice, she quitted the cottage with such an impression of the scene as made her say to Harriet, as they walked away,
>
> 'These are the sights, Harriet, to do one good. How trifling they make every thing else appear! – I feel now as if I could think of nothing but these poor creatures all the rest of the day; and yet, who can say how soon it may all vanish from my mind?'
>
> 'Very true,' said Harriet. 'Poor creatures! one can think of nothing else.'
>
> 'And really, I do not think the impression will soon be over,'

said Emma, as she crossed the low hedge, and tottering footstep which ended the narrow, slippery path through the cottage garden, and brought them into the lane again. 'I do not think it will,' stopping to look once more at all the outward wretchedness of the place, and recall the still greater within.

Upcher was similarly concerned and so among other gestures of goodwill he glazed the cottages and painted them yellow, settled the feud between two families, and persuaded the son of one of his tenant farmers to marry his mistress. On Christmas Day 1813, the servants and their families had dinner together in Upcher's kitchen, their children socialising with his. Abbot Upcher, whose piety matched his name, regularly read the Bible to his servants; he also pulled down the old workhouse and painted the village church. In addition, Charlotte Upcher set up a school and a Female Friendly Society. Repton was sure that the villagers, were they called upon to do so, would 'rise at night to serve the Liberal Patron'.

Upcher also planted trees, and pruned according to Repton's instructions to improve the existing woods. Repton also advised him to extend the woods that the previous owner Flower had planted on the lower slopes of the hills. Upcher embraced this idea with enthusiasm, recording his successes in detail in his journal – indeed, it became one of his favourite pastimes. He studded his land with chestnuts and beeches, birches and poplars, and extended the old woods with mountain ashes, sycamores and oaks. Tree-planting was popular at this time. So much so that the Society for the Encouragement of Arts, Manufactures and Commerce awarded medals for outstanding achievements. The Earl of Moray had raised almost eight million trees on his estate; Thomas Johnes at Hafod in Wales and Upcher's neighbour Thomas Coke at Holkham had nurtured similar millions. Many such landowners cultivated fast-growing species such as larches and firs to cater for the increasing demand for timber; but Upcher's aim, rather than making money from his trees, was to leave his mark on the landscape with specimens that would mature long after his death. Given that the deciduous hardwoods he chose would take several generations to grow to their full height, Upcher was here affirming his belief in the future and in his descendants. The

trees represented longevity and a connection with the earth – an image treasured and admired by his contemporaries. With their roots anchored in the
ground and their majestic crowns swaying in the wind, trees were seen not only
as beautiful but also as symbols of stability and continuity. Portrait painters
such as Johann Zoffany and Gainsborough used venerable old specimens in
their paintings to emphasise their sitters' social importance; Alexander Pope had
thought a tree 'a nobler object than a prince in his coronation robes'.

For Repton, on an estate such as Sheringham only hardwoods expressed
the right message. Others might plant for quick profit, but a gentleman should
concentrate on the slow-growers. Payne Knight agreed with him on this point,
advising in his poem *The Landscape* (1794) to plant oaks and elms in order to
'Banish the formal fir's unsocial shade'. Oak was the favourite. For the poet
William Cowper it was the 'Lord of the woods', and Edmund Burke had
compared the aristocracy to 'the great oaks which shade a country'. They were
the only trees named specifically in Sheringham's Red Book – in the form of
a grove enveloping the house from the back.

Already in 1664, in *Sylva* – the only English bestseller on forestry ever
written – John Evelyn was encouraging landowners to look after their forests
as future timber for the Navy, rather than putting their land into tillage. In times
of war the patriotic symbolism had become even more pointed:

> While Oceans breath may blast a Single tree
> England's combined Oaks resist the Sea.
> Emblem of Strength, increas'd by Unity . . .

Repton wrote in the Red Book, reminding Upcher that Sheringham's oaks not
only symbolised England's naval supremacy, but their 'bent & distorted' shapes
had been wrought by the ocean winds, the same force that would blow England's
ships across the sea to victory against France.

Much of the planting was along the new approach through the Great
Wood, for which Repton had given Upcher precise instructions during his
numerous visits. Although many landowners still built approaches that circuited
their estates to show off their size, this was a mistake, Repton had pointed out:

'The most obvious meaning of an *approach* . . . was simply this – A ROAD
TO THE HOUSE.' Rather than surrounding the park, Sheringham's approach
should offer the prospect of a variegated landscape as well as displaying the
house. Much of the approach should be edged by wooded areas, Repton advised,
and by March 1814 Upcher had extended the existing wood with two small belts
of trees. Repton instructed that small groups of a single species be arranged
together according to their colours, rather than mixing individual trees of
different sorts as picturesque improvers had done. Objecting to the 'reoccurrence
of the same mixture' over and over again, Repton claimed that picturesque
planting was in fact as monotonous as planting only one sort of tree.

He advised Upcher to mix deciduous trees with thorns, which would act
as 'nurses' for the trees, protecting them from grazing deer and cattle. Upcher
planted nine kinds of thorn in clumps of three, mixed in with sycamore and
beech, along the right-hand side of the driveway where the ridge, which the
road followed, dipped suddenly on to the flatter part of the estate. The much
prized view of the sea was mostly hidden by the old woods, so Repton recommended targeted pruning to create 'peeps'. Also, more trees should be planted,
he said, in order to thicken certain areas, and so Upcher included some spruce
and silver firs to 'darken the Wood'. To the left of the driveway he planted
oaks mixed with spruce; the fast-growing softwoods would protect the oaks
from the harsh winds and would be thinned out later to give the hardwoods
more space. Upcher's anxieties about the future seemed forgotten; he wrote
contentedly in his diary on 22 February: 'Prayers, pruning in wood, farming,
domesticated and happy'. When not occupied with estate business he spent time
with his family, sometimes dancing with the children while Charlotte accompanied them on the piano. He and his eldest son also had fun catching rats in
the barn.

The Upchers were no doubt as relieved as anyone else of their class when reports
arrived from France in April 1814 that the allied army had marched into Paris
on 31 March and forced Napoleon to abdicate, restoring the Bourbon monarchy
and putting Louis XVIII on the throne. By May, with Napoleon banished to the
island of Elba, a peace treaty had been signed, and in June the Upchers went to

London to celebrate the end of twenty-one years of almost continuous hostilities. All summer the city was in jubilant mood: public parties were held in the parks, with masquerades at the Vauxhall pleasure gardens, and the prince regent gave many private fêtes; in prominent areas, windows were rented out for fifty guineas to view the celebrities parading in the streets. The Upchers were 'irresistibly compelled' to watch the war heroes marching through the capital. As they arrived in London the prince was organising the biggest celebratory party London had ever seen: the architect John Nash had transformed Hyde Park, Green Park and St James's Park with pagodas, temples, a Chinese bridge and other eastern-style follies. A mock naval battle on the Serpentine in Hyde Park re-enacted the victory at Trafalgar, water rockets spouted and fireworks illuminated the night. The highlight of the party was the sending-up in smoke of the 'Castle of Discord' – a Gothic folly made of canvas symbolising the horrors of war – to re-emerge as the 'Temple of Concord'.

On his return to Sheringham, Abbot Upcher set about sowing more of his heathland with wheat in order to increase profits. He also built a laundry and a lodge for his gamekeeper, and repaired several of the farmhouses on the estate. The most exciting project of the winter of 1814 and the following spring, though, was the completion of the approach to the house, which Upcher believed was Repton's 'masterpiece'. The road ran straight along the 150-foot ridge up to the large bend, a natural focal point that Repton had named 'The Turn'. Here the hill had been excavated to make the descent to the house less steep. Repton had insisted that the road's embankments along the southern boundary be left rough and abrupt, rather than smoothed over or covered with turf or gravel. The road itself, on the other hand, was manmade, and so should be acknowledged as 'a work of art', he pointed out in the Red Book. Once again, as with his advocacy of the neat flower garden, Repton rejected the idea of natural gardening that had prevailed since the days of Lord Cobham at Stowe. His readiness to admit artificiality back into the landscape was a move in the direction of the next generation of gardeners, who would champion geometrical parterres, sculpted terraces and even topiary – features that for a century had displeased anybody who claimed to have taste.

Though the end of the war came as a relief and the improvements to his estate were beginning to pay dividends, Upcher, like many others, became increasingly worried about the country's economy. Two hundred thousand demobilised soldiers were flooding into the already strained labour market and half of the government's revenue was being swallowed up by the interest payments on the debts accumulated during two decades of war. To the farmers' despair trade embargoes were lifted, allowing the import of cheap foreign grain, and as wheat prices plummeted, landowners suffered: Upcher's wheat was selling at only half the wartime price, making his tenants hesitate to sign new leases at the previous rent.* To restrict foreign competition, in early 1815 Parliament passed the controversial Corn Laws whereby foreign wheat was to be sold in Britain only when the home price had reached eighty shillings a quarter. This kept basic food prices artificially high, but Upcher and other landowners believed that without the Corn Laws 'the Agriculture of England must have perish[ed]'. Most of the population, needless to say, was incensed. Riots broke out across the country, and on 17 March that year the unrest hit Norfolk, when a mob turned against Upcher and his neighbour Thomas Coke at an agricultural show in Norwich. Stones and brickbats hailed down on them, forcing them to flee to the nearest inn. There a thousand of the rioters continued their assault and, fearing for their lives, Upcher and Coke fled through a back door, leaving the mayor and the militia to sort out the mayhem.

Three days later, Napoleon, who had escaped from Elba, marched triumphantly into Paris, promising to restart the war. Within three months, however, he had been defeated by the English and Prussian army at the battle of Waterloo and sent into exile on St Helena. Charlotte Upcher, like the rest of Britain, was jubilant: 'This is a happy world after all,' she wrote in her commonplace book; while Repton, who was slowly recovering from a nine-month relapse of his recurring attacks of *angina pectoris*, from which he had been suffering since his carriage accident in 1811, worried that 'kingdoms [were being] raised and kicked down like a child's house of cards'. Perhaps the miseries of war had triggered in the ageing landscape gardener thoughts on his own

---

*Wheat sold for 110–120 shillings per quarter (28 pounds) in 1811 compared to 40–50 shillings in 1815. (Wade Martins, 1980, pp. 11, 14).

mortality. His legacy, the gardens he had taken so much pride in, was an ephemeral one, he knew. 'I should rejoice to have my name recorded by your power of conferring immortality,' he wrote to his old friend the botanist Sir James Edward Smith. But Smith, perhaps doubting Repton's horticultural expertise, politely ignored his request to name a climbing plant after him.

Instead, as we saw in the opening lines of this chapter, it was Jane Austen who immortalised Repton, although not in the way he had aspired to. Linking him with the nouveaux riches, with the morally inferior and with the superficial characters in her novel – all of them 'improvers' – Austen used Repton as a means of criticising the very value system he himself came to despise. More mockery followed in 1816, when Thomas Love Peacock in his novel *Headlong Hall* depicted a landscape designer 'of the first celebrity', one Mr Milestone, who was clearly based on Repton. Again Repton was ridiculed – by implication – this time not for his clients but for gardens that 'are nothing but big bowling greens, like sheets of green paper, with a parcel of round clumps scattered over them . . . and a solitary animal here and there looking as if it were lost'. Peacock's Mr Milestone is ignorant and preposterous, a garden designer who follows unquestioningly the fashion of the day. It must have stung Repton to be cast as a mere 'improver', given that his attachment to tradition and his criticism of society were not unlike Austen's. In fact, in his later designs, at Ashridge, Beaudesert and Endsleigh, all carried out the previous year, his nostalgic view of the past was clearly evident: witness the formal flowerbeds, terraces and secluded gardens he included there. Both Peacock's and Austen's satire was based on Repton's earlier work, so radically different from these later gardens.

At Ashridge in Hertfordshire he designed for the Earl of Bridgewater a garden composed of fifteen sections, evoking the idea of Elizabethan 'garden rooms'. They included a rosarium, a mount garden, topiary and flower-embroidered parterres. At Beaudesert in Warwickshire and at Endsleigh in Devon he had laid out formal flowerbeds, reminiscent of the baroque gardens of the late seventeenth century. In fact Repton had reinvented himself – he surely would now have agreed with Burke and Austen that garden and landscape 'improvements' often destroyed valuable traditions. Such improvements had been regarded as a mark of sophistication, until the French Revolution; then, in the light of the violence committed in its name, Burke had warned that the rush to change old institutions could easily become a destructive exercise unless one kept the 'whole in mind'. Like Burke, Austen had made the link between measured reforms within the state and reforms within a landed estate, between seismic shifts in society and the destruction of old avenues, plantations, even whole villages. Repton had 'destroyed' many a traditional garden during his career, but he came to regard the formal gardens of the sixteenth and seventeenth centuries as symbolic of a better society. His change of direction came too late, though, to save his reputation. Unfortunately for him, his vanity – George III, among others, called him a 'coxcomb' – also made him the perfect target for satire.

Despite this, however, the improvements made to Sheringham were judicious rather than radical or destructive. And Upcher was determined that his legacy should not be 'transient, as the snowflake on the bosom of our ocean', he told Charlotte. To increase the estate's productivity and at the same time provide a safe future for his descendants, he now dedicated his mornings to agricultural matters. On visits to nearby Holkham, where Thomas Coke had achieved an international reputation for his sophisticated farming methods, Upcher admired the weed-free land, declaring that the fields were 'like Gardens'. Coke had invested his profits back into his business instead of frittering them away in London, as so many landowners did. Highly mechanised processes, long-term contracts for his tenants and crop-rotation clauses in their leases had doubled the yields.

Back home, having taken Repton's advice, Upcher put his newly acquired knowledge into practice. In April 1816 the labourers drilled two bushels of barley into the area immediately beyond the flower garden in front of the new house. Upcher could hardly have devised a more visible way of incorporating the working life of his estate into the garden. From the drawing- and dining-rooms the family and their guests would now look out on orderly cornfields instead of a sweeping expanse of lawn. This, of course, was against all the rules of picturesque gardening – only a few years before, Gilpin had dismissed agricultural landscapes because 'the regularity of cornfields disgusts; and the colour of corn, especially near harvest, is out of tune with everything else'. Even Repton, only a decade earlier, had insisted that setting a field in the pleasure grounds of a house was comparable to introducing a 'pig sty into the recesses of the drawing room'.

Given the current scarcity of food, however, a cornfield now signalled patriotic as well as practical intent. Norfolk was at the centre of the food riots at this time, so Upcher knew that he had to feed his workers as well as pay them wages. Elsewhere, tenants unable to pay their rents were abandoning their farms; and to make matters worse, in May a drop in temperature to 5 degrees centigrade marked the beginning of what would become the coldest summer of the century: the harvest promised to be disastrous. Now, the view of corn-fields whose flat, straight lines had so recently been regarded as irreconcilable with picturesque aesthetics, served to express Upcher's hope for better times. In addition, Repton explained in his Red Book, 'at seed time & at harvest it may be enlivened by Men as well as beasts', thereby '<u>humanizing</u>, as well as <u>animating</u> beautiful Scenery'. Just as painters imbued images of agricultural activity with the traditional values of stability and security, so the cornfield was a moral statement, and Upcher was proud of his working estate. Unlike the gardens at Stowe, there was nothing neoclassical about the pastoral scene presented by Sheringham: labourers – ploughing, reaping, harvesting – played an essential role, as portrayed in many of Constable's paintings.*

When Repton and his son arrived at Sheringham in June 1816 for what they called a 'love-visit', they were impressed by Upcher's progress. The main body of the house was well under way and it seemed likely that it would be finished within the original estimate of just over £7000.† By late summer, it would be ready for the plasterers and painters to start work. Although the

---

*Since the outbreak of the war with France in 1793 the number of paintings with rural subjects exhibited at the Royal Academy had risen dramatically. It had become an acceptable subject for art.

†The original estimate was £7195 19s 8d excluding carriage for building materials; by September 1816, when the house was almost finished, expenses had risen to almost £6000, which presum-ably left enough over to keep within budget (Building Account, Sheringham, 1815–17, Norfolk Record Office).

approach had been finished, as had the main tree-planting schemes, Repton was still able to help with many of the finer details. Upcher was pleased that his visitors 'were indefatigable in their exertion to improve [the] grounds, views from the Bower [the house], and thousand other things'. By the end of the year the office wing with the servant hall, kitchen and nursery had been completed. The roofers had finished the slating, the internal walls and ceilings were all in place. The six joiners and carpenters, who had come specially from London to make the doors and windows, had departed. Repton had finalised the layout for the flowerbeds, the kitchen garden had been planted, and the family had eaten the first of their own produce – a dish of peas. The first pieces of furniture – beds, carpets, tables and even books – had been installed; moving-in day was imminent.

But then, in early 1817, a few days after Charlotte and Abbot had inspected the fields and visited their tenants, Upcher came down with a 'violent inflammatory fever', as Charlotte described it in her commonplace book. Charlotte was devastated, writing to Repton that she feared her children might lose 'the most affectionate of fathers'; Sheringham, 'that once happy paradise', meant nothing to her without her husband. Sending helpful instructions on 'what to stop and what to finish' on the estate, Repton tried to ease her pain, but when, amidst the chaos, the clerk of works suddenly died, all building activity stopped. Repton himself was tired and ill. Sensing that his life too was nearing its end, his 'favourite & darling child in Norfolk ceased to be an object of delight'.

On his doctor's recommendation Abbot Upcher left Sheringham and his beloved children in March, staying first with Charlotte's father in Kirby Cane, Norfolk, before moving to Brompton in Kent. The prognosis was not encouraging, and Charlotte sent for their solicitor to make her husband's will. Jane Austen, also ill, was at that moment writing the last words of *Sanditon*, the novel she would never finish. Two months later, she too left her home on the advice of her apothecary, to be looked after by a doctor in Winchester, the nearest city to her. Lying in bed or on a sofa, she enjoyed looking out of the bay window on to her landlord's garden; but despite the rest and medical care her health deteriorated rapidly, and in July she died. Eight months later, Repton died – unexpectedly, before his favourite client. But Upcher was soon to follow and, like Jane Austen, he never returned home, dying at the age of thirty-four in February 1819 of a stroke at a rented cottage in Kent. The day after his death his mourning widow cut off all her long ringlets and intertwined them with locks of her children's hair, and with one of Upcher's. On the ribbon with which she tied the hair together she wrote the word 'united', and laid it around Abbot's neck. For a fortnight she sat next to her dead husband, praying and grieving her loss, before setting off on the sad journey home. When she arrived, Charlotte decided to stay in the old farmhouse, still standing, and filled with memories of happier days. Sheringham was abandoned, still awaiting portico, terraces and flowering plants for the garden. Another twenty years would pass before his son Henry completed Sheringham, and Upcher's dreams were fulfilled.

6

The Genius of Man: Chatsworth

'Art beats nature altogether there.'
Charles Darwin about Chatsworth's Great Conservatory,
28 October 1845

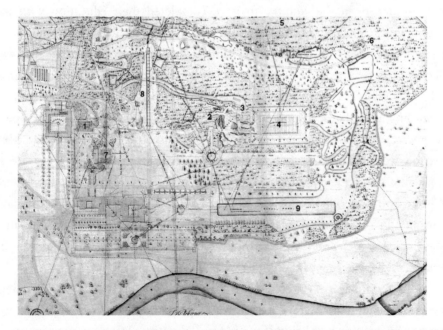

Chatsworth in 1858. 1 Orchid houses built in 1834 2 Rock Garden 3 Coal hole for Great
Conservatory 4 Great Conservatory 5 Flue for Conservatory 6 Pinetum with aboretum and
serpentine walks 7 Converted greenhouse with formal flower garden 8 Cascade
9 Canal pond with Emperor's Fountain

Just after midnight on 8 May 1826 Joseph Paxton arrived by coach from London in Chesterfield in Derbyshire. At half past four in the morning, just before sunrise and after a twelve-mile moonlit walk across the windswept moors of the Peak District, he climbed over the park gates of one of the largest estates in England: Chatsworth. This was the first time the young man saw the garden that he would shape, and that would shape his future, inspiring him to design the Crystal Palace, the most iconic building of nineteenth-century Britain.

The youngest of nine children, the twenty-two-year-old Paxton had left his father's small Bedfordshire farm seven years before to pursue a career in gardening. Driven by the twin passions that would forge his professional life, technology and botany, he had apprenticed himself to a renowned horticulturist. With him Paxton had worked on hothouses and on fruit cultivation, and had perfected his engineering skills with the construction of a large lake. For the last three years, he had worked as an under-gardener at the Horticultural Society garden in London. When he arrived at Chatsworth he was one of the first gardeners in the country to have completed their education with the Horticultural Society, which offered the best training available in Britain. After three years there he had become skilled in practical gardening and was acquainted with the latest developments in botany as well as new technological advances. Since its foundation in 1804 the Society had promoted horticulture according to the latest scientific principles. One of England's most extravagant aristocrats, William Spencer Cavendish, 6th Duke of Devonshire, had seen Paxton working in the gardens of the Society, which adjoined his estate at Chiswick. He had invited him to become superintendent of his gardens at Chatsworth – an opportunity greater than any man in his position could have dreamt of. For an annual salary of £65 Paxton's duties would be to look after the kitchen garden and the pleasure grounds – one of the best-paid jobs on the estate (the housekeeper by contrast earned only £20).

When Paxton clambered down the grassy bank early that May morning, he saw a honey-coloured palace set in a large park. The sandstone house was framed by wooded hills behind, and in front, the River Derwent wove its gentle way across the vast lawns. Paxton wandered through the grounds, laid out as a 'natural landscape' and 'looked around the outside of the house'. From his casual observation one thing was clear: the Duke seemed to care more for architecture than for horticulture. The elegant new wing had just been finished, and the window frames glinted with gold-leaf.

After Paxton had investigated the pleasure grounds, he went to the kitchen garden, a fifteen-minute walk from the house. Finding the gates locked and not yet having received the keys, he scaled the wall and entered the twelve-acre plot. Used to the immaculate state of the Horticultural Society's garden, he thought that Chatsworth's vegetable and fruit looked neglected. The Society's garden at Chiswick boasted the largest collection of fruit in the country, experimental plots for plant cultivation, hothouses and an arboretum, whereas Chatsworth's four pine houses (for pineapples) were in a sorry state, and in the two vineries he found a total of just eight bunches of grapes. The only bright note among all the dilapidation was the sight of some forcing frames for cucumbers, and two good hothouses for growing peaches. But even these were equipped with old-fashioned flues which, as Paxton observed, 'almost burn one end of the house, while the other is nearly cold'. In fact, everything looked outdated. He also noticed that not a single hothouse contained flowers.

As daylight crept into the valley, the estate's gardeners began to arrive. Assuming his new position, Paxton immediately gave them their orders for the day. He then walked back towards the house and asked to be given a tour of the baroque waterworks. Although more than a hundred years old, they still worked and looked spectacular. The most magnificent feature was the Cascade: three hundred yards of water pounding over twenty-four broad steps, gouged out of the slope that ran down from the hills towards the house. Having met his staff, Paxton went for breakfast. This he took at the housekeeper's cottage, where he met his future wife Sarah Brown, who 'fell in love with me, and I with her, and thus I completed my first mornings work at Chatsworth before nine o'clock'.

Like many young men of his generation, Paxton had an imperturbable belief in progress as the long-awaited economic boom, following on from victory in the Napoleonic Wars, was fostering a growing sense of national pride and a conviction in England's ascendancy. Her factories were supplying goods across

Joseph Paxton, 1836

the globe. The defeat of her main economic and political adversary stimulated the belief that Britain was militarily and morally superior to any other power. This new-found optimism marked a departure from the gloom that had hung over the previous decade. During Paxton's childhood, the Luddite riots of 1811/12 and the Peterloo massacre seven years later had sent ripples of fear through many quarters, but by now the prominent radicals had been imprisoned, exiled or sent to Botany Bay. Many factory workers had accepted, at least for now, both their level of pay and the new working conditions brought about by labour-saving machinery. The country was bursting with energy, and men like Paxton were convinced they were living during a time of unparalleled advancement. Industrial activity was reaching a new peak, iron prices were rising, the unemployment rate was falling in many industrial cities. The newspapers predicted a new period of prosperity.

Inventiveness, manufacturing growth and naval supremacy laid the foundation for what would become Victorian Britain. The moneyed middle classes invested in property and speculated, building more houses than ever before. The large villas and sweeping terraces around Regent's Park in London, designed by John Nash and other Regency architects, had just been finished. With their fluted Greek columns, friezes and triumphal arches they provided elegant homes for the nouveaux riches. King George IV declared that at no other point in British history had society been in such a 'thriving condition'. He himself, gluttonous and glorying in his riches, had built one of the most opulent and outlandish palaces in Europe: the Brighton Pavilion. Although high society became renowned for its decadence, this was also the era that saw the emergence of a new generation of ambitious and driven men such as Paxton, who would herald the values of the Victorian age.

Class inequalities were still excessive, young children worked all day in the factories, and slavery was still legal. While manufacturers became million-aires, living and working conditions for the working classes were dismal. Nonetheless, it was possible for a lowly under-gardener like Paxton to be appointed superintendent of one of the largest gardens in the country. The educa-tion he had received at the Horticultural Society gave him the confidence to take up the challenge and to join the ranks of fashionable architects and gardeners who had worked at Chatsworth over the previous two centuries. Sixty years earlier, Capability Brown had razed the intricately patterned parterres that George London and Henry Wise had laid out at Chatsworth in the mid-1690s, while William III was mourning the death of his beloved queen Mary. Brown had replaced the terraces with lawns and trees, softened the line of the river and moved the kitchen garden out of sight; but he had left some of the fountains and ponds, and a canal, as reminders of what had been the grand baroque gardens of the 1st Duke of Devonshire. He had turned Chatsworth into one of the most beautiful landscaped gardens of the 1760s; but since then, it was as if time had stood still.

The 6th Duke's ancestors had spent vast amounts on the garden, but his interests lay in improving the house and collecting books and fine art. A connois-seur, like his mother the flamboyant and notorious Georgiana, 5th Duchess of Devonshire, he was known as a reckless spendthrift. The eldest son of one of the grandest Whig families in Britain, at thirty-five the Duke was one of the richest men in the country and its most eligible bachelor, having inherited estates of almost two hundred thousand acres, which provided him with a yearly income of £100,000. His upbringing, however, had been unconventional – he grew up with siblings both legitimate and illegitimate, under the care of his mother and his father's mistress. Capricious and partially deaf, he was also a chronic hypochondriac, filling his diary with more details about his imagined illnesses than about anything else. In the previous decade, he had given some of the most glamorous parties London had seen. At his house in Chiswick his guests admired his menagerie, consisting of a white elephant, some giraffes and kangaroos. The interiors of his houses were no less extravagant: he spent, on average, more than £4000 a year on furniture alone at Chatsworth and Devonshire House in central London. Gardens were the one area where parsimony ruled: at Chatsworth, the Duke allocated only £600 annually, and that included Paxton's salary. This was just enough for the upkeep of the greenhouses, pleasure grounds and kitchen garden, but did not stretch to any great landscaping schemes.

For the next three years, Paxton used this budget to repair the existing garden and keep it in order.[*] Then, in 1829, he began to build a pinetum, a project that would demonstrate to the Duke his skills and his horticultural talents. On an eight-acre site Paxton introduced more than fifty species, including American junipers and cedars, Japanese pines and the antipodean Norfolk pine, sourcing them from the Horticultural Society, other private gardens and from leading nurseries. He even carried the seeds of the famous Douglas fir – which reached two hundred feet in its native California – from London in his hat. As with the Horticultural Society's arboretum, where he had also worked as an under-gardener, the purpose of the pinetum was to collect and house as many trees as possible – in this case conifers. In fulfilling this aim Paxton made the Duke the owner of the largest pinetum in the country, anticipating the Victorian fashion by twenty years. Impressed by his gardener's skills, the Duke increased his salary from £65 to £226 a year, and upped the garden budget to £2000.

During these first years at Chatsworth Paxton also experimented with hothouses in the kitchen garden. The introduction of exotic plants into

---

[*]Unless otherwise stated, the chronology of the making of the garden and the relationship between Paxton and the Duke are based on their letters, the Duke's diary, account books (all held under the Chatsworth Settlement Trust), and on Paxton's own publications such as the *Horticultural Register* and *Magazine of Botany*.

William Spencer Cavendish, 6th Duke of
Devonshire, 1833–4

England's cold climate had forced gardeners to try out new methods of producing the heat and humidity that many of them needed, and the construction of hothouses and the heating systems to power them effectively had long been discussed in the horticultural world. Early botanists like John Tradescant had insulated new seedlings with dung and covered them with baskets, while others had explored the use of heated walls. The Dutch hothouses made of glass that Queen Mary installed in her garden at Hampton Court had been innovative in the late seventeenth century; but throughout the eighteenth, gardeners had struggled unsuccessfully with brick, wood and glass, producing greenhouses that still failed to admit enough light. Repton had introduced glass-roofed 'flower passages' connecting the house with the greenhouse – an early step towards the modern conservatory. With more flowering plants, shrubs and trees than ever before pouring into Britain from all corners of the expanding Empire, horticulturists were determined to find new solutions.

Living in what his contemporary Thomas Carlyle, for one, called the 'Mechanical Age', Paxton was interested in the technological possibilities that the Industrial Revolution threw up. In particular, he was fascinated by the myriad applications that James Watt's steam engine could be put to. Richard Arkwright had introduced some into his cotton mills in the late eighteenth century; the ironmaster John Wilkinson had used the steam engine in steel production, to power his cylinder-boring process; *The Times* was the first newspaper to be printed on steam-powered printing machines. Paxton wrote to the leading manufacturers of steam engines and boilers enquiring about their potential for heating. The introduction of the new gas lighting and heating into Britain's factories prompted him to considered using gas as a source of smoke-free heat in his new hothouses. And intrigued by the modern construction methods that had led to the creation of vast structures such as iron bridges, he also asked for estimates for iron hothouses.

While Paxton was exploring means of putting the Industrial Revolution to the service of horticulture, others were pushing the boundaries of technological progress even further. To prove its safety, Isambard Kingdom Brunel organised a dinner for more than 150 guests inside the partially finished Thames Tunnel (from Rotherhithe to Wapping). George Stephenson's steam locomotive, the *Rocket*, had covered the distance between Liverpool and Manchester at an unprecedented fifteen miles an hour. Charles Darwin was preparing to leave for South America on the *Beagle*, a voyage that would inspire his seminal work, *The Origin of Species*; and Michael Faraday began his experiments with electricity which he would publish over the next forty years. Like Paxton, many of these men came from relatively poor backgrounds and, driven by talent and ambition, had risen through the ranks, to be respected at the highest levels of society. Robert Arkwright, for example, whose father had in 1769 patented the water frame which improved the 'spinning jenny', was on friendly terms with the Duke.

Whenever the Duke visited Chatsworth, Paxton would proudly show his employer his latest successes, especially the fruit, vegetables and flowers produced in the new hothouses. Pleased with both Paxton and his immaculately kept garden, the Duke began to note the progress in his diary. In 1829 he had given Paxton £400 from his private funds for the construction of the hothouses. The next year, when Paxton showed his employer how he had successfully transplanted a forty-year-old weeping ash, the Duke was even more impressed, and increased the garden budget to £5000 – Paxton spent almost £1000 on plants.

By 1831, five years after Paxton had begun his work at Chatsworth, the kitchen garden possessed nearly thirty hothouses. Instead of heating the hothouses directly with coal fires and flues, Paxton equipped some of them with a system similar to modern central heating. Water was heated up in a boiler and then pumped through a series of pipes into the hothouse. The boiler ensured that the water was maintained at a constant temperature, thus overcoming the problem of the traditional coal-fire method that required continual attention by a gardener. Paxton was not working in isolation; he was very much part of a network of gardeners keen to make horticulture a scientific discipline. The pursuit of scientific knowledge had been transformed from a gentlemanly occupation into a professional endeavour. Though the word 'scientist'* had not yet been coined disciplines such as botany and geology were emerging and societies and related journals were being founded. In 1827 the Society for the Diffusion of Useful Knowledge, nicknamed 'The Steam Intellect Society', was established, followed four years later by the British Association for the Advancement of Science. The fascination with classifying and ordering the world had intensified in the course of the eighteenth century; Samuel Johnson, in the first comprehensive English dictionary, imposed an order on the language; and in France Diderot had published his famous *Encyclopaedia*. The Swedish botanist Carl Linnaeus had revolutionised the classification of plants when he divided them into classes and orders according to their reproductive organs and renamed all known plants with his simple binomial nomenclature.

This new spirit of rationality filtered down into more practical areas, such as plant collection and their care. Paxton immersed himself in the related scientific developments, and within a decade of leaving his father's farm he had educated himself sufficiently to embark on an ambitious project that would launch him into the national horticultural arena. In 1831 he published the first

---

*The *Quarterly Review* reported in 1834 that it had been proposed at meetings of the British Association for the Advancement of Science to call students in search of knowledge about the material world 'scientist'.

issue of the *Horticultural Register*, a magazine catering for the ever-growing interest in plants and gardens. The magazine included scientific explanations of botanical phenomena, as well as a monthly gardening to-do list. Chatsworth was the testing ground for Paxton's experiments – paid for by the Duke – and the magazine was the public forum through which he could broadcast his findings. The *Horticultural Register* was written in a straightforward style and sold at a reasonable price, unlike the periodicals Paxton had found in the library of the Horticultural Society. Leaping at the possibilities offered by the cheaper printing technology, Paxton placed himself at the forefront of the flurry of gardening periodicals becoming available, giving instructions, practical advice and scientific insights.* For the time being his main competitor was John Claudius Loudon's *Gardener's Magazine*, which had been the market leader for five years.

Twenty years older than Paxton, Loudon was a workaholic who had already published several books on gardening, agriculture and hothouses, establishing himself as Britain's leading horticultural writer. His response to the first issue of the *Horticultural Register* was to visit Chatsworth, prudently choosing a day when Paxton was absent. Publishing his verdict in his *Gardener's Magazine*, he declared Chatsworth an 'unsatisfactory place'. Not only did he dismiss the baroque waterworks and the setting of the house, he also claimed that Paxton's ornamental planting in the kitchen garden was in 'bad taste'. In a powerful rebuke in the next issue of the *Horticultural Register*, Paxton attempted to set the record straight, accusing Loudon of descending on Chatsworth with the 'pre-determination to find fault'.

Like Paxton, Loudon was passionate about creating artificial climates, and saw himself as the pioneer in a new world in which exotic plants, birds and fish would be kept in huge glass domes. In his vision, England's gardeners would also be able to keep 'examples of the human species' in their greenhouses – he had in mind people from the tropical rainforests – thus creating living tableaux. On a more practical level, he advocated replacing the flat roofs of

---

*In 1787 William Curtis launched the first horticultural periodical, the *Botanical Magazine*. This was followed by the *Botanical Cabinet*, founded by the nursery Loddiges in 1815, and Loudon's *Gardener's Magazine*, which he had started in 1826.

greenhouses with a ridge-and-furrow construction which would make full use of the changing angles of sunlight during the day. Though this was Loudon's idea, Paxton was the first to test and perfect the system. He arranged the roof sashes in a series of pitches, giving his glasshouses a zigzag silhouette of peaks and troughs. This increased the surface area of glass that would catch the low sunrays in the morning and evening, while the wooden bars forming the rows of ridges broke up the harsh mid-day rays.

In 1832 the Duke wrote in his diary: 'happy here'. It was Chatsworth and his plants that now gave him the greatest pleasure, but politics and his position as Lord Chamberlain – the chief officer of the royal household – kept him all too often in London. His presence at court was important: as Lord Chamberlain he was responsible for state ceremonies and the royal palaces. But his new-found love for gardening together with his growing disillusionment with politics made him increasingly reluctant to leave Chatsworth. The Reform Bill in particular had absorbed much of his time and energy. Remembering the violent riots of twenty years earlier, the Duke and his aristocratic Whig friends were conscious of the threat of revolution and knew that they had to make concessions to the

Paxton's greenhouse with ridge-and-furrow roof

moneyed middle classes so as to prevent them from aligning themselves with the working class. Despite being challenged by the Tories, the bill was finally passed – after a long struggle – in June 1832. It extended the vote to those who rented or owned a house with an annual rental value of £10 or more, thus increasing the electorate by 50 per cent – although this still meant that only one in five men could vote.

At the end of this eventful year, the Duke was struck down by a mysterious illness that made him lame for two years. But the affliction allowed him to spend more time at Chatsworth, where he was happy in Paxton's company. There he was 'wheeled about in the Buxton chair' (an early wheelchair) or hobbled on crutches to the greenhouse, where he could always be sure of finding a new plant in bloom.

By now the relationship between the gardener and his patron was changing. Science, technology and horticulture were Paxton's domain, and the Duke was his pupil. His employer, on the other hand, was an expert on art and architecture, having travelled the continent and seen the landmarks of European culture. His aristocratic friends owned many of the gardens Paxton was competing with, so the Duke decided that it was his turn to teach Paxton. In February 1833 he asked Paxton to accompany him to Dropmore, Lady Grenville's garden in Buckinghamshire, and one of the most fashionable in the country. It was a cold day and Paxton had to sit outside in the rain on the box next to the coachman. The seat inside, next to the Duke, was reserved for his noble friends; Paxton was, after all, still only a gardener. But the chilly journey was worth it. Paxton admired the flowerbeds laid out in scroll-shapes, lutes and swirls, harking back to the formal gardens of the seventeenth century.

Many designers and architects readily embraced progress and technological advances, while at the same time wanting to retain a sense of continuity with the past – history was still the lens through which to view and understand the world, and it had its place in gardens too. Newness could be threatening, and so inventions were often cloaked in familiar garb. Thus manufacturers and craftsmen employed an eclectic array of ornaments borrowed from the past, such as Gothic tracery and baroque carving. In gardening, Repton had already in the last decade of his career advocated formal flowerbeds, and Loudon urged his readers to familiarise themselves with the historical styles. He had included a garden history section in his *Encyclopaedia of Gardening*, as well as often discussing earlier styles in the *Gardener's Magazine*. Dropmore with its patterned parterres stood at the beginning of an era that used history extensively as a source book, quoting from it visually. In literature, medieval romances such as Walter Scott's *Ivanhoe* (1819) popularised the past; the five volumes of Thomas Babington Macaulay's *History of England* would become bestsellers in the middle of the century; and a decade later the Duke's neighbour at Haddon Hall, Lord John Manners, organised themed medieval soirées, romanticising paternalistic relations between landlord and tenant. On one occasion Lord Eglinton of Eglinton Castle in Ayrshire organised a jousting tournament in which his young aristocratic friends, rigged out in armour, pretended to be knights; and artists of the Pre-Raphaelite Brotherhood such as Dante Gabriel Rossetti and John Everett Millais were painting chivalric scenes.

Of all the styles available, the gardener at Dropmore had opted for the formal French parterre; but instead of picking out the patterns in gravel and individual specimens, he had used great swathes of flowers. '[B]eauty in masses', Loudon called this, insisting that a 'grand lesson' could be learned from it. For the first time solid, flat blocks of one sort of flower were used to create a display like a plush carpet, producing an effect quite unlike the picturesque theatrical displays that Repton had devised at Sheringham by mixing flowers of different heights and colours.

Back at Chatsworth the Duke was in turn 'charmed by the flower garden' – all Paxton's work – in front of the converted seventeenth-century greenhouse. Almost a century earlier the grand baroque parterres of George London and Henry Wise had been swept away by Capability Brown, but once again Chatsworth had gone over to symmetry: beds were laid out in neat scrolls, half-moons and other geometrical shapes, cut into the grass and delineated by gravel walks edged with box. The difference was that they were smaller than the earlier baroque parterres, and instead of planting choice specimens like those that had impressed visitors to William and Mary's garden at Hampton Court, Paxton had dedicated each of the compartments carved out of the grass to one colourful species, such as hyacinths or tulips for spring flowering, or hardy greenhouse plants for summer and autumn. As at Dropmore, the beds were brimming with colour, and the whole surface of the two largest beds was now veiled in low-growing moss roses, interrupted only by the straight lines of tall standard roses. At the centre of the design stood a stone ornament like a giant flower pot, in which Paxton displayed his prized seasonal greenhouse plants. 'Planting in masses,' he said, echoing Loudon, created the most dramatic effects in a garden.

With this new fashion for greenhouse flowers planted outside when the season was right, originated the 'bedding system'; it would become ubiquitous in Victorian gardens, dramatically changing the role of the head gardener on large estates. Until now, his job had been the relatively simple one of maintaining the gardens laid out by fashionable landscape designers such as Capability Brown, Humphry Repton or one of their disciples. The emphasis on large blocks of flowering plants and the desire to see blossom all year round, however, now meant that it was up to the gardener to try to bypass the seasons by growing bedding plants in the greenhouses. Only thus could he achieve the required 'annual look'. At a large garden like Chatsworth, to procure enough flowers Paxton had to implement a system of mass production in the hothouses. Like a factory owner, he aimed for the highest possible output and efficiency

Paxton's flower garden in front of the converted greenhouse

levels. Successfully displaying his ability to extract whatever he wanted from nature, he dressed Chatsworth in a striking array of patterns and colours.

In April 1834, the Duke took Paxton to Paris to see the city's great private gardens as well as the Louvre, Versailles and the brand-new glasshouse at the Botanic Gardens, the Jardin des Plantes, which was still under construction – one of the largest to be built so far. Though at times he sent him on errands, like a servant, for much of the visit the Duke treated his gardener as a friend, which allowed Paxton an insider's view of the cultured aristocratic world. Sharp, intelligent but obedient, Paxton was his patron's ideal travelling companion.

Back in England, they continued their tour by visiting the Botanic Gardens at Kew to obtain some specimens and went shopping together at Loddiges, the Hackney nursery that had built its reputation on its immense stock of exotic plants. Paxton bought camellias, dahlias, laurels and rhododendrons. That year alone he spent almost £600 on plants, shrubs and seeds.

In late autumn the Duke 'walked with Paxton, planning' – 'Chatsworthing', as he called it. One of the projects they discussed was the creation of an arboretum. In January 1835 Paxton began to clear forty acres of woodland, to the east above the garden. Far from minding the disruption and mess involved, the Duke could not wait 'to find the pleasure ground up to my neck in mud all over'. Over the next six months Paxton felled thousands of trees; diverted two miles of stream from the surrounding moor to the area designated for the arboretum; laid out a mile-long walk and planted 1670 species of trees. As with the pinetum six years earlier, he combined a scientific with an aesthetic approach. Along the meandering walk he planted the trees in groups according to their botanical classification, which totalled seventy-five different orders. Wooden tallies gave both the Latin and the English name, the year of introduction and native country. The arboretum was designed to encourage visitors to broaden their horticultural knowledge while taking pleasure in the picturesque woods. It would become the largest in Europe, outdoing Loudon's at Derby which would open in 1839, as well as Loddiges' in Hackney.

The Duke called it 'transcendent', and his sister Lady Grenville teased him: 'You and Paxton, sitting under the red rhododendron at Chatsworth, under the shades of palms and pines [give] no thought of your country's weal and woe.' By now the Duke had withdrawn from political life, and the problems his party faced no longer concerned him. The wrangling within the Whig camp had weakened their position in Parliament and with the king, and the resignation of influential Whig grandees such as Earl Grey and Viscount Althorp had left the party without strong leadership. The previous year had seen five prime-ministerial changes creating confusion and instability.* Now in spring 1835, when the ageing Whig Lord Melbourne was reappointed prime minister, he tried to persuade the Duke to become either Lord Chamberlain again or Lord-Lieutenant of Ireland. The Duke declined both posts. Botany had totally eclipsed his interest in politics and in public life. At that moment he was particularly obsessed with the strange beauty of a flower with orange petals shaped like the wings and antennae of a tropical butterfly – *Oncidium papilio*, an orchid that triggered a lifelong passion in the Duke.†

During the previous year the Duke and Paxton had amassed 240 orchid species at Chatsworth, Paxton proudly reported in his latest publishing project, the *Magazine of Botany* – more than any other collector in such a short period. Greedy for their beauty but also for their diversity, the two men had received orchids from other collectors, botanic gardens and from Loddiges, the first nursery to cultivate them commercially. It was an expensive, time-consuming passion, and the rare specimens often died in the smoke and heat of the glasshouse stoves. That they thrived at all was proof of the gardener's skills. To accommodate them, Paxton built three orchid houses, and consequently his hothouse bill doubled – from £495 in 1833 to £1192 for the next year. The largest was equipped with the latest technology: hot-air chambers placed under the potted orchids keeping their roots warm, and perforated water pipes to provide instant humidity. Only a handful of other orchid collections could rival Chatsworth's, and in spring 1835 the owner of one such collection, on the brink

---

*In summer 1834 Earl Grey (Whig) resigned; in July Lord Melbourne (Whig) became prime minister, but in November he was dismissed by the king. The Duke of Wellington (Tory) was prime minister for one month until Sir Robert Peel (Tory) took over in December, but only to resign in April 1835 when Lord Melbourne became prime minister again.
†Now known as *Psychopsis papilio*.

of financial ruin, was forced to sell. The Duke was first in line to buy. At that moment, Paxton was engaged in diverting the stream, clearing the ground for the arboretum and decorating the formal flower garden with elegant Italian columns – as well as publishing his magazines – but the Duke nonetheless told him to down tools and make haste to Kimbolton in Cambridgeshire so as to evaluate the orchids on offer. Paxton reported back that they were 'sumptuous', and so the Duke agreed to pay the asking price of £500. The orchids were his. Spurred on by ambition and a competitive spirit, Paxton wrote back excitedly: '[O]ur collection of orchideae has now mounted completely to the top of the tree. I am fearful some of our neighbours will be a little jealous of our progress – the race now will lay between ourselves, Lord Fitzwilliam and Mr Bateman.'* But their hunger for orchids was far from sated: while Paxton was packing up the newly purchased exotics ready for transport to Chatsworth the two men were already planning their next project: an expedition to India, where their gardener would gather plants never before seen in England.

The sculptural voluptuousness of orchids had captured the minds of men for centuries; the Greeks ate the erotically shaped tubers as an aphrodisiac, calling them *orchis*, meaning 'testicle'. There are twenty-five thousand species across the globe, ranging in size from pin-head to giants weighing more than half a ton. This enormous variety, plus their flamboyant beauty, made them the perfect collectible for the nineteenth-century enthusiast. For the Duke of Devonshire, they also became a vehicle through which to show off his wealth; for Joseph Paxton, to show off his knowledge. Acquiring and displaying natural objects was not a new phenomenon; Renaissance cabinets of curiosity had been the precursors to museums such as John Tradescant's Ark in Lambeth, in south London. But whereas Tradescant had collected anything that was 'strange' – a stuffed dodo, a 'mermaid's hand', a 'piece of human flesh on a bone' – collectors from

---

*Lord Fitzwilliam, the Viscount Milton, kept his orchid collection at Wentworth House in Yorkshire. The orchids *Miltonia* are named in his honour. James Bateman of Knypersley Hall in Staffordshire was also obsessed with the strange beauty of orchids. He provided information for some of the new orchids Paxton introduced in the *Magazine of Botany*. Later Bateman would move his collection to his famous garden at Biddulph Grange near Stoke-on-Trent.

the mid-eighteenth century onwards were fascinated by the natural order and by taxonomy.

The importation of such exotics had been made possible by Britain's expansion as an empire. In the last quarter of the eighteenth century Captain Bligh had brought back orchids from Jamaica, and Joseph Banks had collected them when he had circumnavigated the globe as the naturalist on Captain Cook's *Endeavour*. Nurturing the exchange of plants between the colonies and Britain, Banks had been the driving force in the establishment of botanic gardens in the growing Empire. Now plant hunters used them as base stations for their expeditions. Sending plant hunters to uncharted territories to collect seeds and flowers was dangerous, but collectors such as the Duke were willing to risk their money – and the lives of their gardeners, if necessary – to secure the possession of an undiscovered plant.

The intrepid young man Paxton chose for this adventure was John Gibson, a twenty-year-old under-gardener who had worked in the orchid house at Chatsworth.* With his pockets crammed with letters of introduction, Gibson left the Peak District in April 1835 for an educational tour of the private orchid collections and major nurseries of England, including Loddiges. Paxton wanted to make sure that his young employee learned as much as possible about the species and their cultivation before he set off.

The Duke now sent word to Dr Nathaniel Wallich, the director of the Botanic Garden in Calcutta, who would be supervising Gibson's travel arrangements in India. Paxton picked some fine specimens for Wallich from his greenhouses: the gifts would not only please Wallich but also permit Gibson to test a new type of packing case. The success of this expedition was as dependent on the safe carriage of the plants as it was on the young man's findings themselves. Stored in barrels, boxes or baskets, during the long journey the plants had to be watered and tended through heat wave and blizzard, but until then, most exotics had perished en route. The new 'Wardian cases', however, raised expectations among the horticultural community. Invented by Nathaniel Ward,

---

*Unless otherwise stated, Gibson's travels, the plants he found and his thoughts are based on letters related to the expedition, including Gibson's, Paxton's, the Duke's and Nathaniel Wallich's (Chatsworth, India Correspondence).

Hand-held 'Wardian' case

a London GP, the conception of these miniature 'greenhouses' had been serendipitous. The doctor had placed a cocooned pupa together with some moist earth in a jar, hoping a butterfly would hatch. To his surprise, a fern and a grass seedling grew, because the sealed jar created a self-sustaining environment in which the moisture in the soil evaporated and then condensed again. Ward immediately recognised the potential of his discovery, and built some larger air-tight cases out of wood and glass. He placed some plants in the moist soil, sealed the case, then sent them to Sydney. Remaining unopened for the duration of the journey, so avoiding the risk of damage by salty sea air and water, the moist atmosphere was maintained and the plants arrived in excellent condition. Gibson was one of the first plant collectors to use Wardian cases in earnest.

As he prepared to exchange the dirty London streets for the luscious vegetation of the Khasi Hills north-east of Calcutta, Gibson received one last order from Paxton and the Duke. They asked him to bring back from Burma a flowering evergreen that had become a legend in England: the *Amherstia nobilis*. Its delicate clusters of dazzling red flowers were said to be so beautiful that the tree was offered in sacrifice to Buddha. Nine years earlier Wallich had seen it in full bloom in a Burmese monastery. Having never yet survived transport to England, its successful importation would be the crown jewel in

Chatsworth's collection. On 22 September 1835 John Gibson left England for Calcutta, joining HMS *Jupiter* at Woolwich on a journey that would take nearly six months.

In the meantime, Paxton was preparing his grandest project so far. In expectation of the treasures that Gibson would bring back from India, he had designed the perfect home for the rare plants: the Great Conservatory or, as he often called it, the Great Stove.* After ten years of experimenting with hothouse technology, Paxton was ready to construct something bigger and better than anything yet attempted. The building he envisaged consisted of a central 'nave', 67 feet high, for the largest trees, with two lower side aisles for the smaller species. The whole building would be 277 feet long by 123 wide – a bulbous two-tiered structure in which the ridge-and-furrow walls and roof created the impression of a curving glass shell. The most challenging aspect of the construction would be the single-span roof across the central axis, which was to be seventy feet wide. This design was the culmination of Paxton's expertise in engineering.

Paxton's plan was an audacious one. He had no formal training as an architect or engineer and yet, while leading railway engineers struggled to span the platforms of the new stations,† he was embarking on what would be the largest glass structure in England. His Great Conservatory would be the first glass 'cathedral' in an era that would become famous for its ingenious buildings. Within the next few decades, structures such as the Floral Hall in Covent Garden (1852) and railway stations such as St Pancras in London (1866), whose glass roof would arch a hundred feet over the tracks, would amaze all who saw them. The international race for the biggest glass exhibition buildings began with Paxton's own Crystal Palace in 1851, and culminated in the Palais des

---

*'Stove' meaning 'hothouse' came into use in the late seventeenth century. *Great Stove*: Unless otherwise stated, the building of the Great Stove is based on Chadwick 1961a; Colquhoun 2003; articles in *Gardener's Magazine* and *Illustrated London News*; and Chatsworth Account Books.

†In 1836 Lime Street, the first railway station in Liverpool, opened with what was considered a massive roof span – 55 feet – while London's first mainline railway terminal at Euston (1837) spanned 40 feet.

The Great Conservatory and the surrounding terrace, 1844

Machines in Paris (1889), which achieved a roof span of almost four hundred feet. In 1835, though, no glass structure had spanned seventy feet without the use of supporting columns.

Only one other building had reached a comparable scale: the Antheum at Brighton, a conservatory with a dome spanning over 150 feet. But its gigantic structure gave way just one day after it was completed in 1833. This brought home to Paxton, who had seen it, the enormity of the structural challenge ahead of him, so he asked the estate's foreman carpenter to build a scale model of his designs for the Great Stove. The Duke adored it. He took it to London in December 1835, parading it at horticultural meetings and showing it at Loddiges and to the botanist and horticulturist John Lindley.[*] Showing off was part of the game, of course, and a month later, returning from a visit to the Duke of Bedford's garden at Woburn Abbey, Paxton once again revealed his ambition and competitive spirit. Writing to his wife Sarah, he scoffed at Woburn's attempt to plant an arboretum 'in imitation of Chatsworth', dismissing it as 'a miserable failure'. The Duke of Bedford also wanted a conservatory like the one at

* John Lindley was the assistant secretary at the Horticultural Society and, in 1829, had been appointed the first Professor of Botany at the University of London. He published several books on orchids and would later be called the 'father of orchidology'. In 1841, together with Paxton, he founded the *Gardeners' Chronicle*.

Chatsworth, because, Paxton was sure, the 'old codger [was] jealous of us'.

The spot chosen for the Great Conservatory was located in woodland at some distance from the house. While his men set to work preparing the site, Paxton was adding the last details to his design.

Gibson arrived in Calcutta on 8 March 1836. After the long sea journey, he was excited at the prospect of seeing one of the most famous tropical gardens in the Far East. He was not disappointed. The avenues of palms, and the groves of cinnamon trees were impressive enough, but even more so was the centre-piece, a huge banyan tree, its long aerial roots sweeping the ground beneath, same of them having formed new trees. Most stunning of all was the *Amherstia nobilis*, the tree in which his employer had expressed such an interest. Clothed in its startling red blossom hanging from the branches like glowing lanterns, it struck Gibson as the most beautiful thing he had ever seen. He ran around 'clapping his hands like a boy who has got three runs in a cricket match'.

Gibson had to wait two months before discussing his itinerary with Wallich, who was away in the Assam Hills, so he busied himself looking after the plants he had brought from Chatsworth which, thanks to the Wardian cases, were in remarkably good condition. He also prepared samples of the many flowers he would take home from the Botanic Garden for their transport to Chatsworth. The garden had been founded in 1787 by the East India Company to support agricultural improvements in the area and to break the Dutch monopoly. Now, with the company's increasing military and political hold over India, the garden's role had changed. Botany rather than commerce was the leading concern and Wallich, as director of the garden and a voracious plant hunter himself, had assembled a brilliant collection of flowering shrubs and trees.[*]

When Dr Wallich arrived in Calcutta in May, he immediately organised Gibson's trip to Cherrapunji in the Khasi Hills. Five weeks later Gibson left Calcutta with mixed feelings – he was about to encounter one of the richest

---

[*]One of Gibson's favourites was a huge banana plant, a rare fruit in England. Before the young man left for India, Paxton had been nurturing a dwarf banana, later called *Musa cavendishii*; and as Gibson was sending off his first packages from Calcutta, Paxton was harvesting the first bananas ever grown in England.

botanical treasure troves in India, but to get there he had to negotiate, mainly by boat, three hundred miles of uncharted terrain. He wrote to Paxton about the great numbers of boats that had sunk in this most inhospitable area of the subcontinent (near the modern Bangladeshi border). For fear that the 'Indian savages would kill him for the sake of his goblet and then eat him with his own knife and fork', he left behind his new silver travelling case.

With no map, Gibson had to rely on two local guides during the journey. When travelling downriver, its waters dangerously swelled by the moonsoon rains, he had to lie flat in the middle of the little boat in order to keep stable. He crossed swamps infested with leeches and mosquitoes and his clothes were permanently drenched by the spray from the crashing waterfalls and from the constant rain. Already exhausted when he reached the foothills of the Khasi range, he now had to climb four thousand feet to his base on the Cherrapunji plateau. Almost four weeks after he had left Calcutta, Gibson settled into his little bungalow on this flat grey rock. The warm rain turned puddles into lakes, while below in the misty valley the jungle awaited him. And there could be no doubting why Wallich had sent him here. Wherever he looked, flowers of every size, colour and shape met his gaze. In this paradise, five hundred orchid species alone could be found. For the next few months his home was here, high in the cloud-covered mountains above the steaming forest. Cherrapunji was the wettest place on earth. Gibson's clothes and bedding were never fully dry, but the thought of the orchids kept his spirits up. By the end of his first two weeks, he had already collected fifty species of orchids. Every evening he sat on his veranda, laying out his seeds and plants near large coal fires, in a constant battle against the effects of the humidity and the rain. Despite his solitary existence, he was happy, gaining pleasure from every new flower he found. He wrote eagerly to Wallich about his discoveries: orchids with yellow petals merging into dark-purple lips; *Dendrobium densiflorum* with its dense clusters of yellow blossom; the scarlet orchids he found entwined around the branches of a tree. As he carefully packed his treasures into baskets, his thoughts turned to home; in mid-October he wrote to Wallich: 'I wish they knew in Chatsworth . . . They would jump for joy.'

*

Back in England the Duke declared that he was 'drunk with Chatsworth'. The site for the Great Conservatory had now been cleared, and work had begun. While his men got on with excavating the underground heating chambers and the foundations, Paxton was calculating that he would need forty miles of wooden sash bars to hold the thousands of rectangular glass panels. The bars had to contain the usual grooves into which the glass would be fitted, but he had also specified two more grooves, one on the outside to act as a rainwater channel, and one on the inside to catch the condensation. The cost of producing these by hand would have been enormous, so Paxton designed sash bars that were a standard size and length and, ever inventive, mechanised their production by building a steam-driven machine to cut the triple grooves, saving £1400.

Standardisation was still a relatively novel idea and Paxton was ahead of his time. Perhaps inspired by earlier inventors such as Joseph Bramah (1748–1814) and his one-time apprentice Henry Maudslay (1771–1831) who had introduced precision locks and tools based on standardised and inter-changeable parts, Paxton was the first to apply the idea to architecture. Mechanisation, on the other hand, was widely used in factories. The textile industry had been particularly quick to introduce new machinery to replace manual labour. Looms and spinning machines as well as pumps and drills were all, by now, powered by steam. Applying the same principles to his problem, Paxton had connected a manual grooving machine to a steam engine supplied by Boulton & Watt of Birmingham. In July 1836 he wrote to tell the firm that the steam engine worked, but irregularly, as well as making 'a rumbling noise'. But he continued his experiments, determined to put it right. In September the Duke's favourite niece, Lady Burlington, laid the Great Conservatory's foundation stone.

Although the conservatory was currently Paxton's favourite project, it was not the only thing that preoccupied him. He had also completed the formal flower garden in front of the old converted greenhouse with sixteen statues from the Duke's collection placed on slender stone columns. The hundreds of Portugal laurels that he had bought during the previous two years and trimmed into neat balls – in imitation of the more frost-susceptible orange trees of the formal gardens he had seen with the Duke in Paris – were now six feet high. Along the house, the Broad Walk was lined with outlandishly shaped Chilean monkey-puzzle trees, then still a rarity. Together, all this created a very different image of nature from that of the landscaped garden that had dominated Britain for a century. Here at Chatsworth a new 'artificial' look had taken over, with specimen trees and more formal layouts. Paxton had gone one step further than Repton's declaration that a garden was a 'work of art, using the material of nature'. As Loudon put it, the new style was 'calculated for displaying the art of the gardener'. It was called 'gardenesque'.

Thirty years earlier, at the height of the picturesque craze, this style would have been dismissed as 'unnatural' and 'too regular', but now in his *Magazine of Botany* Paxton was celebrating geometrical beds as the 'creation of art', and suggesting that gardeners had 'gone too far' in their insistence on irregularity. Following Humphry Repton's example, he argued that flowerbeds should be placed close to the house, while picturesque scenes should be at a distance, forming a backdrop to the rest of the garden – like the arboretum and pinetum at Chatsworth.

In order to keep abreast of these fashions the Duke spent much of his time visiting his friends and comparing their gardens with his own. In October 1836 he visited Elvaston Castle near Derby. Here, although the gardener William Barron had only begun planting the year before, the Duke was surprised by what had already been achieved. Never before had a garden been made to look 'mature' so quickly, with ancient yew trees and cedars, a topiary arbour and eleven miles of evergreen hedges – all of which Barron had transported and transplanted to Elvaston. The circular beds were edged with green yew and filled with dwarf dahlias. Everything in the garden was 'artificial', including the many grafted trees – the demonstration par excellence of the 'art' of the gardener, since nature alone could not produce these strange mutations. Barron had grafted topiary 'crowns' on to the tops of yew trees, as well as weeping beech on to upright species, giving them dangling tops. 'Astounding piece of folly & yet wonderful success,' the Duke wrote in his diary on the evening of his visit. In his own garden too, Paxton had successfully defied nature by grafting conical deodar pines with their drooping branches on to tall cedars of Lebanon, and weeping ash on to the pines in the arboretum to make them look 'Asiatic'.*

Gibson, meanwhile, was still at Cherra in what Wallich described to the Duke as 'a continued trance of rapture'. The collection he had amassed, he was certain, would be the largest and most exquisite that had ever crossed the ocean. He could just see the symphony of colour that the scarlet, vermilion, sky-blue and bright-yellow petals of the orchids would create in Chatsworth's hothouses. In January 1837, after five months in complete solitude, he confided in a letter to Paxton that he had almost 'gone wild'. The Duke was thrilled by the 'most delightful letters', which were only now arriving in England, a year after Gibson had written them. At last he and Paxton knew what treasures the young plant hunter had found – and even more exciting, that they had begun their long journey home.

It was in early February 1837 that Gibson arrived back in Calcutta. On seeing his harvest assembled in the Botanic Garden, he proudly wrote to Paxton that he was surprised to see the 'enormous quantity'. Some thirty cases of plants were already on their way, and he too was now ready to depart. On 4 March he left India on the *Zenobia*, with twelve trunks stashed on the poop deck and his cabin crammed with the more delicate beauties – forcing him to sleep sandwiched between cases – as well as baskets full of orchids and plants in bottles. Above him, suspended from the ceiling, orchids still attached to their host tree branches swayed to the movement of the waves. His most precious cargo, two cuttings of *Amherstia nobilis*, a present from Dr Wallich, sat next to him in a chest. One cutting was labelled for the Duke, the other for the director of the East India Company. Never before had so many living specimens been brought to England – of the three hundred exotics that were new, eighty were species of orchids, Paxton later informed William Hooker, the director of the Botanic Gardens at Kew.

When Gibson landed at Plymouth on 14 July 1837, Britain had a new monarch. Three weeks earlier, William IV had died after a reign of only

---

*Paxton also published articles on the scientific principles of grafting in the *Magazine of Botany*, (1836).

seven years, and his niece the eighteen-year-old Princess Victoria had succeeded him. Brought up in a constrained and secluded environment by her domineering mother Princess Mary, Duchess of Kent, Victoria was a serious teenager. Interested in history and declaring that she wanted to 'be good', she had learned her lessons from the excesses of George IV and the unpopularity of her predecessor. In the prime minister Lord Melbourne she found a surrogate father who would assist her in her goal. The old Whig grandee spent several hours a day teaching her his views on history, politics and life, as well as emphasising the importance of her royal duties. As a member of the nobility the Duke of Devonshire was obliged to dine often with the new queen at Buckingham Palace, but he objected to the stifling atmosphere. The queen was thirty years his junior and he found it difficult to hold a conversation with her. Furthermore, he declared her to be 'perfectly ugly'.

A new monarch was not the only change that Gibson found on his return from India. After a series of good harvests had petered out and strains in Britain's relationship with the United States had begun to affect trade, the country was sinking into an economic crisis. While Paxton and the Duke were spending exorbitant sums on prodigious projects such as the Great Conservatory, unemployment rose and people were beginning to starve. The Poor Law Amendment Act of 1834 had abolished 'outdoor relief', but instead the unemployed and ill were forced into workhouses, where conditions appalled many contemporaries. Charles Dickens captured their horrors in *Oliver Twist*, a book that Queen Victoria wanted to read but Lord Melbourne strongly advised against. Despite the widespread suffering, the Duke and Paxton were more concerned about the death of one plant. The *Amherstia nobilis* intended for the Duke had not survived the journey from Calcutta, although the one for the East India Company director was flourishing. Gibson begged Paxton to 'get *Amherstia* down to Chatsworth, or we will lose it', and the Duke, then in London, was 'in a grand fuss' about it. In a desperate attempt to acquire the treasure, he wrote to the chairman of the East India Company offering a deal: Paxton would look after the exotic plant at Chatsworth – '[T]here is not in England a gardener capable of rearing it and propagating it so sure as Mr Paxton'.

On 21 July at nine o'clock in the morning, Paxton arrived at his employer's London home, Devonshire House. The Duke's valet, seeing him approach, called down from a window that he should proceed at once to the Duke, rather than to the newly arrived plant cases. When he entered the Painted Hall, where the *Amherstia nobilis* stood, he found the Duke waiting for him. Paxton was 'to lavish [his] love upon the gem', he said. With no reply yet received from the East India Company to the Duke's proposal, Paxton packed the *Amherstia* ready for transport to Chatsworth. For over ten days, everybody eagerly waited to hear whether the Company would let them take the rare plant. Finally, a letter arrived on the 31st informing the Duke that *Amherstia* could stay at Chatsworth – the chairman agreed that Paxton was the only gardener who could do justice to its magnificence. When the Duke arrived in mid-August at Chatsworth he immediately went to inspect Gibson's treasure, writing in his diary afterwards: 'Garden. Paxton. The *Amherstia* cutting has thrived rapidly. O joy of plants.' The orchids were also doing well, thanks to Paxton's idea of planting them according to their natural habitat, in several houses with different temperatures, humidity levels and degrees of light. The Great Conservatory was also taking shape: the masons had finished the basement walls and most of the small wooden ribs for the curved side aisles were in place.

John Gibson's assiduous hunting had made the orchid collection at Chatsworth the largest and most valuable in the country. Even this, however, failed to satisfy Paxton and the Duke: they now wanted more trees for the pinetum and the arboretum. They had set their hearts on some of the towering pines and firs that one of the Horticultural Society's plant hunters, David Douglas, had sent to the Society in the early 1820s from the west coast of America. Since Douglas's death – he had fallen into a bull pit while collecting plants three years previously – only a few of these trees had been available in England. An expedition would be perilous, but fired by Gibson's success in India, Paxton and the Duke began to plan a new adventure – only this time, as a safety measure, they would send two gardeners.

Accordingly, in March 1838 two young men left Chatsworth to embark on the greatest adventure of their lives. Like John Gibson two and a half years earlier, Robert Wallace and Peter Banks were equipped with plant-gathering tools and a catalogue of advice including a warning about the dangers posed by both bears and women. Arriving in New York a month later, they took a steamboat up the Hudson River to La Chine, near Montreal. There they were joined by a brigade of the Hudson Bay Company, who would accompany them across Canada by canoe. The plan was to reach Fort Vancouver on the west coast by early winter. Except for a few scattered fur-trading posts set up by the Company during the last century, Canada was still a wild and mainly uncharted country. For the next two months they encountered blizzards, strong headwinds and frozen rivers. They carried their boats for miles over bogs, and traversed the rapids on the Winnipeg River. By the end of June they reached Lake Winnipeg, the midway point in their journey.

In August 1838 the Duke left Chatsworth for the Grand Tour, thereby escaping the increasingly suffocating grip of his mistress, whom, since the late 1820s, he had kept in London lavishing her with jewels and expensive clothes. Over the last few months, however, they had rowed so much that she had attempted to stab herself and the Duke felt 'obliged to drink to keep up my spirits'. But now he was lonely and only days after leaving London he wrote in his diary: 'rejoiced at thoughts of Paxton next month'. Without Paxton he was bored: the gardener had become his entertainer and confidant as well as his adviser. During the next six weeks the Duke was in a 'terrible stew' as he waited for Paxton in Geneva, refusing to see any of the main tourist attractions without him. At Chatsworth, meanwhile, Paxton was preparing for his departure – reluctantly, because although he had every confidence in his wife, he was unwilling to leave the building of the Great Conservatory under her supervision.

After eleven years of marriage, Sarah Paxton had become indispensable to her husband's professional life. Without her organisational skills, determination and general assistance he would not have been able to leave Chatsworth so often, accompanying the Duke on his trips and travelling the country in search of the best plants and equipment for the garden. This time, though, the pressure on her was enormous: he would be leaving her in charge of his most ambitious project, and she was heavily pregnant with their fifth child. But having drawn up detailed instructions for Sarah and his workmen, Paxton packed his bags at the end of September and was off. When he arrived in Geneva he had trouble finding the Duke, who had changed residence three times. Bad-tempered at first, he was nonetheless relieved to see Paxton, and in no time at all he declared his gardener the 'grand leader of the band'. They set off on their tour of the Alps, then progressed to Italy where they enjoyed gardens, sculpture and art of all kinds. Overwhelmed by what they saw, Paxton wrote to Sarah: 'I am almost like a steam boiler with the safety valve closed, ready to burst.' As they travelled around, Paxton no longer sat on the coachman's box but inside, next to the Duke. What clearer indicator that his position had changed irrevocably? The Duke was content, though admitting in his diary that at times he was '[a] little bored, for Mr P. sleeps and ruminates sometimes when I wish to converse, but he is everything for me'.

Numerous letters from Chatsworth, most of them from Sarah, kept Paxton and the Duke informed about progress in the garden. A month after he had left England, Paxton received a full update. They had reached a crucial point in the construction of the Great Conservatory: his men were now working on the sophisticated heating system that would create a tropical climate in the midst of the Derbyshire hills. To keep them well out of sight, Paxton had designed all the service and supply equipment to be underground. The labourers had already dug one-fifth of the tunnel that would transport the three hundred tons of coal needed each year to fire the boilers that would heat the glasshouse. The boiler flues would also be underground, taking the fumes to a hidden chimney some distance away, while a seven-mile network of iron piping filled with hot water would also be necessary to heat the Great Conservatory. A boiler manufacturer had been to Chatsworth and estimated that at least six boilers would be needed (the number would rise to eight). At the same time, the carpenters were busy on the curved shell of the conservatory, using Paxton's ingenious technique of warping the timber ribs into the desired shape by bending them over a template. Though the ribs were made only of thin timber boards, then braced together, the method of construction made them stronger than iron – and so reliable, in fact, that the same technique was used for Brunel's wooden viaduct across the Avon in 1845, and for the arches at King's Cross Station in London seven years later.

The workmen steamed ahead. In December Sarah informed her husband that though one of the carpenters had fallen off some scaffolding while screwing a bolt into a rib, to everyone's surprise he hadn't broken a single bone. By New Year 1839 the main structure of the conservatory was in place. Sarah tried to tempt Paxton home: 'Amherstia & daughter are growing most vigorously,' she cajoled, and the orchids, despite the Derbyshire winter, were displaying their kaleidoscopic blooms in the glasshouses. But the Duke still desired his company and would not let him leave. '[W]hat cannot be done this season must be done next,' he insisted. Determined to go to Constantinople, like a stubborn child he refused to go alone, warning Paxton that if he were to leave for England now he would always hold his departure against him. Knowing that his future lay in the Duke's hands, Paxton obliged – although the prospect of seeing the Orient must also have influenced his decision.

Paxton 'wept' when he eventually left for England in April 1839, leaving the Duke, who was feeling his 'own wretched unworthiness', in Geneva. When Paxton arrived at Chatsworth on 11 May he had seen more art, architecture and other cultural landmarks than many an aristocrat. Overwhelmed by the trip, soon after arriving home he found a quiet moment to slip into the house to

Paxton's painting and glazing wagon at the Crystal Palace. The 'contrivance' he used at Chatsworth was probably similar to this.

contemplate the Duke's sculpture collection, where he 'saw a thousand beauties' which he 'had not appreciated before'. The transformation was complete: the farmer's son had become a cultured and educated gentleman.

A week after Paxton's arrival the workmen began fitting the glass panels into the 24,500 sash bars of the Great Conservatory. Again Paxton sourced the best manufacturer available, this time a company in Birmingham, Chance Bros, who six years earlier had introduced a new method of glass production from the continent that increased the maximum panel length possible to three feet.[*] Paxton, though, wanted still larger sheets: if Chance Bros could not add at least another foot, he would 'decline the order'. The threat of losing such a large commission worked: Paxton received glass panels four feet long, the largest ever used in a conservatory. Although unfinished, the building was already attracting attention: in his *Gardener's Magazine* Loudon compared it to a 'cathedral'.

Paxton reported all the successes to the Duke, who was still in Geneva, but at the end of May, just two weeks after Paxton had returned to England, he had to deliver some devastating news. Robert Wallace and Peter Bank, the young gardeners sent to Canada on the plant mission, had never reached Fort Vancouver. After three months of great hardship and privation, their boat had hit a rock in the Columbia River rapids, only a few days' journey from their destination. The boat had capsized, and they had drowned. Paxton, horrified by the 'melancholic news', called the expedition 'a total failure'. Neither he nor the Duke would ever again send a gardener from Chatsworth on a hazardous plant-hunting adventure.

By the early 1840s, the whole of the Great Conservatory was glazed, 'gleaming like a silver sheet' in the sun. The scaffolding had been removed, and the trellises for the climbing plants had been fixed to the ribs. In addition to everything else, Paxton had designed a highly efficient watering system imitating the natural conditions of the tropical rainforest. Hoses could be connected to the pipes so as to shoot jets of water roofwards, which would then fall back to simulate rain.

---

[*]Chance Bros employed continental glass blowers, who produced cylinders of glass which were cut and flattened to sheets while the glass was still hot.

Since he had built the largest hothouse in the world, Paxton was not about to fill it with anything but the biggest and best specimens he could find. Lady Tankerville, from Walton in Surrey, had promised the Duke two enormous palm trees which had outgrown her conservatory. One weighed twelve tons, the *Derby Mercury* reported on 23 September 1840, and had a trunk eight feet in circumference. Even the sanguine Paxton admitted that transporting them would be a 'really gigantic job'. The rest of the horticultural community was sceptical; John Lindley and other botanists advised that moving them would probably result in the trees' death. But the transplantation of mature trees was not a new idea. André Le Nôtre had already practised the technique in the late seventeenth century at Versailles, and Capability Brown had become famous for his great tree-moving schemes at Stowe and elsewhere. The trees had often died; but then Brown, for one, had never studied the anatomy of plants, and his method involved tearing the trees out of the soil, damaging their roots in the process. Paxton, on the other hand, had moved mature trees before and his success had been due to his leaving the roots enveloped in a protective ball of earth. His greatest achievement was the transplanting of a forty-year-old weeping ash from Derby to Chatsworth in 1830. Now, ten years later, the thriving ash was testimony to his skills.

In August 1840 he instructed his carpenters to dismantle the entire glasshouse at Walton, because it was impossible to get the palms through the doorway. Ten labourers then began digging carefully around the first palm, soon assisted by a further six of Lady Tankerville's men – meanwhile, the Duke waited anxiously in London, receiving daily bulletins. Next, the carpenters built a huge case for the palm. Finally, the removal could begin – with the help of a transplanting machine of Paxton's own design, which the workmen at Chatsworth had built. But the earth around the roots had so increased the weight that the ropes and chains snapped before they could lift the first palm on to the waiting cart. After several more attempts, the palm was finally hoisted and secured. It had taken almost four weeks to get this far. Now, the whole neighbourhood watched as eleven horses pulled the massive cargo out on to the road, beginning the two hundred miles to Chatsworth.

Having safely skirted London, disaster struck at St Albans when the wheels of the cart finally gave way, crushed by the weight of the palm. The wheels were fixed and the journey resumed, only to be interrupted several more times by the need to repair or change them again. Eventually the police had to be asked for assistance: the crown of the palm was so wide that some of the turnpike gates had to be removed in order to let it through. Paxton, meanwhile, was rushing back and forth between Chatsworth and the palm, checking its progress as it trundled northwards. At the end of September, two weeks after the accident at St Albans, the first palm arrived at Chatsworth. Paxton had defied his critics and delighted the Duke, who was happy to pick up the enormous transportation bill for £726.

In the years following the construction of the Great Conservatory, Paxton filled his horticultural shrine with thousands of exotic specimens. Between 1840 and 1843 the Duke gave him over £3000 to spend. He ordered many of the plants from the finest nurseries in the country, while others came from Madras, Vera Cruz and other distant shores. Paxton also benefited from the generosity of other gardeners, who had heard of his masterpiece and sent plants that had outgrown their own hothouses. The most generous was Baron Ludwig Hugel who was so excited by the Chatsworth project that he virtually emptied his gardens in Cape Town, sending the contents across the oceans. The collection became so valuable that the under-gardeners had to work out-of-hours shifts to guard the rare plants and 'prevent deprivation'. Paxton, tireless perfectionist that he was, continued to improve his cultivation methods, by shading his plants from the sun's glare with calico, and installing a fumigation machine. The effort was rewarding in more ways than one: on 9 November 1841 Paxton wrote proudly to the Duke, who was in London, that the number of visitors, especially gardeners from England and abroad, was 'extraordinary'.

As well as marvelling at Paxton's 'Great Stove', visitors to Chatsworth also admired the planting of the gardens. There orange beds were edged with bands of blue flowers, yellow beds with purple, scarlet with white, the contrasts serving to further heighten the natural brilliance of the plants. Inspired by the theories of the chemist Michel Eugène Chevreul and by Goethe's recently translated *Theory of Colour* (published in England in 1840), Paxton applied their ideas about complementary colours, contrast and harmony to his plant arrangements.

The success of Chatsworth allowed Paxton to broaden his horizons, as his services became increasingly in demand. The Duke never objected to his accepting other commissions, since Paxton seemed to possess the energy and determination of two. And so in the summer of 1843, when Birkenhead's leading industrialists approached him to design a park for the community, to be controlled by the local authorities, he happily accepted.* Until then, with the exception of the royal parks in London, cities had lacked large public green spaces. With the growth of the new industrial centres, the disappearance of the commons, increasing pollution and poor working conditions in factories, the need for municipal parks was acknowledged for the first time.†

In November 1843, shortly after Paxton took on the Birkenhead commission, the Duke, who was in London, received a letter informing him that Queen Victoria would be visiting Chatsworth in just three weeks. The Duke was not pleased; but needless to say, he obliged, drily commenting to the over-worked Paxton: 'Here is an event.' In reply, Paxton and the steward respect-fully asked if the Duke he would mind not coming up to Derbyshire, since his 'presence would retard what may be necessary to be done'; and would he, instead, remain in London to concentrate on the guest list? This was the biggest event Paxton had ever organised. Moreover, the Peak District in December offered neither the ideal location nor the best climate in which to demonstrate the glory of a garden. The solution, Paxton decided, was to make the Great Conservatory the centre of the spectacle. So the rest of the

*The park at Birkenhead in Cheshire was opened in 1847 and inspired Frederick Law Olmsted's layout for Central Park in New York.
†Recreational facilities for the working classes were still largely discouraged by the ruling elite, concerned that social gatherings might encourage revolutionary ideas. Ten years earlier, however, a Select Committee on Drunkenness had recommended public walks and gardens as an antidote to the evils of alcohol; another Select Committee had declared that public parks, fresh air and space for recreation would improve city dwellers' physical health and moral well-being.

garden was tidied up, the paths were dressed in new white and yellow gravel, and Paxton's men decorated the inside of the house with white and crimson heather.

On 1 December Queen Victoria and Prince Albert arrived to the cheers of a large crowd that had lined the twelve-mile road from Chesterfield to Chatsworth. After lunch the queen asked to see the Great Conservatory. As the royal party, led by the Duke, crossed the garden, they would have seen in the distance the curved glass dome glinting between the trees. Passing by the immaculately trimmed yew hedge enclosing the conservatory area, they walked over the grass terrace – 'free of irregularities', as the *Magazine of Botany* had described it two years earlier – punctuated by circular beds containing specimen plants.

At the doorway to the conservatory, Paxton waited in the cold for the queen and her consort. Welcoming them, he escorted the party into the humid interior. The leaves of giant palms arched high above them, towards the glass roof; aquatic plants grew luxuriantly in their heated tanks, and tender climbers twisted around the trellises. Making her way along the broad central carriageway, then down the two flanking walkways, the queen inspected the plants minutely, while Prince Albert was fascinated by the technical details. Steering them from the temperate zone at one end of the building to the tropical zone at the other, Paxton constantly pointed out the different species. Unlike the potted flowers and trees in other conservatories, these were planted directly into the soil, some of them as deep as ten feet. The royal couple viewed banana trees, cacti such as *Epiphyllum* with their fragrant flowers blooming from leaflike branches, bougainvilleas and *Cinnamomum verum* (cinnamon trees); hibiscus plants in many hues, passionflowers, and *Begonia insignis* with their graceful dangling pink flowers and the strongly scented butterfly-like blossoms of *Hedychium conarium* that had arrived in Gibson's boxes from India. Exotic birds flew over the bamboos and monkeys climbed up and down the banyan tree. Silvery fish darted to and fro in the ponds fringed with papyrus and sculptural arum lilies. In between his floral treasures Paxton had placed rock crystals, like 'mountain[s] of light', catching and refracting the sun's rays; Indian stalactites, moonstones, pyramid-shaped spars and a huge piece of Blue John, the famous purple fluorspar mined in Derbyshire.

The queen was entranced. She thought it the 'most stupendous and extraordinary creation imaginable'. Paxton was a 'genius', she declared. On the second evening of the visit, when darkness enveloped the garden, Paxton instructed his men to light the fourteen thousand oil lamps that they had fastened along the ribs of the conservatory. As it was transformed into what the *Illustrated London News* of 9 December called a 'fairy palace of some eastern tale', the

Illuminated interior of the Great Conservatory for Queen Victoria's visit in 1843

royal couple drove in the Duke's carriage along the central aisle. The entertainment continued outside in the garden, where Paxton orchestrated a sophisticated, hour-long display of illuminations. Three thousand Russian lanterns hung in the trees, the fountains sparkled like liquid diamonds, and the Cascade was lined with an ever-changing ribbon of Bengal lights, from white to blue to red. In a magnificent finale, fireworks lit up the whole park. As almost a hundred members of the British aristocracy, from the Duke of Wellington to Lord Melbourne, sat down to dinner, thousands of members of the public, who had obtained tickets to see the conservatory illuminated, entered the park. Those who could not get in watched the display from outside the gates.

Long after the last guest had gone to bed, in a massive clearing-up operation, two hundred men worked through the night in the extreme cold – Paxton had demanded that everything be immaculate when the royal couple awoke the next morning. The paths were raked, the lawns rolled, the pans of Bengal lights collected; some climbed up into the trees to gather the Russian lanterns, while others swept up the leaves and the rubbish, scattered by the crowd and the wind. So impressed was the Duke of Wellington when at seven the next morning he saw 'the field of battle' completely cleared, that he told the Duke of Devonshire: 'I would like that man of yours for one of my generals'.

The triumph of Queen Victoria's visit was a tribute to Paxton's talents – indeed, to his genius. The orchestration of the illuminations was a tour de force; their beauty testified to his unerring taste. His design and construction of the most sophisticated glass building in the country had demonstrated at every turn his boundless inventiveness. The garden at Chatsworth illustrated to perfection Britain's new-found status as the workshop of the world. The hothouses were equipped with the latest technology. Paxton's analysis of the soil according to new scientific theories had shown him which chemicals and manures would make his plants flourish. The velvet grass, so much admired, had been cut with 'garden engines', the newly invented lawnmowers with rotary blades. The fruit and vegetables eaten by the Duke's guests had been grown in the kitchen garden, where Paxton now produced them on an industrial scale. Every year, for instance, he nurtured three thousand pots of strawberries for the Duke's table. A 'Catalogue of Plants Grown at Chatsworth' of about 1840, compiled for the Duke, records that Paxton was growing in total more than 3500 species of plants.

His extraordinary talent was hailed across the country, and his friends – also great admirers of his work – included the prominent engineers Robert and George Stephenson and Brunel. Respected for his ingenuity, skill and taste, Paxton epitomised many Victorian virtues – not least two of those promulgated by Samuel Smiles in his nineteenth-century bestseller, *Self-Help*: 'perseverance' and being a 'true gentleman'. The last, in particular, had enabled Paxton to transcend class barriers and mix with the upper echelons of society.

As if Paxton wasn't busy enough with the queen's visit, the Duke had also asked him to design a single-jet fountain that would be the highest in the world. He had once seen something like it – at Cassel Wilhelmshöhe in Germany, one of the most spectacular gardens on the continent. To achieve such a spectacle with a gravity-fed fountain, Paxton knew he needed a reservoir high above the house. Once the royal couple had left, he organised a survey of the spot he had in mind, on the moors above the garden. The drop from the new reservoir to Brown's old canal pond, which would become the basin for the new fountain, was almost four hundred feet. According to Paxton's calculations, this would provide enough power to create a jet over two hundred and fifty feet high, making it sixty feet higher than the one at Cassel. A month later the Duke and Paxton fought their way through a gale to the area chosen for the reservoir – even the Duke was 'half frightened by the immense work', he confided to his diary on 18 January 1844. Paxton's men would have to move one hundred thousand cubic yards of earth by spade and wheelbarrow, cut a two-and-a-half-mile ditch into the moor to collect spring- and rain-water to fill the new reservoir, as well as chisel up to fifteen feet into the solid rock to lay the pipes. As always, the Duke was impatient to see the project finished. This time it was the visit of Tsar Nicholas, the Emperor of Russia, in the summer, that put the pressure on Paxton: the Duke wanted to dedicate the fountain to his old acquaintance. The men worked frantically, day and night, to complete what Paxton referred to in the *Magazine of Botany* as the 'monster fountain'. Meanwhile, he was studying and testing hydraulics and pneumatics, asking leading engineers to confirm his results.

Though the fountain was finished in time, the emperor never saw it, having decided to visit the Duke at his London home instead. By July the Duke was feeling 'low and nervous' – not because the emperor had cancelled his visit to Chatsworth, but because his agent had told him that he was £1 million in debt. Years of extravagance had caught up with him. Always reckless with money, he had spent such a huge amount during the previous decade on his garden and house that more than half his annual income was now eaten up by interest payments. The improvements at Chatsworth had cost him more than £300,000, of which £33,000 had been swallowed up by the construction of the Great Conservatory alone. But if the garden was the source of his financial woes, it was also, as ever, his consolation. Paxton was ready to demonstrate the power of the new Emperor Fountain: the water in the reservoir was only two feet deep, but once the valves had been opened the jet shot up to a mighty two hundred and sixty-seven feet. Here indeed was the world's highest fountain. 'O Paxton!' wrote the Duke in his diary later that day. 'It is a glorious success. The most majestic object.' Trusted friend as well as gardener par excellence, Paxton had succeeded in cheering him up. And it was to him that the Duke now turned for help in his financial crisis.

After working through the accounts, Paxton's solution was simple: the Duke should sell off some of his other estates. His employer promptly followed his instructions. Making Paxton his official financial adviser, he admitted: 'It is well I follow your advice in small as well as great things.' Paxton himself regarded his latest promotion as his 'grandest triumph' in his long succession of 'grand undertakings', he told his wife. Selling the estates would take some time, but the ageing Duke knew that disaster had been averted. In December 1844 Paxton sold the first estate for £100,000, and the second a year later for almost £500,000 – to George Hudson, the 'Railway King'.* Now solvent, the Duke could start spending again on the garden at Chatsworth.

The next task was to finish the Rock Garden, which Paxton had begun two years earlier. Inspired by their travels through the Alps, the vast rockery to the west of the Great Conservatory now covered six acres. Rock garden enthusiasts had experimented with a variety of styles. Some set out to exploit the natural features of the landscape, as at Hawkstone. Others sought to recreate naturalistic stone formations, like the rock garden at Blenheim. Yet others had attempted scale models of the Alps: Lady Broughton at Hoole House near Chester had decorated the spiky rocks in her lawn with snow made from crushed white spar and marble. None of these approaches suited Paxton: what he had in mind was the total transformation of the smooth lawns

*These were the Yorkshire estates Baldersby and Londesborough.

Humphry Repton's design for the flower garden at Sheringham. Instead of designing rolling lawns right up to the house, Repton envisaged a more manicured scene. There is a 'flower passage' and a conservatory to the left, trellises to the right, and circular and kidney-shaped flowerbeds that are edged in by the low basket-like fences

The formal flower garden at Beaudesert illustrates Humphry Repton's nostalgic view of the past. This is typical of his designs in the last years of his professional life, when he harked back to the geometrical layouts of Elizabethan and baroque gardens

The view from the dining room at Sheringham on to a ploughed cornfield shows how
Humphry Repton integrated agricultural life into the garden. He added people and cattle to
'animate' the scene. The temple can be seen in the distance

John Constable's paintings of rural labourers expressed a yearning for a rustic idyll
that can be seen in the art and literature of the period as well as in garden designs such
as those by Humphry Repton for Sheringham

Chatsworth, Derbyshire, in 1828, two years after Joseph Paxton began to work there

John Gibson, the gardener Joseph Paxton chose to
travel to India to collect orchids and other exotic
plants, brought back the evergreen tree *Amherstia
nobilis* from the Botanic Garden in Calcutta

Victoria regia (now *Victoria amazonica*) flowered for the first time in
England under Joseph Paxton's care at Chatsworth in 1849

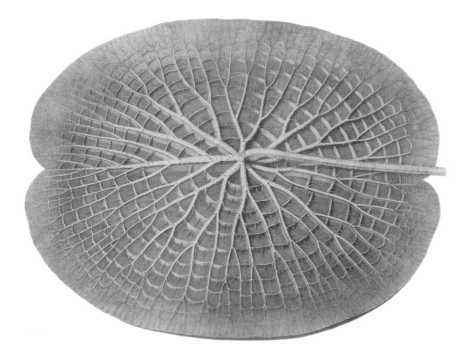

The underside of the lily leaf shows nature's masterful engineering.
The protruding veins, which give the leaves strength and stop them from buckling,
inspired Joseph Paxton to design the Lily House at Chatsworth and then Crystal Palace
with a flat ridge-and-furrow roof

Joseph Paxton's Crystal Palace was a much enlarged version of the Lily House at Chatsworth

The south border in Gertrude Jekyll's garden at Munstead Wood shows the
painterly way in which she planted herbaceous borders

The Great Plat at Hestercombe is one of Gertrude Jekyll and Edwin Lutyens' masterpieces. Elizabethan and Jacobean architectural elements, such as balustrades, paved walks and steps, combined with Jekyll's natural planting became the epitome of an English garden

Woman Before a Cottage by Arthur Claude Strachan. For Gertrude Jekyll and many of her contemporaries the flower-clad cottage symbolised a peaceful rural life untainted by urban influences and industrialisation. It was this image that she wanted to convey in most of her gardens

From the mid-nineteenth century, artists, writers and gardeners once again began to admire old-fashioned plants. In *Ophelia*, for instance, John Everett Millais depicted flowers such as daisies, *Lythrum salicana* and white lilies. Gertrude Jekyll used many of the same flowers in the borders at Hestercombe

The Arts and Crafts Movement was inspired by the many flower references in Shakespeare's work. This is the frontispiece to *Flowers from Shakespeare's Garden* by Walter Crane (1906)

at Chatsworth into a dramatic rockscape that would demonstrate his mastery of nature. At Hawkstone visitors had worshipped the 'genius of place'; Paxton and the Duke wanted to celebrate the 'genius of man'.

Paxton needed huge boulders. Although Chatsworth had no natural rocks, an abandoned quarry above the estate offered just what he was after. But how to transport them? Again he applied his breadth of knowledge and ingenuity to the matter in hand, contriving a steam-powered machine to transport the rocks and winch them into place. By 1844 he had created towers of rough stones stacked up to forty feet high and cemented together. 'Art has been triumphant,' one visitor exclaimed; and the Duke wrote, 'The spirit of some Druid seems to animate Mr Paxton in these bulky removals.' With the hard landscaping in place, the gardeners now filled the cracks and crannies with soil and planted the delicate alpine flowers that Paxton had so coveted in Switzerland. The addition of straight walks and arches highlighted the artificiality of the 'natural' scene. The masterstroke, completely blocking the main path, was a huge boulder which, at the touch of a mechanism, swivelled like a revolving door, revealing another path leading to a replica of a seventeenth-century 'copper tree' – a water joke that sprayed unwary visitors with eight hundred water jets.

A year later, the Duke faced a dilemma: should he allow a new railway to be built through his land? Britain was in the grip of railway fever. Since the 1830s over two thousand miles of track had been laid, costing speculators a total of £67 million, and now Parliament had authorised plans for yet more lines, on which an estimated two hundred thousand men were working. Paxton had long been captivated by the railways, and it was he who proposed linking Chatsworth and its environs to the network. Over the previous decade he himself had speculated in railway shares, investing a total of £35,000. He had, as Charles Dickens wrote, 'the command of every railway and railway influence in England and abroad, except the Great Western; and he is in it heart and purse'.

The Chatsworth railway scheme became Paxton's new pet project. He was appointed provisional director of the Manchester, Buxton, Matlock and

Midland Junction Railway (MBMMJR), a small company with a cumbersome name, and invested some of his own money in it. The intention was to connect Manchester with the existing line between Derby and London, and at the same time to link Chatsworth with the main railway network. Because of the problems involved in laying tracks in the Peak District, Paxton appointed his friend George Stephenson, inventor of the *Rocket*, as surveyor in hope of finding a solution. There were two possible routes: either directly through the Duke's land or through the neighbouring estate at Haddon Hall. The owner of Haddon Hall, the Duke of Rutland, was outraged at the thought of the noisy, smelly railway running so close to his ancient mansion. Assuming he would find an ally in his neighbour and friend, the Duke of Devonshire, he opposed the plan. But Paxton's employer had changed his allegiances, now deferring to his gardener rather than to his aristocratic friends. After long discussions with Paxton he decided he would support the scheme, and would invest £50,000 if the line were to pass through Chatsworth. Unlike his noble neighbour, he welcomed this symbol of modernity.

In March 1848 Louis Philippe of France, having been forced to abdicate, sought asylum in England. A wave of revolutions was spreading across Europe. The Duke feared, as did most of his class, that the unrest in France and Italy and in cities such as Berlin, Vienna and Budapest would ignite radical movements in Britain. When he learned that the Chartists were preparing for a mass procession in London on 10 April, to take their petition for universal male suffrage and annual Parliaments to Westminster for the third time, he called for his gardener. Paxton tried to calm him, but such was the Duke's anxiety that Paxton agreed to go to the capital himself to investigate the situation on the streets.

The London Paxton found was indeed preparing for a violent demonstration, and on an enormous scale: the queen had moved her household to the Isle of Wight, shopkeepers had barricaded their shops and many public buildings and banks had been sandbagged. Eight thousand soldiers, four thousand policemen and thousands of special constables were out on the streets. When Paxton eventually saw the Chartist crowd, he was surprised by how much smaller it was than he had expected. The security forces, recruited largely from the middle classes, easily outnumbered them. In face of the opposition the government had mounted, the Chartist leader, Feargus O'Connor, called off the demonstration. Unlike the French bourgeoisie, who had played a significant role in the Revolution, their British counterparts had been sufficiently appeased by the Reform Bill in 1832 to want no part in a Chartist protest. The Chartists felt they had been sold out by the middle classes.[*] Having wagered that the protest would come to nothing, Paxton went to his broker and picked up £500, boasting to his friends later: 'That's the way to profit by a panic.' On 13 April the Duke wrote with relief in his diary: 'There will be an end of all destructions of rank and property in England.'

By 1849 the economy was picking up and the increasing trade with the expanding Empire was bringing a degree of prosperity. A decade earlier the journalist and radical campaigner William Cobbett had declared: 'I defy you to agitate a fellow with a full stomach'; now, at the end of the 'hungry forties', real wages were rising and rumblings of discontent had died down. The threat of an English revolution was past. Preoccupied as ever with his own concerns, the Duke could enjoy normal life again. The most exciting bit of news had been that the railway would be coming to the nearby village of Rowsley, just two miles from Chatsworth.

On 4 June the first train pulled into Rowsley station. Chatsworth had been open to the public free of charge for many generations, but now, large groups of working-class people from the growing industrial cities of Derby, Sheffield, Bradford, Leeds, Birmingham and Leicester were able to visit for the first time. One of the first groups to arrive comprised two thousand teetotallers from Sheffield brought by Thomas Cook, an idealist and lay preacher who had been organising excursions for the poor for the last eight years in order to improve their moral well-being. Some of them must have had a long wait as the under-gardeners had been instructed to show parties of no more than twenty around the gardens, staggered at five-minute intervals. Entry to the Great Conservatory, however, was only by special permission from Paxton or the Duke. In the first year after the railway opened, eighty thousand visitors walked

[*]Six weeks earlier, in February 1848, Karl Marx and Friedrich Engels had published the *Communist Manifesto*.

through the gates of Chatsworth, making it one of the largest tourist attractions in the country.

Paxton was proud of his achievements, but for all his horticultural triumphs there were still some things that remained beyond his grasp. One of these concerned a giant water lily. For the last six years he had been trying, without success, to germinate its seeds. Only a handful of botanists had seen the exuberant lily flowering in its native habitat in South America, and no one had ever seen it in England. The seeds originated in British Guiana, where the botanist Sir Robert Schomburgk had seen the plant in all its glory in 1837. He had despatched seeds to England, along with drawings depicting a plant covering the water all around it with six-foot-diameter leaves and flowers made up of hundreds of white and pink petals. It was one of the most extraordinary plants ever discovered, and the horticultural world had been dazzled. They gave it an appropriately regal name, *Victoria regia*.* Every gardener in the country who could get hold of the rare seeds did his best to nurture a seedling; but like Paxton they all failed – except for one.

   In July 1849, a month after the railway reached Chatsworth, William Hooker, the director of the Botanic Gardens at Kew, informed Paxton that they had managed to grow some seedlings. They would distribute between thirty and forty of them to eminent gardeners across the country, of whom Paxton was one. The race to get *Victoria regia* to flower had begun. For the next three weeks Paxton concentrated on building a tank for the plant, which he hoped would simulate its natural habitat as far as possible. To make sure 'that the plant should feel the removal as little as possible', he told Hooker, he would pick up the seedling himself, and so at six o'clock in the morning on 3 August 1849, his forty-sixth birthday, he arrived at Kew. The seedling displayed no sign of its giant potential, and fitted into a container smaller than a hatbox. Paxton rushed to Euston to catch the new train to Rowsley, which had reduced the journey time from fifteen hours to just ten.† At Chatsworth, in preparation for

---

Victoria regia is now called *Victoria amazonica*.

†A piece of information we owe to Robert Aughtie, one of Paxton's under-gardeners at Chatsworth, who noted down the new travel times in his diary.

the lily's arrival, the workmen had begun to heat up the water in one of the large hothouse tanks. In the centre of the three-foot deep tank, they put a mound of loam and peat to accommodate the roots, gently heated by the pipes running through it. A small wheel in one of the corners kept the water in constant motion, producing the soft ripples of the lily's native rivers. A week later the water had reached the right temperature, of 30 degrees centigrade and the lily took possession of its new home.

By the end of September it had already outgrown its tank, so Paxton built a new one. Nineteen bright-green leaves, the largest of which was over three feet in diameter, had uncurled from their spiky, furled-up balls, and were now gently floating on the water's surface. Paxton was becoming increasingly excited. He seemed to be ahead of the race – the lilies at Kew were not growing at all. Only the long Derbyshire winter nights worried him: *Victoria regia* needed light as well as heat. Gaslight was just not bright enough – if only, Paxton remarked to the Duke on 1 October, electricity were available to provide those few extra hours of light every morning and evening. His aspirations, though, were ahead of his time. The use of electricity, as he well knew, was still at an experimental stage – the light-bulb and dynamo were yet to be invented.

As it turned out, however, the lily didn't seem to mind the long hours of darkness, and on 1 November a large prickly bud appeared above the surface of the water. The leaves were now nearly five feet across – the outside rim turned up like the edges of a tray, contrasting the crimson hairy underside with the smooth green surface. One evening, a week later, the bud opened to reveal a flower of a flawless white, with the fragrance of a ripe fruit. Letters reporting every detail of the plant's progress had been flying between Paxton and the Duke, who was staying at his estate in Ireland; that night Paxton wrote: 'no words can describe the grandeur and beauty' of the plant. The following evening the flower displayed its vibrant pink centre, and expanded fully during the night. The outside petals were now lying flat on the water's surface, like a halo around the prominent pink centre. On the third evening the flower had faded, but more buds were appearing. Paxton invited Hooker to come and admire his wondrous achievement, tempting him with 'the sight [. . . that] is worth a journey of a thousand miles'. He did not have to entice him; horticulturists from across the country flocked to Chatsworth, including Hooker and John Lindley. Everyone wanted to see *Victoria regia* in full bloom.

The Duke finally arrived at Chatsworth ten days after the first flowering. As he crossed the dark wintry gardens, he saw his hothouse illuminated in the distance.* Paxton the impresario had created the perfect stage for this spectacle. Inside, the air was warm and a soft light played on the 'stupendous' lily. Paxton was already there, together with Lindley, admiring the giant plant. Its floating leaves were not only huge but also incredibly strong, and to prove it the Duke put Paxton's seven-year-old daughter, Annie, on one of them. An artist from the *Illustrated London News*, invited along to witness Paxton's success, captured the scene, recording it for the whole country to see, and for posterity.

Annie Paxton on the leaf of *Victoria regia*, 1849. Note the waterwheel in the corner behind Annie

A few weeks later it was clear that the lily needed a yet larger tank and the Duke and Paxton decided that it deserved its own house. So Paxton set to work. Intrigued by the astonishing load-bearing capacity of the lily's flat leaves, he studied the networks of radiating veins on their undersides, perceiving that

*Under-gardener Robert Aughtie noted in his diary on 20 and 26 November 1849 how the glasshouse was illuminated for important guests as the flowers opened only in the evening (Harley and Harley,1992, pp. 169–70).

it was their 'cross-bars' that stopped the leaves from 'buckling'. This he translated into his first horizontal ridge-and-furrow roof. The Lily House was, as Paxton explained, 'not the production of a momentary consideration of the subject'; on the contrary, it had evolved over twenty years of experimentation, but his observation of the leaves' anatomy had inspired him to depart from his sloping or curving ridge-and-furrow roofs. The leaves were a 'beautiful example of natural engineering', he would tell the Society of Arts in a lecture delivered in November the next year. The Lily House encapsulated perfectly the coming together of Paxton's twin passions: horticulture and engineering. In this one building he had incorporated all the glasshouse features he had pioneered over the years. As well as the new flat ridge-and-furrow roof, it housed sophisticated ventilation and heating systems, and the ingenious 'Paxton Gutter' for collecting rain and condensation. Paxton had used hollow iron columns that supported the roof but also doubled as drains, plus floorboards with gaps between them to get rid of the dust. At the centre was the large circular tank for *Victoria regia*, surrounded by eight smaller tanks for other aquatic plants. It was the most efficient and economic glasshouse Paxton had ever built.

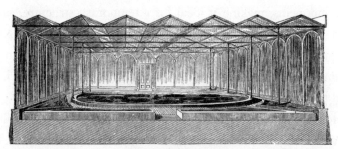

Figure 4.—Interior View.

Figure 5.—Perspective View of the Exterior.

Interior and exterior of the Lily House, 1850

While Paxton was putting the finishing touches to the Lily House in April 1850, the Building Committee of the Royal Commission for the Great Exhibition were struggling to agree among themselves on the design of a building whose purpose would be to house the 'Exhibition of the Works of Industry of All Nations'. Due to open on 1 May 1851, it would be the world's first large-scale international exhibition ever held; and the timeframe was tight. Prince Albert supported it with passion, believing it would provide a showcase for the achievements of nineteenth-century man while displaying Britain's industrial might. When Paxton finally turned his attention to the notion of submitting his own design, it was almost too late, and it took all his and the Duke's networking to secure him an extension to the deadline. As ever, he had been too busy, but as a man whose 'very leisure would kill a man of fashion', as Dickens put it, he was determined to find the time. On 7 June 1850 he drove to Hyde Park to survey the proposed site. On the 11th, while he was attending a dull committee meeting of the Midland Railway of which he was a director, his mind wandered to the exhibition. A few scribbles later, on a bit of blotting paper, he had drawn a blotchy sketch of what looked like several Lily Houses stacked together. An idea quickly formed. Like the Lily House, the design would be based on standardised components, making it ideal for a temporary structure, since all the parts could be prefabricated off site, then assembled in Hyde Park. Not a single brick, not an ounce of mortar, would be needed – only wood, iron and glass. This building would inaugurate a new era of architecture, in which standardisation and prefabrication would become markers of modernity.

Paxton spent the next weeks in a frenzy of designing, calculating, and drawing. Well aware of the enormity of the task he had set himself, he invited leading engineering and glass manufacturers to assist with the construction details and costings. On the evening of 15 July, he sent a telegram to his wife in Derby: his design had been approved. Nine days later, when Paxton and the Duke arrived at Chatsworth, seven hundred visitors were waiting to cheer them. This was the first time the Duke had seen the new Lily House. He was 'enchanted' – it was, as he wrote in his diary on the 24th, 'the parent of the exhibition house'. He also mused on the fact that, although Paxton had won one of the most prestigious commissions of the industrial age, he remained 'the unaltered gardener'; and Paxton was the first to acknowledge the Duke's 'fostering hand'.

After weeks of rain, the Crystal Palace opened on a bright and sunny day in May 1851, on time and on budget. Traffic jams from the city centre to Hyde Park brought London to a standstill, and crowds lined the streets. In Hyde Park itself three hundred thousand people gathered to watch Queen Victoria and Prince Albert arrive. Paxton led the royal procession through the sunlit building. Inside were displayed the myriad products of Victorian Britain: locomotives, hydraulic cranes, steam-driven ploughs, scale models of suspension bridges . . . Among the thousands of exhibits were a bed that functioned as an alarm clock and a cricket catapult. One focal point was an enormous neo-Gothic altar clad in machine-carved ornaments – another demonstration of the possibilities of mechanisation. Over the next six months this vision of progress, invention, industry and, above all, belief in man was presented to six million visitors. The *London Illustrated News* declared the exhibition a wonder of the world, as amazing as the pyramids; others heralded it as a cathedral of material

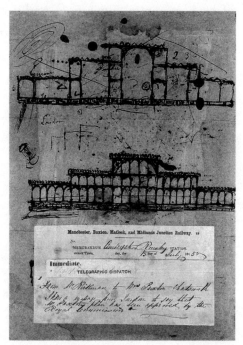

Paxton's sketch for the Great Exhibition.
Ink on blotting paper, June 1850

progress. There were, however, a few designers, writers and architects, such as John Ruskin and William Morris, who were appalled by what they perceived as ostentation and excess. This small group of critics objected in particular to such exhibits as an eighty-blade pocket-knife, beehives in the form of dolls' houses and a tableau of stuffed kittens having a tea-party. In their opinion, mechanisation had gone mad, and instead of pointing to greater efficiency and improved design, the cheaply decorated trivia that crammed the exhibition's galleries were the epitome of vulgarity. The majority of visitors did not share their disapproval – on the contrary they were impressed by what they saw: to them both the Palace and its contents trumpeted Britain's manufacturing superiority to the world.

Whenever Paxton went to Hyde Park he was noticed by visitors; 'Look, look, there's Mr Paxton' was a familiar cry. He had become a celebrity, and the Duke of Devonshire was happy to 'parade the architect about' and bask in his limelight. Inspired by an exotic plant and encouraged by his own patronage, his protégé had created the most important building of the century. The three mature elms around which Paxton had built the Crystal Palace were a reminder of his horticultural inspiration. And it was in the gardens at Chatsworth, that England's twin personae – 'workshop of the world' and 'green and pleasant land' – had become one.

7

Our England Is a Garden: Hestercombe

'The message will be of nature and men.'
William Richard Lethaby, *Architecture, Mysticism and Myth*, 1892

'Go to nature, in all singleness of heart . . . Wild nature tamed but not degraded under the hand of Man.'
John Ruskin, *Modern Painters*, 1843

'We must turn this land from the grimy backyard of a workshop into a garden.'
William Morris in his lecture, 'Art and the Beauty of the Earth', 13 October 1881

On 14 August 1903,[*] Edwin Landseer Lutyens, a successful architect in his mid-thirties with expressive and elegant hands, was sitting on a train bound for Taunton in Devon, writing letters as he always did when he travelled. The purpose of the journey was to discuss with the Honourable Edward William

[*] Unless otherwise stated, the chronology of the making of Hestercombe and Lutyens' schedule are based on the letters between him and his wife Emily (RIBA) and Jekyll's notebooks (Godalming Museum).

Berkeley Portman and his wife Constance Mary the enlargement of their garden at Hestercombe, Somerset. On arrival at the station, Lutyens was most likely met by a servant and driven the four-mile journey to Hestercombe in Portman's smart green and yellow Cadillac. Indicative of Portman's wealth, the house, nestling among the folds of the Quantock Hills, was surrounded by a thirty-five-acre landscaped garden. Designed in the mid-eighteenth century, it was laid out in a steep-sided valley around a serpentine lake to the north of the house. Follies ranging from a thatched Witch House to a classical temple were dotted along the periphery. South of the house in front of the drawing-room windows, the previous garden architect, one Henry Hall, had laid out a formal Victorian Terrace with a tiered fountain at its centre and four rectangular beds planted with annuals, forming a neat but garish carpet.

While the landscaped garden largely retained its original charm, the house was less prepossessing. Built in the late eighteenth century in a plain classical style, it had been extended and 'embellished' in the 1880s in a way that both destroyed its original proportions and introduced incongruous architectural elements such as parapets and an ornate Renaissance-inspired tower. A 'very bad house architecturally', was Lutyens' verdict. The house, however, was not his concern; he had been commissioned to extend the garden below the Victorian Terrace. This part of the garden drew the eye outwards across the landscape to a stunning view over Taunton vale, but the site itself was challenging. Stretching down from the terrace, it formed a series of swells sloping from north to south as well as from east to west, making terracing complicated and a single-level garden too expensive. With a few days in hand, Lutyens had plenty of time to look around, consider the options and assess the depth of Portman's purse before drawing up a scheme.

Considered by many of his rivals to be almost predatory in seeking commissions, Lutyens had doubtless gathered information about his new client before meeting him, so he probably already knew that Edward Portman was in line to inherit a fortune and the title of viscount from his father, who owned thousands of acres of countryside as well as the Marylebone Estate in London. Portman himself already owned well over ten thousand acres, and unlike many other landowners, who had been hard hit by a series of agricultural depressions at the end of the previous century, would 'have more money than which he knows what to do with', Lutyens was sure. While others had suffered from the bad harvests, growing international competition and the effects of cheap imports from the newly opened-up North American prairies, Portman's model dairy business and his own breed of prize-winning Devonshire cattle were still making a profit. Nonetheless, Portman could not expect to remain immune, any more than could his fellow aristocrats, to the social and economic changes that were taking place.

The heir-in-waiting was forty-seven years old, a tall, sturdy man with a fashionably thick moustache adorning a fleshy face. He had a reputation as a hospitable host, a good sportsman and a paternalistic landlord – he was interested in agricultural reform and the moral well-being of his tenants. A 'real good sort', Lutyens called him. As well as taking an active part in the local agricultural associations, sitting on the board of the local hospital to which he was a generous benefactor, chairing numerous societies and serving as Master of the Taunton Hunt for some years, he was known for spending his money on 'eating, hospitals and cattle breeding'. His wife Constance Mary also busied herself with local charitable causes, earning from Lutyens the nicknames 'Lady Bountiful' and 'bazaar opener to the county'.

In many respects, the Portmans still lived in a manner similar to their ancestors. But the world around them was changing. Unlike his grandfather, who had held the post of Lord Lieutenant of the county of Somerset on the strength of no other qualification than that he was a baron, Portman's route to this kind of eminence was slightly more complicated. In the wake of the Local Government Act of 1888, which introduced elected county councils, it was a council committee that appointed Portman to the posts of Deputy Lieutenant of Somerset and Justice of the Peace for Dorset. Indeed, the centuries-old system of local government in which the aristocracy ruled as non-elected oligarchs had come to an end. This change had been fuelled in part by the widespread criticism of landowners' treatment of tenant farmers, which had turned into an attack on the very legitimacy of the landed classes' right to govern. The increasing levels of rural poverty had led to calls for greater state intervention on behalf of workers, and the imposition of direct taxes on estates and on unearned income. In 1884 the Third Reform Act, introduced by Gladstone's government in response to radical pressure groups, extended the household vote to the counties (though women were still excluded). Taking little interest in politics, Portman, however, seemed unperturbed by the shifting political climate; to him little seemed to have changed, as he continued to enjoy the deference that his standing and wealth brought him in the local community. Lutyens described his house as 'a typical self satisfied comfortable English sporting-squire of a house and place'; no epithets could have better described its owner.

In 1903 Lutyens was the leading country-house architect, fêted by those rich enough to afford country houses of a style that evoked the old English manor house with steep-hipped roof and irregular silhouette, while at the same time boasting up-to-the-minute luxuries such as electricity and plumbed-in bath-rooms. He was also dedicated to the idea that a building should relate to its landscape through the use of local materials and vernacular craft techniques. In this he was often associated with the Arts and Crafts Movement, whose dislike of industrial production during the second half of the nineteenth century had led it to emulate the craftsmanship of the Middle Ages. Lutyens had also become increasingly interested in the work of the Renaissance architect Andrea Palladio, as well as that of Christopher Wren pursuing what Lutyens called the 'high game' of classicism.

Edwin Lutyens. Drawing by Phipps, *c.* 1906

As part of his architectural work, Lutyens also designed gardens, a skill he had learned from Gertrude Jekyll. Twenty-five years his senior, Jekyll had been introduced to Lutyens at a tea party in Surrey in 1889, the same year he had set up as an independent architect at the tender age of nineteen. They would have seemed an unlikely team. Whereas Lutyens had yet to establish a reputation, Jekyll was already well known in the world of gardening. Born into a wealthy middle-class family, she could have chosen, as did so many of her class and generation, to restrict her artistic skills to a little embroidery and painting during leisure hours. Instead, much more serious about her creativity, she had been one of the first women to study at the South Kensington School of Art in London, with the aim of training as a painter. Inspired by her travels through Europe and by the Arts and Crafts Movement, she had also worked in interior decoration, in metalwork and embroidery, until her short-sightedness forced her to abandon her plans. But having always loved flowers, she then put all her artistic knowledge into gardening – into painting with 'living' colours. Lutyens' first impression of her was of a short, plump woman who chose her words with care; she wore a black felt hat from which sprang a black cock's tail-feather, 'curving and ever prancing forwards'. Though she said little to him on that first afternoon, Jekyll had taken to the bright young man; over the next few years, on 'voyages of discovery' in and around the country lanes, she imparted to him her love of the Surrey countryside, her knowledge of traditional craft techniques, of vernacular architecture and of gardening.

Two years after her death in 1932, in his foreword to a biography by her nephew Francis Jekyll, Lutyens still fondly remembered their trips around Surrey and Sussex in Jekyll's pony and trap, with him forced by the reins to one side of the driving seat and terrified by her perilous driving style (caused by her myopia). Searching out old farmhouses and cottages, they would stop to discuss 'their modest methods and construction', while Jekyll pointed out pretty cottage gardens or clusters of wild flowers growing at the roadside. Since their first meeting, Jekyll had published five books and innumerable articles on gardening, and had become one of the country's leading experts. Together the two of them had established an informal partnership in which Lutyens would design the house and the basic layout of the garden while Jekyll would fill in the rest of the canvas.

Gertrude Jekyll sketched by Edwin Lutyens, c.1896

Having missed out on the customary public school education on account of illness, Lutyens at first lacked benefactors, but Jekyll had introduced him to her extensive network of contacts and played a key part in his rise to fame. As one rival noted: 'Miss Jekyll has pretty well run him and now he is doing a roaring trade.' In the early years of their partnership Lutyens' role had been that of eager pupil. He was often intimidated by Jekyll's use of long words, which she had once observed were useful 'engines of warfare of the nature of the battering ram'. For her part, Jekyll admired his talent and enjoyed working with him. The difference between him and other architects, she said, was as 'between quicksilver and suet'. But Jekyll – or 'Bumps', or 'Woozle' or 'Mother of all Bulbs', as Lutyens called her – was more than just a source of commissions; she was also the 'best friend a man could ever have found'.

Things had changed since the early days of their relationship, though, and where Jekyll had once been the one to attract new clients, now as Lutyens travelled to Hestercombe in 1903 it was he who was the public face of the partnership. One reason for this reversal of roles was Lutyens' marriage to Emily, the eccentric and stern-looking daughter of Earl Lytton. This had elevated Lutyens' social position and acquainted him with a number of wealthy family friends who soon became clients. Another reason was that Jekyll, now almost

Edwin Lutyens and Gertrude Jekyll sketched by Edwin Lutyens, 1896

sixty, was becoming increasingly disinclined to travel too far from her home at
Munstead Wood in Surrey because of her short-sightedness – this had worsened over the past few years, bringing on severe headaches from eye-strain.
These days she was happy to let Lutyens visit the designated site, where he
would normally make his first drawings, or in the train on the way back to his
London office. Then he would report back to her, whereupon she might be
induced to make the trip herself. If the garden was too far afield, she would
ask him for detailed information about the situation, the surrounding landscape
and the condition of the soil. Then, with the salient facts at their disposal, they
would discuss Lutyens' initial sketches. Once they had finalised the layout, Jekyll
would draw up her planting plans, with a view to filling the garden with colour
and scent.

Jekyll had developed much of her style by experimenting in her own garden at
Munstead Wood. In contrast to Victorian 'carpet bedding' such as Paxton's
garish flowerbeds at Chatsworth or William Nesfield's ornate parterres of
coloured gravel, she designed herbaceous borders that looked both natural and
informal. Though she often used circular or rectangular beds, she would group
her flowering plants in irregular clumps so that they seemed to weave in and
out of each other, rather than arranging them in symmetrical patterns and great

swathes of one colour. Jekyll's combination of geometrical beds with picturesque planting bore a strong resemblance to what Repton had been aiming for
at the end of his career. But whereas Repton had presented his flowers in a
theatrical, highest-to-lowest conical arrangement or in ground-covering
schemes, in Jekyll's borders they rose and fell, apparently at random, in an
undulating movement. Furthermore, in contrast to Repton, who had often
included unrealistic designs in his Red Books, featuring in close proximity
flowers that would never bloom together, Jekyll had the necessary horticultural
skills to translate her ideas into gardens that would always work. She knew how
to paint with flowers. She also used her botanical knowledge to devise gardens
based mainly on hardy perennials – orchestrating their flowering periods to
perfection – instead of depending on the still popular annuals that had to be
ripped out twice a year and exchanged for new plants grown in greenhouses.

Having had a chance to size up both the site and his hosts, Lutyens wrote excitedly from Hestercombe to his wife Emily: '[M]oney abounds.' Portman had
even installed electric lighting, powered by a water-wheel, as early as 1897 when
the generation of electricity was still in its infancy. Lutyens was counting on a
generous budget. His design encompassed the area south of the house below
the Victorian Terrace, and consisted of a formal square walled garden on six
levels.* Working with the lie of the land rather than against it, he made the
most of the awkward site by proposing a sunken plot at the centre, with narrow
ascending terraces on each side. Each of the six levels would feature Jekyll's
long herbaceous borders and grass walks. As well as providing a clever solution to the difficulties presented by the terrain, the centre of the sunken area,
125 feet square, would reflect the width of the existing terrace, thus relating the

*Unless otherwise stated, the description of Hestercombe is based on Edwin Lutyens' designs
and Gertrude Jekyll's planting plans, copies of which are held at RIBA (the originals are in
the Reef Point Collection at the University of California, Berkeley). They are also based on
Jekyll's notebooks at the Godalming Museum, as well as on her plans at the Somerset Record
Office; H. Avray Tipping's articles in *Country Life*; Lawrence Weaver, *Houses and Gardens by
E. L. Lutyens*, London, Country Life, 1913; and Philip White (ed.), *An Illustrated Guide to
Gertrude Jekyll's Planting Design for the Formal Garden at Hestercombe*, Taunton, Hestercombe
Gardens Trust, 2004.

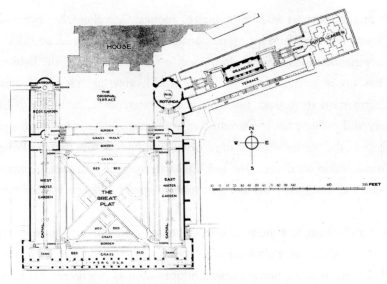

Edwin Lutyens' plan of the garden at Hestercombe

new design to the old and giving the whole a sense of unity. Standing on the Victorian Terrace, the Portmans would be able to look down on to the new beds. To the left and right, Lutyens proposed two narrow water channels – the Rill Gardens or Water Gardens – stretching along the entire length of the new section. He also wanted to connect this part of the grounds with the eighteenth-century landscaped garden to the north: his solution was to mirror the layout of the house, which had a wing running diagonally (north-east) from the south façade. A paved terrace in front of it would extend like an arm towards a small raised and walled area at the east end of the garden (the Dutch Garden) which would give access to the landscaped part. At the centre of the paved terrace Lutyens planned to build an orangery; below it and the small walled plot would be a gently descending lawn.

Lutyens estimated the cost at £10,000, plus his fees which were to be 5 per cent of the commission. But Edward Portman was reluctant to 'rush and spend money' before he had inherited his father's fortune. Instead, he asked whether something could be done for just £1000.* Lutyens was unperturbed; he prided himself on being able to persuade his clients, whatever their initial

*Considering that a High Court judge earned in the region of £5000 in 1913–14 while a cleaner's annual income was under £30, this was still a large amount of money.

ideas on budgets, to part with large sums of money. One client, he once boasted, 'didn't know how to spend his money until he met me'. Indeed, so calculating were Lutyens' methods that he often tried to find out whether the lady of the house 'has any influence and if so what?' And having spoken with Constance Mary Portman on 16 August, his last day at Hestercombe, he wrote to Emily: '[T]o-day will prove what her strength of influence is. She is for the 10,000£!!' When he left, the matter was still unresolved, but he was sure that the Portmans would commission his design. He had 'a wonderful way with clients', remarked one of his assistants, and 'always got them to spend what he wanted them to spend'.

Over the next few months, Lutyens made frequent trips to see Jekyll at Munstead. His visits were always jovial: she would entertain him with generous meals, homemade cakes, home-brewed liquors such as elderberry wine, as well as 'nonsense games and comfy all round'. Although Lutyens' responsibility as architect was to draw up the garden layout and Jekyll's to think up the planting schemes, neither saw their role as distinct from the other's. '[B]oth these crafts must meet and overlap and work together, the architect and gardener must have some knowledge of each other's business,' Jekyll argued. So both contributed ideas to all aspects of the task in hand, resuming by letter where their conversations left off and swapping revised plans, with their revisions scribbled all over them, until they agreed upon the scheme.

By spring 1904, the Portmans had awarded Lutyens and Jekyll the commission. Constance Mary Portman, it turned out, had persuaded her husband to spend more than he had originally planned on a substantial design including the sunken garden and the small walled plot to the east, but not the Orangery. On 7 April, Lutyens visited the site again, and the following week he invited a group of workmen from Hestercombe to his London office in order to discuss the drawings. As usual, Lutyens was busy on a variety of projects, and complained when the builders arrived: 'Everybody wants me.' Keeping them waiting, he wrote hastily to Emily who was away, telling her that the builders were in the next room and that he felt 'dreadfully pushed', especially since his friend Edward Hudson had invited himself to dinner and was expected within ten minutes.

Eventually, after having explained his plans for Hestercombe to the workmen, Lutyens was ready to receive the large, laconic Hudson. Having inherited a printing business from his father, Hudson had founded the magazine *Country Life* seven years earlier. Week after week, wealthy lawyers, businessmen, bankers and their wives would leaf through the glossy pages, admiring the country houses of Britain in all their seemingly timeless tranquillity. For these men and women a place in the country represented rising social status as well as an escape from the city – something that many of Lutyens and Jekyll's clients also sought. Hudson himself had asked Lutyens to build his house, Deanery Garden in Berkshire, a few years before, and now the architect was building *Country Life*'s new offices in Tavistock Street in London. Both lacking the formal education expected of men of their eminence, they felt a certain affinity with each other that would extend into a lifelong friendship. Hudson's admiration for Lutyens' work led him to assert that Lutyens was the best architect since Wren and, convinced of his friend's talent, he did his utmost to promote his work. The friends and acquaintances he recommended him to had included the Portmans, and he regularly publicised Lutyens and Jekyll's work in *Country Life*. Jekyll wrote a column in the magazine called 'Garden Notes' and each of their major buildings and gardens had been – and would continue to be – featured in a section called 'Country Homes and Gardens Old and New'. Alongside historical houses mostly built before 1740, Lutyens and Jekyll's collaborations were presented almost as if they too were part of England's heritage. Certainly, like any Tudor, Elizabethan, Jacobean or early Georgian home or estate, their projects conveyed a romantic vision of traditional rural England.

The articles in the 'Country Homes' section featured the historical aspects of the properties illustrated and presented them as the *homes* of England's cultivated classes, conveying the belief, first, that life in the country was better than in the city; and second, that the best way to pass one's time was as an English country gentleman. The magazine embodied a lifestyle of leisure consisting of tea parties on the terrace and croquet on the lawn, interrupted only by horse-riding, hunting, fishing and gardening. Here in the illustrations of Hudson's publication the countryside promised a healthy and wholesome way of life; but most importantly, *Country Life* reinforced the importance to the self-made plutocrat of a country house and garden. Though the land may no longer have represented a sure investment, the estate remained a symbol of ancestry that such people were keen to ape. And if a Lutyens–Jekyll design was not suitable the wealthy reader could always find his or her dream home in the full-page illustrated property advertisements alongside the articles. By 1904 the middle classes' urge to escape from the hectic pace of life in London, its poverty and squalor, to a rural weekend retreat, was widespread. It was further encouraged by easier access to the shires via more comfortable and faster trains and via the motor-car, which had first been introduced to the English public at the Crystal Palace exhibition of 1896.

Whether for the nouveaux riches or for aristocrats like Portman, Lutyens and Jekyll's houses and gardens combined the luxury of a country retreat with a sense of tradition. At home in the landscape, their gardens exuded a timeless dignity. Carefully incorporating traditional craft techniques and local materials, Lutyens' designs made it difficult to discern the old from the new. They could draw on English garden styles dating back to the sixteenth and seventeenth centuries in such a way as to give each garden a patina of permanence. For the aspiring, this created the illusion of well-established roots, while for the Portmans it affirmed their place in history.

At the end of April Lutyens returned to Hestercombe where work had already begun on the gardens. In order to create the six terraces the ground had to be levelled, and thousands of tons of rubble and rough pink stone, sourced from the estate, had to be trundled in by horse and cart to create the walls. With the earthworks under way, Lutyens made numerous visits to the site over the next few months, checking that everything was being executed according to his instructions. To some architects, overseeing the labouring would have seemed dull, but ever since he was a boy Lutyens had enjoyed watching the local builders at work and he had a deep respect for traditional techniques. As a member of the Artworkers' Guild and as a 'pupil' of Gertrude Jekyll, Lutyens had come to appreciate the Arts and Crafts principle that vernacular craftsmanship was both superior to modern techniques and a more honest way of working.

Assiduously, Lutyens kept Jekyll informed of progress, and in October, he made what he hoped was his last trip of the year to 'get Hestercombe done with', before leaving for a fishing holiday in Norway. Fishing holidays were one of the few absences from work that Lutyens allowed himself, but first he wanted to redesign the large sunken plot so as to emphasise the diagonal axes rather than the straight lines of the terrace. So he connected the steps at each corner of the main terrace with two intersecting diagonal grass walks instead of parallel paths, and replaced the planned rectangular flowerbeds with four triangular ones.

Having waited for Lutyens' new layout to be implemented, Jekyll was finally able to send the first plant plans on 1 December 1904. Drawn to a scale of one-sixteenth of an inch to a foot, the plans outlined the position and shape of each plant grouping and the number of plants that should fill each bed, leaving little creative freedom for the two head gardeners and their fifteen-strong team of garden hands. Two weeks later she sent what would be the first of many batches of plants from her own garden, including dwarf lavender, rock pinks and the silvery cotton lavender – *Santolina* – which would eventually fill the beds bordering the terrace walls. Although Jekyll employed at any one time between eleven and twenty men in the garden and nursery at Munstead Wood, she neither raised plants for profit nor exploited her commissions to expand her nursery trade. In fact, her nursery was more a labour of love, driven by the desire to provide plants for her own garden as well as those of her friends and clients. In contrast to the money-grabbing Lutyens, Jekyll warned one client: 'My prices should not be quoted to your nursery or they may assume a grievance against me for "underselling the trade".'

The new design was more dynamic than Lutyens' first. The intersecting diagonal walkways were laid out in grass and edged with stone, creating the four triangular sections. These were then further subdivided by stone borders into triangular, square and L-shaped flowerbeds. Flanking the whole plot on all four sides would be the ascending terraces filled with flowering plants. The layout resembled sixteenth- and early seventeenth-century garden designs that had been depicted in pattern-books such as Didymus Mountain's *Gardener's Labyrinth* (1577), and Gervase Markham's *The Country Farm* (1615), both of which became popular again when the architect Reginald Blomfield reproduced

designs from them in 1892 in his book *The Formal Garden in England*. To reinforce the link with the past even further, Lutyens called this part of the garden
the 'Great Plat', using the sixteenth-century word for 'plot'.

Like Lutyens, Blomfield and other garden architects often used historical precedents as their inspiration. During the last twenty years there had been
an explosion of interest in Italian and English Renaissance gardens, resulting
in the publication of many books on the subject. There had been some debate
as to which was superior, the Italian or English Renaissance style. Blomfield,
the most vocal of the architects, passionately advocated the simplicity of the
English garden. He claimed that the developments on the continent were
'nothing to us' – 'the point is, what has been done in England'. In line with
this thinking, many rejected the ornamental parterres of mid-nineteenth-century
gardens by designers such as William Nesfield and Charles Barry on the grounds
that they were too ornate, that they were monumental interpretations of Italian
Renaissance and French baroque gardens. Instead, they turned to the plainer
English designs, using as models pictorial sources as well as preserved gardens
from the late sixteenth and early seventeenth centuries. Francis Inigo Thomas,
for example, the garden designer who illustrated Blomfield's *Formal Garden in
England*, had laid out Athelhampton in Dorset ten years before in a typically
early Elizabethan series of enclosures – like outdoor rooms – with arbours,
raised walks and box-edged parterres.

Architects and gardeners differed, of course, in their vision of how a
garden should be. Of central concern was the balance between architecture and
nature. On one side of this debate stood Blomfield and Thomas who believed
that stone balustrades, raised terraces and flights of steps, which gave a garden
its basic geometry, should dominate. They demanded a linear, symmetrical
design with paved and gravel pathways and statuary harking back to the rigid
formality of Elizabethan days. At the other end of the spectrum was the well-
known gardener and writer William Robinson, who advocated a 'wild' garden.
Jekyll had worked with him on his magazine *The Garden* and had contributed
a chapter to his second book, *The English Flower Garden* (1883). In contrast to
earlier garden theorists such as Loudon and Paxton who had insisted that horticulture should express the artistry of the gardener, Robinson and Jekyll argued

that one should learn from nature and put its lessons into practice in the flowerbed. Declaring that art should never be imposed on nature, Robinson's mantra of the 'right plant for the right place' revolutionised English gardening, emphasising the importance of the right soil, adequate drainage and the correct amount of sun in the positioning of plants; aesthetically pleasing plans drawn up by a designer who gave little consideration to environmental factors should be avoided. Jekyll was equally vehement in her claim that 'No artificial planting can ever equal that of nature . . . one can learn from it the great lesson of the importance of moderation and reserve, of simplicity of intention and direction of purpose.'

Both would have agreed with John Ruskin's verdict on the Victorians' predilection for forming geometric patterns and monograms out of low-growing annuals, which were nothing more than an 'assembly of unfortunate beings, pampered and bloated above their natural size, stewed and heated into diseased growth; corrupted by evil communication into speckled and inharmonious colours'. This bedding-out system degraded flowers, reducing them, as Robinson insisted, 'to crude colour without reference to the natural forms of beauty'. Hardy perennials, bulbs and naturalised exotics should form the main body of the garden, not greenhouse-nurtured annuals. Similarly, William Morris had admitted that he would 'blush with shame' at the very thought of them.

As a partnership, Lutyens and Jekyll bridged this divide by combining Blomfield's formal architecture with Robinson's natural planting. The gardeners at Hestercombe, for example, would place seeds in the nooks and crannies of the walls and steps while they were under construction, so that as the seeds germinated and grew the hard lines of the stone would soften. To the same end, Lutyens used local stone in its rough unworked state in order to emphasise the natural qualities of the material and counterbalance the artificiality of the manmade structures. Weathering and moss would do the rest. Though his layout was inspired by historical examples, Lutyens, unlike Blomfield, was also led by nature, allowing the landscape to inform the design. Like Harold Peto, for whom he had worked when he had first left art school, he also took the lie of the land as the inspiration for his designs. In his own garden at Iford Manor

in Wiltshire Peto had made the most of what nature had provided and transformed a steep valley into descending terraces.

Within the geometrical beds that Lutyens devised, Jekyll arranged her
flowers to 'look happy and at home, and make no parade of conscious effort'.
Thus even in this most formal part of Hestercombe – the central beds of the
Great Plat – the overlapping groups of bright-pink peonies, scarlet phlox, blue
delphiniums and red gladioli, though smartly framed by glossy bergenias,
created a more natural feel. Like Robinson, Jekyll hated the showmanship of
Victorian planting. Complaining about the fashion for neat ribbon borders
of blue, yellow and scarlet, she wrote, 'One cannot but deplore the amount of
misdirected labour in the preparation, planting and maintenance that wretched
thing entailed'; but, she continued, 'It was not the fault of the plants themselves that they were unfairly used, and . . . if the scarlet geranium reigned
supreme it was not the geranium's fault that it was made to sit upon the throne.'

Lutyens and Jekyll's gardens recalled the decaying formal gardens of past
times, in which the hard geometry had been broken by wild-growing flowers
and shrubs that had let nature regain the upper hand. Of those old gardens
Jekyll said: 'Kindly nature clothes the ruin with her own beauty.' Looking weathered and ancient, their own gardens seemed to have existed since Tudor times.
In a sense they combined four centuries of garden design in which the formal
terraces of Hatfield represented one aspect, while Hawkstone's tangled thickets
and unkempt shrubberies and the theatrical flowerbeds of Sheringham imbued
the other. In a world in flux, they created beautiful gardens that appeared to
have endured the passage of time.

In the early months of 1905, news arrived of revolution in Russia. One of
Lutyens' clients, Princess Dolgorouki, was married to a Russian; but despite
receiving letters from her husband in Russia describing his fears of attack by
riotous miners, she remained more interested in the plans for her luxurious
weekend retreat at Nashdom in Buckinghamshire. The Portmans, similarly
unconcerned by political events abroad, continued with life as usual, attending
charitable functions and presenting prizes at agricultural fairs. Locally, the
Portmans remained as popular as ever, at least on the surface – the *Somerset*

County Gazette regularly fawned on the couple. The issue of 7 April 1906, referring to the perceived crisis over rural depopulation as farm labourers migrated to the towns and cities, stated: 'If there were more landlords of Mr Portman's sort about there would be no difficulty in keeping people in the country.'

However, while the Portmans managed to retain their prominence within the local community, the growing popularity of the socialist movement led to critics of the landowning classes becoming ever more vociferous. Writers such as H. G. Wells and George Bernard Shaw, both members of the Fabian Society, expressed their discontent in their literary works as well as in political pamphlets. Shaw, who had given numerous lectures on his socialist ideals of equality, on the abolition of private property and on universal suffrage, was particularly vitriolic in his attacks on aristocrats like Portman, whom he regarded as perpetuating a system of injustice, however benevolent or paternalistic some may have been in their treatment of their tenants. This antipathy towards the aristocracy even began to filter into children's literature, such as Kenneth Grahame's *The Wind in the Willows* which describes a village under invasion by a radical mob (depicted as weasels) and the irresponsible behaviour of the reckless aristocrat Toad of Toad Hall, who exploits his estate and his tenants in order to finance his expensive lifestyle. Unlike the romantic Arts and Crafts Movement or Lutyens and Jekyll, whose work was steeped in history, critics such as Shaw believed it was time to turn away from the past. Wells, in particular, insisted that only by taking a firm grip on the future could one change society.

No more concerned than Portman by events in the wider world, Lutyens concentrated on his projects, particularly Hestercombe, which he had been visiting regularly while the structural features of the garden were being completed. By July 1905, he was sure that 'the garden is going to be a success'. About this time he was invited to a dinner party at the Portmans'. Lutyens already knew some of the guests, but two that he had not met before were Mrs Portman's sons from her first marriage. As one had inherited from an uncle the title of Viscount de Vesci as well as large estates in Ireland and Kent, Lutyens doubtless wanted to make a good impression on the potential new client.

Compared to his fellow male guests who wore smart country tweeds

during the day and black tail-coats for dinner, Lutyens, as usual, looked decidedly scruffy. Indifferent to clothes, he would never think to add some colour
or elegance by wearing a silk tie in the evening, but always appeared in suits
with matching waistcoats of grey serge or tweed. His wife Emily complained
that his clothes smelled and looked creased, imploring him to avoid spilling his
drinks down his shirt or scorching the backs of his trouser legs by standing too
close to the fire. Even though he exuded professional confidence and was
considered by his friends to be a charming companion who 'possessed the faculty
of making everybody seem younger', at parties Lutyens was deeply shy. But
since social events offered an important opportunity to acquire new clients as
well as to cement his relationships with existing ones, he had developed a technique for overcoming his natural disposition, which was to adopt an attitude of
'bubbling friendliness' and draw funny sketches or dream homes for his fellow
guests' amusement.

Soon afterwards the Portmans left for Scotland and the shooting season,
while Lutyens was busy in Northamptonshire with a job at Ashby St Ledgers,
a manor house belonging to the politician and millionaire Ivor Guest, cousin
of the Duke of Marlborough and later 1st Viscount Wimborne. Known as 'the
paying Guest' because of the conspicuous way in which he displayed his fortune,
he was one of Lutyens' richest clients. Lutyens reported to Emily that Guest
had acquired 'two motors and a heap of smart horses, polo ponies and a perfect
army of men servants, with a groom of the chambers' – he was glamorous and
urbane as well as wealthy, and belonged to the 'smart set'. Portman was more
modest, and though he too indulged in the occasional luxury such as his Cadillac,
his life revolved around the management of his estate, interrupted by the
shooting season in Scotland and brief trips to London where he maintained a
town house. On the whole, Portman was old-fashioned in his outlook and
lifestyle – land and what it yielded were his main source of income, not just a
sideline or dalliance as it was for someone like Guest. Fifty years earlier,
Portman's lifestyle would have been the norm for an upper-class man, but now
many had dispensed with their estates and settled for just a country house; for
them, as for Wilde's Lady Bracknell in *The Importance of Being Ernest*, land
had 'ceased to be either a profit or a pleasure. It gives one position, and prevents

one from keeping it'. While Portman found cattle-breeding an exciting occupation and enjoyed managing his land, the new generation of aristocrats was more interested in the trappings of country life – the glamorous house and garden that would provide the setting for parties or a retreat from town.

The death of Queen Victoria in 1901 ended, at least symbolically, an era that had been drawing to a close for some time; the new order was represented by aristocrats such as Guest, and other wealthy patrons of Lutyens, including bankers and American industrial heirs – who had come to Britain and married into old English families. For them, cars, yachts and expensive holidays on the Riviera were *de rigueur*. The change was encouraged partly by Edward VII's hedonistic lifestyle and his championing of an ostentatious court life. As his grandson the Duke of Windsor later observed, the king's choice of friends heralded 'the birth of a new era . . . High office or ancient lineage were no longer the sole criteria of status. Beauty, wit, wealth, sophistication – these had now become valid passports to the Sovereign's intimate circle.' Whereas his mother Queen Victoria had celebrated domesticity and family values, Edward indulged in parties and luxuries. The difference between mother and son became all the clearer when he converted what had been Victoria's private chapel at Balmoral into a billiard room for his rich friends' amusement. Many aristocrats deeply resented the influx of British and foreign plutocrats who were enjoying the king's favours and flaunting their wealth in a manner that was considered vulgar and showy.

The vision of England that Edward Portman cherished, on the other hand, could be seen in his garden, harking back to a not-so-distant past when the nobility ruled the country. The image of a garden untainted by modernity or foreign influence was emphasised by Jekyll's choice of plants, of which she sent more in October 1905 for the walls and beds around the Great Plat. Although she used many flowering plants that were originally introduced into England from abroad, Jekyll particularly liked native English ones such as columbine, foxgloves and pinks. 'Some of the most delightful of all gardens are the little strips in front of roadside cottages,' she once said, and her schemes were based on years of observing the wayside verges, the cottage gardens and the dry-stone walls in her home county of Surrey. They were impossible to pass, she said, 'without learning or observing something new', and this 'simple and tender charm that one may look for in vain in gardens of greater pretension' was what she aimed for in her own. She instructed the gardeners at Hestercombe to plant lavender, rock pinks and catnip into the stonework. The effect was a seemingly wild tangle of plants that looked as if they had been growing there for years, evoking the traditions which, she said, 'make our English waysides the prettiest in the temperate world'.

Jekyll's writings and her choice of plants reflected a more widely held belief that the cottage stood for an ancient rural culture unaffected by urban life and its associated corruption and depravity. In the nineteenth century, painters had idealised the rose-clad cottage nestling in a garden of hollyhocks, sunflowers and old fruit trees as a symbol of Englishness. In 1891, an exhibition of garden paintings at the Fine Art Society in London was hailed as a lesson in patriotism. The *Illustrated London News* had written: '[I]n looking on the yew hedges, the grass walks, and the ancestral elms and twisted apple trees, we feel the continuity of our national life, and recognise how each succeeding generation or family has been linked together by a love of flowers and nature.' The depiction of rural life by painters such as Arthur Claude Strachan and Helen Allingham was much admired. More intimate and domestic than those of Constable, their paintings often showed women and children in cottage gardens, or farmers coming home at the end of the day: sanitised scenes of a small bucolic world in tune with tradition. Rather than taking vegetable plots and tools as her subject-matter, Allingham preferred hollyhocks, sweet peas, roses and marigolds. One contemporary garden writer has summed up the symbolic power of the cottage garden thus: 'The common flowers of a cottager's garden tell of centuries of collaboration' between man and nature. The fact that many of these plants originated in far grander gardens and were also subject to fashion, percolating down over the decades into the vernacular culture, was largely ignored by artists as well as by Jekyll and members of the Arts and Crafts Movement.

To many like Jekyll, 'real' England was under threat. Industry, the car and faster trains were encroaching, destroying unspoilt rural England. 'In the older days, London might have been at a distance of two hundred miles. Now one never can forget that it is at little more than an hour's journey,' Jekyll wrote. She conceded: 'It is impossible to grudge others the enjoyment of its [the countryside's] delights'; but 'one cannot but regret, that the fact of its being now thickly populated and much built over, has necessarily robbed it of its older charms of peace and retirement'. The previous year, in 1904, she had published her book *Old West Surrey*, which recorded the practices 'of our working folk' – before they disappeared, as she feared. Refusing to use modern appliances herself – even a typewriter, which would have eased the strain on her eyes – she bemoaned the willingness of rural workers to throw out their

I.—THE VILLAGE. OLD STYLE.

II.—THE VILLAGE. NEW STYLE.

The Village Old Style and the Village New Style. George Morrow, *Punch*,
11 September 1907

'solid furniture of pure material and excellent design' in favour of 'cheap pretentious articles, got up with veneer and varnish and shoddy material'.

At the end of the nineteenth century this fear that the spread of urban influences would eradicate the nation's heritage triggered the foundation of the Folklore Society and William Morris's Society for the Protection of Ancient Buildings. The National Trust had been established in 1895, to record and conserve England's indigenous culture and places of historic interest and natural beauty. In horticulture, the mass production of greenhouse plants, including hybrids, was increasingly seen as a symptom of an over-commercialised world. Seed companies began to increase their stocks of traditional species such as delphinium and wallflower, in an attempt to preserve or reintroduce old-fashioned plants, and campaigns were mounted, for instance, to find species that had grown in Jacobean gardens.

At Hestercombe, Jekyll used rock pinks and white columbine to cascade down the walls of the Great Plat, while planting white foxgloves and the native iris in the beds below. In addition, however, she used new hybrids and exotic plants as long as they were hardy and could be left to grow as if in the wild, thereby recreating at least the informality so typical of a cottage garden. Just as Jekyll dressed Portman's garden in flowers that conjured up images of Englishness, writers too had turned to the rural idyll for an image of the nation. Building on a long tradition in English literature, Alfred Tennyson's poetry in the mid and late nineteenth century celebrated nature and village life. Equally, Thomas Hardy's early novels painted a nostalgic picture of stable rural life. For Hardy, the cottager was the last link with medieval England in a society under threat from the encroachment of modern life. The setting of his Wessex novels answered city dwellers' longing for a rural idyll; it resonated so deeply that Hardy revised the texts for later editions, giving a greater prominence to the landscape. Further, he provided a 'map' of Wessex which was included in the collected edition of his novels, as by then 'Wessex societies' had sprung up, and enthusiasts toured the county to identify the landmarks in the novels. Villages were increasingly seen not just as a haven from the city but as the repository of the moral character of the nation – to the extent that William Morris, in his socialist Utopian novel *News from Nowhere*, conceived

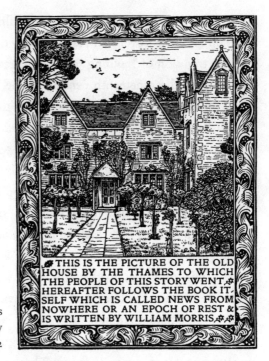

THIS IS THE PICTURE OF THE OLD HOUSE BY THE THAMES TO WHICH THE PEOPLE OF THIS STORY WENT. HEREAFTER FOLLOWS THE BOOK IT-SELF WHICH IS CALLED NEWS FROM NOWHERE OR AN EPOCH OF REST & IS WRITTEN BY WILLIAM MORRIS.

Frontispiece of William Morris's *News from Nowhere*. Engraving by W. H. Hooper, 1892

a future London as a happy 'rural' community in which crafts, agriculture, traditional architecture and old-fashioned gardens replaced the present squalid conditions. Now, at the beginning of the twentieth century, the Poet Laureate Alfred Austin again popularised 'Old England' with his book *Haunts of Ancient Peace*. The *Daily News* commented: 'Under its spell we lose for a time the brick-and-mortar civilisation that sometimes seems all pervading, and gladly fly with the writer . . . to the green lanes and fields outside our prison.'

This nostalgia for an idyllic past was often accompanied by a critique of the city, which was reinforced by the growing evidence of urban poverty, bad housing and pollution reported in publications such as social reformer Charles Booth's *Life and Labour of the People in London** and chocolate-manufacturer and philanthropist Seebohm Rowntree's study of poverty in

*Booth began his surveys in 1886 and the results were published between 1889 and 1903, with the final seventeen-volume report in 1902–3. In *Poverty: A Study of London Town Life* (1901) Rowntree investigated wages, food, housing and health. He would later become a close friend of Lloyd George and produced reports for him.

York (1901). Other progressive industrialists such as George Cadbury and William Hesketh Lever had responded to the current climate by reviving the English tradition of building model villages for their workers. Already in the first half of the nineteenth century, some landowners had provided 'model cottages' for their tenants. One such was the Duke of Devonshire for whom Joseph Paxton, between 1838 and 1842, rebuilt the village of Edensor on the Chatsworth estate, supplying each house with water and sewerage as well as a garden.* The Duke had been inspired by Blaise Hamlet near Bristol, with its picturesque thatched cottages designed by John Nash for the pensioners on the estate (completed in 1811).† In a similar spirit, Cadbury and Lever wanted to provide good quality modern accommodation for their workers. While Nash's cottages at Blaise imitated a traditional hamlet and Edensor's eclectic mix of styles evoked the past with Tudor, Norman, Gothic and Italianate houses, Cadbury and Lever favoured a 'medieval' style of archi-tecture. Designed to mimic aspects of medieval communities, Cadbury's village, Bourneville, just outside Birmingham, included a village green and he even organised 'ancient' feasts. Though Jekyll agreed with Cadbury that bringing factory workers 'out to the land' where they 'might pursue the most natural and healthful of all recreations, that of gardening', was of great benefit to them, she did not welcome the idea of more of the countryside being swallowed up by new towns, however well they might imitate the image she held so dear. Nevertheless, the idea proved so popular that in spring 1905 a committee of reformers, town planners and architects who were planning the first 'garden city' at Letchworth in Hertfordshire invited the public to view an exhibition of new workers' cottages built in a variety of 'old-fashioned' styles that included rough-cast walls, half-timbering, dormer windows and gables. By October that year, when Jekyll sent her plant plans to the head

---

*John Robertson, Loudon's draughtsman, designed ten of the cottages in Edensor, but Paxton oversaw the construction of them and was responsible for the infrastructure, such as drainage, roads and gardens.

†In 1796 Humphry Repton had produced a Red Book for Blaise Castle. By the time Nash started on the hamlet, most of Repton's improvements, such as new carriage roads across the park and a Gothic entrance gate with lodge, had been implemented.

One of the cottages at Edensor on
the Chatsworth estate.

gardener at Hestercombe, more than sixty thousand people had visited the
new houses.

Though Lutyens was too busy with country-house commissions – at least
for the moment – to take much interest in the new garden cities, to the amusement of his clients he did play his own 'town game'. This involved inventing
'lovely townscapes' for the estates he was working on, in which he would place
such items as windmills, canals, shops and horses – though they were never
intended to get any further than his sketch pad. Jekyll too enjoyed this game.
As 1905 drew to a close, Lutyens visited her at Munstead Wood where she was
busy with half a dozen or more garden commissions in addition to Hestercombe.
Her daily schedule was divided by meals and naps into one-and-a-half-hour
periods, and even in the evenings she would be working on plant orders or
embroidering a bedspread. Most of her friends accepted that she often had no
time for social calls – she was not easily distracted from her work. Lutyens,
however, was an exception. He was always welcomed, his visits providing an
opportunity to talk about work and enjoy each other's company.

Such trips also provided rare moments of respite for Lutyens. Driven
both by his ambition and by his desire to provide his wife with the kind of
lifestyle to which she had been accustomed before their marriage, he had little
time or energy for anything other than work: '[P]ray that I may work well for

Art and Emmy, Emmy and Art,' he wrote. When he was not visiting clients or building sites, he was standing at the drawing-board, smoking his pipe, pausing only for short, silent dinners – Emily read while he did the crossword – before returning to his desk to work late into the evening. Feeling that the family came second to his work, Emily wrote: 'I get so afraid lest we drift further apart, instead of growing closer. I don't think you feel it quite as I do, for your work is so much to you.' Even when he was travelling, Lutyens used the time spent on the train to draw up new schemes when not writing letters to clients, though he always found a moment for a note to Emily. He had no plans to return to Hestercombe before the end of the year; the Portmans were away in Scotland for Christmas and he was working on a number of other projects that needed his attention. However, not long after visiting Gertrude Jekyll at Munstead, he was called back to Hestercombe to attend to the rabbits, which were 'hard at it eating the fig trees which must be stopped'.

Soon after Edward and Constance Mary Portman's return to Hestercombe, there was a general election in January 1906. It resulted in a landslide victory for the Liberal Party, as well as twenty-nine seats going to the newly formed Labour Party. For the aristocracy this was disastrous; since the Liberal Party had split twenty years earlier over the question of Irish devolution, it was no longer dominated by landowners. Many aristocrats – including Portman's grandfather – had left the Party at that point, and it now consisted of wealthy businessmen, trade unionists, professional politicians and members of the working class. The new prime minister, Henry Campbell-Bannerman, spoke of the need to 'make the land less of a treasure house for the rich and more of a treasure house for the nation'. The message, for Portman and others, could not have been clearer.

In response, seventy peers formed a secret organisation called the Apaches as a stronghold of aristocratic power, promising to use their position in the House of Lords to fight against Liberal reforms. Others established the Central Landowners' Association with the aim of defending their agricultural interests. Portman, however, despite the Liberals' support for an increase in direct taxes on ground rents, death duties and 'unearned increments', still felt secure. Like

Anthony Trollope's Archdeacon Grantly in *The Last Chronicle of Barset* (1867), Portman might have said: 'Land gives so much more than the rent. It gives position and influence and political power, to say nothing about the game.' For the time being, at least in the House of Lords, the aristocratic voice remained strong enough to veto those radical reforms that might threaten Portman's way of life. It was not politics, therefore, that occupied his mind, as Labour MPs demanded votes for women, but his garden; and on 25 April Lutyens was summoned to Hestercombe to discuss extending his scheme yet further. 'I have to go to Portman as soon as possible,' he wrote to Emily; 'they want me to stay.'

When he arrived, the garden was in full bloom. Some of the violets, narcissi and lilies-of-the-valley had been used to decorate the marquee in which two hundred breeders and farmers had lunched two weeks before at Portman's cattle and sheep sale. The auction had been lucrative and each guest had received a buttonhole in blue and white – Portman's colours. Ten days later Lutyens announced to Emily: 'Portman has accepted my garden extension schemes. £2000 which is good – and it comprises an Orangery which will be fun to build and good to look at.' Wooed by the prospect of more money, he continued: 'She [Mrs Portman] is so nice and friendly and Portman [same].'

Two and a half months later, in July 1906, Jekyll received Lutyens' final plan of the gardens, showing the new Orangery at the centre of the East Terrace that linked the Great Plat to the little raised garden called the Dutch Garden. Included in the plans were details of the drainage and water supply, due to be installed within five weeks. Designed in Lutyens' classical 'Wren style', the Orangery would be the only new garden building at Hestercombe. Its large arched windows would overlook the lawn. The walls were to be built of rubble-stone, whose rough surface Lutyens contrasted with the artificiality of the polished stonework in which he picked out the base of the building, the window arches, the pillars flanking the doors and the corners. The natural unworked stone would link the Orangery to the dividing wall between the east and west sections of the gardens. This, with its strong plain buttresses, was the most rugged construction in the garden. Elsewhere, too, Lutyens had played with contrasts: the rough walls of the Great Plat, for instance, counterpointed the smooth ashlar that he had used for the niches, arches and

The Orangery at Hestercombe, *Country Life*, 1908

balustrades, as well as architectural details such as the coping around the Rotunda.

By the end of the year the Orangery was finished, and in January 1907 Hestercombe came alive again. Edward Portman arrived back from Dorset where he had spent Christmas at his father's mansion, Bryanston, and his wife returned from India where she had been visiting her brother, the Governor of Madras. Jekyll sent the plans for the flowerbeds that were to feature in front of the Orangery, and some time later went to Hestercombe to see it for herself. The 'big trees in the grass slopes' through which the sun shone in brilliant patches made this east part of the garden, she thought, 'wonderful, big and quiet'. In comparison to the planting of the Great Plat and its terraces, the whole of this section was less formal. The two-acre site consisted mainly of a sloping lawn, levelled in two places for croquet, tennis and bowls, and divided by trees planted in ascending heights to give the impression of an amphitheatre. The informality was elegantly set off by the classical grandeur of the Orangery. On the terrace, in front, geometrical grass shapes framed by flagstones echoed the linearity of Lutyens' 'Wrenaissance' building.

To the east of the Orangery, high above the lawn, was the small square

Dutch Garden, designed on a more intimate scale than anything else. In March, having received Jekyll's plans and plants, the gardeners began work on it. As with the Great Plat, Lutyens had laid the plot out symmetrically, but here the flowerbeds were divided by paved paths instead of grass. By using flowers and shrubs of a similar colour, Jekyll linked the planting of each of the central beds with the outside border. Again as with the Great Plat she relied mainly on perennials, many of which had exuberant foliage, in order to create a garden that would look beautiful for much of the year. Her favourite, the low-growing grey *Stachys lanata*, provided a permanent silvery ribbon around each of the beds, while hostas with their voluptuous heart-shaped leaves filled them with a luminous green. Clumps of catmint, dwarf lavender and China roses created a wash of mauves and pinks, while spiky *Yucca filamentosa* gave the whole a striking sculptural structure.

In the central diamond-shaped bed dwarf lavender and rosemary predominated, while the outer borders echoed the mauves of the four inner

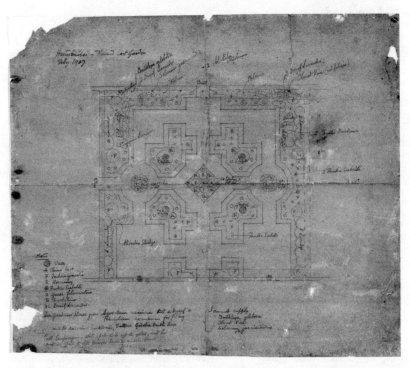

Gertrude Jekyll's planting plan for the raised Dutch Garden, 1907

beds – here, drifting into blues with swathes of lavender and the sculpted blue blossoms of *Clematis davidiana*. The spiky globe thistles (*Echinops*) and sea hollies (*Eryngium oliverianum*) mirrored these shades and provided the verticals. The pinks of the China roses were repeated in the heart-shaped blooms dangling from the arched branches of dicentras and in the vivid pink of the fuchsias. Also in the outer border, the broad brush strokes of the golden-yellow Jerusalem sage (*Phlomis fruticosa*) counterpointed the lilac-blue scheme; nearby, the orange-yellow ball-like blooms of *Buddleja globosa* struck a warm note against the stonework of the north-facing wall. Jekyll also used a selection of annuals to augment the perennials – she did not dislike annuals *per se*, just the way they had been used as ground covering ('carpet bedding') in the Victorian garden. So she instructed the gardeners to grow from seed pale-yellow, pink and white snapdragons, gentle blue *Ageratum houstonianum*, both tall and dwarf, and the purple *Trachelium caeruleum*. They were to fill any remaining spaces with double roses, providing further pink highlights. Not a scrap of ground was to be wasted.

The Dutch Garden, *Country Life*, 1908

By spring 1907 the gardeners were still working on the Dutch Garden as well as executing Jekyll's plans for the planting of the Pergola marking the southern boundary between the Great Plat and the countryside beyond. At more than two hundred feet long it was a massive structure. Lutyens' design incorporated pairs of round and square pillars of rough local stone which supported heavy oak crossbeams. Old-fashioned climbing roses, woodbine and varieties of vines would cover it, softening its lines as well as providing a shaded walk at this end of the garden. Like the sundial at the centre of the Great Plat which she praised 'not only as a distinctive ornament, but also as a link with the old gardens of our Tudor ancestors', the Pergola was intended to trigger associations with 'the pleached alley of the Tudor gardens when young trees of hornbeams or Wych-elm were trained over a tunnel-shaped trellis or laths'.

In her plantings, Jekyll also liked to use flowering plants associated with earlier centuries, mirroring the work of other artists, poets and writers who since the early nineteenth century had often chosen medieval and Elizabethan flowers as motifs. Tennyson, for instance, celebrates the sunflower, hollyhock and tiger-lily in one of his early poems 'Song.' Later, Shakespeare's work became something of a horticultural encyclopaedia, as it included abundant references to old-fashioned species. It inspired members of the Arts and Crafts Movement – who used them in book illustrations and textile designs as well as in their gardens – and garden owners like the Duchess of Warwick at Eastern Lodge in Essex, who devised a 'Shakespeare border' in which each plant was labelled with the relevant quotation. The Pre-Raphaelite Brotherhood also contributed to the popularity of these old-fashioned flowers. Millais's *Ophelia* (1852), for example, depicts Shakespeare's daisies, slender *Lythrum salicaria*, and white lilies.

And so Jekyll grew drifts of rosemary, lavender and lilies, flowers used in the medieval *hortus conclusus*, together with pinks, which had been popular in knot gardens such as those at Hatfield. In the composition and arrangement of her plants she was influenced by her training at the South Kensington School of Art and by her knowledge and skill as an accomplished embroiderer: her aim, in her gardens, was to 'use the plants [so] that they shall form beautiful pictures'. For her, a collection of plants no more made a garden than the colours in a paintbox created a painting. 'Merely having them' was not enough. The gardener, she advised, should regard the soil as the canvas and the flowers as pigments, and take it from there. The overriding rule was to be alive to colour harmonies and combinations, which she took to a masterly level. Gardening 'in its best expression, may well rank as one of the fine arts', she wrote.

For the Great Plat borders below the Victorian Terrace, Jekyll created an impressionistic picture predominantly in blue, white, grey and mauve. Having chosen her palette of plants, which included the grey *Stachys* and *Santolina*, blue globe thistle and clematis, mauve catmint and lavender as well as white pinks and clouds of *Gypsophila paniculata*, she set them in a gentle transition from one hue to the next, interspersed with bold inserts of yellow Jerusalem sage and clumps of bright-pink *Sedum spectabile*. Having studied the work of painters such as Turner as well as Chevreul's theories on colour harmonies and contrasts that had formed the basis of many a Victorian parterre, here she combined a nuanced progression of hues – a practice favoured by contemporary gardeners – with the Victorian fashion of contrasting flowers of complementary colours. So she also placed bright-yellow *Verbascum phlomoides* and *Achillea compacta* next to blue *Campanula carpatica*. Elsewhere she used grey-leaved plants such as *Senecio cineraria* (silver ragwort) to set off the pure brilliance of the blues and pinks surrounding them, while white tree lupins (*Lupinus arborius*) helped to heighten the pale pink of soapwort (*Saponaria officinalis*). Unlike the painter, however, the gardener had the flowering seasons of her live pigments to consider. So Jekyll gave substance to the garden with strong-foliaged plants such as the shiny-leafed *Choisya ternata*, while positioning white everlasting sweet peas and clematis, which bloomed in mid- to late summer, in such a way as to mask the fading remains of earlier flowering plants. Every flower and shrub was placed with the careful foresight needed to create succeeding waves of blooms, and she expected the gardeners to follow her instructions exactly – for it was this planning that made the 'difference between a garden that is utterly commonplace and one that is full of beauty and absorbing interest'.

By high summer 1907, the beds were awash with colour and the air heavy with scent. From the two Rill Gardens, each stretching along the entire length of the Great Plat, came the soothing, cooling sound of water. Spurting into pools from the mouths of the classical masks set into the top of the arches at the north end of the Rill Gardens, the water then rippled down the narrow channels. At regular intervals pairs of tiny pools or 'tanklets' flanked the rills which were edged by stones. This linearity was softened by Japanese water irises and wild aquatic flowers such as blue water forget-me-not (*Myosotis palustris*) and pale-pink flowering rush (*Butomus umbellatus*), while sculptural arum lilies grew in the pools. 'The wide, paved ledges make pleasant walking ways,' wrote Jekyll; 'at even intervals they turn, after the manner of the gathered ribbon strapwork of ancient needlework, and enclose circular tanklets giving the opportunity of a distinct punctuation with important plants.'

Lutyens had not visited for some months. He was becoming increasingly concerned about the impact that the American stock-market panic was having on his commissions. As share prices plummeted that summer in New York, the London stock market followed. In August, one of his clients cancelled the building of a country house because he had lost £10,000 in just a fortnight. The financial crisis together with the cumulative effect of the Liberal government's

The west Rill Garden with the narrow channels and little 'tanklets', *Country Life*, 1908

policies – including the promised higher land taxes and increase in death duties – affected Lutyens' entire clientele, rich businessmen and aristocracy alike. 'No one has any money now,' he wrote glumly to Emily. And aware that his country-house commissions might not sustain him, he began to consider other options. The colonies offered one possibility – there was always the need for government buildings and private houses for the British administrators – while at home he noted the boom in garden cities, informing Emily on 8 August: 'I see there is going to be a bill for the planning of towns. I do wish I could have a say in it. Herbert Jekyll [Gertrude's brother], being the head of the new traffic and road department, may be able to help me.'

Jekyll, meanwhile, decided to take a holiday on the south coast with Emily. Lutyens, as usual, was too busy to take any time off: 'I have LOTS to do, lots undone,' he wrote to Emily, at the same time telling her to look after Jekyll. She 'wants to be comfy', he wrote; '[M]ake her feel she may go to bed when she likes and don't let her feel "out" of it.' A few days later he wrote again: 'Don't forget Bumps likes to go to bed early and then spend time in her room each day doing things. This means a table or something. If there is no table she will delight in inventing a substitute – ask her if she would like a carpenter to wait on her.' He had also warned Emily that Jekyll liked to travel with a great deal of paraphernalia, including drawing-boards, writing materials and holdalls full of stationery. Sure enough, when she arrived, Emily informed her husband on 22 August: 'Bumps [was] laden with delicious funny odd luggage which she would unpack all by herself at once.'

Typically Lutyens preferred to stay at home and work rather than join what he called their 'party of suffragettes'. By contrast, Emily and her friend Mrs Webbe (wife of the cricketer A. J. Webbe), who was also on holiday with them, would have been glad to call themselves suffragettes. Unfulfilled by her marriage, Emily had thrown herself into the women's movement, joining the Women's Social and Political Union founded in 1903 by Emmeline Pankhurst. She also regularly visited the Lock Hospital in London where she read fairy stories to the prostitutes who were being treated there for venereal diseases. She even went pamphleteering on the beach with Mrs Webbe on later holidays. But Jekyll herself did not associate with the movement. On the contrary, despite earning a living as a professional gardener and writer she preferred to call herself an amateur. Nor did she use her public position to fight for recognition of women's increasingly professional contribution to gardening. Despite the existence of a number of successful women writers on the subject and the establishment of schools for 'lady gardeners',* it was still not considered appropriate for women of a certain class to earn a living. In response, such women remained reticent about calling themselves professionals and adopted a self-effacing, modest tone in their work. Jekyll had lived most of her life in the reign of Victoria, so perhaps it wasn't surprising that such attitudes were firmly ingrained in her. Throughout her published work she sought to emphasise her practical, rather than intellectual, skills, and in this way maintained an acceptable image of decorum.†

By January 1908, Lutyens had little more to do at Hestercombe than to check that everything was running smoothly and that the Portmans were satisfied. Although Jekyll still had more batches of plants to send, another arriving in February, it was clear to them both that Hestercombe had turned out to be one of their most sophisticated co-productions. In April Lutyens received recognition as a leading authority on gardens when he was asked to give a speech at the Architectural Association. The invitation should have filled him with pleasure, but instead he felt so uncertain of what to say that he hurried to Munstead Wood to go over his notes with Jekyll, hoping, he confided to Emily, 'to improve my . . . speech'. He dreaded the event, telling Emily that he was so nervous that 'my hand shook'. Amidst the anxiety of preparing the talk,

---

*Theresa Earle and Alecia Amherst were both successful authors; Ellen Willmott, an heiress who spent her fortune on her gardens, was the first woman member of the Linnean Society; while Lady Warwick established the Lady Warwick Agricultural Association for Women in 1898 and Frances Wolseley set up the Glynde School for Lady Gardeners in 1902, of which Jekyll was a patron (Bennett, 2000, pp. 124–38).

†Jekyll's first book, *Wood and Garden* (1899), was subtitled *Notes and Thoughts, Practical and Critical, of a Working Amateur*. In the introduction she wrote (p. 1): 'I lay no claim to literary ability; or to botanical knowledge, or even to knowing the best practical methods of cultivation; but I have lived among outdoor flowers for many years, and have not spared myself in the way of actual labour.'

Lutyens also became increasingly unsettled about political events. On 3 April the prime minister Henry Campbell-Bannerman had resigned. 'I am so sorry Asquith is Prime Minister,' Lutyens wrote three days later. Asquith's loyalties were not with the landed classes, who were still Lutyens' main source of income. More worrying yet was that Asquith had appointed the radical Welshman David Lloyd George as Chancellor of the Exchequer. This orphaned son of a schoolteacher was regarded by most of the aristocracy as 'that damned Welsh attorney' or 'dirty little rogue'. Now Lloyd George was in a position to draft new reforms – radical enough, forty years later, to be recognised as the basis of the Welfare State. And he lost no time: in July 1908 the Old Age Pensions Act became law; and this was only the beginning.

Lutyens may have been alarmed, but the Portmans clearly were not sufficiently worried to air their concerns or to take any action. Blind to the 'frost' that would strip them of their 'fine foliage of pretences', as H. G. Wells would warn in 1909 in his novel *Tono Bungay*, Edward Portman and his wife continued with their seasonal round of prize-giving and charitable events. In fact Wells, who came from a family of gardeners* and had grown up observing the lifestyles of the aristocracy, might well have been writing about the Portmans in his portrayal here of people who refused to recognise that the old order was changing. 'The great houses stand in their parks still, the cottages cluster respectfully around on their borders', but, he continued, the 'hand of change rests on it all, unfelt, unseen' like a late autumn day. At about this time *Country Life* – in all likelihood Edward Hudson himself – had been in contact with the Portmans to ask whether they would like their garden to be featured in the magazine.† No doubt pleased to figure in a publication that continued to celebrate both their way of life and their status, they agreed. In the two articles that appeared in successive issues in October 1908, the author, H. Avray Tipping, a well-known writer on architecture and gardens, wrote enthusiastically on

---

*Wells's grandfather had been head gardener at Penshurst Place in Kent and his father worked at Redleaf, also in Kent.

†We do not know whether Hudson contacted the Portmans directly, but it was standard practice for him to look around a property or garden before deciding whether he would commission an article (Cornforth, 1988, p. 41).

Lutyens' ability to fuse the demands of art and nature. Moreover, he held Hestercombe up as a model for all, for it proved that 'an architect can be in unison with Nature, that a formal garden can form part of a landscape'. Equally significant, Tipping commented, was Lutyens' skill at evoking the past without becoming subservient to the architectural traditions he was drawing on.

Though Tipping missed little in his praise of the layout, the design and the planting techniques, no mention of Gertrude Jekyll was made in either article. It was unlikely, though, that Jekyll would have minded. She never sought the limelight; her sole concern was that she and Lutyens create a garden that would offer that sense of 'stepping into another world – a comforting world of sympathetic restfulness that shuts out all bustle and hurry, and induces a sense of repose and invigorating refreshment'. Even as winter was approaching, her flowerbeds continued to provide foliage and blooms for the family's enjoyment. The peace of the Portman household, however, was about to be threatened: Lloyd George was preparing a budget that would shock Liberals as well as Tories in its bold attack on the aristocracy. Not even Portman would be able to ignore it.

Six months later, in April 1909, Lloyd George introduced the 'People's Budget', intended in part to fund the new Pensions Act and the increasingly competitive arms race with Germany. Lloyd George, who had always hated what the landed classes stood for, was determined to free the ordinary people from the 'oppression of the antiquated, sterilising and humiliating system of land tenure'. His 'social reform' budget also looked ahead to the introduction of schemes such as unemployment insurance and tax reductions for people with children. And all of this was to be financed by the wealthy. Every time an estate changed hands, whether through death, transferral or purchase, a duty of 20 per cent would be payable on the capital gains. In addition, the Chancellor proposed to tax the rich more heavily and to levy a 'super-tax' – an additional sixpence in the pound – on higher incomes.[*] Even some members of his own

*Lloyd George established the idea of progressive taxes when he proposed that people earning over £5000 per annum should pay an additional tax on their income above £3000.

party were startled by Lloyd George's proposals; it was 'not a Budget but a revolution: a social and political revolution of the first magnitude', one Liberal peer commented. More unnerving still for Portman was the growing hostility that Lloyd George and another ambitious young minister, Winston Churchill, were showing towards the House of Lords, the last bastion of aristocratic power. Although in recent years increasing numbers of peerages had been granted to men of business, finance and industry, landowners still formed the majority.[*] As early as 1909 Churchill was demanding the abolition of the Upper House; it was, he declared, 'an institution absolutely foreign to the spirit of the age and to the whole movement of society'.

For his part, Lutyens felt the full impact when his worst fears were realised and his country-house commissions began to decline. He knew that if Lloyd George's budget was accepted by the Lords it would be a disaster for him. He had already, the previous year, turned to new types of projects, having agreed to design a number of very different buildings including two churches and the central square for the new Hampstead Garden Suburb in London. But he still preferred working for private clients – with individuals there were no committees to complicate matters. In July he went once again to Hestercombe to see the finished garden. It had been less than five years since the first plant had taken root in the Great Plat, yet already the garden looked as if it had stood there for centuries, a remnant of a more stable past. As he and Portman stood fishing on the riverbank later that day, perhaps they reflected on how much had changed since Lutyens first saw Hestercombe. Even Portman had been roused into action: he was planning to lead a demonstration against the budget at Blandford in Dorset. Within days of Portman's rally, Lloyd George gave a speech at Limehouse in London in which he attacked the aristocracy for their greed and self-interest. Not long afterwards, in a speech delivered at Newcastle, he asked whether it was right that the peers, these 'five hundred . . . ordinary men, chosen accidentally from among the unemployed', should be able to override the elected government, who represented the judgement 'of millions of people who are engaged in the industry which makes the wealth

---

[*]In 1909 there were 147 landowners in the House of Lords, but there were also '39 Captains of Industry, 35 Bankers and 35 Railway Directors too' (Camplin, 1978, p. 119).

of the country'. Appalled at 'that cad L. George' criticising the aristocracy, Lutyens wrote to Emily: 'Feudalism only fails 1.) where the lord is bad and 2.) more generally when the vassals have democratic leanings and work for themselves.'

In November that year the House of Lords took the unprecedented step to veto the budget. For now it seemed that Portman and his fellow peers had won, but their victory would be short-lived. Appealing to popular sentiment Lloyd George called a general election. The Liberals won, which later led to the budget being forced through.

In his first *Country Life* article on Hestercombe, Tipping celebrated the interweaving of art and nature, stating that although 'man has distinctly asserted his empire over this set of enclosures and compartments', nature has nonetheless been allowed 'free agency within recognised limits'. Now, one year on, it seemed as if the garden might soon constitute the limits of Portman's dominion. Just as the walls of the Great Plat separated the sunken garden from the surrounding landscape, Portman had for years shored up the barrier that shielded him from modernity and reform. The importance of ancestry and of the traditional order infused the whole garden. Like *Country Life*, Hestercombe continued to convey an image of rural England cut off from the current of events; Hestercombe was ensconced in tradition. As E. M. Forster observed two decades later, the middle classes having 'strangled the aristocracy' continued to copy their way of living because they remained 'haunted by the ghost of its victim'. And so Hestercombe would become the quintessential English garden, inspiring generations of gardeners right up to the present day. Though it marked the beginning of the end of the era of the great country-house garden, its particular combination of the formal and the natural continues to shape the small gardens of suburbia and rural England alike.

Appendix

All seven gardens are open to the public and, to different degrees, are still recognisable as we have described them. Some have undergone restoration programmes intended to recreate the layouts, planting schemes and original buildings, while others have evolved and matured, successfully integrating elements from different eras. Here we describe what is left of the original gardens and briefly outline what has happened since their heyday. We include details of other gardens that contain similar features, layouts or plants, or have some other connection with the gardens that are the subject of this book.

Chapter 1 Hatfield House, Hertfordshire

Robert Cecil's ornamental knot gardens and spectacular waterworks were destroyed at the end of the seventeenth century. John Tradescant left Hatfield three years after Cecil's death, eventually being appointed by Charles I as Keeper of the Gardens, Vines and Silkworms at Oatland Palace in Surrey. He continued to collect exotic plants and curiosities, which were exhibited from 1629 at England's first public museum, the Ark in South Lambeth, London, which was filled with the rarities that he and his son had brought back from their voyages to Russia, Algeria and Virginia. The nucleus of his collection can still be seen at the Ashmolean Museum in Oxford.

In the mid-nineteenth century the gardens at Hatfield underwent major changes when the 2nd Marquis of Salisbury created new terraces, parterres, walls and a maze. In keeping with the Victorian predilection for historical styles, he wanted to reinstate a Jacobean feel – though, as was common, he showed no great concern for historical accuracy. The terraces, for example, were built higher and wider than Robert Cecil's originals. When the Dowager Lady Salisbury came to live at Hatfield in the 1970s with her late husband the 6th Marquis, she began to reorganise and replant the garden. She included a seventeenth-century knot garden, grassed terraces, two mounts and a new kitchen garden. Although none of the original planting schemes survived, she used seventeenth-century sources as a basis for the restoration; the knot, for example, would have been typical of its time, and she used only plants that would have been available to Tradescant.

No grand Elizabethan or Jacobean garden survives in its entirety in England. To see the playful waterworks that delighted royalty and courtiers of the time, the English visitor has to travel to Italy. Two gardens in particular are relevant to the story of Hatfield.

Villa d'Este

The garden at the Villa d'Este is most famous for its theatrical waterworks, situated at different levels of the wide ascending terraces. Myriad fountains, cascades, pools and a water organ dazzled Renaissance visitors. Built in the hilly terrain twenty miles west of Rome between 1560 and 1575 for Cardinal Ippolito d'Este, it epitomises what Cecil wanted to recreate at Hatfield. Many of the waterworks are still functioning.

Villa Lante

Fifty miles north-east of Rome, this is one of the most stunning Italian Renaissance gardens. It was completed by 1573 for Cardinal De Gambara. Built into a hillside, the tiered terraces command sweeping views across the surrounding landscape. The entire garden is based on classical proportions – circles and squares and other geometric shapes dominate the terraces, one of which is a water parterre. With his penchant for outdoor living, the Cardinal created a garden in which to entertain his guests with spectacular water features and *al fresco* dining at the Fountain Table, which still exists. The visitor today can admire the Fountain of Lights and the sinuous stepped cascade, the Water Chain.

Lyveden, Northamptonshire

The finest example of an Elizabethan water garden, where the moat or canal was used as a decorative feature that surrounded the parterre. As at Theobalds and the Island at Hatfield, visitors would have been able to admire the garden from boats. Today one can still follow the spiral paths to the top of the 'snail mounts' for a fine view across the landscape, including the New Bield. Little more than a shell, the lodge has remained untouched for four centuries; its roof and interior decoration are still missing – it was never finished after its owner Thomas Tresham died in 1605. Mountain Jennings, Cecil's gardener, went to Lyveden for inspiration and Tresham's wife sent fruit trees to Hatfield from their famous orchard.

Chapter 2 Hampton Court, Surrey

When Mary's sister Anne became queen after William III's death in 1702, she made Henry Wise the Royal Gardener, instructing him to destroy much of the work he had just finished. Disliking not just her late brother-in-law but the smell of box too, Anne ordered Wise to get rid of much of the parterre in the Fountain Garden. All of William's fountains except for the main one were dismantled, and Marot's elegant parterre patterns were exchanged for plain grass. Queen Anne thus wiped out the most magnificent baroque garden in the country.

Hampton Court ceased to be a popular residence for the monarchs that followed, and when Capability Brown was made Royal Gardener at Hampton Court in 1764 he was able to maintain the gardens for an annual £100 – a fraction of the £5000 that their maintenance had cost William and Mary. Brown retained the Canal and the straight avenues, and left other parts of the main design intact too. But he did stop clipping the evergreens in the Privy and

Fountain Gardens, allowing them to grow large and unruly. The only visual evidence today of his work at Hampton Court is the Great Vine, which he planted in 1768 in what was formerly Mary's part of the garden.

The Privy Garden was meticulously restored during 1991–5, and today visitors can see how the parterre would have looked in 1702. Wise's turf patterns, sand alleys, evergreens, shrubs and flowers have been reinstated, as well as Tijou's railings and screens, of which some have been painted grey and gold again. Nothing of the planting of Mary's flower garden survives, but there are plans to replant parts of it; its division into three sections remains the same. In the Fountain Garden only the Canal and the avenues suggest the grandeur of William and Mary's time. The area where the geometrical Wilderness used to be is now famed for its spring bulbs (only a maze testifies to the original planting), but the Chestnut Avenue with its rows of trees on each side still marches northwards. The restoration of the garden continues, including the gradual replacement of the trees in the avenues.

Versailles, France

Still encapsulating the baroque splendour of its past, Versailles recalls Louis XIV's passion for his garden, and André Le Nôtre's imposing designs continue to impress. The elaborate parterres descending from the palace towards the Grand Canal are still best admired from above – from the palace itself or from the top terrace. Flanking them and the Grand Canal are many wildernesses. Enclosed by high hedges, they lead to small clearings which feature fountains and statues.

Het Loo, Netherlands

Het Loo in the heart of the Netherlands, north of Arnhem, was begun before William and Mary left for England as their summer residence and hunting lodge. It epitomises the more intimate Dutch style in gardening. Enclosed and on a much smaller scale than Versailles or Hampton Court it shows the relative privacy and domesticity of the Dutch court. Like the parterre in the Fountain Garden, the parterres at Het Loo were designed by Daniel Marot, but instead of laying out the intricate patterns in turf as at Hampton Court, he used box and gravel. Destroyed in the eighteenth century to make way for a landscaped park, the parterres were restored to their past glory for Het Loo's three-hundredth anniversary in 1984.

Chapter 3 Stowe, Buckinghamshire

When Richard Grenville succeeded to the estate of his uncle Viscount Cobham in 1749, as well as eradicating the remaining formal elements from the landscape and the vestiges of geometrical design, he changed and relocated many of the temples, statues and paths. Like his uncle he was passionate about the garden, and even when, many years later, he was seriously ill he insisted on being wheeled around to inspect the building works. Stowe remained popular with tourists and underwent many alterations until 1848, when the 2nd Duke of Buckingham and Chandos was forced to sell the estate because of debt. Although his son was able to keep the house and pleasure grounds, the garden staff was streamlined from forty to four. In 1921–2 the estate, including the house and garden, was sold, to become Stowe School. Recognising the importance of the garden, the school repaired some of the buildings and the pupils did much of the gardening, but over the next six decades the dilapidation grew too widespread and in 1989 the garden was transferred to the ownership of the National Trust.

With this began an extensive restoration programme which continues to the present day. Many of the old trees have been felled and replaced, casts of the original statues have been introduced and many buildings such as the Temple of Venus and the Grecian Temple (now known as the Temple of Concord and Victory) have been restored. Some features were demolished by Cobham's heirs, such as Vanbrugh's Pyramid, but over thirty buildings and monuments survive, – although some have been altered – including the famous ha-ha, Vanbrugh's Rotunda and the Hermitage. In the Elysian Fields the visitor can admire Kent's landscape, which still boasts the Temple of British Worthies and the Temple of Ancient Virtue, though its counterpart the Temple of Modern Virtue has not survived the passage of time and in Hawkwell Field Gibbs's Gothic Temple, the Temple of Friendship and the Palladian Bridge still stand. Appropriately, the tallest building in the garden is still Cobham's monument, though many vistas on to it are now obscured by overgrown trees. Stowe remains one of the most celebrated eighteenth-century landscape gardens in Britain.

Rousham, Oxfordshire

William Kent began to work on Rousham in 1737. It is his best-preserved landscape garden; and having escaped the hand of any later designers, it is entirely his. Visitors can still enjoy features such as the cascade in Venus Vale, as well as the artificial ruins and serpentine walks. The survival of original documents with plant lists and instructions has permitted the accurate restoration of the eighteenth-century planting scheme, which includes flowering shrubs along the margins of the evergreens, dispelling once and for all the myth that landscaped gardens had no flowers in them.

Stourhead, Wiltshire

Another famous landscaped garden, created between 1741 and 1780 by the banker Henry Hoare II. Damming the River Stour to create a large irregular-shaped lake, Hoare also commissioned temples, a grotto and other garden buildings that were meant to be seen on a prescribed route. Subsequent owners have made some changes to the gardens, but the essence and structure remain intact, as do many of the original ornamental temples and monuments. Today visitors can walk the same paths, enjoying the views along the Fir Walk as they catch glimpses of the Pantheon and the famous Grotto.

Chiswick House, London

Designed by William Kent and Charles Bridgeman, Chiswick was home to Lord Burlington, who spearheaded the Palladian movement in England through his patronage of Kent and the architect Colen Campbell. Designed to resemble the Roman countryside, the garden was also famous for its classical temples. It is now a public park, retaining much of its original structure, and is currently being restored.

Chapter 4 Hawkstone Park, Shropshire

After Richard Hill's death in 1808 his heir made no major changes to the land-scape, except to extend the park and add two drives. By the end of the nine-teenth century the family was bankrupt, and the estate was broken up in the early twentieth century. The Hall was sold to the religious order the Redemptionists, part of the park became a golf course and many of Hill's follies, views and paths deteriorated.

In 1990, when the Hawkstone Park Hotel – the old inn – was sold, the new owners decided to restore the overgrown parkland. Unlike eighteenth-century visitors who began their tour at Neptune's Whim, crossing over to Red Castle before exploring the Grotto, the Hermitage and the Swiss Bridge, visit-ors today begin at the Greenhouse and finish at Reynard's Walk. Neptune's Whim has not been restored, and Red Castle remains closed to the public. Though many of the tableaux such as the Scene at Otaheite and the Turkish Tent have been lost, follies such as the Hermitage – minus its hermit – have been restored. Health and safety regulations have led to many paths being fenced off and diverted – visitors no longer have to straddle dangerous crevasses. But the long tunnel to the Grotto has been cleared and the views from Reynard's Walk to the ruin retain their charm.

Today, Hawkstone is the most complete 'sublime' garden in Britain, but there are others featuring many elements that, in their day, would have been similar to Hill's designs.

Hafod, Cardiganshire, Wales

The garden of Thomas Johnes, cousin of 'improver' Richard Payne Knight, is one of the few that played with the notion of the sublime to the extent that Hawkstone did. Begun in 1783, the year Richard Hill inherited Hawkstone, Hafod too became a major tourist attraction in the late eighteenth century. Inspired by William Mason, Richard Payne Knight and Uvedale Price, Johnes ensured that his garden would be included in the second edition of William Gilpin's *Observations on the River Wye* (1789) by visiting the indefatigable vicar armed with a portfolio of drawings. Built along a river gorge, the garden features a waterfall, 'alpine' scenes and a rustic bridge. The restoration began in the 1990s and is ongoing.

Painshill, Surrey

Built by Charles Hamilton in the mid-eighteenth century, Painshill is a landscaped garden with a large circuit walk and many Gothic follies, including a temple, a tower and a ruined abbey. There is also a Grotto whose quartz and 'stalactite' interior has been restored, and a rebuilt Turkish Tent. An Amphitheatre of trees and shrubs and the restored flowerbeds in the Elysian Plain offer good examples of 'theatrical planting'.

Studley Royal and Fountains Abbey, North Yorkshire

Few gardens included real ruins like Hawkstone Park did, but one of the most spectacular one is Fountains Abbey at Studley Royal. In 1767, when he purchased the neighbouring estate, William Aislabie incorporated the twelfth-century Cistercian abbey into the picturesque landscaped garden, which also included a formal water garden that his father had devised in the early eighteenth century. Today visitors can still enjoy the geometrically laid out gardens with their stunning view over the abbey.

Chapter 5 Sheringham Park, Norfolk

Until 1986 Sheringham Park was owned by the Upcher family, who continued to maintain the landscape according to Repton's Red Book. In the mid-nineteenth century they had begun to plant rhododendrons along the main approach to the house, and a hundred years later the collection had grown to more than sixty species and hundreds of varieties. In 1975 the Temple was built, its design inspired by Repton's drawing but its exact position not quite as indicated in the Red Book. Thus Repton's 'favourite work' was finally completed, except for the flower garden which has never been realised.

When the National Trust took the estate over in the mid-1980s, their restoration work initially concentrated on the removal of *Rhododendron ponticum*, which had overgrown large parts of the park, impeding the views along the drive. Since then, many dead trees have been replaced and walks for visitors have been laid out in the woods. In its faithfulness to Repton's designs Sheringham is unique; no other client followed his instructions so meticulously as did Abbot Upcher and his descendants. To this day, Sheringham features many of the views depicted in its Red Book.

Repton's legacy is most visible in the many surviving Red Books. Some are in the private collections of the estate owners, while others are kept in record offices, archives and libraries.

Woburn Abbey, Bedfordshire

The Red Book of Woburn (1805) was one of the most sumptuous Repton ever produced. His proposals for the Duke of Bedford included the park and the specialist gardens such as the American and Chinese gardens, the arboretum, the rosary, the menagerie and hothouses. Repton felt that his designs were almost fully realised at Woburn. Today there is also a large deer park, the 'naturalised' Bason Pond and a Chinese Dairy. Repton's approach from the village of Woburn to the house remains as he planned it, the shortest route and the most scenic.

Endsleigh, Devon

Designed in 1814, also for the Duke of Bedford, Endsleigh was one of Repton's last commissions and also one of his most formal designs. Laid out along the banks of the River Tamar, the garden features a grassed terrace with raised flowerbeds. The geometric shapes evoke a past that Repton had turned to in his growing conservatism. Today the garden has been restored according to his drawings.

Chapter 6 Chatsworth, Derbyshire

Joseph Paxton worked at Chatsworth until the Duke's death in 1858. He continued with his other projects too, such as the rebuilding of the Crystal Palace at Sydenham in south London, and became MP for Coventry. Many of his additions to the garden at Chatsworth remain: the Emperor Fountain, the conservatory wall, some orchid houses and the Rock Garden testify to his passion. *Victoria amazonica* still flourishes, but in the Display Greenhouse built in 1970, not in the Lily House. Paxton's Great Conservatory, however, did not survive the economic constraints imposed on the estate after the First World War. After several attempts to dismantle it, it was Paxton's grandson who, in May 1920, with the help of two hundred pounds of explosive, destroyed the masterpiece. What remains is the coal tunnel, partially excavated in 2003, and the foundation walls within which the late 11th Duke and the Dowager Duchess planted a maze.

The Arboretum is still there, though the planting is no longer arranged by botanical classification. Since the late 1950s, many garden buildings and Paxton's Rock Garden have been restored. The foundation walls of the Canal Pond have been reclayed and rebuilt. Many new features have been added such as the Serpentine Hedge, the Pleached Limes and the Kitchen, Cottage and Sensory Gardens.

Edensor, Derbyshire

Next to Chatsworth is Edensor, the 'model village' which Paxton, assisted by Loudon's draughtsman John Robinson, rebuilt during 1838–42. Designed in a mix of architectural styles, it displays Paxton's interest in architecture as well as demonstrating his concern for social welfare: all the cottages were equipped with running water, sewerage, drainage and small gardens.

Palm House, Royal Botanic Gardens, Kew

Though not designed by Joseph Paxton himself, the Palm House shows his influence in the magnificence of the curvilinear glasshouse. It was commissioned by the director of the Royal Botanic Gardens, William Hooker, who had seen the Great Conservatory at Chatsworth. He wanted a glasshouse of a similar size for his growing collection at Kew and asked the architect Decimus Burton and the manufacturer Richard Turner to design and construct it. The Palm House was finished in 1848. Many of the plant species Paxton and the Duke grew at Chatsworth can be seen at Kew and in spring, the delicate blossom of *Amherstia nobilis* still dazzles visitors today.

Chapter 7 Hestercombe, Somerset

Two years after Lutyens and Jekyll finished the garden, in 1909, Edward Portman died. His wife remained in the house until 1944, when the whole estate was sold. When Somerset County Council acquired the house and garden in 1973, Lutyens and Jekyll's planting scheme and layout were submerged in a tangle of overgrowth and had deteriorated considerably. But thanks to Jekyll's plant plans, found in the gardeners' potting-shed, it was possible to restore the garden to its former beauty.

The house is now the headquarters of the Somerset Fire Brigade, but the gardens are open to the public. After major restoration work, still ongoing, visitors can today wander through more than 150 years of garden history: the mid-eighteenth-century landscaped garden (which includes numerous follies and the Great Cascade); the Victorian Terrace and shrubbery, and the restored Lutyens and Jekyll garden. The Great Plat and the Dutch Garden look today as they would have looked in Edward Portman's day. Hestercombe continues to demonstrate the sophisticated appeal of informal planting in an architectural layout.

Jekyll's legacy can be felt in many gardens today: her use of flowers and shrubs as if 'pigment' in an Impressionist painting; her way of planting to soften structural elements; her passion for finding the right plant for the right place. Hestercombe has influenced famous gardens such as Hidcote in Gloucestershire and Sissinghurst in Kent, but also innumerable hobby gardeners who have integrated her vision into country and city gardens large and small.

Iford Manor, Wiltshire

Once home to Harold Peto, the prominent Edwardian architect. The garden at Iford Manor was built by Peto himself and is another excellent illustration of an architectural layout combined with informal planting. Inspired by Italian Renaissance gardens and situated in a steep valley, the garden consists of a series of terraces. Rock and water gardens, statues and a cloister add texture to the scene, while flowering plants spill out of the walls and paving. Many of the original plants still flourish there, such as Italian cypresses, wisterias, phillyreas and martagon lilies. The garden has been restored by the current owners to look as it did when Peto designed it.

Athelhampton, Dorset

Designed by Francis Inigo Thomas, an advocate of Reginald Blomfield's architectural style of formal gardening, Athelhampton was laid out after 1891. It includes a walled garden divided into compartments, with simple geometric flowerbeds and topiary. In comparison to Hestercombe, which it predated by several years, the planting is more plain and formal, with the emphasis on its architectural layout. Over the last forty years, the garden has been restored.

Sissinghurst, Kent

Writer and gardener Vita Sackville-West was inspired by Gertrude Jekyll's garden at Munstead Wood which she visited as a child. Together with her husband, writer and critic Harold Nicolson, she went on to create one of the most evocative gardens of the twentieth century. The epitome of the English garden, it combines 'outdoor rooms' with rich planting schemes that would have impressed Jekyll in their subtle colour transitions and endless variety. Nicolson planned the layout of the garden, while Sackville-West devised the informal planting. Taken over by the National Trust in the 1960s and restored, this small, intimate garden continues to delight visitors today.

Bibliography

Much of our research is based on the work of other historians and biographers, who have painstakingly collected, transcribed and interpreted the many letters, account books, bills and plant lists that have helped to bring our narrative alive. Without them this book could not have been written.

Publications used in more than one chapter are listed either in the General section or under the chapter in which they first appear.

AO	Accounts of the Office of Works (at TNA)
BL	British Library
DC	Directors' Correspondence
HH	Hatfield House
HMC	Historical Manuscripts Commission (at TNA)
Kew	Royal Botanic Gardens, Kew
LC	Records of the Lord Chamberlain (at TNA)
LS	Records of the Lord Steward (at TNA)
RIBA	Royal Institute of British Architects
TNA	The National Archives

Manuscripts and Other Unpublished Sources

Bedfordshire Record Office
L30/9a/1, ff.164–75, Jemima, Marchioness Grey, Letterbook, 5 July 1748

British Library
Add. 5842 f.130, anon., probably John Whaley, in the 'Journal of John Dodd's Tour' (1735)
Add. 20101 f.69, William Talman, 12 Sept. 1699
Add. 37919 f.90, Humphry Repton to William Wyndham, 3 July 1808
Add. 47030 ff.156–9, Lord Perceval to Daniel Dering, 14 Aug. 1724
Add. 57806 f.76, Anne Grenville to Richard Grenville, 1750
Add. 62112 Humphry Repton's Memoir, unpubl. MS
Add. 72339 ff.147–8, John Tradescant to William Trumbull, 21 October 1610
Lansdowne Papers
Sloane Papers

Chatsworth Settlement Trust
Account Books; Catalogue of Plants Grown at Chatsworth, *c.* 1840; 6th Duke's Diaries; 6th
Duke's Group of Correspondence; 2nd Series of Correspondence; the Great Conservatory
at Chatsworth, 21 Sept. 1891; India Correspondence; Paxton Group of Correspondence;
Vouchers in Bundles, 1827–8; James White, unpublished notebook; uncatalogued material;
maps

Godalming Museum
Gertrude Jekyll's Notebooks

Hampton Court Curatorial Office
G. D. Heath, 'William and Mary Chronology', compiled from: Records of the Lord
Chamberlain; Records of the Lord Steward, Records of the Privy Council; State Papers
(all held at the National Archives)
Travers Morgan, 'Royal Parks Historical Survey: Hampton Court and Bushy Park', London,
Dept of Environment, 1983
Terry Gough, 'The Privy Garden at Hampton Court', unpubl. dissertation

Hatfield House
Most of the MSS are also available on microfilm in the British Library:
Accounts; Bills; Cecil Papers; Estate Papers; Family Papers; R. T. Gunton, 'The Building of
Hatfield House', 1895, unpubl. MS; maps

Hestercombe Gardens Trust
'The Portmans and Hestercombe', unpubl. MS

Huntington Library, San Marino, USA
Correspondence of Humphry and William Repton
Stowe Papers, Temple Accounts: Estate Accounts and Household Accounts

National Archives
Accounts of the Office of Works, 1688–1702 (Hampton Court)
Historical Manuscripts Commission: Earl of Carlisle MSS, 15th Report, App. pt VI; Hatfield
    MSS, vol. IX; Hatfield MSS, vol. XIV; Salisbury MSS, vol. XX; Salisbury MSS, vol. XXI;
    Earl of Westmorland MSS, 10th Report, App. pt IV
Records of the Lord Chamberlain (Royal Household), 1688–1702
Records of the Lord Steward (Royal Household), 1688–1702
State Papers Domestic, James I
Treasury Papers, 1689–1702 (Hampton Court)

Norfolk Record Office
Sheringham Estate Papers
Printed extract from the Sheringham Inclosure Act, 26 July 1811;
Abbot Upcher, 'Sherringhamia', 1813–16
Personal papers of Charlotte Upcher
maps

Private Collections
Bygott Collection, held at Shropshire Archives
Hawkstone Survey, 1787

Royal Botanic Gardens, Kew
Directors' Correspondence

Royal Institute of British Architects
Copies of Reef Point Collection (originals held at University of California, Berkeley, USA)
Edwin Lutyens Family Papers
Humphry Repton, Red Book for Sheringham, 1812

Shropshire Archives
Attingham Collection; maps

Somerset Record Office

Gertrude Jekyll's Planting Plans for Hestercombe; photographs

Stowe Gardens Estate Office, National Trust

Jane Evans, 'Descriptions compiled from Seeley's guide books to Stowe Gardens, 1744–1838', n.d.

Land Use Consultants, *Stowe Gardens Survey*, prepared for the National Trust supported by English Heritage, 1992

Richard Wheeler, 'Icons and Emblems', unpubl. conference paper, n.d.

—— 'William Kent and the Faerie Queene', unpubl. conference paper, n.d.

—— 'Stowe. Framework Conservation Plan, pt b: The Garden', Stowe, National Trust, 1999

Maps and garden plans

West Sussex Record Office

Uppark Papers

York City Archives

MSS T/4, Jonathan Gray, 'Tour in the Western Counties and South Wales', 1802

General

Aiton, William T., *Hortus Kewensis*, London, 1789 (and later edn, 1811–13)

Beer, E. S. de (ed.), *The Diary of John Evelyn*, Oxford, Clarendon Press, 1955

Black, Jeremy, *Eighteenth-century Britain, 1688–1783*, Palgrave, London, 2001

Brewer, John, *The Pleasures of the Imagination. English Culture in the Eighteenth Century*, London, HarperCollins, 1997

Briggs, Asa, *A Social History of England*, London, Penguin, 1999

—— *The Age of Improvement, 1783–1867*, London, Longman, 2000

Brown, Jane, *The Art and Architecture of English Gardens*, London, Weidenfeld & Nicolson, 1989

Campbell-Cluver, Maggie, *The Origins of Plants*, London, Headline, 2001

Cave, Kathryne, Kenneth Garlick and Angus MacIntyre (ed.), *The Diary of Joseph Farington*, New Haven and London, Yale University Press, 1978–84

Charlesworth, M., *The English Garden. Literary Sources and Documents*, Mountfield, East Sussex, Helm Information, 1993

Defoe, Daniel, *A Tour through the Whole Island of Great Britain* (first publ. 1724–6), abridged and ed. P. N. Furbank and W. R. Owens, New Haven and London, Yale University Press, 1991

Desmond, Ray, *Bibliography of British Gardens*, Winchester, St Paul's Bibliographies, 1984

Elliott, Brent, *Flora. An Illustrated History of the Garden Flower*, London, Scriptum Editions, 2001

Fearnley-Whittingstall, Jane, *The Garden. An English Love Affair*, Weidenfeld & Nicolson, London, 2002

Fleming, Laurence, and Alan Gore, *The English Garden*, London, Michael Joseph, 1980

Freyberger, Betsy G., *The Changing Garden. Four Centuries of European and American Art*, Berkeley, University of California Press, 2003

Girouard, Mark, *Life in the English Country House*, New Haven and London, Yale University Press, 1978

Gribbin, John, *Science. A History, 1543–2001*, London, Penguin, 2003

Hardyment, Christina, *Literary Trails. Writers in Their Landscapes*, London, National Trust, 2000

Harvey, John, *Early Nurserymen*, London, Phillimore, 1974

Hobhouse, Penelope, *Plants in Garden History. An Illustrated History of Plants and Their Influence on Garden Styles*, London, Pavilion, 1997

—— *The Story of Gardening*, London, Dorling Kindersley, 2002

Hunt, John Dixon, and Peter Willis (ed.), *The Genius of the Place. The English Landscape Garden, 1620–1820*, Cambridge, Mass., and London, MIT Press, 2000

Jacques, David, *Georgian Gardens. The Reign of Nature*, London, Batsford, 1993

Laird, Mark, *The Flowering of the Landscape Garden. English Pleasure Grounds, 1720–1800*, Philadelphia, University of Pennsylvania Press, 1999

Latham, Robert, and William Matthews (ed.), *The Diary of Samuel Pepys*, London, G. Bell, 1970

Malins, Edward, *English Landscaping and Literature, 1660–1840*, London, Oxford University Press, 1966

Margoliouth, H. M. (ed.), *The Poems and Letters of Andrew Marvell*, Oxford, Oxford University Press, 1927

Mosser, Monique, and Georges Teyssot (ed.), *The History of Garden Design. The Western Tradition from the Renaissance to the Present Day*, London, Thames & Hudson, 2000

Mowl, Timothy, *Gentlemen and Players. Gardeners of the English Landscape*, Stroud, Sutton Publishing, 2000

Porter, Roy, *English Society in the Eighteenth Century*, London, Penguin, 1990

Quest-Ritson, Charles, *The English Garden. A Social History*, London, Viking, 2001

Schama, Simon, *Landscape and Memory*, London, Fontana Press, 1996

Thacker, Christopher, *The History of Gardens*, London, Croom Helm, 1985

Thomas, Keith, *Man and the Natural World. Changing Attitudes in England 1500–1800*, Penguin, London, 1984

Thompson, E. P., *The Making of the English Working Class*, Penguin, London, 1980

Uglow, Jenny, *A Little History of British Gardening*, London, Chatto & Windus, 2004

Whyte, Ian D., *Landscape and History since 1500*, London, Reaktion Books, 2002

Williamson, Tom, *Polite Landscapes. Gardens and Society in Eighteenth-century England*, Baltimore, Johns Hopkins University Press, 1995

Chapter 1 Hatfield House

Roy Strong's *The Renaissance Garden in England* is still the seminal book on the period and provides a comprehensive overview with much detail. The essays in the anthology *Patronage, Culture and Power. The Early Cecils 1558–1612* edited by Pauline Croft give a wide-ranging account of the Cecil family's passion for gardens and architecture. Anybody interested in John Tradescant will appreciate Prudence Leith-Ross's exhaustive study of him and his son. Her book has been invaluable for identifying plants and their modern names. Lawrence Stone's *Family and Fortune* gives insight into the Cecils' financial situation. For a chronological reconstruction and details of the building of Hatfield and the gardens R. T. Gunton's unpublished collection of related manuscripts has been indispensable.

Adams, William Howard, *Nature Perfected. Gardens through History*, Abbeville Press, New York, London and Paris, 1991

Airs, Malcom, '"Pomp or Glory": The Influence of Theobalds', in Croft (ed.) 2002

Andrews, Martin, 'Theobalds Palace: The Gardens and Park', in *Garden History*, vol. 21, no. 2 (winter 1993)

Brown Phelps, Henry, and Sheila V. Hopkins, *A Perspective of Wages and Prices*, London and New York, Methuen, 1981

Bullen, A. H. (ed.), *Thomas Middelton: The Works*, Nimmo, 1885–6

Butler, Ewan, *The Cecils*, London, Frederick Muller, 1964

Caus, Salomon de, *Les Raisons des Forces Monuvantes*, Paris, 1624

Cecil, David, *The Cecils of Hatfield House*, London, Cardinal, 1973

Coward, Barry, *The Stuart Age, England 1603–1714*, London, Longman, 2000

Croft, Pauline, 'The Reputation of Robert Cecil: Libels, Political Opinion and Popular Awareness in the Early Seventeenth Century', in *Transactions of the Royal Historical Society*, 6 series, vol. 1, London, 1991

—— (ed.), *Patronage, Culture and Power. The Early Cecils 1558–1612*, New Haven and London, Yale University Press, 2002

—— *King James*, London, Palgrave Macmillan, 2003

Curie, Christopher K., 'Fishponds as Garden Features, c. 1550–1750', in *Garden History*, vol. 18, no. 1 (spring 1990)

Davies, Godfrey, *The Early Stuarts, 1603–1660*, Oxford, Clarendon Press, 1976

Gapper, Claire, John Newman and Annabel Ricketts, 'Hatfield: A House for a Lord Treasurer', in Croft (ed.) 2002

Gunther, Robert William Theodore, *Early British Botanists and their Gardens*, Oxford, Oxford University Press, 1922

Harington, John, *Nugae Antigua*, London, Vernor & Hood, 1804

Harrison, William, *The Description of England*, New York, Dover Publications, 1994 (first publ. 1577)

Harvey Woods, H. (ed.), *John Marston: The Plays*, Edinburgh and London, Oliver & Boyd, 1934–9

Haynes, Alan, *Robert Cecil, Earl of Salisbury*, London, Peter Owen, 1989

Henderson, Paula, 'Overlooking the Garden', in *Country Life*, vol. 128ii (19 May 1988)

—— 'Adorning the Arbour', in *Country Life*, vol. 184i (8 Mar. 1990)

—— 'Sir Francis Bacon's Water Gardens at Gorhambury', in *Garden History*, vol. 20, no. 2 (Dec. 1992)

—— 'Secret Houses and Garden Lodges', in *Apollo*, vol. 146i (Jul. 1997)

—— 'A Shared Passion: The Cecils and Their Gardens', in Croft (ed.) 2002

Herford, C. H., and Percy Simpson (ed.), *Ben Jonson*, Oxford, Clarendon Press, 1925–56

Hulse, Lynn, '"Musique which Pleaseth myne Eare": Robert Cecil's Musical Patronage', in Croft (ed.) 2002

Humphries, Sydney (ed.), *Bacon's Essays*, London, Adam & Charles Black, 1912

Hunt, John Dixon, *Garden and Grove. The Italian Renaissance Garden in the English Imagination: 1600–1750*, London and Melbourne, J. M. Dent, 1986

Jacques, David, 'The *Compartiment* System in Tudor England', in *Garden History*, vol. 27, no. 1 (1999)

Jeffrey, Edward (ed.), *Paul Hentzner's Travels in England, during the Reign of Queen Elizabeth*, Strawberry Hill, 1797 (first publ. 1598)

Kishlansky, Mark, *A Monarchy Transformed: Britain 1603–1714*, London, Penguin, 1997

Knowles, James, '"To Raise a House of Better Frame": Jonson's Cecilian Entertainments', in Croft (ed.) 2002

Lasdun, Susan, *The English Park, Royal, Private and Public*, London, André Deutsch, 1991

Lazzaro, Claudia, *The Italian Renaissance Garden*, New Haven and London, Yale University Press, 1990

Leith-Ross, Prudence, *The John Tradescants. Gardeners to the Rose and Lily Queen*, London, Peter Owen, 1998

Lockyer, Roger, *The Early Stuarts: A Political History of England 1603–1642*, London and New York, Longman, 1999

Loomie, A. J., 'Sir Robert Cecil and the Spanish Embassy', in *Bulletin of the Institute of Historical Research*, vol. 42 (1969)

MacGregor, Arthur, *The Ashmolean Museum. A Brief History of the Museum and Its Collections*, Oxford, Ashmolean Museum, 2001

Markham, Gervase, *The English Husbandman*, London, J. Browne, 1613

—— *Country Contentments: or The Husbandmans Recreations (The English Housewife)*, London, J. Harison, 1633–7

McClure, Norman Egbert (ed.), *The Letters of John Chamberlain*, Philadelphia, American Philosophical Society, 1939

Morgan, Luke, 'Landscape Design in England circa 1610: The Contributions of Salomon de

Caus', in *Studies in the History of Gardens and Designed Landscapes*, vol. 23, no. 1 (Jan.–Mar. 2003)

Mortensen, Peter, *The Time of Unmemorable Being. Wordsworth and the Sublime 1787–1805*, Copenhagen, Tusculanum Press, 1998

Mukerji, Chandra, 'Reading and Writing with Nature: A Materialistic Approach to French Formal Gardens', in *Consumption and the World of Goods*, ed. John Brewer and Roy Porter, London, Routledge, 1994

Munby, Lionel, *Hatfield and Its People*, Hatfield, WEA, 1959

Naunton, Robert, Sir, *Fragmenta Regalia. Memoirs of Elizabeth*, London, Charles Baldwin, 1824

Nevinson, J. L., *The Embroidery Patterns of Thomas Trevelon*, Walpole Society, Oxford, Oxford University Press, vol. 41 (1966–8)

Newman, John, and Caroline Stanley-Millson, 'Blickling Hall: The Building of a Jacobean Mansion', in *Architectural History*, vol. 28 (1985)

Nicolson, Adam, *Power and Glory: Jacobean England and the Making of the King James Bible*, London, HarperCollins, 2003

Nuttall, Peter A., *Thomas Fuller: The History of Worthies of England*, AMS Press, New York, 1965

Parkinson, John, *Paradisi in Sole Paradisus Terrestris*, London, H. Lownes & R. Young, 1629

Pearsall Smith, Logan (ed.), *Life and Letters of Sir Henry Wotton*, Oxford, Clarendon Press, 1907

Pomian, Krzysztof, *Collectors and Curiosities. Paris and Venice, 1500–1800*, Cambridge, Polity Press, 1990

Prest, John, *The Garden of Eden. The Botanic Garden and the Re-creation of Paradise*, New Haven and London, Yale University Press, 1981

Shelton, Anthony A., 'Renaissance Collections and the New World', in *The Cultures of Collecting*, ed. John Elsner and Roger Cardinal, London, Reaktion Books, 1997

Smith, Alan G. R. (ed.), *The 'Anonymous Life' of William Cecil, Lord Burghley*, Lewiston and Lampeter, Edwin Mellen Press, 1990

Somerset, Anne, *Unnatural Murder. Poison at the Court of James I*, London, QPD, 1997

Sorbière, Samuel, *A Voyage to England*, London, J. Woodward, 1709

Spedding, James (ed.), *The Letters and Life of Francis Bacon*, London, Longmans, Green, Rader & Dyer, 1868

Spenser, Edmund, *The Faerie Queene*, ed. A. C. Hamilton, London, Longman, 2001

Stewart, Alan, *The Cradle King. A Life of James VI and I*, London, Chatto & Windus, 2003

Stone, Lawrence, 'The Building of Hatfield House', in *Architectural Journal*, vol. 112 (1956)

—— *Family and Fortune. Studies in Aristocratic Finance in the Sixteenth and Seventeenth Centuries*, Oxford, Clarendon Press, 1973

Strong, Roy, *A Celebration of Gardens*, London, HarperCollins, 1991

—— *The Renaissance Garden in England*, London, Thames & Hudson, 1998

Stubbes, Philip, *The Anatomy of Abuses*, ed. Frederick Furnivall, New Shakespeare Society, London, 1877–9 (first publ. 1583)

Sturdy, David, 'The Tradescants at Lambeth', in *Journal of Garden History*, vol. 2, no. 1 (Oct.–Dec. 1982)

Summerson, John, 'The Building of Theobalds, 1564–1585', in *Archaeologia, or Miscellaneous Tracts relating to Antiquity*, Society of Antiquarians, vol. 97 (1959)

Sutton, M. James, 'The Retiring Patron: William Cecil and the Cultivation of Retirement, 1590–1598', in Croft (ed.) 2002

Temple, Sir Richard Carnac, *The Travels of Peter Mundy in Europe and Asia, 1608–1667*, vol. 3, pt 1 (1634–7), London, Hakluyt Society, 1919

Waldstein, Baron, *The Diary of Baron Waldstein. A Traveller in Elizabethan England*, trans. G. W. Groos, Thames & Hudson, London, 1981 (first publ. 1600)

Whalley, Robin, and Anne Jennings, *Knot Gardens and Parterres*, London, Barn Elms, 1998

Williams, Gordon, *A Dictionary of Sexual Language and Imagery in Shakespearean and Stuart Literature*, London, Athlone Press, 1994

Williams, Penry, *The Later Tudors. England 1547–1603*, Oxford, Oxford University Press, 2002

Wilson, Arthur, *The History of Great Britain. Being the Life and Reign of King James I*, London, Richard Lownds, 1653

Woodhouse, Elizabeth, 'Spirit of the Elizabethan Garden', in *Garden History*, vol. 27, no. 1 (1999)

Woods, May, *Visions of Arcadia. European Gardens from Renaissance to Rococo*, London, Aurum Press, 1996

Chapter 2 Hampton Court

No one interested in Hampton Court should miss Simon Thurley's impeccably researched *Hampton Court: A Social and Architectural History* – the most comprehensive and up-to-date study of the palace and gardens. Since the restoration of the Privy Garden in the 1990s a number of articles and books on the subject have been published. Jan Woudstra's research on the planting scheme of the Privy Garden and David Jacques's work on its construction have been invaluable.

Amherst, A. *History of Gardening in England*, London, Bernard Quaritch, 1895

Anon., *The Royal Diary, Or King William's Interior Portrait*, London, 1702

Baridon, Michael, 'The Scientific Imagination and the Baroque Garden', in *Studies in the History of Gardens and Designed Landscapes*, vol. 18, no. 1 (spring 1998)

Batey, Mavis, and Jan Woudstra, *The Story of the Privy Garden at Hampton Court*, London, Barn Elms, 1996

Bevan, Bryan, *King William III. Prince of Orange, the First European*, London, Rubicon, 1997

Bowen, Marjorie, *The Third Mary Stuart*, London, John Lane, 1929

Burnet, Gilbert, *Bishop Burnet's History of his Own Time from the Restoration of Charles II to the Treaty of Peace at Utrecht, in the Reign of Queen Anne*, London, William Smith, 1838

Claydon, Tony, *William III*, London, Longman, 2002

Colvin, H. M. (ed.), *The History of the King's Works, 1660–1782*, London, HMSO, 1976

Couch, Sarah M., 'The Practice of Avenue Planting in the Seventeenth and Eighteenth Centuries', in *Garden History*, vol. 20, no. 2 (Dec. 1992)

den Hartog, Elizabeth, and Carla Teune, 'Gaspar Fagal (1633–88): His Garden and Plant Collection at Leeuwenhorst', in *Garden History*, vol. 30, no. 2 (winter 2002)

Doebner, Richard (ed.), *Memoirs of Mary Queen of England (1689–1693) together with her Letters and Those of James II and William III to the Electress Sophia of Hanover*, London, David Nutt, 1886

Downes, Kerry, *Sir John Vanbrugh: A Biography*, London, Sidgwick & Jackson, 1987

Dutton, Ralph, *English Court Life from Henry VII to George II*, London, B. T. Batsford, 1963

Erlanger, Philippe, *Louis XIV*, London, Phoenix, 2003

Evelyn, John, *The Compleat Gard'ner; Or Directions for Cultivating and Right Ordering of Fruit-Gardens and Kitchen-Gardens*, London, Matthew Gillyflower, 1693

Gibson, J., 'A Short Account of Several Gardens near London, 26 January 1691', in *Archaeologia, or Miscellaneous Tracts relating to Antiquity*, Society of Antiquarians, vol. 12 (1796)

Green, David, *Gardener to Queen Anne. Henry Wise, 1653–1738, and the Formal Garden*, London and New York, Oxford University Press, 1956

Grimblot, Paul (ed.), *Letters of William III and Louis XIV and of Their Ministers, 1697–1700*, London, Longman, 1848

Groen, Ben, 'De Codex Regius Honselaerdicensis', in *Het Landgoed Leeuwenhorst bij Noordwijkerhout. Kastelenstichting Holland en Zeeland Jaarboek 2003*, ed. Elizabeth den Hartog, The Hague, Kastelenstichting Holland en Zeeland, 2003

Gunter, R. T. (ed.), *Early Science in Oxford. The Life and Work of Robert Hooke*, Oxford, R. T. Gunter, 1935

Harris, John, *William Talman. Maverick Architect*, London, George Allen & Unwin, 1982

Harris, Walter, *A Description of the King's Royal Palace and Gardens at Loo*, London, R. Roberts, 1699

Hatton, Ragnhild (ed.), *Louis XIV and Absolutism*, London, Macmillan, 1976

Hill, Christopher, *The Century of Revolution, 1603–1714*, London and New York, Routledge, 2002

Hook, Judith, *The Baroque Age in England*, London, Thames & Hudson, 1976

Jacques, David, 'The History of the Privy Garden', in *The King's Privy Garden at Hampton Court Palace, 1689–1995*, ed. Simon Thurley, London, Apollo Magazine, 1995

—— and Arend Jan van der Horst, *The Gardens of William and Mary*, London, Christopher Helm, 1988

James, John, *The Theory and Practice of Gardening*, London, Bernard Lintot, 1728

Jardine, Lisa, *Ingenious Pursuits. Building the Scientific Revolution*, London, Little, Brown, 1999

—— *On a Grander Scale. The Outstanding Career of Sir Christopher Wren*, London, HarperCollins, 2002

Jessop, L., 'The Club at the Temple Coffee House – Facts and Supposition', in *Archives of Natural History*, vol. 16, pt 1 (Feb. 1989)

Jones, J. R., *Country and Court. England, 1658–1714*, London, Edward Arnold, 1978

—— 'The Building Works and Court Style of William and Mary' in *Journal of Garden History*, vol. 8, nos 2, 3 (Apr.–Sept. 1988)

Jong, Eric de, '"Netherlandish Hesperides", Garden Art in the Period of William and Mary, 1650–1702', in *Journal of Garden History*, vol. 8, nos 2, 3 (Apr.–Sept. 1988)

Keynes Geoffrey (ed.), *The Works of Sir Thomas Browne*, London, Faber & Faber, 1964

Law, Ernest, *The History of Hampton Court Palace*, London, George Bell & Sons, 1891

London, George, and Henry Wise, *The Retir'd Gard'ner, translation of Le Jardinier Solitaire, or, Dialogues between a Gentleman and a Gard'ner*, London, Jacob Tonson, 1706

Luttrell, Narcissus, *A Brief Historical Relation of State Affairs, from September 1678 to April 1714*, Oxford, Oxford University Press, 1857

Mariage, Thierry, *The World of André Le Nôtre*, Philadelphia, University of Pennsylvania Press, 1999

Miller, John, *The Life and Times of William and Mary*, London, Weidenfeld & Nicolson, 1974

Ray, John, *The Ornithology of Francis Willughby*, London, John Martyn, 1678

Rose, Craig, *England in the 1690s. Revolution, Religion and War*, London, Blackwell, 1999

Sprat, Thomas, *History of the Royal Society*, London, J. Martyn, 1667

Strong, Roy, *Royal Gardens*, London, BBC Books, 1992

Switzer, Stephen, *Iconographia Rustica*, London, 1742 (first publ. 1718)

Tenison, Thomas, *A Sermon Preached at the Funeral of her Late Majesty Queen Mary in Westminster Abbey*, Chiswell, London, 1695

Thompson, E. M. (ed.), *The Correspondence of the Family of Hatton, 1601–1704*, London, Camden Society, vol. 23 (1878)

Thurley, Simon, 'William III's Privy Garden at Hampton Court Palace: Research and Restoration', in *The King's Privy Garden at Hampton Court Palace, 1699–1995*, ed. Simon Thurley, London, Apollo Magazine, 1995

—— *Hampton Court: A Social and Architectural History*, New Haven and London, Yale University Press, 2003

Tinniswood, Adrian, *His Life so Fertile. A Life of Christopher Wren*, London, Pimlico, 2002

Waller, Maureen, *Ungrateful Daughters*, London, Hodder & Stoughton, 2002

Warton, Guy, *Louis XIV's Versailles*, London, Viking, 1986

Whistler, Laurence, *The Imagination of Vanbrugh and his Fellow Artists*, London, B. T. Batsford, 1954

Wijnandis, D. O., 'Hortus Auriaci: The Gardens of Orange and their Place in Late Seventeenth-Century Botany and Horticulture', in *Journal of Garden History*, vol. 8, nos 2, 3 (Apr.–Sept. 1988)

Woodbridge, Keith, *Princely Gardens. The Origins and Development of the French Style*, London, Thames & Hudson, 1986

Woudstra, Jan, 'The Planting of the Privy Garden', in *The King's Privy Garden at Hampton Court Palace, 1699–1995*, ed. Simon Thurley, London, Apollo Magazine, 1995

Wren, Christopher, *Parentalia, or Memoirs of the Family of the Wrens*, London, T. Osborne & R. Dodsley, 1750

Wren Society, Oxford, printed for the Wren Society at the Oxford University Press, 1924–43

Zee, Henry van der, and Barbara van der Zee, *William and Mary*, London, Macmillan, 1973

Chapter 3 Stowe

Stowe is one of the most written-about gardens in the country. One of the leading authorities is George Clarke, and this chapter is all the better for his extensive research. We have made full use of his articles in the *Stoic*, the Stowe School magazine, as well as his comprehensive collection of contemporary visitors' accounts published as *Descriptions of Lord Cobham's Gardens at Stowe, 1700–1750*. Michael Gibbon's and Richard Wheeler's research has also been particularly useful. Peter Willis's superb study of Charles Bridgeman's life and work has proved invaluable. For the chronology of the making of the garden we have largely relied on Land Use Consultant's extensive *Stowe Gardens Survey* held at the Estate Office at Stowe.

Batey, Mavis, 'The Way to View Rousham by Kent's Gardener', in *Garden History*, vol. 11, no. 2 (1983)

Beckett, John, *The Rise and Fall of the Grenvilles*, Manchester and New York, Manchester University Press, 1994

Berry, Reginald, *A Pope Chronology*, London, Macmillan, 1988

Bevington, Michael, 'The Development of the Classical Revival at Stowe', in *Architectura*, vol. 21, no. 2 (1991)

Bickham, George, *The Beauties of Stow; Or a Description of the Pleasant Seat and Noble Gardens of the Right Honourable Lord Viscount Cobham*, London, E. Owen, 1750

Black, Jeremy, *Walpole in Power*, Stroud, Sutton Publishing, 2001

Brownell, Morris R., *Alexander Pope and the Arts in Georgian England*, Oxford, Oxford University Press, 1978

Burgess, C. F. (ed.), *The Letters of John Gay*, Oxford, Clarendon Press, 1966

Cathcart, Charles, 8th Lord, 'Diary', transcribed in Clarke (ed.) 1990 (original in Earl Cathcart's private collection)

Clarke, George, 'The History of Stowe – IV, Sir Richard Temple's House and Gardens', in the *Stoic*, vol. 23, no. 2 (Mar. 1968)

—— 'Early Gardens at Stowe', in *Country Life*, vol. 145i (2 Jan. 1969)

—— 'The History of Stowe – VII, The Vanbrugh–Bridgeman Gardens', in the *Stoic*, vol. 23, no. 6 (Jul. 1969)

—— 'The History of Stowe – X, Moral Gardening', in the *Stoic*, vol. 24, no. 3 (Jul. 1970)

—— 'The History of Stowe – XIII, Kent and the Eastern Gardens', in the *Stoic*, vol. 24, no. 6 (Jul. 1971a)

—— 'The History of Stowe – XIV, Lancelot Brown's Work at Stowe', in the *Stoic*, vol. 25, no. 1 (Dec. 1971b)

—— 'Military Gardening at Stowe', in *Country Life*, vol. 151ii (18 May 1972)

—— 'The History of Stowe – XVI, The Grenville Family', in the *Stoic*, vol. 25, no. 3 (Jun. 1972)

—— 'Grecian Taste and Gothic Virtue: Lord Cobham's Gardening Programme and Its Iconography', in *Apollo*, vol. 97 (Jun. 1973)

—— 'William Kent. Heresy in Stowe's Elysium', in *Furor Hortensis*, ed. Peter Willis, Edinburgh, Elysium Press, 1974

—— 'Signor Fido and the Stowe Patriots', in *Apollo*, vol. 122ii (Oct. 1985a)

—— 'Where Did All the Trees Come From? An Analysis of Bridgeman's Planting at Stowe', in *Journal of Garden History*, vol. 5, no. 1 (1985b)

—— (ed.), *Descriptions of Lord Cobham's Gardens at Stowe, 1700–1750*, Dorset, Buckinghamshire Record Office, 1990

—— 'The Moving Temples of Stowe: Aesthetics of Change in an English Landscape over Four Generations', in *Huntington Library Quarterly*, vol. 55 (1992)

Cobbett's Parliamentary History of England, London, Hansard, *1733–7*, vol. 9 (publ. 1811); *1737–9*, vol. 10 (publ. 1812); *1739–41*, vol. 11 (publ. 1812); *1741–3*, vol. 12 (publ. 1812)

Coffin, David R., 'Venus in the Eighteenth-century English Garden', in *Garden History*, vol. 28, no. 2 (2000)

Coombs, David, 'The Garden at Carlton House of Frederick Prince of Wales and Augusta Princess Dowager of Wales', in *Garden History*, vol. 25, no. 2 (winter 1997)

Cooper, Anthony Ashley, 3rd Earl of Shaftesbury, *Characteristics of Men, Manners, Opinions, Times*, ed. John M. Robertson, New York, Bobbs-Merrill, 1974 (first publ. 1709)

Coxe, William, *Memoirs of the Life and Administration of Sir Robert Walpole*, London, T. Cadell & W. Davies, 1798

Dézallier d'Argenville, Antoine-Joseph, *The Theory and Practice of Gardening* (first publ. as *La Théorie et la pratique du jardinage*, 1709), trans. John James, London, Geo. James, 1712

Downes, Kerry, *Sir John Vanbrugh. A Biography*, London, Sidgwick & Jackson, 1987

Elwin, Whitwell, and William John Courthope (ed.), *The Works of Alexander Pope*, vol. 3, London, John Murray, 1881

Fabricant, Carole, 'Binding and Dressing. Nature's Loose Tresses: The Ideology of Augustan Landscape Design', in *Studies in Eighteenth-century Culture*, vol. 8 (1979)

'The Faire Majestic Paradise of Stowe' (editorial), in *Apollo*, vol. 97 (Jun. 1973)

Friedman, Terry, *James Gibbs*, New Haven and London, Yale University Press, 1984

Gerrard, Christine, *The Patriot Opposition to Walpole. Politics, Poetry and National Myth, 1725–1742*, Oxford, Clarendon Press, 1994

Gibbon, Michael, 'The History of Stowe – VI, Lord Cobham's House', in the *Stoic*, vol. 23, no. 4 (Dec. 1968)

—— 'The History of Stowe – IX, Gilbert West's Walk through the Gardens in 1731', in the *Stoic*, vol. 24, no. 2 (Mar. 1970)

—— 'The History of Stowe – XI, Lord Cobham's Garden Buildings, pt 1: Vanbrugh, Gibbs, Kent', in the *Stoic*, vol. 24, no. 4 (Dec. 1970)

—— 'Stowe, Buckinghamshire: The House and Garden Buildings and Their Designers', in *Architectural History*, vol. 20 (1977)

Hammond, Brean, *Pope and Bolingbroke. A Study of Friendship and Influence*, Columbia, University of Missouri Press, 1984

Harrison, C., P. Wood and J. Gaiger (ed.), *Art in Theory 1648–1815*, Oxford, Blackwell, 2000

Hervey, John, Lord, *Memoirs of the Reign of George the Second. From His Accession to the Death of Queen Caroline*, ed. John Wilson Croker, London, Bickers & Son, 1884

Hinde, T., *Capability Brown. The Story of a Master Gardener*, London, Hutchinson, 1986

Hotman, François, *Franco-Gallia: Or, an Account of the Ancient Free State of France, and Most Other Parts of Europe, before the Loss of Their Liberties*, London, 1721

House of Lords, Journals of the, London, HMSO, vol. 21 (1718–21); vol. 24 (1732–5)

Hunt, John Dixon, 'Emblem and Expressionism in the Eighteenth-century Landscape Garden', in *Eighteenth-Century Studies*, vol. 4 (1971)

—— *William Kent. An Assessment and Catalogue of his Designs*, London, A. Zwemmer, 1987

Hussey, Christopher, 'Stowe, Buckinghamshire I', in *Country Life*, vol. 102 (12 Sept. 1947)

—— 'Stowe, Buckinghamshire II', in *Country Life*, vol. 102 (19 Sept. 1947)

—— 'Stowe, Buckinghamshire III', in *Country Life*, vol. 102 (26 Sept. 1947)

—— *English Gardens and Landscapes 1700–1750*, London, Country Life, 1967

Kemp, Betty, *Sir Robert Walpole*, London, Weidenfeld & Nicolson, 1976

Langford, Paul, *Walpole and the Robinocracy*, Cambridge, Chadwyck-Healey, 1986

—— *A Polite and Commercial People, England 1727–1783*, Oxford, Oxford University Press, 1992

Llanover, Lady (ed.), *The Autobiography and Correspondence of Mary Granville, Mrs Delany*, vol. 2, London, Richard Bentley, 1862

Lubbock, Jules, *The Tyranny of Taste. The Politics of Architecture and Design in Britain, 1550–1960*, New Haven and London, Yale University Press, 1995, p. 113

Lyttelton, George, *Letters from a Persian in England to His Friend at Isapahan*, London, J. Millan, 1735

Mack, Maynard, *Alexander Pope. A Life*, New Haven and London, Yale University Press, 1985

Milles, Jeremiah, *An Account of the Journey that Mr Hardness and I took in July 1735*, transcribed in Clarke (ed.) 1990 (original at the British Library, BL Add. MS 15776, ff.2–10)

Monk, Samuel Holt (ed.), *Five Miscellaneous Essays by Sir William Temple*, Ann Arbor, University of Michigan Press, 1963

Müller, Ulrich, 'Rousham: A Transcription of the Steward's Letters, 1738–42', in *Garden History*, vol. 25, pp. 2 (winter 1997)

Lady Sophia Newdigate's Journal, 1748, transcribed in Clarke (ed.) 1990 (original at Warwick County Record Office, CR 1841/7, ff.3–5)

O'Malley, Theresa, and Joachim Wolschke-Bulmahn (ed.), *John Evelyn's 'Elysium Britannicum' and European Gardening*, Washington, Dumbarton Oaks Reserch Library and Collection, 1998

Penn, John, *History and Descriptive Account of Stoke Parke in Buckinghamshire*, London, W. Bulmer, 1813

Plumb, John, *Sir Robert Walpole*, London, Cresset Press, 1956

Richardson, Samuel, in Appendix to 3rd edn of Daniel Defoe, *A Tour through the Whole Island of Great Britain*, 1742, repr. in Clarke (ed.) 1990

Robinson, John Martin, *Temples of Delight. Stowe Landscape Gardens*, London, National Trust, 2002

Rogers, Pat, *Essays on Pope*, Cambridge, Cambridge University Press, 1993

Rose, George Henry, *A Selection from the Papers of the Earls of Marchmont, 1685–1750*, London, John Murray, 1831

Schulz, Max F., 'The Circuit Walk of the Eighteenth-century Landscape Garden and the Pilgrim's Circuitous Progress', in *Eighteenth-Century Studies*, vol. 15, no. 1 (1981)

Seeley, B., *A Description of the Gardens of the Lord Viscount Cobham at Stow in Buckinghamshire*, Northampton, W. Dicey, 1744

Sherburn, George (ed.), *The Correspondence of Alexander Pope*, Oxford, Clarendon Press, 1956

Smith, J. (ed.), *The Grenville Papers*, London, John Murray, 1852

Southwell, Edward, 'Account of my Journey begun 6 August 1724', transcribed in Clarke (ed.) 1990 (original at Yorkshire Archaeological Society, MS328, ff. 5–6)

Steuart, Henry, *The Planter's Guide*, London, William Blackwood & Sons, 1848 (first publ. 1827)

Stowe Landscape Gardens, London, National Trust, 1997

Stroud, Dorothy, *Capability Brown*, London, Faber & Faber, 1975

Switzer, Stephen, *The Nobleman, Gentleman, and Gardener's Recreation; Or an Introduction to Gardening, Planting, Agriculture*, London, B. Barker & C. King, 1715

Thompson, E. P., *Whigs and Hunters. The Origin of the Black Act*, London, Allen Lane, 1975

Tinniswood, Adrian, *The Polite Tourist*, London, National Trust, 1998

Turner, Roger, *Capability Brown and the Eighteenth-century English Landscape*, Chichester, Phillimore, 1999

Vertue, George, *Notebook 3*, 1733, vol. 22, Walpole Society, Oxford, Oxford University Press, 1934

Walpole, Horace, *Anecdotes of Painting in England*, London, Henry G. Bohn, 1862

Warton, Joseph (ed.), *The Works of Alexander Pope*, n.p., J.J. Tourneisen, 1803

Webb, Geoffrey (ed.), *The Complete Works of Sir John Vanbrugh*, vol. 4, London, Nonesuch Press, 1928

West, Gilbert, *Stowe. The Gardens of the Right Honourable Richard Lord Viscount Cobham*, London, L. Gilliver, 1732

Wheeler, Richard, 'The Gardens of Stowe and West Wycombe. Paradise and Parody?', in *Apollo*, vol. 45ii (Apr. 1997)

Whistler, Laurence, *The Imagination of Vanbrugh and his Fellow Artists*, London, B. T. Batsford, 1954

Williams, Harold (ed.), *The Correspondence of Jonathan Swift*, Oxford, Clarendon Press, 1963

Willis, Peter, 'Jacques Rigaud's Drawings of Stowe in the Metropolitan Museum of Art', in *Eighteenth-Century Studies*, vol. 6 (1972)

—— 'Creator of the English Garden. Charles Bridgeman's Tools and Techniques', in *Country Life*, vol. 153 (17 May 1973)

—— (ed.), *Furor Hortensis*, Edinburgh, Elysium Press, 1974

—— 'Charles Bridgeman and Sir John Vanbrugh. Aspects of a Partnership', in *Landscape Design*, vol. 126 (May 1979)

—— *Charles Bridgeman and the English Landscape Garden*, Newcastle-upon-Tyne, Elysium Press, 2002

Wilson, Michael, *William Kent. Architect, Designer, Painter, Gardener, 1685–1748*, London, Routledge, 1984

Woodbridge, Kenneth, 'William Kent as Landscape Designer. A Reappraisal', in *Apollo*, vol. 100 (Aug. 1974)

—— 'William Kent's Gardening. The Rousham Letters', in *Apollo*, vol. 100 (Oct. 1974)

Wotton, Sir Henry, *The Elements of Architecture, Collected . . . from the Best Authors and Examples*, London, John Bill, 1624

Periodicals
Guardian
Old Whig
Spectator
Stoic
Tatler
The Morning Post and Daily Advertiser

Chapter 4 Hawkstone Park

Of all the gardens in this book Hawkstone is the least documented, so we have relied on contemporary visitor accounts as well as on the *Shrewsbury Chronicle* over a period of thirty years. Edwin Sidney's biography of Richard Hill, published in 1839, like so many nineteenth-century biographies has to be used with caution. Rather than drawing from Sidney's character descriptions, we have used only the letters and diary entries from which he quotes. Adrian Tinniswood's *The Polite Tourist* and Ian Ousby's *The Englishman's England* are very readable studies of the emergence of tourism in England. For the picturesque, Malcolm Andrews' and John Dixon Hunt's work is indispensable, and for William Gilpin Carl Paul Barbier's book is the most comprehensive.

Andrews, Malcolm, *The Search for the Picturesque: Landscape, Aesthetics and Tourism in Britain, 1760–1800*, Stanford, Stanford University Press, 1990

—— *The Picturesque. Literary Sources and Documents*, East Sussex, Helm Information, 1994

Barbier, Carl Paul, *William Gilpin. His Drawings, Teaching and Theory of the Picturesque*, Oxford, Clarendon Press, 1963

Bateman, John, *The Great Landowners of Great Britain and Ireland*, Leicester, Leicester University Press, 1971 (first publ. 1876)

Batey, Mavis, 'The English Garden in Welsh', in *Garden History*, vol. 22, no. 1 (summer 1994)

—— 'The Picturesque: An Overview' in *Garden History*, vol. 22, no. 2 (summer, 1994)

Benn Tony (ed.), *Thomas Paine: Common Sense and The Rights of Man*, London, Phoenix Press, 2000

Bermingham, Ann, *Landscape and Ideology. The English Rustic Tradition, 1740–1860*, London, Thames & Hudson, 1987

Binnie, G. M, *Early Dam Builders in Britain*, London, Thomas Telford, 1987

Boswell, James, *The Journal of a Tour to the Hebrides with Samuel Johnson*, ed. L. F. Powell, London, J. M. Dent, 1958

Broadley, A. M., *Dr Johnson and Mrs Thrale*, London, John Lane, 1910

Brown, Ford K., *Fathers of Victorians: The Age of Wilberforce*, Cambridge, Cambridge University Press, 1961

Burke, Edmund, *A Philosophical Enquiry*, Oxford, Oxford University Press, 1998 (first publ. 1757)

—— *Reflections on the Revolution in France*, London, Penguin, 1968 (first publ. 1790)

Burnet, Thomas, *The Sacred Theory of the Earth*, London, John Hooke, 1719 (first publ. 1681)

Butcher, Edmund, *An Excursion from Sidmouth to Chester in the Summer of 1803*, London, H. D. Symonds, 1805

Campbell Dixon, Anne, 'Hermits for Hire', in *Country Life*, vol. 182ii (2 Jun. 1988)

Copley, Stephen, and Andrew Edgar (ed.), *David Hume: Selected Essays*, Oxford, Oxford University Press, 1996

Daniels, Stephen, *Fields of Vision. Landscape Imagery and National Identity in England and the United States*, Princeton, Princeton University Press, 1993

Davenport-Hines, Richard, *Gothic. Four Hundred Years of Excess, Horror, Evil and Ruin*, London, Fourth Estate, 1998

Donne, John, *Poems*, London, John Marriot, 1633

Gilmour, Ian, *Riot, Risings and Revolution. Governance and Violence in Eighteenth-century England*, Pimlico, London, 1992

Gilpin, William, *Observations, Relative Chiefly to Picturesque Beauty, Made in the Year 1772, on*

Several Parts of England; Particularly the Mountains and Lakes of Cumberland, and Westmoreland, London, R. Blamire, 1786

—— *Three Essays: on Picturesque Beauty; on Picturesque Travel; and, on Sketching Landscape: to which is Added a Poem, on Landscape Painting*, London, R. Blamire, 2nd edn, 1794

—— *Observations on the Western Part of England, Relative Chiefly to Picturesque Beauty*, London, T. Cadell & W. Davies, 1798

—— *Observations on Several Parts of the Counties of Cambridge, Norfolk, Suffolk, and Essex. Also on Several Parts of North Wales, Relative Chiefly to Picturesque Beauty, in Two Tours, the Former Made in . . . 1769, the Latter in . . . 1773*, London, T. Cadell & W. Davies, 1809

—— *Forest Scenery*, London, Sampson Low, Marston, Searle & Rivington, 1879 (first publ. 1791)

Godber, Joyce, 'The Marchioness Grey of West Park, Bedford', *Bedfordshire Historical Record Society*, vol. 47 (1968)

Gomme, Andor, 'The Building of Hawkstone Hall: A Reconsideration of the Evidence', in *Archaeological Journal*, vol. 141 (1984)

Gore-Brown, Robert, *Chancellor Thurlow. The Life and Times of an Eighteenth-century Lawyer*, London, Hamish Hamilton, 1953

Harris, Eileen, 'Hunting for Hermits', in *Country Life*, vol. 182ii (26 May 1988)

Harwood, Edward S., 'Luxurious Hermits', in *Studies in the History of Gardens and Designed Landscapes*, vol. 20, no. 4 (winter 2000)

Hill, George Birbeck (ed.), *Boswell's Life of Johnson together with Boswell's Journal of a Tour to the Hebrides and Johnson's Diary of a Journey into North Wales*, Oxford, Clarendon Press, 1964

Hobsbawm, E. J., *The Age of Revolution 1789–1848*, New York and Toronto, Mentor, 1962

Hulbert, Charles, *Nature's Beauties and Wonders displayed in Shrewsbury, Hawkstone Park and the Isle of Man, etc*, London, W. Baynes & Son, 1825

Hunt, John Dixon, *The Figure in the Landscape: Poetry, Painting, and Gardening during the Eighteenth Century*, Baltimore and London, Johns Hopkins University Press, 1976

—— *Gardens and the Picturesque: Studies in the History of Landscape Architecture*, Cambridge, Mass., and London, MIT Press, 1992

—— *The Picturesque Garden in Europe*, London, Thames & Hudson, 2003

Hutchinson, William, *An Excursion to the Lakes, in Westmoreland and Cumberland, August 1773*, London, L. Wilkie, 1774

Jones, Barbara, *Follies and Grottoes*, London, Constable, 1953

Kerkham, Caroline, 'Hafod: Paradise Lost', in *Journal of Garden History*, vol. 2, no. 4 (Oct.–Dec. 1991)

Knapp, Oswald G. (ed.), *The Intimate Letters of Hester Piozzi and Penelope Pennington, 1788–1821*, London, John Lane, 1914

Lewis, W. S. (ed.), *Horace Walpole's Correspondence*, New Haven and London, Yale University Press, 1937–61

Macfarlane, Robert, *Mountains of the Mind. A History of a Fascination*, London, Granta, 2003

Manwaring, Elizabeth Wheeler, *Italian Landscape in Eighteenth-century England*, London, Frank Cass, 1965

Markham, Sarah, *John Loveday of Caversham, 1711–1789. The Lives and Tours of an Eighteenth-century Onlooker*, Salisbury, Michael Russell, 1984

Mason, William, *The English Garden, A Poem, Published in Four Books*, London, Goldney & Ward, 1778–81

Mavor, William, *The British Tourist's or Traveller's Pocket Companion through England, Wales and Ireland*, London, Richard Phillips, 1809

McQuiston, Julian R., 'Sir Richard Hill: Shropshire Evangelist', in *Shropshire Archaeological Transactions*, vol. 58 (1965–8)

Middleton, Terry, 'Caves and Mines of Hawkstone Park, Salop', in *Cave Science*, vol. 14, no. 3 (Dec. 1987)

Miller, Naomi, *Heavenly Caves. Reflections on the Garden Grotto*, London, George Allen & Unwin, 1982

Milton, John, *Paradise Lost*, London, Basil Montagu Pickering, 1873 (first publ. 1667)

—— *Poems*, facsimile of 1645 edn, Oxford, Clarendon Press, 1924

Moir, Esther, *The Discovery of Britain. The English Tourist 1540–1840*, London, Routledge, 1964

Mortensen, Peter, *The Time of Unmemorable Being. Wordsworth and the Sublime 1787–1805*, Copenhagen, Tusculanum Press, 1998

Oswald, Arthur, 'Beauties and Wonders of Hawkstone I', in *Country Life*, vol. 124i (3 Jul. 1958)

—— 'Beauties and Wonders of Hawkstone II', in *Country Life*, vol. 124i (10 Jul. 1958)

Ousby, Ian, *The Englishman's England. Taste, Travel and the Rise of Tourism*, London, Pimlico, 2002

The Parliamentary History of England, London, Hansard, vols 22–33 (publ. 1814–18)

Pollock, John, *Wilberforce*, London, Constable, 1977

Porter, Roy, *Enlightenment. Britain and the Creation of the Modern World*, London, Penguin, 2000

Price, Uvedale, *Thoughts on the Defence of Property. Addressed to the County of Hereford*, Hereford, 1797

Pückler-Muskau, Prince, *Tour in England, Ireland and France*, Philadelphia, Carey, Lea & Blanchard, 1833

Pugh, R. B. (ed.), *The Victoria History of the Counties of England: Shropshire*, London, University of London Press, 1973

Radcliffe, Ann, *A Sicilian Romance*, London, T. Hookham, 1790

Rodenhurst, T., *A Description of Hawkstone, the Seat of Sir Richard Hill*, Shrewsbury, T. Wood, 1784, 1786; London, John Stockdale, 1799, 1807.

Rousseau, Jean-Jacques, *The Confessions of J.-J. Rousseau: with the Reveries of the Solitary Walker*, London, J. Brew, 1783

Salmon, Joseph Wittingham, *Moral Reflections in Verse, Begun in Hawkstone Park*, Nantwich and Drayton, E. Snelson, 1796

—— *The Beauties of Hawkstone Park*, London, E. Hodson, 1817

Schama, Simon, *Citizens. A Chronicle of the French Revolution*, London, Penguin, 1989

Shropshire Gazetteer, Wem, T. Gregory, 1824

Sidney, Edwin, *The Life of Sir Richard Hill*, London, R. B. Seeley & W. Burnside, 1839

—— *The Life of Lord Hill*, London, John Murray, 1845

Sitwell, Edith, *The English Eccentrics*, London, Faber & Faber, 1933

Skrine, Henry, *Two Successive Tours throughout the Whole of Wales*, London, Elmsley & Bremner, 1798

Southam, H., and R. Davies, *The Hawkstone Handbook. An Illustrated Guide to Hawkstone Park*, Shrewsbury, L. Wilding, 1905

Thorne, R. G., *The History of Parliament*, London, Secker & Warburg, 1986

Tice, Frank, *The History of Methodism in Cambridge*, London, Epworth Press, 1966

Tinniswood, Adrian, *The Polite Tourist. A History of Country House Visiting*, London, National Trust, 1998

Tovey, Duncan C. (ed.), *The Letters of Thomas Gray*, London, George Bell & Sons, 1900

Trinder, Barrie, *The Industrial Revolution in Shropshire*, London, Phillimore, 1973.

—— *The Making of the Industrial Landscape*, London, Phoenix Giant, 1982

Warner, Revd Richard, *A Walk through Wales in August 1797*, Bath, R. Cruttwell, 1802

—— *A Tour through the Counties of England and the Borders of Scotland*, Bath, R. Cruttwell, 1799

Whately, Thomas, *Observations on Modern Gardening*, London, 1770

Wickham Legg, L.G. (ed.), *A Relation of a Short Survey of 26 Counties, Observed in a Seven Weeks Journey Begun on August 11, 1634 by a Captain, Lieutenant and an Ancient*, London, F. E. Robinson & Co., 1904

Wigstead, Henry, *Remarks on a Tour to North and South Wales in the Year 1797*, London, W. Wigstead, 1800

Wilberforce, Robert, and Samuel Wilberforce, *The Life of William Wilberforce*, London, Bungay, 1838

Wilson, William, *A Missionary Voyage to the Southern Pacific Ocean in the years 1796–1798*, London, T. Chapman, 1799

Wordsworth, William, *The Prelude, or Growth of a Poet's Mind*, London, Edward Moxon, 1850

Wraxall, Sir N. W., *Historical Memoirs of His Own Time*, London, Richard Bentley, 1836

Wren, Christopher, 'Report on Westminster Abbey in 1713 to Dean Atterbury', in *Wren Society*, vol. 11 (1934)

Wu, Duncan, *Wordsworth's Reading 1770–1799*, Cambridge, Cambridge University Press, 1993

Periodicals

Annual Register

Shrewsbury Chronicle, 1782–1802

Spectator

Chapter 5 Sheringham Park

Here we must mention Stephen Daniels in particular, who produced a prodigious body of work on Humphry Repton. In addition we have used much of Repton's own writings and his Red Book for Sheringham (which is held at RIBA, as well as Edward Malins's beautifully rendered facsimile from the manuscript). For Abbot Upcher's life, his journal 'Sherringhamia' (held at the Norfolk Record Office, as well as being transcribed and edited by Susan Yaxley) and excerpts from his diary (as published in Emma Pigott's memoirs of her mother Charlotte Upcher) have been our main sources. Alistair Duckworth's study *The Improvement of the Estate*, on Jane Austen and landscapes, has been invaluable, as has Mark Laird's superbly researched *The Flowering of the Landscape Garden*.

Austen, Jane, *Sense and Sensibility*, London, Penguin, 1995 (first publ. 1811)

—— *Pride and Prejudice*, London, Penguin, 1998 (first publ. 1813)

—— *Mansfield Park*, London, Penguin, 1996b (first publ. 1814)

—— *Emma*, London, Penguin, 1996a (first publ. 1816)

—— *Northanger Abbey*, London, John Murray, 1818

Barrell, John, *The Dark Side of the Landscape. The Rural Poor in English Painting 1730–1840*, Cambridge, Cambridge University Press, 1980

Bartell, Edmund, *Observations upon the Town of Cromer, Considered as a Watering Place*, London and Cromer, John Parslee, 1800

Batey, Mavis, 'In Quest of Jane Austen's "Mr Repton"', in *Garden History*, vol. 5 (1977)

—— *Jane Austen and the English Landscape*, London, Barn Elms, 1996

Beckett, R. B. (compiled and annotated by), *John Constable's Discourses*, Ipswich, Suffolk Record Office, vol. 14, 1970

Bending, Stephen, 'William Mason's "An Essay on the Arrangements of Flowers in Pleasure Grounds"', in *Journal of Garden History*, vol. 9, no. 4 (1989)

Bermingham, Ann, 'The Picturesque and Ready-to-wear Femininity', in *The Politics of the Picturesque*, ed. Stephen Copley and Peter Garside, Cambridge, Cambridge University Press, 1994

Byng, John, *The Torrington Diaries*, ed. C. Bruyn, Andrews London, Eyre & Spottiswoode, 1936

Carter, George, Patrick Goode and Kedrun Laurie, *Humphry Repton. Landscape Gardener, 1752–1818*, exhibition catalogue, Norwich, Sainsbury Centre for Visual Arts, 1982

Clarke, Michael, and Nicholas Penny (ed.), *The Arrogant Connoisseur: Richard Payne Knight, 1751–1824*, Manchester, Manchester University Press, 1982

Daniels, Stephen, 'Humphry Repton and the Morality of Landscape', in *Valued Environments*, ed. John R. Gold and Jacquelin Burgess, London, George Allen & Unwin, 1982

—— 'Cankerous Blossom. Troubles in the Later Career of Humphry Repton Documented in the Repton Correspondence in the Huntington Library', in *Journal of Garden History*, vol. 6, no. 2 (1986)

—— 'The Political Iconography of Woodland in Later Georgian England', in *The Iconography of Landscape*, ed. Denis Cosgrove and Stephen Daniels, Cambridge, Cambridge University Press, 1988

—— 'Landscape Design and the Idea of Improvement 1730–1900', in *Historical Geography of England and Wales*, ed. R. A. Dodgson and R. A. Butlin, London, Academic Press, 1990

—— *Fields of Vision. Landscape Imagery and National Identity in England and the United States*, Princeton, Princeton University Press, 1993

—— 'On the Road with Humphry Repton', in *Journal of Garden History*, vol. 16, no. 3 (autumn 1996)

—— *Humphry Repton. Landscape Gardening and the Geography of Georgian England*, New Haven and London, Yale University Press, 1999

Dixon Hunt, John, 'Humphry Repton and Garden History', in *Journal of Garden History*, vol. 16, no. 3 (autumn 1996)

Duckworth, Alistair, *The Improvement of the Estate. A Study of Jane Austen's Novels*, Baltimore, Johns Hopkins University Press, 1974

Everett, Nigel, *The Tory View of Landscape*, New Haven and London, Yale University Press, 1994

Garnett, David (ed.), *The Novels of Thomas Love Peacock*, London, Rupert Hart-Davis, 1948

Goldsmith, Oliver, *The Poems*, London, Longman, 1969

Gowan-Longstaffe, Todd, *The London Town Garden, 1740–1840*, New Haven and London, Yale University Press, 2001

Hayman, Richard, *Trees: Woodlands and Western Civilisation*, London, Hambledon & London, 2003

Henrey, Blanche, *British Botanical and Horticultural Literature before 1800*, London, Oxford University Press, 1975

Hussey, Christopher, 'Sheringham Hall, Norfolk, Part I', in *Country Life*, vol. 121i (31 Jan. 1957)

—— 'Sheringham Hall, Norfolk, Part II', in *Country Life*, vol. 121i (7 Feb. 1957)

Hyams, Edward, *Capability Brown and Humphry Repton*, London, J. M. Dent, 1971

Kent, Nathaniel, *Hints to Gentlemen of Landed Property*, London, G. Nicol, 1799

Laird, Mark, 'Corbeille, Parterre and Treillage: The Case of Humphry Repton's Penchant for the French Style of Planting', in *Journal of Garden History*, vol. 16, no. 3 (1996)

Lane, Maggie, *Jane Austen's England*, London, Robert Hale, 1986

Loudon, John Claudius, *The Landscape Gardening and Landscape Architecture of the Late Humphry Repton*, London, Longman & Co., 1840

Mackie, Charles, *Norfolk Annals*, Norwich, *Norwich Chronicle*, 1901

Malins, Edward, *The Red Books of Humphry Repton*, facsimile of the Red Books of Sheringham, Antony House and Attingham, London, Basilisk Press, 1976

Marshall, P. J., and J. A. Wood (ed.), *The Correspondence of Edmund Burke*, Cambridge, Cambridge University Press, 1968

Mason, Robert Hindry, *History of Norfolk*, London, Wertheimer & Co., 1882–5

Meade-Fetherstonhaugh, Margaret, and Oliver Warner, *Uppark and Its People*, London, George Allen & Unwin, 1964

Murray, Venetia, *High Society in the Regency Period, 1788–1830*, London, Penguin, 1999

Payne Knight, Richard, *The Landscape, a Didactic Poem In Three Books, Addressed to Uvedale Price*, London, W. Bulmer, 1794

Pigott, Emma, *Memoirs of the Honourable Mrs Upcher of Sheringham*, London, Harrison & Sons, *c.* 1860

Pratt, Samuel Jackson, *Gleanings in England. Descriptive of the Countenance. Mind and Character of the Country*, London, A. Strahan, 1801

Price, Uvedale, *Essays on the Picturesque*, London, Mawman, 1810 (first publ. 1794)

Prince, Hugh, 'Art and Agrarian Change, 1710–1815', in *The Iconography of Landscape*, ed. Denis Cosgrove and Stephen Daniels, Cambridge, Cambridge University Press, 1988

Repton, Humphry, *Sketches and Hints on Landscape Gardening*, London, W. Bulmer, 1794

—— *Observations on the Theory and Practice of Landscape Gardening*, London, J. Taylor, 1803

—— *An Enquiry into the Changes of Taste in Landscape Gardening*, London, J. Taylor, 1806

—— *Fragments on the Theory and Practice of Landscape Gardening*, London, T. Bensley, 1816

Rigby, Edward, *Holkham, Its Agriculture*, Norwich, Burks & Kinnebrook, 1817

Rousseau, Jean-Jacques, *The Confessions of J.-J. Rousseau: with the Reveries of the Solitary Walker*, J. Brew, London, 1783

Rowlandson, Thomas, and William Combe, *The Tour of Doctor Syntax in Search of the Picturesque*, London, Methuen & Co., 1903 (first publ. 1812)

Smith, Lady, *Memoirs and Correspondence of Sir James Edward Smith*, London, Longman, 1832

Southey, Robert (ed.), *The Works of William Cowper*, London, Baldwin & Cradock, 1835–7

Spence, Joseph, *Observations, Anecdotes, and Characters of Books and Men*, ed. James M. Osborn, Oxford, Clarendon Press, 1966

Stroud, Dorothy, *Humphry Repton*, London, Country Life, 1962

Wade Martins, Susanna, *A Great Estate at Work: The Holkham Estate and Its Inhabitants in the Nineteenth Century*, Cambridge, Cambridge University Press, 1980

White, Gilbert, *The Garden Kalendar 1751–1771* (facsimile of MS in the BL), London, Scolar Press, 1975

Williams, Raymond, *The Country and the City*, London, Chatto & Windus, 1973

Wordsworth, William, *Lyrical Ballads with Other Poems*, London, Longman, 1800

Yaxley, Susan (ed)., *Sherringhamia: The Journal of Abbot Upcher 1813–16*, Stibbard, Larks Press, 1986

Periodical

The Times

Chapter 6 Chatsworth

The timing of the publication of Kate Colquhoun's biography of Joseph Paxton, *A Thing in Disguise*, seemed almost too good to be true. Her extensive and impeccable research on the thousands of letters of Paxton and the 6th Duke of Devonshire has made our search for documents at the Chatsworth archives so much easier, and without her book we would have missed some of the fascinating details. Similarly, James Lees-Milne's *The Bachelor Duke*, a very readable account of an extraordinary man, has pointed us in the right direction. We have drawn extensively on Paxton's own writing, especially from the *Magazine of Botany*, which provided much of the information on the horticultural aspects and on his methods of work. For contemporary developments in gardening, Brent Elliott's *Victorian Gardens* has been a useful source.

Adam, William, *The Gem of the Peak, Or Matlock, Bath and Its Vicinity*, London, Longman, 1838 (plus edns of 1843, 1845, 1851)

Beckett, Derrick, *Brunel's Britain*, Newton Abbot, David & Charles, 1980

Bloom, Clive, *Violent London: Two Thousand Years of Riots, Rebels and Revolts*, London, Sidgwick & Jackson, 2003

Briggs, Asa, *Victorian People: Some Reassessments of People, Institutions, Ideas and Events, 1851–1867*, London, Odhams Press, 1954

—— *Iron Bridge to Crystal Palace. Impact and Images of the Industrial Revolution*, London, Thames & Hudson, 1979

Burkhardt, Frederick, and Sydney Smith (ed.), *The Correspondence of Charles Darwin*, Cambridge, Cambridge University Press, 1985–93

Cannadine, David, 'The Landowner as Millionaire: The Finances of the Dukes of Devonshire, c. 1800–1926', in *Agricultural History Review*, vol. 24, pt 2 (1976)

Cavendish, W. G. S., 6th Duke of Devonshire, *Handbook of Chatsworth and Hardwick*, London, privately printed, 1845

Chadwick, George F., 'The Great Stove at Chatsworth', in *Architectural History*, vol. 4 (1961a)

—— *The Works of Sir Joseph Paxton, 1803–1865*, London, Architectural Press, 1961b

Clark, Frank, 'Nineteenth-century Public Parks from 1830', in *Garden History*, vol. 1 (Sept. 1972)

Colquhoun, Kate, *A Thing in Disguise. The Visionary Life of Joseph Paxton*, London, Fourth Estate, 2003

Conway, Hazel, *People's Parks: the Design and Development of Victorian Parks in Britain*, Cambridge, Cambridge University Press, 1991

Davis, John R., *The Great Exhibition*, Stroud, Sutton Publishing, 1999

Desmond, Raymond, 'Victorian Garden Magazines', in *Garden History*, vol. 5, no. 3 (1977)

Devonshire, Deborah, Duchess of, *The Garden at Chatsworth*, London, Frances Lincoln, 1999

Dickens, Charles, 'The Private History of the Palace of Glass', in *Household Words*, vol. 43 (18 Jan. 1851)

Elliott, Brent, *The Royal Horticultural Society: A History, 1804–2004*, London, Phillimore, 2004

Flanders Darby, Margaret, 'Joseph Paxton's Water Lily', in *Bourgeois and Aristocratic Cultural Encounters in Garden Art, 1550–1850*, ed. Michael Conan, Washington, Dumbarton Research Library, 2002

Gates, Barbara T., 'Ordering Nature: Revisioning Victorian Science Culture', in *Victorian Science in Context*, ed. Bernhard Lightman, Chicago, University of Chicago Press, 1997

Gloag, John, *Mr Loudon's England*, Newcastle-upon-Tyne, Oriel Press, 1970

Granville, A. B., *The Spas of England and Principal Sea Bathing Places*, London, Henry Colburn, 1841

Hadfield, Miles, *A History of British Gardening*, London, John Murray, 1979

Hall, George, *The History of Chesterfield*, London, Whitaker & Co., 1839

Hall, S. C., 'A Day at Chatsworth', in *Art Journal* (1851)

Hansen, Eric, *Orchid Fever. A Horticultural Tale of Love, Lust and Lunacy*, London, Methuen, 2001

Harley, Bessie, and Jessie Harley, *A Gardener at Chatsworth: Three Years in the Life of Robert Aughtie, 1848–1851*, Self-Publishing Association, 1992

Herbert, Gilbert, *Pioneers of Prefabrication. The British Contribution in the Nineteenth Century*, Baltimore, Johns Hopkins University Press, 1978

Hix, John, *The Glasshouse*, London, Phaidon, 1996

Hobhouse, Hermione, *The Crystal Palace and the Great Exhibition*, London and New York, Athlone Press, 2002

Hobsbawm, E. J., *Industry and Empire. From 1750 to the Present Day*, London, Penguin, 1969

Hooker, W., and W. Fitch, *Victoria Regia, or Illustrations of the Royal Water Lily*, London, Reeve & Benham, 1851

James, Lawrence, *The Rise and Fall of the British Empire*, London, Abacus, 1998

Jewitt, Llewellynn, *Illustrated Guide to Chatsworth*, Buxton, J. C. Bates, 1872

Lees-Milne, James, *The Bachelor Duke. A Life of William Spencer 6th Duke of Devonshire, 1790–1858*, London, John Murray, 1998

Lemmon, Kenneth, *The Golden Age of Plant Hunters*, London, Phoenix House, 1968

Leveson Gower, Frederick, *Bygone Years*, John Murray, London, 1905

Loudon, John Claudius, *Remarks on the Construction of Hot-Houses*, London, 1817

—— *Comparative View of the Curvilinear & Common Mode of Roofing Hot-Houses*, London, 1818

Mabey, Richard (ed.), *The Oxford Book of Nature Writing*, Oxford, Oxford University Press, 1995

Markham, Violet, *Paxton and the Bachelor Duke*, London, Hodder & Stoughton, 1935

McCracken, Donald P., *Gardens of Empire. Botanical Institutions of the Victorian Empire*, London and Washington, Leicester University Press, 1997

Mundy, Harriet (ed.), *The Journal of Mary Frampton: from the year 1779 until the year 1846*, London, Sampson Low & Co., 1885

Paxton, Joseph, *A Pocket Botanical Dictionary*, London, 1840

——, *The Cottager's Calendar of Gardening Operations*, London, The Gardeners' Chronicle, 1859

—— and John Lindley, *Paxton's Flower Garden*, London, 1850–3

Pudney, John, *The Thomas Cook Story*, London, Michael Joseph, 1953

Reeve, Henry (ed.), *The Greville Memoirs*, London, Longmans, Green & Co., 1888

Reinikka, Merle A., *A History of the Orchid*, Coral Gables, Florida, University of Miami Press, 1972

Rolt, L. T. C., *Victorian Engineering*, London, Allen Lane, 1970

Smiles, Samuel, *Self-Help. With Illustrations of Character, Conduct, and Perseverance*, Oxford, Oxford University Press, 2002 (first publ. 1859)

Spielmann, M. H., *The History of 'Punch'*, London, Paris and Melbourne, Cassell & Co., 1895

Taylor, William, 'Living in Glasshouses: Vegetality and the Curvilinear Forcing Houses of the Early Nineteenth Century', in *Journal of Garden History*, vol. 15, no. 4 (1995)

—— 'The Cultivation of Reason: Functionalism and the Management of Nature', in *Journal of Garden History*, vol. 18, no. 2 (1998)

Ward, Nathaniel Bagshaw, *On the Growth of Plants in Closely Glazed Cases*, London, 1852 (first publ. 1842)

Warner, Tim, 'The Railway that Never Was', in *Derbyshire Life and Countryside*, vol. 54 (Jan. 1989)

Wilson, A. N, *The Victorians*, London, Hutchinson, 2002

Periodicals
Annual Register
Cottage Gardener and Country Gentleman
Derby Mercury
Gardeners' Chronicle
Gardener's Magazine
Horticultural Register
Illustrated London News
Leicester Journal
Magazine of Botany
Transactions of the Society of Arts, Manufactures and Commerce

Chapter 7 Hestercombe

Gertrude Jekyll was an indefatigable writer, and her voice and opinions resound in her many publications, some of which have recently been reprinted. For Edwin Lutyens, Jane Ridley's biography has been invaluable, as have her and Clare Percy's *Letters of Edwin Lutyens*, which pointed to many letters that we would otherwise have missed. Philip White's guide to Gertrude

Jekyll's planting schemes at Hestercombe is a wonderful source for anybody interested in the restoration of Hestercombe and the horticultural details

Batey, Mavis, 'Gertrude Jekyll and the Arts and Crafts Movement', in *Gertrude Jekyll: Essays on the Life of a Working Amateur*, ed. M. Tooley and P. Arnander, Witton le Wear, Michaelmas Books, 1995

Bennett, Sue, *Five Centuries of Women and Gardens*, London, National Portrait Gallery, 2000

Bisgrove, Richard, *The Gardens of Gertrude Jekyll*, London, Frances Lincoln, 1992

Blomfield, Reginald, *The Formal Garden in England*, London, Macmillan & Co., 1892

Brown, Jane, *Miss Gertrude Jekyll*, exhibition catalogue, London, Architectural Press, 1981

——— *Gardens of a Golden Afternoon*, London, Allen Lane, 1982

——— *The English Garden in Our Time. From Gertrude Jekyll to Geoffrey Jellicoe*, London, Antique Collectors' Club, 1986

Butler, A. S. G., *The Architecture of Sir Edwin Lutyens*, London, Country Life, 1950

Camplin, Jamie, *The Rise of the Plutocrats. Wealth and Power in Edwardian England*, London, Constable, 1978

Cannadine, David, *The Decline and Fall of the British Aristocracy*, New Haven and London, Yale University Press, 1990

Clayton-Payne, Andrew, and Brent Elliott, *Victorian Flower Gardens*, London, Weidenfeld & Nicolson, 1988

Colls, Robert, and Philip Dodd (ed.), *Englishness: Politics and Culture 1880–1920*, London, Croom Helm, 1986

Cook, E. T., and Alexander Wedderburn (ed.), *The Works of John Ruskin*, London, G. Allen, 1902–12

Cornforth, John, *The Search for a Style: Country Life and Architecture, 1897–1935*, London, André Deutsch in association with Country Life, 1988

Ensor, R. C. K., *England, 1870–1914*, Oxford, Clarendon Press, 1988

Festing, Sally, *Gertrude Jekyll*, London, Viking, 1991

Forty, Adrian, *Objects of Desire: Design and Society since 1750*, London, Thames & Hudson, 1995

Gilbert, B., *Lloyd George. A Political Life*, London, Batsford, 1987

Girouard, Mark, *The Victorian Country House*, New Haven and London, Yale University Press, 1979

Gorer, Richard, 'The Puzzle of Repton's Roses', in *Country Life*, vol. 171i (11 Mar. 1982)

Grigg, John, *Lloyd George: The People's Champion, 1902–1911*, London, Eyre Methuen, 1978

Helmreich, Anne, *The English Garden and National Identity*, Cambridge, Cambridge University Press, 2002

Hinge, David, 'Gertrude Jekyll: 1843–1932. A Bibliography of Her Writings', in *Journal of Garden History*, vol. 2, no. 3 (Jul.–Sept. 1982)

Hobhouse, Penelope, *Gertrude Jekyll on Gardening*, London, National Trust and William Collins, 1983

Holdsworth, William, *A History of English Law*, London, Methuen, 1982

Hussey, Christopher, *The Life of Edwin Lutyens*, London, Country Life, 1950

—— 'The Making of *Country Life*', in *Country Life*, vol. 141i (12 Jan. 1967)

Jekyll, Francis, *Gertrude Jekyll: A Memoir*, London, Jonathan Cape, 1934

—— and G. C. Taylor (ed.), *A Gardener's Testament. A Selection of Articles and Notes by Gertrude Jekyll*, London, Country Life, 1937

Jekyll, Gertrude, 'Gardens and Gardens-Craft', in *Edinburgh Review*, vol. 377 (Jul. 1896)

—— *Wood and Garden*, London, Longmans, Green & Co., 1899

—— *Home and Garden*, London, Longmans, Green & Co., 1900

—— *Wall and Water Gardens*, London, Country Life, 1901

—— *Old West Surrey*, London, Longmans, Green & Co., 1904

—— *Colour in the Flower Garden*, London, Country Life, 1908

—— *Garden Ornament*, Woodbridge, Antique Collectors' Club, 1982 (first publ. 1918)

—— 'The Garden: Changes of Fashion in Gardening', in *Nineteenth Century and After*, vol. 104, no. 618 (Aug. 1928)

King, Francis, *The Well Considered Garden*, New York, Charles Scribner's Sons, 1915

Lethaby, William Richard, *Architecture, Mysticism and Myth*, London, Percival & Co., 1892

Lewis, Cherry (ed.), *Gertrude Jekyll. The Making of a Garden: An Anthology*, Woodbridge, Garden Art Press, 2000

Lutyens, Mary, 'Sir Edwin Lutyens', in *Lutyens: The Work of the English Architect Sir Edwin Lutyens*, exhibition catalogue, Hayward Gallery, London, Arts Council of Great Britain, 1981

Mandler, Peter, *The Fall and Rise of the Stately Home*, New Haven and London, Yale University Press, 1997

Marsh, J., *Back to the Land. The Pastoral Impulse in England from 1880 to 1914*, London, Quartet Books, 1982

Massingham, Betty, *Miss Jekyll. Portrait of a Great Gardener*, London, Country Life, 1966

Matthew, H. C. G., 'The Liberal Age', in *The Oxford Illustrated History of Britain*, ed. Kenneth A. Morgan, Oxford, Oxford University Press, 1997

Maude, Pamela, 'Portrait of a Perfectionist. Edward Hudson, the Founder of *Country Life*', in *Country Life*, vol. 141i (12 Jan. 1967)

Mayberry, T. W., *Orchard and the Portmans*, Taunton, T. W. Mayberry, 1986

Middlemas, Keith, *The Life and Times of Edward VII*, London, Weidenfeld & Nicolson, 1972

Milne O. P., 'Reminiscences on Sir Edwin Lutyens', in *Architectural Association Journal*, vol. 74, no. 829 (Feb. 1959)

Moore, S. T., *History of Bryanston* n.p., 1993

Morris, William, *Hopes and Fears for Art: Five Lectures Delivered in Birmingham, London and Nottingham, 1878–1881*, London, Ellis & White, 1882

—— *Art and Beauty: A Lecture Delivered at Burslem Town Hall*, London, Longmans & Co., 1898

Murray, Bruce K., *The People's Budget 1909/10: Lloyd George and Liberal Politics*, Oxford, Clarendon Press, 1980

Ottewill, David, *The Edwardian Garden*, New Haven and London, Yale University Press, 1989

Paul, Andrew, 'The Restoration of Hestercombe', in *Landscape Design*, no. 132 (Feb. 1981)

Percy, Clare, and Jane Ridley (ed.), *The Letters of Edwin Lutyens*, London, Collins, 1985

Rhodes James, Robert (ed.), *Winston Churchill: His Complete Speeches, 1897–1963*, New York and London, Chelsea House Publishers, 1974

Ridley, Jane, *Edwin Lutyens. His Life, His Wife, His Work*, London, Pimlico, 2003

Robinson, William, *The English Flower*, London, Hamlyn Publishing, 1985 (first publ. 1883)

Tankard, Judith, and Michael Van Valkenburgh, *Gertrude Jekyll. A Vision of Garden and Wood*, London, John Murray, 1989

—— and Martin A. Wood (ed.), *Gertrude Jekyll at Munstead Wood*, Strand, Sutton, 1996

Tennyson, Lord Hallam (ed.), Alfred Tennyson, *Poems*, London, Macmillan, 1907

Thompson, F. L. M., *English Landed Society*, London, Routledge & Kegan Paul, 1963

Thompson, Paul, *The Edwardians*, London, Weidenfeld & Nicolson, 1976

Tipping, H. Avray, 'Hestercombe I – The Seat of the Hon. Edward W. Berkeley Portman', in *Country Life*, vol. 24, no. 614 (10 Oct. 1908)

—— 'Hestercombe II – The Seat of the Hon. Edward W. Berkeley Portman', in *Country Life*, vol. 24, no. 615 (17 Oct. 1908)

Tooley, M., and P. Arnander, *Gertrude Jekyll: Essays on the Life of a Working Amateur*, Witton le Wear, Michaelmas Books, 1995

Trollope, Anthony, *The Last Chronicle of Barset*, London, Penguin Classics, 2002 (first publ. 1867)

Weaver, Lawrence, *Houses and Gardens by E. L. Lutyens*, London, Country Life, 1913

Wells, H. G., *Tono Bungay*, London, Macmillan & Co., 1912 (first publ. 1909)

White, Philip (ed.), *An Illustrated Guide to Gertrude Jekyll's Planting Design for the Formal Garden at Hestercombe*, Taunton, Hestercombe Gardens Trust, 2004

Wiener, Martin, *English Culture and the Decline of the Industrial Spirit 1850–1980*, London, Penguin, 1981

Wilde, Oscar, *Collins Complete Works of Oscar Wilde*, London, HarperCollins, 1999

Williams, Robert, 'Edwardian Gardens. Old and New', in *Journal of Garden History*, vol. 13, nos 1, 2 (spring/summer 1993)

Windsor, Duke of, *A King's Story: The Memoirs of HRH the Duke of Windsor KG*, London, Cassell, 1951

Periodicals

Bailey's Magazine of Sports and Pastimes

Illustrated London News

Somerset County Gazette

Picture Credits

Colour sections

Plan of Old Palace, Hatfield: 1607, Marquess of Salisbury

Striped and double anemones: Johann Weinemann, 1734–47. *Flora*, Brent Elliott, Royal Horticultural Society

Lilium martagon: Pieter van Kouwenhoorn, 1630. *Flora*, Brent Elliott, Royal Horticultural Society

Fritillaria meleagris: Pieter van Kouwenhoorn, 1630. *Flora*, Brent Elliott, Royal Horticultural Society

Hampton Court: Leonard Knyff, c.1703. The Royal Collection © Her Majesty the Queen Elizabeth II

Het Loo: Romeyn de Hooghe, published by Petrus Persoy, c.1698. Rijksmuseum, Amsterdam

Orangery Garden and hothouse: Mulder and de Lespine, c.1690. The Library, Wageningen Agricultural University

Auricular Royal: James Sowerby, The Florist's Delight, 1790. Royal Horticultural Society

Great Parterre, Longleat: Robert Thacker, c.1704. Marquess of Bath, Longleat House, Warminster, Wiltshire

The Rotunda and Queen's Theatre: Jacques Rigaud, 1681–1754. Christies Images/Bridgeman Art Library

A Conversation of Virtuosi . . . at the King's Arms: Gawen Hamilton, 1735. National Portrait Gallery, London

Scything: Gardens of Chiswick House from the West, Pieter Andreas Rysbrack, 1640–1748. English Heritage Photo Library

Windmill at Wijk by Duurstede: Jacob van Ruisdael. c.1670. Rijksmuseum, Amsterdam

Coalbrookdale by Night: Philip de Loutherbourg, 1801. Science Museum, London/Bridgeman Art Library

Illustrations in the text

Hatfield

33   Mount Parnassus: *Les raison des forces mouvants*, Salomon de Caus, 1624. British Library

34   Solar-powered fountain: *Les raison des forces mouvants*, Salomon de Caus, 1624. British Library

36   Sketch of waterworks: Thomas Wilson, 1611, The National Archives, London

37   The island in the East Garden: Letters and papers published in the Calendar of State Papers Domestic, James I, 1611–1618. The National Archives, London

Hampton Court

46   Versailles: Pierre Lepautre, 1660–1744. Giraudon/Bridgeman Art Library

48   William of Orange: After Peter Lely, 1677. National Portrait Gallery, London

48   Queen Mary: After William Wissing, c.1690. National Portrait Gallery, London

49   Hampton Court: Hendrick Denckerts, c.1630. The Royal Collection © Her Majesty the Queen Elizabeth II

57   Fountain Garden: Daniel Marot, 1689. Museum Boymans-van Bueningen, Rotterdam

59   Wilderness: Nicholas Hawksmoor, c.1710–14. Courtesy of the Trustees of Sir John Soane's Museum, London/Bridgeman Art Library

76   Reconstruction of Privy Garden in 1695: Daphne Ford, *The King's Privy Garden at Hampton Court*, Simon Thurley, ed., Apollo, 1995/© By courtesy of the Trustees of Sir John Soane's Museum

81   Design for gates: B. Gentot after Tijou, 1693. The Guildhall, London

83   Privy Garden: c.1714, English School. Courtesy of the Trustees of Sir John Soane's Museum, London/Bridgeman Art Library

84   The Great Parterre, Longleat: Robert Thacker, 1704. Marquess of Bath, Longleat House, Warminster, Wiltshire

Stowe

89   Richard Temple, Viscount Cobham: After Jean-Baptiste van Loo c.1740. National Portrait Gallery, London

91   View of Stowe: Charles Bridgeman, c.1719. British Library

93   Vanbrugh's Pyramid: Jacques Rigaud, c.1733. The Governors of Stowe School, Photographic Archives

94   Ha-ha: Sketch by Felix Kelly, *The Georgians at Home*, Longmans, Green and Co, 1967. British Library

99   Detail from Bridgeman's plan: *Fifteen Views of Stowe*, Jacques Rigaud, issued by Sarah Bridgeman, 1793. The Governors of Stowe School, Photographic Archives

107   Elysian Fields: Thomas Rowlandson, 1805. The Governors of Stowe School, Photographic Archives

109   River Alder: J. C. Nattes, 1805. The Governors of Stowe School, Photographic Archives

Hawkstone Park

Sheringham Park

201   Flower garden at Nuneham Courtenay: Paul Sanby, 1777. Private Collection/Bridgeman Art Library

202   Hardenberg Basket for Lady Suffield at Blickling Hall: John Adey Repton, 1823. Blickling Hall

Chatsworth

215   Map of Chatsworth, 1858: Devonshire Collection, Chatsworth. Reproduced by permission of the Chatsworth Settlement Trustees

218   Joseph Paxton: Henry Perronet Briggs, 1836. Devonshire Collection, Chatsworth. Reproduced by permission of the Chatsworth Settlement Trustees

221   William Spencer Cavendish, 6th Duke of Devonshire: Carelli, 1833–4. Devonshire Collection, Chatsworth. Reproduced by permission of the Chatsworth Settlement Trustees

225   Greenhouse with ridge-and-furrow roof: *Paxton's Magazine of Botany*, 1836. Royal Horticultural Society

228   Flower garden in front of the old greenhouse: *Paxton's Magazine of Botany*, 1836. Royal Horticultural Society

233   Wardian case: 1842. British Library.

235   The Great Conservatory at Chatsworth: English School, 1844. *Illustrated London News* Picture Library, London/Bridgeman Art Library

245   Painting and glazing wagon: English School, 1850. *Illustrated London News* Picture Library, London/Bridgeman Art Library

251   Interior Great Conservatory: English School, 1843. *Illustrated London News* Picture Library, London/Bridgeman Art Library

260   Annie Paxton: English School, 1849. *Illustrated London News* Picture Library, London/Bridgeman Art Library

261   Lily House at Chatsworth: *Gardener's Chronicle*, 1850. Royal Horticultural Society

263   Paxton's sketch for the Great Exhibition: Joseph Paxton, 1850. Victoria and Albert Museum, London/Bridgeman Art Library

Hestercombe

268   Edwin Lutyens: Phipps, *c.*1906. RIBA

270   Gertrude Jekyll: Edwin Lutyens, *c.*1896. RIBA

271   Lutyens and Jekyll: Edwin Lutyens, 1896. RIBA

273   Plan of garden at Hestercombe: Edwin Lutyens, 1908. *Country Life* Library

285   Village Old Style/New Style: George Morrow, 1907. *Punch* or the London Charivari/Punch Collection

287   Frontispiece of William Morris's *News from Nowhere*: W. H. Hooper, 1892. Private Collection/Bridgeman Art Library

ADDRESSES AND OPENING TIMES

Hatfield House

Hatfield
Hertfordshire AL9 5NQ
tel. 01707 287010
www.hatfield-house.co.uk
Opening times of the gardens
Easter Saturday–end September:
Park and West Garden: 11a.m.–5.30p.m.
East Garden: open only on Monday 11a.m.–5.30p.m.

Hampton Court

Surrey KT8 9AU
tel. 0870 752 7777
www.hrp.org.uk
Opening times of the gardens
The Wilderness, Tiltyard and Rose Garden:
All year: 7a.m.–dusk
Gardens and Maze:
April–October: 10a.m.–6p.m.
End October–March: 9.30a.m.–4.30p.m.; Monday 10.15a.m.–4.30p.m.

Stowe

Buckingham
MK18 5EH
tel. 01280 822850
www.nationaltrust.org.uk
Opening times of the gardens
March–October: Wednesday–Sunday 10a.m.–5.30p.m.
November–February: Saturday and Sunday only, 10a.m.–4p.m.

Hawkstone Park

Weston-under-Redcastle
Shropshire SY4 5UY
tel. 01939 200611
www.hawkstone.co.uk

Opening times of the park
January–March: Saturday and Sunday only, 10a.m.–3p.m.
April–May: Wednesday–Sunday 10a.m.–4p.m.
June–mid-September: every day 10a.m.–4p.m.
Mid-September–October: Wednesday–Sunday 10a.m.–4p.m.
Extended opening hours and activities during school holidays

Sheringham Park

Upper Sheringham
Norfolk
NR26 8TB
tel. 01263 823778
01263 821429 (Infoline)
www.nationaltrust.org.uk
Opening times of the park
All year: dawn–dusk

Chatsworth

Bakewell
Derbyshire DE45 1PP
tel. 01246 582204
www.chatsworth.org
Opening times of the gardens
Mid-March–May: 11a.m.–6p.m.
June–August: 10.30a.m.–6p.m.
September–mid-December: 11a.m.–6p.m.

Hestercombe Gardens

Cheddon Fitzpaine
Taunton
Somerset
TA2 8LG
tel. 01823 413923
www.hestercombegardens.com
Opening times of the gardens
All year: 10a.m.–6p.m.

Acknowledgements

There are three people without whom this book would never have happened: Leo Hollis who had the idea, shared it and then generously gave it to us; Adam Wishart who thought of us when Leo explained to him that a ha-ha was more than just a ditch, then came up with the title and introduced us to the greatest of agents; and Patrick Walsh, our lovely agent whose deft advice was always appreciated and who – through everything – dealt with us with steadfast humour. If at times he despaired he never showed it.

We have received much generous and dedicated help from so many people – all have contributed to the making of this book. Foremost we are indebted to all the garden owners, gardeners, archivists and curators who own or work in 'our' seven gardens – they have turned this project into the most pleasurable pursuit an author can possibly imagine. In particular we would like to thank: at Hatfield the late 6th Marquess of Salisbury and the Dowager Lady Salisbury for permitting us to use their fabulous archive and the very helpful Robin Harcourt-Williams for his time, knowledge and patience in answering all our many pernickety questions. At Hampton Court, Susanne Groom, the curator, was incredibly helpful and not only gave us a great tour through the garden, but actually measured the Fountain Parterre so that we had the correct dimensions before we hit our deadline; thanks also to Toby Cosgrove who sent us a plan for the garden. At Stowe we are especially grateful to Michael Bevington, Octavia Tulloch and Barry Smith, and, most of all, to Richard Wheeler whose generosity of time and information and lively description of the garden and its makers will always be remembered. At Hawkstone we would like to thank Gill White for sending us photographs and books as well as trying to track down the copyright for some of the images in the guidebook; and the park warden, Roger Whitehouse, who gave us much of his time, driving and walking us across the park, as well as guiding us through the confusing warren of tunnels and paths on Grotto and Terrace Hill. At Sheringham our thanks go to the head warden, Keith Zealander, for a wonderful long walk through the park and his detailed information on the restoration programme. Working at

Chatsworth has been a real treat, and our sincere thanks go the 11th Duke of Devonshire and the Trustees of the Chatsworth Settlement; everybody there was extremely helpful – in particular Andrew Peppitt, who also patiently answered the many questions which arose once we had left the archives. At Hestercombe we would like to thank the Hestercombe Gardens Trust for their help, especially Kim Legget for assisting us with our queries.

Equally we would like to thank the following people and institutions: Peter Bamford at the Cheshire Record Office for his endeavours to find some information about Joseph Salmon; the staff at the Rare Books and Manuscript Department of the British Library; Sophie Chessum at the National Trust; Helen Clifford who taught us to love the eighteenth century; the staff at Colindale Newspaper Library; Nick Davies; Anne-Louise Fisher; the staff at Godalming Museum; Peter Goodchild for pointing us to the *Hawkstone Survey*; Keith Goodway for his information on William Emes; Paula Henderson; Mr and Mrs Heber-Percy for generously bringing parts of their archive to London from Shropshire; Philip Johnson at the York City Archive; the staff at the Lindley Library; the ever-helpful staff at the London Library; the librarians at the RIBA British Architectural Library, particularly Alison Chew and Eleanor Gawne, and Catriona Cornelius for pursuing late reference checks for us. Jennie Macve at the Hafod Trust; Rebecca Marshall at the National Trust; Lesley Price at the School of Oriental and African Studies for information on Richard Hill in connection with the London Missionary Society; the staff at the National Archives; the staff at the Norfolk Record Office; Kevin Rogers; the organisers and speakers at the William Kent at Stowe Study Day (May 2003) for providing a fascinating set of conference papers; the staff at the Herbarium of the Royal Botanic Gardens, Kew; the staff at the Shropshire Archives, in particular Samantha Mager; Joannne Nutt at the Wedgwood Museum; Clare Parson at Wilberforce House Museum; Philippa Rawlinson at the National Trust; C. A. Rudkin at the Parliamentary Archives; the staff at the Somerset Record Office; Caroline Upcher; Olga Ward; the staff at the West Sussex Record Office; and the staff at the York City Archive. Last, but not least, we would like to thank everybody who helped and supported us at Time Warner: Ursula Mackenzie, Sue Phillpott, Viv Redman and Linda Silverman.

We are grateful to the following institutions for granting us permission to quote from their manuscripts: Bedfordshire and Luton Archives and Records Service; the British Library; Edward V. Bygott; Lord Cathcart; the Duke of Devonshire; Godalming Museum; The Huntington Library, San Marino, California; Historic Royal Palaces; National Archives; Norfolk Record Office; private collector; Royal Institute of British Architects, British Architectural Library; the present Lord Salisbury; Shropshire Archives; Somerset Record Office; the Trustees of the Royal Botanic Gardens, Kew; West Sussex Record Office; and York City Archive.

Each of us would like to thank our friends and relatives who have read different drafts of the manuscript or contributed in some way, small or large, to making this book what it is.

Andrea: Thank you to Isabel Allen for sharing her love for Jane Austen; Pru and Stan Baker; Jessica Bartling for bearing my moaning; Kate Colquhoun for writing a great book and becoming a friend; Antonina Gern; Nick Leech for his horticultural forbearance and knowledge; Lord Edward Manners and Saskia Nixdorf for letting me stay in the most beautiful house in the country; Julia Sen (das Ellerbeker Herzchen) for her comments on some of the chapters and for writing stories about 'Herr Neckermann'; Stefan Turnbull and Tim Tzouliadis for their search for titles and Tim for his sound judgement and critique on the drafts; Eva Wishart for reading some chapters and the late David Wishart for his love of the picturesque and the treasures in his library; Trixi Wulf for her fine 'legal' advice; and my parents Brigitte and Herbert Wulf who have always allowed me to dream – thank you for all the hours you spent reading through drafts and for making the dramas seem less serious. My biggest and most heartfelt thanks go to Adam Wishart, my storyteller, who has read every word and survived the past three years with a big smile on his face, although it must sometimes have been unbearable. Thank you for carrying me through the difficult times and thank you for making me fly in the good ones.

Emma: Thank you to all my family for their lively interest and erudite observations, not to mention their never-ending fund of historical anecdotes; to my friends for their enthusiastic encouragement; to my colleagues on the GLAADH project and at the Open University for their curiosity and generosity of knowledge, especially Cath King; and to my mum, Sunniva Gieben, for her reassuring words and invaluable help as I juggled writing with pregnancy and then the birth of my daughter. Most of all I want to say a huge thank you to my dad, Bram Gieben, for always being there to read and reread endless drafts, for his wise comments, sharp editorial eye and witty asides; and to my husband, El Mostafa Gamal, for his unswerving support, thoughtful reflections and long-suffering patience while gardens and history took over our lives. Thank you.

This book is dedicated to our daughters: Linnéa who is the princess of the castle; and Leila, the most wonderful blossoming of life spring could have brought.

Notes

Introduction

ix   *My dear sir:* Thomas Love Peacock, *Headlong Hall* (1816), in *The Novels of Thomas Love Peacock*, ed. David Garnett, London, Rupert Hart-Davis, 1948, p. 23.

     of first celebrity: And following quotes, Ibid., pp. 18, 22–3.

xiii *very ingenious Mathematician':* Walter Harris, *A Description of the King's Royal Palace and Gardens at Loo*, London, R. Roberts, 1699, p. 47.

xiv *All gardening is landscape:* Joseph Spence, *Observations, Anecdotes, and Characters of Books and Men*, ed. James M. Osborn, Oxford, Clarendon Press, 1966, anecdote 606, vol. 1, p. 252.

     [a] sort of delightful: Edmund Burke, *A Philosophical Enquiry*, Oxford, Oxford University Press (first publ. 1757), 1998, p. 67.

xv   *Art beats nature:* Charles Darwin to J. S. Henslow, 28 Oct. 1845, *Correspondence of Charles Darwin*, eds. Frederick Burkhardt and Sydney Smith, Cambridge, Cambridge University Press, 1987, vol. 3, p. 260

xvi *use plants [so] that:* Gertrude Jekyll, *Colour in the Flower Garden*, London, Country Life, 1908, pp. vi, 9

Chapter 1 Hatfield House

1   *numerous aristocrats:* The descriptions of Theobalds and its garden are based on contemporary travel accounts: *Paul Hentzner's Travels in England, during the Reign of Queen Elizabeth*, ed. Edward Jeffrey, Strawberry Hill, 1797 (first publ. 1598); *The Diary of Baron Waldstein. A Traveller in Elizabethan England*, trans. G. W. Groos, Thames & Hudson, London, 1981 (first publ. 1600); Jacob Rathgeb, (1592), in Malcom Airs, '"Pomp or Glory": The Influence of Theobalds', in *Patronage, Culture and Power. The Early Cecils 1558–1612*, ed. Pauline Croft, New Haven and London, Yale University Press, 2002, pp. 13–15; and

Roy Strong, *The Renaissance Garden in England*, London, Thames & Hudson, 1998, pp. 51–6.

2   *built to envious show:* Quoted in James M. Sutton, 'The Retiring Patron: William Cecil and the Cultivation of Retirement, 1590–1598', in Croft 2002, p. 162.

3   *a surly, sharp sour:* Lady Russell to Robert Cecil, quoted in Ewan Butler, *The Cecils*, London, Frederick Muller, 1964, p. 105.

   it was unwholesome: John Mylles about Cecil, before 25 Feb. 1601, TNA HMC, Hatfield MSS, vol. XIV, p. 162.

   dissembling smoothfaced dwarf: Pauline Croft, 'The Reputation of Robert Cecil: Libels, Political Opinion and Popular Awareness in the Early Seventeenth Century', in *Transactions of the Royal Historical Society*, 6th series, vol. 1 (1991), p. 47.

4   *a courtier from his cradle:* Sir Robert Naunton, *Fragmenta Regalia. Memoirs of Elizabeth*, London, Charles Baldwin, 1824, p. 138.

   nourished [Cecil] with the milk: Arthur Wilson, *The History of Great Britain. Being the Life and Reign of King James I*, London, Richard Lownds, 1653, p. 43.

   a nursery of lust: Lucy Hutchinson, quoted in Anne Somerset, *Unnatural Murder. Poison at the Court of James I*, London, QPD, 1997, p. 28.

5   *a lethargy of pleasure:* Giovanni Carlo Scaramelli to the Doge and Senate of Venice, 25 Aug. 1603, quoted in Alan Stewart, *The Cradle King. A Life of James VI and I*, London, Chatto & Windus, 2003, p. 175.

   £1100 on these festivities: And more information regarding the party: expenses at Theobalds for the 5 days of entertainment ending 28 July 1606 (HH Family Papers, vol. III).

   tree with taffeta leaves: John Chamberlain to Dudley Carlton, 5 Oct. 1606, in *The Letters of John Chamberlain*, ed. Norman Egbert McClure, Philadelphia, American Philosophical Society, 1939, vol. 1, p. 232.

6   *had women and indeed wine too:* John Harington to Mr Secretary Barlow, Jul. 1606, in John Harington, *Nugae Antiquae*, London, Vernor & Hood, 1804, vol. 1, p. 349.

   humbled himself before her: Ibid., p. 350.

   rudely made war with: Ibid., p. 349.

   follow the fashion: Ibid.

   every man should blow: Ibid., p. 352.

7   *borrowed one day's retreat:* Cecil to Sir Thomas Lake, 15 Apr. 1607, TNA State Papers Domestic, James I 14/27/7.

   [U]pon what part of: Cecil to Lake, 15 Apr. 1607, Ibid.

9   *Burghley's books:* Elizabeth Woodhouse, 'Spirit of the Elizabethan Garden', in *Garden History*, vol. 27, no. 1 (1999), p. 27.

10 *some things about:* Tibbot Gorges to Cecil, 10 Sept. 1608, TNA HMC, Salisbury MSS, vol. XX, p. 233; and for paintings, architectural drawings, mosaics and statues see *Life and Letters of Sir Henry Wotton*, ed. Logan Pearsall Smith, Oxford, Clarendon Press, 1907, vol. 1, pp. 412, 419–20.

10 *The country is your Orb:* James I, quoted in John Dixon Hunt, *Garden and Grove. The Italian Renaissance Garden in the English Imagination: 1600–1750*, London and Melbourne, J. M. Dent, 1986, p. 110.

11 *pick some such observations:* Cecil to Sir Michael Hicks, 14 Aug. 1605, BL Lansdowne 89/48.

12 *[T]hanks are no requital:* Lady Tresham to Cecil, 27 Oct. 1609, transcribed in R. T. Gunton, 'The Building of Hatfield House', 1895, HH unpublished MS., p. 29.
    new extensions: Lawrence Stone, 'The Building of Hatfield House', in *Architectural Journal*, vol. 112 (1956), pp. 111–13.
    by this proportion: HH Estate Papers Accounts 8/8 (Family Papers vol. III).

13 *the one that manages:* Spanish ambassador to Philip III, 17 Jan. 1606, quoted in A. J. Loomie, 'Sir Robert Cecil and the Spanish Embassy', in *Bulletin of the Institute of Historical Research*, vol. 42 (1969), p. 34.
    this little man . . . . Ibid., p. 41; see also pp. 39, 56.
    most expensive building: Hatfield would finally cost £38,848, Stone 1956, p. 128.

14 *vain commodity which:* William Harrison, *The Description of England*, New York, Dover Publications, 1994 (first publ. 1577), p. 255.
    mak[ing] you lose your: Samuel Sorbière, *A Voyage to England*, London, J. Woodward, 1709, p. 64.

15 *Since I see you now determined:* Sir Henry Butler to Cecil, 2 Apr. 1608, TNA HMC, Hatfield MSS vol. XX, p. 123.
    Not [as] Robin Goodfellow: Lionel Munby, *Hatfield and Its People*, Hatfield, WEA, 1959, bk 1, pp. 15–17.

16 *succeed Salisbury [Cecil], and:* The Letters and Life of Francis Bacon, ed. James Spedding, London, Longmans, Green, Rader & Dyer, 1868, vol. 4, p. 74.
    pryvie: Ibid., p. 52.
    plott to be made: Ibid., p. 52.
    to speak of them: Ibid., p. 76.

17 *knot gardens in the West Garden:* Description of the West Garden based on HH Bills 38, transcribed in Gunton 1895, pp. 218–20.

19 *viewing platforms:* HH Accounts 9/24, transcribed in Ibid., pp. 54–5; the raising of them, HH Cecil Papers 143/122, transcribed in Ibid., p. 93.
    laying the grass quarters: HH Bills 38, transcribed in Ibid., p. 218.
    Contemporary 'recipes': Gervase Markham, *The English Husbandman*, London, J. Browne, 1613, pt.2, p. 125.

20 *Britain Burse:* HH Cecil Papers Accounts 160/1 (Family Papers vol. III); Alan Haynes, *Robert Cecil, Earl of Salisbury*, London, Peter Owen, 1989, p. 178; Lawrence Stone, *Family and Fortune. Studies in Aristocratic Finance in the Sixteenth and Seventeenth Centuries*, Oxford, Clarendon Press, 1973, pp. 102–5.

20   *All other places give:* James Knowles, '"To Raise a House of Better Frame": Jonson's Cecilian Entertainments', in Croft, 2002 p. 191.

king's £600,000 debt: Barry Coward, *The Stuart Age, England 1603–1714*, London, Longman, 2000, p. 139, and Stewart 2003, p. 238.

to make money of anything: Harington to Cecil, 11 Jan. 1609, TNA HMC, Salisbury MSS, vol. XXI, p. 3.

about estimating what might: HH Bills 27, transcribed in Gunton 1895, p. 221.

Robert Lyming's estimate: From 25 May 1609, transcribed in Ibid., pp. 45–6, and Stone 1956, pp. 114–17.

21   *Thomas Wilson's estimate:* From 29 May 1609, transcribed in Gunton 1895, p. 47.

may bee changed and alltered: Robert Bell to Wilson, 26 Sept. 1609, transcribed in Ibid., p. 24.

unless I understand: Lyming to Wilson, 18 Jan. 1610, transcribed in Ibid., p. 35.

dispute: Wilson to Cecil, 1607, quoted in Stone 1956, p. 106, and Stone 1973, p. 67.

slimmed-down building scheme: 'Things to be done at Hatfield at the main house, by my Lord's appointment', 28 Jul. 1609, transcribed in Gunton 1895, p. 48.

changes were cancelled: Stone 1956, p. 116.

will be as strong & substantial: Lyming to Wilson, 1 Oct. 1609, transcribed in Gunton 1895, p. 25.

Wilson and Inigo Jones: Stone 1956, p. 118.

digging, carting & carrying: HH Bills 38, transcribed in Gunton 1895, p. 223.

22   *stones & flints:* Lyming to Wilson, 1 Oct. 1609, transcribed in Ibid., p. 26.

a sufficient complement: Captain Avery Philips to Cecil, Oct. 1609, transcribed in Ibid., p. 30.

his continual Residence: Bell to Wilson, 26 Sept. 1609, transcribed in Ibid., p. 24.

23   *bird of Arabia:* HH Cecil Papers Accounts 160/1 (Family Papers vol. III); and Adam Nicolson, *Power and Glory: Jacobean England and the Making of the King James Bible*, London, HarperCollins, 2003, p. 18.

24   *repairs to the parsonage:* HH Estate Papers 8/8 and Cecil Papers Accounts 160/1 (Family Papers vol. III).

Great Contract: Roger Lockyer, *The Early Stuarts: A Political History of England 1603–1642*, London and New York, Longman, 1999, pp. 117–29; Pauline Croft, *King James*, London, Palgrave Macmillan, 2003, pp. 75–82; Haynes 1989, pp. 194–208; Coward 2000, pp. 138–44; Stewart 2003, pp. 238–43; and TNA HMC, Salisbury MSS, vol. XXI.

25   *two little square buildings:* HH Accounts 9/24, transcribed in Gunton 1895, pp. 54–5.

at some remote angle of: John Worlidge, *Systema Horticulturae*, 1677, quoted in Roy Strong, *A Celebration of Gardens*, London, HarperCollins, 1991, p. 99.

conceited dishes: Gervase Markham, *Country Contentments: or The Husbandmans Recreations (The English Housewife)*, London, J. Harison, 1633–7, p. 122.

25   *artificial cinnamon sticks:* Ibid., pp. 122–31.

26   *banquets in corners:* Ben Jonson, 'Cynthia's Revels', (1600–1) in *Ben Jonson*, ed.
      C. H. Herford and Percy Simpson, Oxford, Clarendon Press, 1925–56, vol. 8, p. 109;
      Thomas Middleton, *Your Five Gallants* (1604–7), in *Thomas Middleton: The Works*, ed.
      A. H. Bullen, Nimmo, 1885–6, vol. 6, p. 13.

26   *to stirre up appetite:* John Marston, *The Insatiate Countess* (1610), in *John Marston: The
      Plays*, ed. H. Harvey Woods, Edinburgh and London, Oliver & Boyd, 1934–9, vol. 3.
      kindles and nourishes concupiscence: Dr Mayerne's medical report on Sir Robert Cecil,
      quoted in Stone 1973, p. 51.
      unparallel lust and hunting: Sir D'Ewes about Cecil, quoted in Stone 1973, p. 51.
      whereby messengers may be sent: H. Renaldes to Cecil, n.d. [*c.* 1609], TNA HMC, Salisbury
      MSS, vol. XXI, p. 185. Nothing more is known of what this conveyance was.
      Lyming at Blickling Hall: John Newman and Caroline Stanley-Millson, 'Blickling Hall:
      The Building of a Jacobean Mansion', in *Architectural History*, vol. 28, 1985.

27   *Hatfield's garden buildings:* HH Accounts 9/24, transcribed in Gunton 1895, p. 55; HH
      Bills 58/1.
      take away all jealousies: Proposition of the French ambassador, Feb. 1610, TNA HMC,
      Salisbury MSS, vol. XXI, pp. 203–4.
      first party at Hatfield: HH Estate Papers Accounts 160/1 (Family Papers vol. III).

28   *straightening the river:* HH Accounts 9/24, transcribed in Gunton 1895, p. 62.
      [I]t hathe plessed my Lord: And the following quotes regarding John Tradescant's order
      of plants, Tradescant to William Trumbull, 21 Oct. 1610, BL Add. 72339 ff.147–8; also
      transcribed in Prudence Leith-Ross, *The John Tradescants. Gardeners to the Rose and Lily
      Queen*, London, Peter Owen, 1998, p. 313.

30   *strange discourses:* James I to Cecil, 6 Dec. 1610, TNA HMC, Salisbury MSS, vol. XXI,
      p. 265.
      I rather write than: James I to Cecil, Ibid. p. 265.
      Cecil's debts: Stone 1973, p. 60.
      tennis balls amongst them: James I to the Privy Council, 7 Dec. 1610, TNA HMC, Salisbury
      MSS, vol. XXI, p. 266.
      heated letters: Letters between James I and Cecil, Ibid., pp. 263–8.
      Cecil's visit to the queen: HH Special Bills Bundle 46 (Family Papers vol. IV).
      green velvet hangings: HH Estate Papers Box G/13 (Family Papers vol. IV).
      thousand . . . effects of water: Pope Gregory XIII's comment on the waterworks at the
      Villa Lante, quoted in Claudia Lazzaro, *The Italian Renaissance Garden*, New Haven and
      London, Yale University Press, 1990, p. 252.

31   *Sturtivant's visit:* Wilson to Cecil, 27 Jan. 1611, transcribed in Gunton 1895, p. 258.
      Caen stone: TNA HMC, Salisbury MSS, vol. XX, p. 231.
      thirty thousand vines: Wilson to Cecil, 5 Feb. 1611, transcribed in Gunton 1895, p. 38.

31 *the vineyard:* HH Gen 3/20, transcribed in Gunton 1895, p. 86; and HH Bills 69, transcribed in Ibid., p. 235.

the most considerable rarity: John Evelyn, 11 Mar. 1643, *The Diary of John Evelyn*, ed. E. S. de Beer, Oxford, Clarendon Press, 1955, vol. 2, p. 80.

profitable sideline: There are numerous references in the Hatfield accounts to gardeners who sold plants to Cecil: e.g., Mountain Jennings; John Gardener (cherry trees), HH Accounts 160/1; Robert Wroth (oaks), HH Agents' Accounts Apr.–Sept. 1611, all transcribed in Gunton 1895, pp. 118, 140.

beyond seas: And the following quotes regarding Cecil's plant orders from abroad, HH Bills 24; HH Bills 15; Wilson to Roger Houghton 25 Feb. 1610; HH Bills 36; HH Bills 38, all transcribed in Gunton 1895, pp. 211, 193, 36, 249, 224, 222.

32 *hyndereth the passage:* A Note of his Lordships business done at Hatfield, 17 May 1611, TNA State Papers Domestic, James I 1/63/88, 17 May 1611, transcribed in Gunton 1895, p. 80.

more shallow: Ibid., p. 81.

a rocke and twice: HH Accounts 160/1 and List of Work, 1 Jul. 1611, transcribed in Gunton 1895, pp. 155, 84.

33 *£200 on food:* HH Accounts 160/1 (Family Papers vol. IV); at Theobalds he had spent £500 on the five-day party.

Mount Parnassus: As described by the Duke of Saxony, quoted in Strong 1998, pp. 90–1.

35 *de Caus's commission:* A recent article by Luke Morgan, 'Landscape Design in England circa 1610: The Contributions of Salomon de Caus', in *Studies in the History of Gardens and Designed Landscapes*, vol. 23, no. 1 (Jan.–Mar. 2003), pp. 2–6, suggests that since his first bill was dated 31 Jan. 1611 (HH 58/3), de Caus was already working at Hatfield in 1610. This is not correct: the bill was dated according to the 'old style' calendar in which the year started on 25 Mar. The correct date (new style) for the first bill is therefore 31 Jan. 1612.

I beseech your Lordship: John Dacombe to Cecil, quoted in Stone 1973, p. 32.

every journey brings new: Wilson to Cecil, 25 Nov. 1611, TNA State Papers Domestic, James I, 14/67, f.62, transcribed in Gunton 1895, p. 40.

36 *like to have the great:* Ibid., p. 40.

37 *of a small river:* Sorbière 1709, p. 64.

four pretty slight arbours: And following quote, HH Cecil Papers 143/122, transcribed in Gunton 1895, p. 90.

for the passage over: Ibid., p. 90.

Easter 1612: Ibid., p. 91.

38 *cast metal leaves:* HH Bills 58, transcribed in Ibid, 1895, p. 282.

not pleasing: HH Cecil Papers 143/122, transcribed in Ibid., p. 95.

adventure of maintenance: HH Family Papers vol. IV.

39 *the very Book of Nature:* Kepler quoted in Peter Mortensen, *The Time of Unmemorable Being. Wordsworth and the Sublime 1787–1805*, Copenhagen, Tusculanum Press, 1998, p. 25.

No needs there Gardiner: Edmund Spenser: The Faerie Queene, ed. A. C. Hamilton, London, Longman, 2001 (1st edn of bks I–III 1590, of bks IV–VI 1596), bk III, canto VI, v. 34, p. 347.

for all the Moneths: Francis Bacon, *Of Gardens*, 1625, in *Bacon's Essays*, ed. Sydney Humphries, London, Adam & Charles Black, 1912, p. 253.

Grand Staircase: HH Bills 58/1.

40 *cloake bag:* And the following quotes, Tradescant's itinerary and bills, HH Gen. 11/25 and HH Bills 58, transcribed in Gunton 1895, pp. 289–96; also Leith-Ross 1998, pp. 29–38.

41 *Cecil's collapse:* Haynes 1989, p. 209; Butler 1964, p. 137.

destructively explosive laxatives: Stone 1973, p. 52.

[I]t is on all hands: Sir John More to Sir Ralph Winwood, quoted in Haynes 1989, p. 209; John Chamberlain to Sir Dudley Carleton, in McClure 1939, vol. 1, pp. 346–7.

somewhat thinner than: Earl of Shrewsbury to Hicks, 23 Jan. 1612, BL Lansdowne 92/79.

42 *king's refusal:* Haynes 1989, p. 209.

progress in the garden: HH Cecil Papers 143/122, HH Bills 58/1; HH Bills 69 transcribed in Gunton 1895, pp. 90–2,219; HH Estate Papers Box G/13 (Family Papers vol. IV).

43 *Cecil at Bath:* For a contemporary description of Cecil's time in Bath, TNA HMC, Earl of Westmorland MSS, 10th Report, App. pt 4, 1612, pp. 12–16; Stone 1973, pp. 50–5.

higher than the navel: Cecil to William Cecil, 8 May 1612, BL Lansdowne 92/100.

blue & livid spots: TNA HMC, Earl of Westmorland MSS, p. 13.

scorbute grass: Shrewsbury to Hicks, 13 May 1612, BL Lansdowne 92/101.

to gather so much of: Ibid.

quintessence of honey: Countess of Shrewsbury to Hicks, dated before 24 May 1612, BL Lansdowne 92/102.

filthy froth: Croft 1991, p. 47.

payment for physicians: HH Estate Papers Box G/13 and HH Estate Papers 71 (Family Papers vol. IV).

44 *for mowing of the courts:* HH Bills 69 and HH Estate Papers Bills 71 (Family Papers vol. IV).

mourning 'cloaks': Estate Papers Bills 71 (Family Papers vol. IV).

Chapter 2 Hampton Court

47 *trading ships:* Thierry Mariage, *The World of André Le Nôtre*, Philadelphia, University of Pennsylvania Press, 1999, p. 101.

double bottomed monarchy: Bishop Burnet's History of his Own Time from the Restoration of Charles II to the Treaty of Peace at Utrecht, in the Reign of Queen Anne, London, William Smith, 1838, vol. 5, p. 525.

Description of William: Ibid., vol. 5, p. 702; and Anon., *The Royal Diary, Or King William's Interior Portrait*, London, 1702, p. 41.

48   *the gaiety and:* Burnet 1838, vol. 5, p. 525.

observed the errors: Ibid., vol. 5, p. 702.

was all fire: Ibid., vol. 5, p. 702; and John Miller, *The Life and Times of William and Mary*, London, Weidenfeld & Nicolson, 1974, p. 43.

gave too much occasion: Quoted in Ralph Dutton, *English Court Life from Henry VII to George II*, London, B. T. Batsford, 1963, p. 156.

great vivacity and cheerfulness: Burnet 1838, vol. 5, p. 525.

49   *noisy world full:* *Memoirs of Mary Queen of England (1689–1693). Together with her Letters and those of James II and William III to the Electress Sophia of Hanover*, ed. Richard Doebner, London, David Nutt, 1886, p. 11.

so filled with: Evelyn, 24 Jan. 1684, *The Diary of John Evelyn*, ed. E. S. de Beer, Oxford, Clarendon Press, 1955, vol. 4, p. 363.

50   *the present fashion:* Samuel Pepys, 22 Jul. 1666, *The Diary of Samuel Pepys*, ed. Robert Latham and William Matthews, London, G. Bell, 1970, vol. 7, p. 213.

badly neglected: Mary to Agnes van Wassenaer-Obdam, 5 Mar. 1689, quoted in Simon Thurley, *Hampton Court: A Social and Architectural History*, New Haven and London, Yale University Press, 2003, p. 151.

gardening as therapy: Maureen Waller, *Ungrateful Daughters*, London, Hodder & Stoughton, 2002, p. 280.

a proper improvement: Christopher Wren, *Parentalia, or Memoirs of the Family of the Wrens*, London, T. Osborne & R. Dodsley, 1750, p. 326.

51   *Sir Christopher Wren hath:* Newsletter of 2 Mar. 1689, *The History of the King's Works, 1660–1782*, ed. H. M. Colvin, London, HMSO, 1976, vol. 5, p. 155.

reapaire unto Hampton Court: TNA LC 5/149; and for the move to Hampton Court, TNA LS 1/31, transcribed in Heath 'William and Mary Chronology'.

[M]y heart is not: Doebner 1886, p. 11.

account opened: TNA AO 1/2482/295.

little Knacks: Wren 1750, p. 262.

Building certainly ought: Ibid., p. 262.

52   *Works of Filigrand:* Ibid., p. 262.

London's career and travels: Stephen Switzer, *Iconographia Rustica* (1st publ. 1718), 1742, pp. 70–81; Ben Groen, 'De Codex Regius Honselaerdicensis', in *Het Landgoed Leeuwenhorst bij Noordwijkerhout Kastelenstichting Holland en Zeeland Jaarboek 2003*, ed. Elizabeth den Hartog, The Hague, Kastelenstichtung Holland en Zeeland, 2003, p. 81; David Green, *Gardener to Queen Anne. Henry Wise, 1653–1738, and the Formal Garden*, London and New York, Oxford University Press, 1956, pp. 4–12.

53　*London's salary:* TNA AO 1/2482/298.

Brompton Park Nursery: Evelyn described the Brompton Park Nursery in a two-page advertisement, in *The Compleat Gard'ner; Or Directions for Cultivating and Right Ordering of Fruit-Gardens and Kitchen-Gardens*, London, Matthew Gillyflower, 1693; Evelyn, 24 Apr. 1694, de Beer 1955, vol. 5, p. 176; Keith Thomas, *Man and the Natural World. Changing Attitudes in England 1500–1800*, Penguin, London, 1984, p. 224.

perhaps as much as: Switzer 1742, p. 79.

Talman's and Wren's salaries: TNA AO 1/2482/298 and Adrian Tinniswood, *His Life so Fertile. A Life of Christopher Wren*, London, Pimlico, 2002, p. 302.

54　*Workshops:* TNA Work 5/55 ff.19, 92.

London's lodgings: In Dec. 1700 the Hampton Court locksmith worked on the locks at London's bedchamber and kitchen, TNA Work 5/51 f.502, and Wren had lodgings at Hampton Court at least from the 1670s; Tinniswood 2002, p. 208.

against the French King: TNA PC 2/73, transcribed in Heath 'William and Mary Chronology'.

lost no time . . . either: And the following quote, Switzer 1742, p. 77.

estimate for hothouse: Matthew Bankes to John Bale, 25 Apr. 1689, BL Sloane 4062 f.231.

55　*spacious Garden with fountaines:* Evelyn, 16 Jul. 1689, de Beer 1955, vol. 4, p. 645.

the entertaining so soon: Burnet 1838, vol. 5, p. 525.

Louis XIV's finances: Guy Warton, *Louis XIV's Versailles*, London, Viking, 1986, pp. 50, 175–6.

56　*[F]or good Proportion:* William quoted in Wren 1750, p. 326.

£25,000: TNA AO 1/2482/295 and TNA AO 1/2482/298.

men and horses to Ireland: TNA PC 2/73, transcribed in Heath 'William and Mary Chronology'.

ordered everything that: Daniel Defoe, *A Tour through the Whole Island of Great Britain* (first publ. 1724–6), abridged and ed. P. N. Furbank and W. R. Owens, New Haven and London, Yale University Press, 1991, p. 72.

very ingenious Mathematician: Walter Harris, *A Description of the King's Royal Palace and Gardens at Loo*, London, R. Roberts, 1699, p. 47.

57　*Marot's parterre:* David Jacques, 'The History of the Privy Garden', in *The King's Privy Garden at Hampton Court Palace, 1699–1995*, ed. Simon Thurley, London, Apollo Magazine, 1995, p. 27; and Travers Morgan, 'Royal Parks Historical Survey': Hampton Court and Bushy Park, London, Dept of Environment, 1983 (held at Curatorial Office, Hampton Court), p. 29.

mathematical instruments: TNA AO 1/2482/298.

£1500 for lead and solder: Ibid.

58　*trenches and . . . ditches:* Ibid and TNA Work 5/55 ff.24, 28, 35, 45, 51.

It is a silly superstition: William quoted in Ernest Law, *The History of Hampton Court Palace*, London, George Bell & Sons, 1891, vol. 3, p. 4.

60   *examining and surveying:* Wren 1750, p. 326.

accident at Kensington: Narcissus Luttrell, *A Brief Historical Relation of State Affairs, from September 1678 to April 1714*, Oxford, Oxford University Press, 1857, vol. 1, p. 606.

accident at Hampton Court: The numbers of deaths and of injured workmen vary in the different sources: Luttrell 1857, vol. 1, p. 616; Thurley 2003, p. 171; Wren Society 1927, vol. 4, pp. 72–4.

troubled: Robert Hooke's diary entry about Wren's distress: R. T. Gunter (ed.), *Early Science in Oxford: The Life and Work of Robert Hooke*, Oxford, R. T. Gunter, 1935, p. 171.

made me go often: Mary to William, Dec. 1689, Wren Society 1930, vol. 7, p. 136.

Hampton Court enquiry: Plus the dispute between Wren and Talman and the following quotes: Treasury Minute Book, transcribed in Wren Society 1927, vol. 4, pp. 73–4.

61   *the reports:* These have not survived, but since work continued immediately it is evident that no recriminations were levelled against Wren.

progress in the Fountain Garden: TNA AO 1/2482/298.

62   *The Prince is gone:* Mary quoted in Marjorie Bowen, *The Third Mary Stuart*, London, John Lane, 1929, p. 92.

to see so little devotion: Doebner 1886, p. 11.

Gardens operat upon humane: John Evelyn to Sir Thomas Browne, 28 Jan. 1660, in *The Works of Sir Thomas Browne*, ed. Geoffrey Keynes, London, Faber & Faber, 1964, vol. 4, p. 275.

Mary had left: Mary left Hampton Court on 16 Oct. 1689, returning on 31 May 1690 (Heath 'William and Mary Chronology').

63   *cataloguing the four hundred plants: Horti Regii Hamptoniensis hybernacula sunt ornate*, BL Sloane 2928. Another catalogue of plants grown at Hampton Court in 1690 was compiled by Dr Robert Gray: *Horti Regii Hamptoniensis exoticarum*, BL Sloane 3370 ff. 1–8.

description of the hothouses: Bale to Duchess of Beaufort, 1 Sept. 1692, BL Sloane 4062 f.246.

cut flowers: D. O. Wijnandis, 'Hortus Auriaci: The Gardens of Orange and their Place in Late Seventeenth-century Botany and Horticulture', in *Journal of Garden History*, vol. 8, nos 2, 3 (Apr.–Sept. 1988), pp. 80, 84; and in London, TNA AO 1/2482/298.

64   *some of my old botanick acquaintances:* Charles Hatton to Christopher Hatton, 26 Apr. 1690, transcribed in *The Correspondence of the Family of Hatton, 1601–1704*, ed. E. M. Thompson, London, Camden Society, vol. 23 (1878), p. 148.

report on hothouses: Bale to Duchess of Beaufort, 1 Sept. 1692, BL Sloane 4062 f.246.

Mary's garden: There are no clear dates for the planting of the three main plots; but since her garden had been walled off by Mar. 1690 and her hothouses had been filled by early Mar. with the plant collection from Holland, it is likely that London planted her garden at the same time.

transfer himself: TNA AO 1/2482/298.

in my own country: Doebner 1886, p. 28.

65　*women should meddle:* Ibid., p. 23.

　　[D]uring the absence of: Mary to Agnes van Wassenaer-Obdam, quoted in Thurley 2003, p. 182.

　　French are in the Channel: Mary to William, 24 Jun. 1690, and other letters with updates on building progress 12 and 26 Jul., quoted in Wren Society 1930, vol. 7, p. 136.

　　If they have, Sire: Henry van der Zee and Barbara van der Zee, *William and Mary*, London, Macmillan, 1973, p. 317.

　　found him . . . in perfect: And the following quotes, Doebner 1886, p. 33.

66　*[T]he king and I were:* Mary, quoted in Bowen 1929, p. 228.

　　gardener's feast: TNA Work 5/55 f.285.

　　special walkways: Thurley 2003, p. 182.

　　arbour with fir rails: TNA AO 1/2482/298.

　　work in the Privy Garden: TNA Work 5/55 ff.222, 233.

67　*figures like lace-patterns:* J. Gibson, 'A Short Account of Several Gardens near London, 26 January 1691', in *Archaeologia, or Miscellaneous Tracts relating to Antiquity*, Society of Antiquarians, vol. 12 (1796), p. 181.

　　London's invoice: TNA AO 1/2482/298.

　　dismantling of sheds: TNA Work 5/55 f.351.

　　plants from abroad: David Jacques and Arend Jan van der Horst, *The Gardens of William and Mary*, London, Christopher Helm, 1988, pp. 174–5; TNA AO 1/2482/298; Wijnandis 1988, p. 82; Elizabeth den Hartog and Carla Teune, 'Gaspar Fagal (1633–88): His Garden and Plant Collection at Leeuwenhorst', in *Garden History*, vol. 30, no. 2 (winter 2002), p. 201.

68　*faithful Records:* Thomas Sprat, *History of the Royal Society*, London, J. Martyn, 1667, p. 61.

　　horticultural publications: Thomas 1984, pp. 225–31.

　　[W]e have wholly omitted: John Ray, *The Ornithology of Francis Willughby*, London, John Martyn, 1678, preface, A4.

69　*should take care of:* Moses Cook, quoted in Charles Quest-Ritson, *The English Garden. A Social History*, London, Viking, 2001, p. 101.

　　Foreigne plants raised: BL Sloane MS 3343 ff.5–7.

　　progress in the garden: Jacques and van der Horst 1988, pp. 65, 68.

　　earth-moving 'engines': Defoe 1991, p. 72.

70　*maintenance contracts:* TNA AO 1/2482/298.

71　*William's trusted Secretary:* Craig Rose, *England in the 1690s. Revolution, Religion and War*, London, Blackwell, 1999, pp. 85–6.

　　Let the Queen rule: William, quoted in Bowen 1929, p. 253.

　　The commons [used me]: William to the Earl of Halifax, quoted in Miller 1974, p. 115.

　　Marot's designs: There are several references to changes made at the 'French Man's' instruction in the accounts for Aug. and Oct. 1691, TNA Work 5/55 ff.319, 331, 341.

72   *he was now going:* Burnet 1838, vol. 4, p. 606.

    How reasonable were her: Thomas Tenison, *A Sermon Preached at the Funeral of her Late Majesty Queen Mary in Westminster Abbey*, Chiswell, London, 1695, pp. 16–17.

73   *'directions' at the gardens:* And London's work practice, Switzer 1742, p. 81.

    Talman on the road: His riding charges at Hampton Court, TNA AO 1/2482/295 and TNA AO 1/2482/296.

    You cannot form: William to the Grand Pensionary Heinsius, 11 and 21 Jan. 1698, transcribed in Paul Grimblot (ed.), *Letters of William III and Louis XIV and of Their Ministers, 1697–1700*, London, Longman, 1848, vol. 1, pp. 147, 150.

74   *Portland and London:* Green 1956, p. 17.

    visit the gardens . . . which: William to the Earl of Portland, 3 Feb. 1698, transcribed in Grimblot 1848, vol. 1, p. 156.

    dead and dirty: Portland to William, 1 Mar. 1698 (19 Feb. in the English calendar), transcribed in Ibid., pp. 192–3.

    to make excursions: William to Portland, 25 Feb. 1698, transcribed in Ibid., p. 204.

75   *never been more vexed:* William to Portland, 2 Mar. 1698, transcribed in Ibid., p. 219.

    The King of England: Count Tallard to Louis XIV, 9 May 1698, and Louis XIV to Count Tallard, 10 Apr. 1698 (1 Apr. in the English calendar), transcribed in Ibid., pp. 466, 357.

    conversing cheerfully: Portland to William, 4 May 1698 (24 Apr. in the English calendar), transcribed in Ibid., p. 443.

    draft peace treaty: William to Heinsius, 31 May 1698, transcribed in Ibid., vol. 2, p. 25.

    follow the hounds: And following quotes, Portland to William, 17 May 1698 (7 May in the English calendar), transcribed in Ibid., vol. 1, pp. 494–5.

    Le Nôtre: Roy Strong, *Royal Gardens*, London, BBC Books, 1992, p. 33.

76   *Talman's estimate:* 18 Jan. 1699, Wren Society 1927, vol. 4, p. 65; for the corresponding bill handed in after the work was finished in Dec. 1699, TNA T1/67 ff.96, 98 and George London's last bill for work done in summer 1699, TNA T1/67 f.105.

    Wise's estimate: 12 Feb. 1699, Wren Society 1927, vol. 4, p. 65.

77   *I have made use:* William Talman, 12 Sept. 1699, BL Add. 20101 f.69.

78   *progress in the garden:* For details on Wise's work, bill for Dec. 1699 for 'Several works done and performed' in Bushy Park by Henry Wise, TNA T1/67 f.107.

    the King began with: Defoe 1991, p. 65.

    to lye: Post Boy, no. 709 (21 Oct. 1699), and Luttrell 1857, vol. 4, p. 553.

    Castle Howard commission: Kerry Downes, *Sir John Vanbrugh. A Biography*, London, Sidgwick & Jackson, 1987, pp. 26–7, and Laurence Whistler, *The Imagination of Vanbrugh and his Fellow Artists*, London, B. T. Batsford, 1954, pp. 35–9.

79   *William watching the engineer:* And the nightshifts, TNA Work 5/51 ff.508, 493.

    remainder of the time: M. A. Laugier's 'Essay on Architecture' (1753), quoted in Keith Woodbridge, *Princely Gardens. The Origins and Development of the French Style*, London, Thames & Hudson, 1986, p. 223.

79   *the water more plentifully:* And maintenance, Jacques and van der Horst 1988, p. 83.

Installation of statues: This began in spring 1700, but the *Borghese Warrior* was installed only in Jul. 1701.

to preserve many of: Letters and estimates between Lord Ranelagh, Wren and Talman dated 16, 30 and 31 Jul. 1700, Wren Society 1927, vol. 4, p. 66.

work in the Privy Garden: TNA Work 5/51 ff.333–72.

80   *utmost mortification:* And the following quotes, William to Heinsius, 16 Nov. 1700, transcribed in Grimblot 1848, vol. 2 pp. 477–8.

five hundred workmen: TNA Work 5/51 f.523, and Wise's bill for 8 Aug. 1700–12 Feb. 1701, Ibid. f.548 (10,488 solid yards).

platforms . . . 13,700 cubic yards: Wise's bill for 12 Feb.–24 Apr. 1701, for 'the second sinking', TNA Work 5/52 ff.571, 575v (13,796 solid yards).

wooden model: TNA Work 5/51 f.416v.

iron railings: TNA Work 5/52 ff.265, 266.

81   *4 new stays:* Ibid. 5/52 f.296.

82   *turf laid:* Wise's bill for 12 Feb.–24 Apr. 1701, Ibid. f.572.

work in the Privy Garden: Ibid. ff.297, 297v, 310, 311.

lowering of the Privy Garden: Wise's bill for 30 Jun.–30 Oct. 1701, Ibid. f.581 (20,352 solid yards).

plumber: Ibid. ff.323, 340v, 344.

83   *completion of parterre:* And the following details about the planting of it, Wise's bill for 30 Jun.–30 Oct. 1701, Ibid. ff.581–3; and Jan Woudstra, 'The Planting of the Privy Garden', in *The King's Privy Garden at Hampton Court Palace 1699–1995*, ed. Simon Thurley, London, Apollo Magazine, 1995, pp. 43–77.

turf, cut from the common: George London and Henry Wise, *The Retir'd Gard'ner, translation of Le Jardinier Solitaire, or, Dialogues between a Gentleman and a Gard'ner*, London, Jacob Tonson, 1706, vol. 2, p. 779, and Wise's bill for 30 Jun.–30 Oct. 1701, TNA Work 5/52 f.581.

84   *fibrous root flowers:* Wise's bill for 8 Aug. 1700–12 Feb. 1701, TNA Work 5/51 f.549.

planting scheme: For contemporary planting schemes, John James, *The Theory and Practice of Gardening*, London, Bernard Lintot, 1728, p. 259; Tradescant's plant lists, Prudence Leith-Ross, *The John Tradescants. Gardeners to the Rose and Lily Queen*, London, Peter Owen, 1998, pp. 252–92; since most annuals and perennials would have been grown from seed, there are no surviving bills for them. The plants listed here had been used by George London for the Great Parterre at Longleat, Woudstra 1995, p. 66; and the Catalogue of Seeds, 1700/1701, BL Sloane 795 ff.65, 66, transcribed and identified by their Latin names in Terry Gough, 'The Privy Garden at Hampton Court', unpubl. dissertation, App. 1.

85   *orange trees.* TNA Work 5/51 f.513.

low walls: TNA Work 5/52 ff.411v, 426, 272v.

little gentleman: Miller 1974, p. 195.

85 *I am drawing towards:* William, quoted Ibid., p. 195.
 scarce decent: Burnet, quoted in Waller 2002, p. 366.

Chapter 3 Stowe

88 *delightfull:* Perceval to Daniel Dering, 14 Aug. 1724, BL Add. 47030, f.157.
 classical garden buildings: Michael Bevington, 'The Development of the Classical Revival at Stowe', in *Architectura*, vol. 21, no. 2 (1991).
 House of Lords: Journals of the House of Lords, 1718–21, London, HMSO, vol. 21, n.d., and for biographical details, John Beckett, *The Rise and Fall of the Grenvilles*, Manchester, Manchester University Press, 1994.
 baronetcy from James I: Beckett 1994, p. 13.
 greatest Whig in the army: Quoted in John Martin Robinson, *Temples of Delight. Stowe Landscape Gardens*, London, National Trust, 2002, p. 34.

89 *much entertain'd with:* John Vanbrugh to Jacob Tonson, 1 Jul. 1719, transcribed in *The Complete Works of Sir John Vanbrugh*, ed. Geoffrey Webb, London, Nonesuch Press, 1928, vol. 4, p. 112.

90 *A Man of Polite:* Joseph Addison, in the *Spectator*, no. 411 (21 Jun. 1712).

91 *six nights in seven:* William Congreve about Cobham, in 'The Faire Majestic Paradise of Stowe', editorial in *Apollo*, vol. 97 (Jun. 1973), p. 542.
 most sought-after Whig: Kerry Downes, *Sir John Vanbrugh: A Biography*, London, Sidgwick & Jackson, 1987, p. 84.
 Bridgeman at Blenheim and Stowe: Bridgeman began in 1709 at Blenheim, and there is a receipt for 'Mr bridgmans man' from 1714 in the Stowe accounts, Peter Willis, *Charles Bridgeman and the English Landscape Garden*, Newcastle-upon-Tyne, Elysium Press, 2002, pp. 4, 109, 34–5.

92 *Nothing is more irregular:* Perceval to Dering, 14 Aug. 1724, BL Add. 47030, f.157.
 You think twenty times: Ibid.

93 *Why may not a Whole:* Addison, in the *Spectator*, no. 414 (25 Jun. 1712).
 the capital stroke: 'On Modern Gardening', in Horace Walpole, *Anecdotes of Painting in England*, London, Henry G. Bohn, 1862, vol. 3, p. 800.

94 *French ha-ha:* Antoine-Joseph Dézallier d'Argenville, *The Theory and Practice of Gardening* (first publ. as *La Théorie et la pratique du jardinage*, 1709); trans. John James, London, Geo. James, 1712 and Willis 2002, pp. 19–21.
 all the adjacent Country: Stephen Switzer, *The Nobleman, Gentleman, and Gardener's Recreation: Or an Introduction to Gardening, Planting, Agriculture*, London, B. Barker & C. King, 1715, p. xiv.

95 *fleas and gnats:* And the following quotes, Perceval to Dering, 14 Aug. 1724, BL Add. 47030, ff.156–7.
 finest seat in England: Ibid., f.156.

95   *with great taste:* Charles Howard to Lord Carlisle, 15 Jun. [1732?], TNA HMC, Earl of
Carlisle MSS, 15th Report, App. pt. VI, p. 91.

Garden to Garden: Alexander Pope to Robert Digby, 12 Aug. [1725?], in *The Correspondence
of Alexander Pope*, ed. George Sherburn, Oxford, Clarendon Press, 1956, vol. 2, p. 314.

If any thing under: Pope to John Knight, 23 Aug. 1731, Ibid., vol. 3, p. 217.

96   *talk'd only as a:* John Gay to Jonathan Swift, 3 Feb. 1723, *The Letters of John Gay*, ed.
C. F. Burgess, Oxford, Clarendon Press, 1966, p. 43.

My gardens improve more: Pope to William Fortescue, 17 Sept. 1724, in Sherburn 1956,
vol. 2, p. 257.

Pope's poem: which praised Cobham and Burlington, *Epistle to Burlington*, 1731.

A man . . . not only: Pope to Ralph Allen, 30 Apr. 1736, Sherburn 1956, vol. 4, p. 13.

through the King's mouth: John, Lord Hervey, *Memoirs of the Reign of George the Second.
From His Accession to the Death of Queen Caroline*, ed. John Wilson Croker, London,
Bickers & Son, 1884, vol. 1, p. 44.

Fop at the Toilet: Pope, *Epistle to Dr Arbuthnot*, 1734, ll. 328–9, in *The Works of Alexander
Pope*, ed. Whitwell Elwin and William John Courthope, London, John Murray, 1881, vol.
3, p. 266.

97   *Guglielmo:* John Dixon Hunt, *William Kent. An Assessment and Catalogue of his Designs*,
London, A. Zwemmer, 1987, p. 13.

Apollo of arts: Horace Walpole 1862, vol. 3, p. 776.

Master Carpenter: Willis 2002, p. 64.

the Kings Gardner: George Vertue, *Notebook* 3, 1733, Walpole Society, Oxford, Oxford
University Press, 1934, vol. 22, p. 69.

garden of vice: Richard Wheeler, 'Icons and Emblems', and 'William Kent and the Faerie
Queene', unpubl. conference papers, Stowe Estate Office (n.d.); and Gilbert West, *Stowe:
The Gardens of the Right Honourable Richard Lord Viscount Cobham*, London, L. Gilliver,
1732.

98   *Mysterious Orgies:* And following quotes, West 1732, ll. 168–9, 196, 220.

Randibus: Jeremiah Milles, *An Account of the Journey that Mr Hardness and I took in July
1735*, transcribed in George Clarke (ed.), *Descriptions of Lord Cobham's Gardens at Stowe,
1700–1750*, Dorset, Buckinghamshire Record Office, 1990, p. 65.

99   *What is left to do:* ('Ce que reste a faire serat a mon avis le plus noble de toute') Lord
Charles Cathcart, diary, 18 Aug. 1730, private collection of Earl Cathcart, transcribed in
Clarke 1990, p. 29, trans. by the authors.

Bridgeman and Kent: As no accounts have survived for this period there is no evidence
of how the work in the Elysian Fields was allocated between Bridgeman and Kent, but
George Clarke puts forward a persuasive argument that they collaborated on the design;
(George Clarke, 'The History of Stowe – XIII, Kent and the Eastern Gardens', in the
Stoic, vol. 24, no. 6 (Jul. 1971a), p. 268; and 'William Kent. Heresy in Stowe's Elysium',
in Peter Willis (ed.), *Furor Hortensis*, Edinburgh, Elysium Press, 1974, pp. 49–55.)

100   *no nobleman['s] Gardens:* Vertue 1934, p. 140.

Fabriques [buildings]: Sir Henry Wotton, *The Elements of Architecture, Collected . . . from the Best Authors and Examples*, London, John Bill, 1624, p. 109.

forms wholly irregular: Five Miscellaneous Essays by Sir William Temple, ed. Samuel Holt Monk, Ann Arbor, University of Michigan Press, 1963, pp. 29–30.

A dead and standing: Marvell, 'The Mower against Gardens', l. 6, in *The Poems and Letters of Andrew Marvell*, ed. H. M. Margoliouth, Oxford, Oxford University Press, 1927.

Art is onely Natures: John Evelyn, quoted in Theresa O'Malley and Joachim Wolschke-Bulmahn (ed.), *John Evelyn's 'Elysium Britannicum' and European Gardening*, Washington, Dumbarton Oaks Research Library and Collection, 1998, p. 17. The unpublished manuscript was written in the 1650s.

Marks of scissors upon: Addison, in the *Spectator*, no. 414 (25 Jun. 1712).

amiable Simplicity: Pope, in the *Guardian*, no. 173 (29 Sept. 1713).

mockery: Anthony Ashley Cooper, 3rd Earl of Shaftesbury, *Characteristics of Men, Manners, Opinions, Times*, ed. John M. Robertson, New York, Bobbs-Merrill, 1974 (first publ. 1709), treatise 5, pt 3, section 2, p. 125.

patrons' libraries: Willis 2002, p. 69.

Consult the Genius of: Pope, *Epistle to Burlington*, 1731, ll. 57, 65, 50–6 in Elwin and Courthope (ed.) 1881, vol. 3, pp. 175–6.

101   *The vast parterres:* Ibid., ll. 73–6, p. 177.

not having the taste: Ibid., notes, p. 177.

Diversion of the Royal: Announcement in the *London Journal*, 1 May 1731. The Serpentine was begun in Sept. 1730 and the invoice submitted in Jun. 1732, Willis 2002, p. 96.

102   *at the request of Bridgeman:* Vertue, 1934, p. 69.

excise scheme: Paul Langford, *A Polite and Commercial People, England 1727–1783*, Oxford, Oxford University Press, 1992, p. 29; Jeremy Black, *Walpole in Power*, Stroud, Sutton Publishing, 2001, pp. 37–8; and *Cobbett's Parliamentary History of England 1733–7*, London, Hansard, 1811, vol. 9, pp. 1–9.

The rising tempest: Henry Goodricke, quoted in Black 2001, p. 37.

menaced, insulted: Cobbett's Parliamentary History of England, 1733–7, vol. 9, p. 8.

103   *out of order:* Cobham to Alexander, Earl of Marchmont, 30 Dec. 1734, transcribed in George Henry Rose, *A Selection from the Papers of the Earls of Marchmont, 1685–1750*, London, John Murray, 1831, vol. 2, p. 57.

And you; Brave COBHAM!: Pope, *Epistle to Cobham*, 1734 (written in 1733), ll. 262–5 in Elwin and Courthope (ed.) 1881, vol. 3, p. 72.

Tho I have not: Cobham to Pope, 1 Nov. 1733, repr. in Sherburn 1956, vol. 3, p. 391.

Rumpsteak Club: Proceedings of the Rumpsteak Club, 1734, transcribed in Rose 1831, vol. 2, pp. 19–20; and Christine Gerrard, *The Patriot Opposition to Walpole. Politics, Poetry and National Myth, 1725–1742*, Oxford, Clarendon Press, 1994, p. 33.

what crimes were alleged: And the following quotes, 'Debate in the Commons on

Mr Sandys' Motion', 13 Feb. 1734, *Cobbett's Parliamentary History of England, 1733–7*, vol. 9, pp. 325–6.

104   *Squire Gawky:* George Clarke, 'The History of Stowe – XVI, The Grenville Family', in the *Stoic*, vol. 25, no. 3 (Jun. 1972) p. 113; and Beckett 1994, p. 26.

excellent spirits: George Berkeley, quoted in *Stowe Landscape Gardens*, London, National Trust, 1997, p. 64.

[P]erfect in the Pleasing: Congreve about Cobham, quoted in Maynard Mack, *Alexander Pope. A Life*, New Haven and London, Yale University Press, 1985, p. 612.

105   *[I]t is enchanted ground:* And following quote, George Berkeley, quoted in *Stowe Landscape Gardens* 1997, p. 64.

Addison's essay: George Clarke, 'The History of Stowe – X, Moral Gardening', in the *Stoic*, vol. 24, no. 3 (Jul. 1970), pp. 113–21.

the good of their country: And following quotes, Addison, in the *Tatler*, no. 123 (21 Jan. 1710).

'vice' or 'virtue': And the 'Choice of Hercules', in Wheeler unpubl. conference papers at Stowe Estate Office, n.d.

[F]or the benefit of: Addison, in the *Tatler*, no. 97 (22 Nov. 1709).

106   *immortal reputation:* Ibid.

Lord Cobham . . . says I: Lady Suffolk, quoted in *Stowe Landscape Gardens* 1997, p. 66.

Lyttelton's inheritance: Old Whig, 10 Apr. 1735.

Kent's work for the royals: David Coombs, 'The Garden at Carlton House of Frederick Prince of Wales and Augusta Princess Dowager of Wales', in *Garden History*, vol. 25, no. 2 (winter 1997), p. 156; and Willis 2002, p. 97.

once a year: Ulrich Müller, 'Rousham: A Transcription of the Steward's Letters, 1738–42', in *Garden History*, vol. 25, no. 2 (winter 1997), p. 178.

rough levell: William White to the owner, General Dormer, 28 Nov. 1738, transcribed in Ibid., p. 181.

Nothing further shall be: White to Dormer, 13 Mar. 1739, transcribed in Ibid., p. 183.

107   *[I]f Mr Kent don't come:* John MacClary to Sir Clement Cottrell (Dormer's heir), 15 Feb. 1741, transcribed in Ibid., p. 186.

Mr Kent can be: Dormer to Cottrell, 21 Jul. 1741, transcribed in Ibid., p. 187.

108   *inscriptions:* George Clarke, 'Signor Fido and the Stowe Patriots', in *Apollo*, vol. 122ii (Oct. 1985a), p. 250, and John Dixon Hunt, 'Emblem and Expressionism in the Eighteenth-century Landscape Garden', in *Eighteenth-Century Studies*, vol. 4 (1971), pp. 299–301.

after Mr Kent's notion: And following quotes, Thomas Richardson to Lord Carlisle, 23 Dec. 1734, TNA HMC, Earl of Carlisle MSS, 15th Report, App. pt VI, p. 143.

109   *leaped the fence:* Walpole 1862, vol. 3, p. 801.

plants at Carlton House: From the nursery bills for Carlton House, Household Accounts of Frederick Prince of Wales, transcribed in Coombs 1997, pp. 168–77.

110   *you think the laurel:* MacClary to Cottrell, 1750, transcribed in Mavis Batey, 'The Way to View Rousham by Kent's Gardener', in *Garden History*, vol. 11, no. 2 (1983), p. 124; and for Kent's shrubberies, Mark Laird, *The Flowering of the Landscape Garden. English Pleasure Grounds, 1720–1800*, Philadelphia, University of Pennsylvania Press, 1999, pp. 36–45.

110   *Bridgeman's plant supplies:* Accounts 1718/19 and 1721/2, in *Stowe Gardens Survey* 1992, p. 80, and George Clarke, 'Where Did All the Trees Come From? An Analysis of Bridgeman's Planting at Stowe', in *Journal of Garden History*, vol. 5, no. 1 (1985b), p. 75.
      mature horse chestnuts: Stowe Gardens Survey 1992, p. 80.
      Paradise Garden in Oxford: Clarke 1985b, p. 77, and App., pp. 79–82.
      'I don't know [where]: MacClary to Cottrell, 15 Feb. 1741, in Müller 1997, p. 186.

111   *abounds with lasting Beauties:* Samuel Richardson, in App. to 3rd edn of Daniel Defoe, *A Tour through the Whole Island of Great Britain*, 1742, repr. in Clarke 1990, p. 87.
      Kent stopped working: The accounts for much of the period when Kent worked at Stowe have been destroyed or lost, but it is thought that he stopped working there around 1736–7, although a number of his designs remained to be executed. (Michael Gibbon, 'The History of Stowe – XI, Lord Cobham's Garden Buildings, pt 1: Vanbrugh, Gibbs, Kent', in the *Stoic* vol. 24, no. 4 (Dec. 1970), p. 181; T. Hinde, *Capability Brown. The Story of a Master Gardener*, London, Hutchinson, 1986, p. 26.)

112   *a very pretty young:* Lady Irwin to Lord Carlisle, 20 May 1736, TNA HMC, Earl of Carlisle MSS, 15th Report, App., pt VI, p. 172.
      the Boy Patriots' speeches: Given in Apr. 1736. *Cobbett's Parliamentary History of England 1733–7*, vol. 9, pp. 1221–3.
      chief promoter: Lady Irwin to Lord Carlisle, 22 Feb. 1737, TNA HMC, Earl of Carlisle MSS, 15th Report, App., pt VI, p. 177.
      perpetually with the Prince: Hervey 1884, vol. 2, p. 367; for Lyttelton's appointment, Ibid., vol. 3, pp. 269–70, 285.
      busts at Carlton House: The invoice was certified by William Kent, 31 Aug. 1736, in Coombs 1997, p. 159.
      headless figure: Wheeler, 'Icons and Emblems', unpubl. conference paper, Stowe Estate Office, n.d.
      beautifull Nature: Anon., probably John Whaley, in 'Journal of John Dodd's Tour', 1735, BL Add. 5842 f.130.
      I am every hour: Pope to Martha Blount, 4 Jul. 1739, Sherburn 1956, vol. 4, p. 185.

113   *insuperable corruption:* And following quote, Pope, *Epilogue to the Satires*, Dialogue 2, 1738, notes, p. 329, in *The Works of Alexander Pope*, ed. Joseph Warton, J. J. Tourneisen, 1803, vol. 4, p. 329.
      the folly and wickedness: Cobham to Earl of Stair, 18 Aug. 1739, transcribed in Rose 1831, vol. 2, p. 148.

113   *Jenkins' pickled ear:* Cobbett's *Parliamentary History of England*, 1737–9, London, Hansard, 1812, vol. 10, pp. 638–9.

    we should go into: Lyttelton's speech in the Commons, 8 Feb. 1739, *Cobbett's Parliamentary History of England 1739–41*, London, Hansard, 1812, vol. 11, p. 311.

    very well, but very: John Selwyn to Thomas Townshend, 10 Mar. 1739, William Coxe, *Memoirs of the Life and Administration of Sir Robert Walpole*, London, T. Cadell & W. Davies, 1798, vol. 3, p. 519.

114   *Hawkwell Field:* Clarke 1971a, p. 271.

115   *two fine Cows, two:* John MacClary to Cottrell, 1750, transcribed in Batey 1983, p. 128.

    gadding Heifers: West 1732, p. 237.

    William Love: Stowe Gardens *Survey* 1992, App. 11: 'Stewards, Clerks of Works and Head Gardeners'.

    free from the vanity: John Penn, *History and Descriptive Account of Stoke Parke in Buckinghamshire*, London, W. Bulmer, 1813, p. 34.

    Gibbs's commissions: Terry Friedman, *James Gibbs*, New Haven and London, Yale University Press, 1984, pp. 13–20.

116   *Tip top Clubbs:* Vertue 1934, p. 120.

    terribly scar'd: Quoted in Willis 2002, p. 70.

    ten guineas: Cobham's Account Book 1736–41, Friedman 1984, p. 292.

117   *pavilion for army colleague:* Milles, Jul. 1735, transcribed in Clarke 1990, p. 61.

    art is the ape of nature: Robinson 2002, p. 77.

    Temple of Liberty: Stowe Temple Estate Accounts, box 69, bundle 2a, 1741, Huntington Library (the temple was then referred to as the Gothic Temple); for Stowe Papers and Cobham's Account Books, see also Friedman 1984, p. 292.

118   *a real Whig:* Viscount Molesworth in the preface to François Hotman, *Franco-Gallia: Or, an Account of the Ancient Free State of France, and Most Other Parts of Europe, before the Loss of Their Liberties*, London, 1721.

    half Church half Tower: Jemima, Marchioness Grey, Letterbook, 5 Jul. 1748, Bedfordshire Record Office, L30/9a/1, ff.164–75.

    for the Removal of: Cobbett's *Parliamentary History of England, 1739–41*, vol. 11, pp. 1359–64, 1370–2.

119   *Bolingbroke:* Gerrard, 1994, p. 108

    King Alfred as a symbol: Ibid., pp. 154–161.

    Old Gothic Pile: George Lyttelton, *Letters from a Persian in England to His Friend at Isapahan*, London, J. Millan, 1735, p. 71.

    a Sudden Shower interrupts: Anonymous description of Stowe, 1738, transcribed in Clarke 1990, p. 76.

    magnificent bridge: Ibid., and Friedman 1984, p. 293.

120   *great favourite:* And following quotes, Ralph Verney, Dec. 1741, quoted in Hinde, 1986,

p. 23; and for employment, *Stowe Gardens Survey* 1992, App. 11: 'Stewards, Clerks of Works and Head Gardeners'.

121   *irregularities in the accounts:* Leonard Lloyd to Cobham, 6 Apr. 1742, Stowe Temple Estate Accounts, box 69, bundle 2a, Potts's Accounts, Mar. 1741, Huntington Library; and George Clarke, 'The History of Stowe – XIV, Lancelot Brown's Work at Stowe', in the *Stoic*, vol. 25, no. 1 (Dec. 1971b), pp. 18–19.

to apprehend: Stowe Temple Estate Accounts, box 69, bundle 12, Lloyd's Accounts, 17 Nov. 1742, Huntington Library.

who could continue: Penn 1813, pp. 33–4.

121   *Brown at Stowe:* Brown handed in his first accounts in Mar. 1741, Hinde 1986, p. 19.

Brown as clerk of works: Clarke 1971b, pp. 19–20.

Brown's character: From contemporary accounts, quoted in Roger Turner, *Capability Brown and the Eighteenth-century English Landscape*, Chichester, Phillimore, 1999, pp. 58–9.

filling up tree holes: Accounts 1743/4, in *Stowe Gardens Survey* 1992, p. 34.

removal of parterre: Accounts 1741, 1743 and 1744, Ibid., pp. 33–4, 112.

unmeasurable: Stowe Temple Estate Accounts, box 69, bundle 7, 1743/4, Mar. 1744, Huntington Library.

One large room: Quoted in Dorothy Stroud, *Capability Brown*, London, Faber & Faber, 1975, p. 39.

Brown for Wotton: Turner 1999, p. 57.

122   *abused by ye carting:* Stowe Temple Estate Accounts, box 69, bundle 13, Apr.–May 1744, Huntington Library.

Or is this gloom: James Thomson, *The Seasons* (Autumn), revised edn publ. 1746, ll. 1037–42.

guidebooks: Adrian Tinniswood, *The Polite Tourist*, London, National Trust, 1998, p. 99.

plain Account: Benton Seeley, *A Description of the Gardens of the Lord Viscount Cobham, at Stow in Buckinghamshire*, Northampton, W. Dicey, 1744, Preface.

123   *Brown married:* On 22 Nov. 1744, Turner 1999, p. 57.

like ten thousand angels: The Grenville Papers, ed. J. Smith, London, John Murray, 1852, vol. 1, p. 19.

squander[ing] the public: Pitt's speech in the Commons, 10 Dec. 1742, *Cobbett's Parliamentary History of England, 1741–3*, London, Hansard, 1812, vol. 12, pp. 1035, 1033.

124   *23,500 cubic yards:* Based on the accounts and calculated in Clarke 1971b, p. 21.

125   *grass amphitheatre:* Stowe Temple Estate Accounts, box 69, bundle 10, 29 Nov. 1746; bundle 11, 25 Apr. 1747, Huntington Library; and *Lady Sophia Newdigate's Journal*, 1748, transcribed in Clarke 1990, p. 178.

iron roller: Willis 2002, p. 111.

gave me no absolute: And following quotes, Lancelot Brown to Cobham, 24 Feb. 1747, quoted in Clarke 1971b, p. 21.

125   *That thin, decayed:* Mary Pendarves (Mary Delany) to Anne Granville, 3 Mar. 1739, in
       The Autobiography and Correspondence of Mary Granville, Mrs Delany, ed. Lady Llanover,
       vol. 2, London, Richard Bentley, 1862, p. 43.

126   *the house of Discord:* Ann Granville, 1746, quoted in Clarke 1990, p. 186.
       designer of the Grecian Temple: Our thanks to Michael Bevington for pointing us to *The
       Morning Post and Daily Advertiser* 'Anecdotes of Mr Brown, the Gardener', 30 July 1774.
       the most beautiful . . . form: Joshua Reynolds, the *Idler*, 1759, quoted in Turner 1999,
       p. 33.

127   *the line of beauty:* William Hogarth, *The Analysis of Beauty*, section 7, 'Of Lines' (1753),
       repr. in *Art in Theory 1648–1815*, ed. C. Harrison, P. Wood and J. Gaiger, Oxford,
       Blackwell, 2000, pp. 496–7.
       tree-moving: Accounts 1746 and 1747; the accounts for 1752 also list repairs to the 'tree
       carriages', *Stowe Gardens Survey* 1992, p. 103; and Henry Steuart, *The Planter's Guide*,
       London, William Blackwood & Sons, 1848 (first publ. 1827), p. 32–3.

128   *the worst:* Jemima, Marchioness Grey, Letterbook, 5 July 1748, Bedfordshire Record
       Office, L30/9a/1, ff.164–75.
       trees for the Grecian Valley: Clarke 1971b, p. 21.
       'Black Act' of 1723: E. P. Thompson, *Whigs and Hunters. The Origin of the Black Act*,
       London, Allen Lane, 1975, p. 223.
       Cobham and the poachers: Ibid., p. 21.

129   *[I]t does not signifie to read:* Hester Grenville, 1748, quoted in *Stowe Landscape Gardens*
       1997, p. 67.

130   *she had cry'd all night:* And following quotes, Anne Grenville to Richard Grenville,
       recounting the conversation with Lady Cobham, 1750, BL Add. 57806, f.76.
       big enough: Ibid.

Chapter 4 Hawkstone Park

131   *On 25 July 1774:* The description of Dr Johnson's visit to Hawkstone is based on his
       account in George Birbeck Hill (ed.), *Boswell's Life of Johnson together with Boswell's
       Journal of a Tour to the Hebrides and Johnson's Diary of a Journey into North Wales*,
       Oxford, Clarendon Press, 1964, vol. 5, p. 434; and Mrs Thrale's diary entry in A. M.
       Broadley, *Dr Johnson and Mrs Thrale*, London, John Lane, 1910, pp. 178–82.
       Dr Johnson's appearance: Based on Boswell's account of Johnson's typical outfit on their
       tour to the Hebrides the year before: James Boswell, *The Journal of a Tour to the Hebrides
       with Samuel Johnson*, ed. L. F. Powell, London, J. M. Dent, 1958, p. 5.

132   *nothing but hideous:* L. G. Wickham Legg (ed.), *A Relation of a Short Survey of 26 Counties,
       Observed in a Seven Weeks Journey Begun on August 11, 1634 by a Captain, Lieutenant and
       an Ancient*, London, F. E. Robinson & Co., 1904, p. 41.
       houling Wilderness: Daniel Defoe, *A Tour through the Whole Island of Great Britain* (first

publ. 1724–6), ed. P. N. Furbank and W. R. Owens, Yale University Press, New Haven and London, 1991, p. 241.

132 *'hook-shoulder'd' and 'ill design'd':* Marvell, 'Upon the Hill and Grove at Bill-borow', in *The Poems and Letters of Andrew Marvell*, ed. H. M. Margoliouth, Oxford, Oxford University Press, 1927, vol. 1, p. 56, ll. 11, 13.

as if nature had: Evelyn, c. May 1646 (Kalendarium), de Beer 1955, vol. 2, p. 507.

warts, and pockholes: Donne, *An Anatomie of the World*, 'The First Anniversary', in John Donne, *Poems*, London, John Marriot, 1633, p. 245, l. 300.

133 *turbulent pleasure, between fright:* And following quotes, Hill 1964, p. 434.

135 *He loved Shropshire:* Richard Hill's speech after his re-election, *Shrewsbury Chronicle*, 10 June 1796.

Tories call me Whig: Hill, quoted in Edwin Sidney, *The Life of Sir Richard Hill*, London, R. B. Seeley & W. Burnside, 1839, p. 285.

to feed the hungry: Hill's speech to Parliament, 16 June 1783, *The Parliamentary History of England, 1782–3*, London, Hansard, 1814, vol. 23, p. 1019.

Roger de Coverley: Sir N.W. Wraxall, *Historical Memoirs of His Own Time*, London, Richard Bentley, 1836, vol. 4, pp. 712–13.

a lover of hospitality: Hill's speech to Parliament, 16 Jun. 1783, *The Parliamentary History of England, 1782–3*, vol. 23, p. 1019.

136 *Peace at all events:* Hill's speech to Parliament 21 Feb. 1783, quoted in Sidney 1839, p. 310.

tottering nation: Hill's speech to Parliament, quoted in Ibid., p. 290.

next to peace: Hill's speech to Parliament, 27 Feb. 1782, *The Parliamentary History of England, 1781–2*, 1814, vol. 22, p. 1083.

'Tis time to part: Paine, *Common Sense* (1st publ. 1776), in *Thomas Paine: Common Sense and The Rights of Man*, ed. Tony Benn, London, Phoenix Press, 2000, pp. 24, 18.

137 *the 360-acre park:* The park was exactly 363 acres, according to the *Hawkstone Survey*, 1787, vol. 2, section 1.

into a sort of paradise: Thomas Erskine about Hill's changes at Hawkstone, quoted in Sidney 1839, p. 425.

138 *destroyers rather than builders:* Christopher Wren, 'Report on Westminster Abbey in 1713 to Dean Atterbury', in Wren Society 1934, vol. 11, p. 16.

the Gothic style: Richard Davenport-Hines, *Gothic. Four Hundred Years of Excess, Horror, Evil and Ruin*, London, Fourth Estate, 1998, pp. 77–83.

139 *skeleton:* Sidney 1839, pp. 10–11.

that excellent old book: Hill's speech to Parliament, 5 Dec. 1783, *The Parliamentary History of England, 1783–5*, 1815, vol. 24, p. 41, also p. 358; *1781–2*, 1814, vol. 22, p. 276; *1797–8*, vol. 33, 1818, p. 685.

weakened his character: William Wilberforce about Hill, reported by Joseph Farington, 11 Jul. 1813, *The Diary of Joseph Farington*, ed. Kathryne Cave, Kenneth Garlick and Angus

MacIntyre, Yale, New Haven and London, Yale University Press, vol. 12, 1983, p. 4394.

scriptural Killigrew: R. G. Thorne (ed.), *The History of Parliament*, London, Secker & Warburg, 1986, vol. 4, p. 199.

139 *fleece their flocks:* Hill to Sir Rowland Hill, 30 Jul. 1767, Shropshire Archives 549/50.

idle, non-resident clergy: Hill's speeches to Parliament, 1782, in Sidney 1839, p. 299 and 4 Dec. 1783, *The Parliamentary History of England, 1783–5*, 1815, vol. 24, p. 111.

140 *religion of the heart:* John Wesley, quoted in E. P. Thompson, *The Making of the English Working Class*, London, Penguin, 1980, p. 391.

'fanatic' madmen: Hume, 'Of Superstition and Enthusiasm' (first publ. 1741–2), in *David Hume: Selected Essays*, ed. Stephen Copley and Andrew Edgar, Oxford, Oxford University Press, 1996, p. 39.

cold manner: Sidney 1839, p. 447.

all trees of noblest: John Milton, *Paradise Lost*, London, Basil Montagu Pickering, 1873 (first publ. 1667), bk 4, ll. 217–63.

141 *present/ A different picture:* William Mason, *The English Garden, A Poem, Published in Four Books*, London, Goldney & Ward, 1778–81, bk 1, ll. 214–15.

hide/ The view: Ibid., bk 1, ll. 206–7.

a variety of shapes: Hawkstone Survey, 1787, vol. 1, p. 4.

irregularly . . . exhibiting much wildness: Ibid., vol. 1, p. 3.

Admit it partially: Mason 1778–81, bk 1, ll. 211–12.

142 *The principal defect:* Philip Yorke, 'Memorandums of a Journey into Staffordshire, 1748', in Joyce Godber, *The Marchioness Grey of West Park, Bedford*, Bedfordshire Historical Record Society, vol. 47, 1968, p. 136.

mean canal which: Mrs Thrale's description of Hawkstone in 1774, in Broadley 1910, p. 62.

show the advantages: Thomas Whately, *Observations on Modern Gardening*, London, 1770, p. 1.

Emes introduces himself to Hill: Since the excavation of the lake was well under way on 1 May 1784, we assume that Emes must have started at least at the beginning of the year: T. Rodenhurst, *A Description of Hawkstone, the Seat of Sir Richard Hill*, Shrewsbury, T. Wood, 1784, p. 47.

small brook: We are indebted to Roger Whitehouse, the park warden at Hawkstone, for the information about the brook and the height of the dams.

143 *[T]here can be no happiness:* Hill's reply to a libel, quoted in Sidney 1839, p. 418.

first gratification: Erskine about Hill, quoted Ibid. p. 425.

144 *Gilpin's sermons:* Shrewsbury Chronicle, 22 Apr. 1791.

mountains – lakes – broken grounds: William Gilpin, *Observations, Relative Chiefly to Picturesque Beauty, Made in the Year 1772, on Several Parts of England; Particularly the Mountains and Lakes of Cumberland, and Westmoreland*, London, R. Blamire, 1786, p. 81.

144   *a sacred thing:* William Gilpin, *Observations on Several Parts of the Counties of Cambridge, Norfolk, Suffolk, and Essex. Also on Several Parts of North Wales, Relative Chiefly to Picturesque Beauty, in Two Tours, the Former Made in . . . 1769, the Latter in . . . 1773*, London, T. Cadell & W. Davies, 1809, p. 122.

capable of being illustrated: William Gilpin, *Three Essays: on Picturesque Beauty; on Picturesque Travel; and, on Sketching Landscape: to which is Added a Poem, on Landscape Painting*, London, R. Blamire, 2nd edn, 1794, p. 1.

145   *a sort of delightful:* Edmund Burke, *A Philosophical Enquiry*, Oxford, Oxford University Press 1998, (first publ. 1757), p. 67.

146   *improved by practice:* Hume, '*Of the Standard of Taste*' (first publ. 1757), in Copley and Edgar 1996, p. 147.

147   *romantic scenes:* Rodenhurst 1784, p. 12.

148   *miserable hut:* Shropshire Archives, court case, 731/4/5/1 (Bygott Collection but held at the Shropshire Archives).

The cottage offends: William Gilpin, *Forest Scenery*, London, Sampson Low, Marston, Searle & Rivington, 1879 (first publ. 1791), p. 293.

the verdict: Shropshire Archives, court case, 731/4/5/1.

a vast number of: Rodenhurst 1784 (1786, 1799, 1807).

149   *lengthening both ends of:* William Emes to Hill, 10 May 1786, quoted in Arthur Oswald, 'Beauties and Wonders of Hawkstone, 1', in *Country Life*, vol. 124i (3 Jul. 1958), p. 21. The original letter is held at the Shropshire Archives, but is currently lost.

£15,000: Thorne 1986, vol. 4, p. 200. Hill's annual income just from his estates in and around Hawkstone was almost £7000 in 1787, *Hawkstone Survey*, 1787, vol. 2, section 15.

150   *steep dingle:* Rodenhurst 1786, p. 34.

coaches: *Shrewsbury Chronicle*, 11 Mar. 1786.

inaugural dinner: Ibid., 7 Jul. 1787.

151   *gentleman's seat:* Jonathan Gray, 'Tour in the Western Counties and South Wales', 1802, York City Archives, MSS T/4, and Henry Skrine, *Two Successive Tours throughout the Whole of Wales*, London, Elmsley & Bremner, 1798, p. 180.

gay parties: York City Archives, Gray 1802, MSS T/4.

journey times: *Shrewsbury Chronicle*, 26 Jul. 1788.

Prices for yacht: Ibid., 19 Apr. 1788.

152   *the savages:* Horace Walpole to William Cole, 16 Jun. 1781, in *Horace Walpole's Correspondence*, ed. W. S. Lewis, New Haven and London, Yale University Press, 1937, vol. 2, p. 275.

jumping up backwards: Ibid., vol. 2, p. 275.

six days are enough: Hill's comments on the Sabbath, quoted in Sidney 1839, pp. 283, 449, 354, and Hill's speeches to Parliament, 22 Jul. 1784 and 26 Mar. 1795, *The Parliamentary History of England, 1783–5*, 1815, vol. 24, p. 1233, and *1794–5*, 1818, vol. 31, p. 1433.

153   *raging storms:* Burke 1998, p. 75.

that confusion and horrid uproar: This is a description of a similar 'cannon induced' experience in the Lake District. William Hutchinson, *An Excursion to the Lakes, in Westmoreland and Cumberland, August 1773*, London, L. Wilkie, 1774, p. 71.

take the wind out: Thorne 1986, vol. 4, p. 199.

Hillisms: John Pollock, *Wilberforce*, London, Constable, 1977, p. 70.

horrid traffic in: Hill on abolition, *Shrewsbury Chronicle*, 20 Apr. 1792.

154   *his most hearty assent:* Hill's speech to Parliament, 18 Feb. 1796, *The Parliamentary History of England, 1795–7*, 1818, vol. 32, p. 748.

£500 annual rent: Hill had parliamentary consent to enclose the commons, had he wanted to, *Hawkstone Survey* 1787, vol. 2, section 15.

my death-bed will not: Pamphlet, quoted in Sidney 1839, pp. 418–19.

[M]ost unwilling to plunge: Wilberforce, 23 Aug. 1789, Robert Wilberforce and Samuel Wilberforce, *The Life of William Wilberforce*, London, Bungay, 1838, vol. 1, p. 242.

spotless white hat: That's how Jonathan Gray saw him in 1802, Gray 1802, MSS T/4.

serenade his guests: Sidney 1839, p. 501, and Edmund Butcher, *An Excursion from Sidmouth to Chester in the Summer of 1803*, London, H. D. Symonds, 1805, p. 174.

walk and ramble among: Hill's party for Lord Thurlow at Hawkstone, Robert Gore-Brown, *Chancellor Thurlow. The Life and Times of an Eighteenth-century Lawyer*, London, Hamish Hamilton, 1953, p. 290.

retire up into: Wilberforce, 5 Sept. 1789, Wilberforce and Wilberforce 1838, p. 244.

penal reform: Pollock 1977, p. 93.

155   *the most stupendous edifice:* And the following quotes, Asa Briggs, *The Age of Improvement, 1783–1867*, London, Longman, 2000, p. 113.

a world of monsters: Burke to his son, 10 Oct. 1789, quoted in Edmund Burke, *Reflections on the Revolution in France*, London, Penguin, 1968 (first publ. 1790), p. 14.

barbarities: Hill, quoted in Sidney 1839, p. 416.

the foulest and most: William Pitt, quoted in Simon Schama, *Citizens, A Chronicle of the French Revolution*, Penguin, London, 1989, p. 687.

the nation [France] . . . which: Hill's speech to Parliament, quoted in Sidney 1839, pp. 433–4.

156   *religious eye:* Joseph Wittingham Salmon, *The Beauties of Hawkstone Park*, London, E. Hodson, 1817, p. xii.

Since GOD is Love: Joseph Wittingham Salmon, *Moral Reflections in Verse, Begun in Hawkstone Park*, Nantwich and Drayton, E. Snelson, 1796, p. 98.

157   *god's spiritual kingdom:* Ibid., p. vii.

rapture and devotion: Salmon 1817, p. xiii.

to be good and useful: Hill, quoted in Sidney 1839, p. 491.

Break their wills: Wesley, quoted in Thompson 1980, p. 412.

family of love: Wilberforce and Wilberforce 1838, p. 244.

157 *Hill's paternalism: Shrewsbury Chronicle,* 20 Feb. 1795.

158 *Hill's speech to Parliament:* 30 Dec. 1794, *The Parliamentary History of England, 1794–5,* 1818, vol. 31, pp. 1034–5.

increase their attention: Uvedale Price, *Thoughts on the Defence of Property. Addressed to the County of Hereford,* Hereford, 1797, p. 28.

159 *their abhorrence of tumult:* The Papers of the London Corresponding Society, quoted in Ian Gilmour, *Riot, Risings and Revolution. Governance and Violence in Eighteenth-century England,* Pimlico, London, 1992, p. 397.

would rather live on: Hill, quoted in Sidney 1839, p. 418.

£5000: Thorne 1986, vol. 4, p. 200.

160 *rare instance:* Skrine 1798, p. 181.

distinguished guests: The description of the royal visit is based on an article in the *Shrewsbury Chronicle,* 19 Aug. 1796.

three hothouses: Hawkstone Survey 1787, vol. 1, section 2, p. 2.

Reynard's Walk: Was built after 1787 and before 1796, as it was not mentioned in the *Hawkstone Survey* 1787, but in the *Shrewsbury Chronicle* on 19 Aug. 1796 and in the 1799 guidebook.

161 *much pleased with: Shrewsbury Chronicle,* 19 Aug. 1796.

the Colossus at Rhodes: Wesley quoted in Barrie Trinder, *The Industrial Revolution in Shropshire,* London, Phillimore, 1973, p. 185.

a dessert service: Shrewsbury Chronicle, 25 Aug. 1797.

mist arising from: Revd Richard Warner, *A Tour through the Counties of England and the Borders of Scotland,* Bath, R. Cruttwell, 1802, vol. 2, p. 188.

rivers of lava: Joseph Banks, quoted in Esther Moir, *The Discovery of Britain. The English Tourist 1540–1840,* London, Routledge, 1964, p. 99.

overpower the soul: Burke 1998, p. 75.

momentary bursts of: Revd. Richard Warner, *A Walk through Wales in August 1797,* Bath, R. Cruttwell, 1799, p. 215.

the idea of the final: Ibid., p. 288.

162 *the defence of the country: Shrewsbury Chronicle,* 16 and 30 Mar. 1798.

the sun shone upon them: Ibid., 12 Oct. 1798.

tiresome uniformity: Warner 1802, p. 164.

look well in a picture William Gilpin, *Observations on the Western Part of England, Relative Chiefly to Picturesque Beauty,* London, T. Cadell & W. Davies, 1798, p. 328.

childishly artificial: Warner 1802, vol. 2, p. 173.

old-fashioned family: Ibid., vol. 2, p. 174.

163 *introduce the gospel:* William Wilson, *A Missionary Voyage to the Southern Pacific Ocean in the years 1796–1798,* London, T. Chapman, 1799, p. xcvi.

163 *paths skirting precipices:* Warner 1802, vol. 2, p. 175.

most beautiful and solemn: Ibid., p. 176.

164   *ten thousand diamonds:* Ibid., p. 162.

      extremely well managed: Ibid., p. 176.

165   *novel, grand, beautiful:* Ibid., p. 177.

166   *peaceful hermitage: Il Penseroso,* in John Milton, *Poems,* facsimile of 1645 edn, Oxford, Clarendon Press, 1924, ll. 167–76, p. 44.

      Contemplative life is not: Pope to Francis Atterbury, 20 Nov. 1717, in Sherburn 1956, vol. 1, p. 454.

167   *withdraw the reality:* 'Notes and Queries', quoted in Anne Campbell Dixon, 'Hermits for Hire', in *Country Life,* vol. 182ii (June 1988), p. 161.

      rotten through age: Butcher 1805, p. 177.

      women and children: Gray 1802, MSS T/4.

      disgusting and unnatural: Butcher 1805, p. 177.

168   *horror of solitude:* Hill 1964, vol. 5, p. 434.

      terrace alps: Salmon 1817, p. 25.

      beyond description: Skrine 1798, p. 176.

      wide chasms . . . strike you: Rodenhurst 1784, p. 19.

169   *I climb the rocks:* Jean-Jacques Rousseau, *The Confessions of J.-J. Rousseau: with the Reveries of the Solitary Walker,* London, J. Brew, 1783, vol. 2, 'Walk 7', p. 295.

      Britain's first true rock climb: Robert Macfarlane, *Mountains of the Mind. A History of a Fascination,* London, Granta, 2003, p. 84.

      no rocks nor Mountains: Thomas Burnet, *The Sacred Theory of the Earth,* London, John Hooke, 1719 (first publ. 1681), vol. 1, pp. 90–1.

170   *these Heaps of Stone:* Ibid., p. 195 (see also pp. 191–8).

      most solemn, the most: The Letters of Thomas Gray, ed. Duncan C. Tovey, London, George Bell & Sons, 1900, vol. 1, p. 38.

      pregnant with religion: Ibid., p. 42.

      [P]recipices, mountains, torrents: Walpole to Gilbert West, 28 Sept. 1739, *Horace Walpole's Correspondence,* ed. W. S. Lewis, New Haven and London, Yale University Press, 1948, vol. 13, p. 181.

      rising on the left: A Sicilian Romance, London, T. Hookham, 1790, vol. 2, p. 114.

      by some vast effort: Sidney 1839, p. 4, and Rodenhurst 1784, p. 26.

171   *kissing the toe of:* Hill to Wilberforce, quoted in Sidney 1839, p. 473.

      trade was like: Hill's speech to Parliament, 16 Apr. 1790, *The Parliamentary History of England, 1789–90,* 1816, vol. 28, p. 687.

172   *a large company of friends:* The description of the party is based on an article in the *Shrewsbury Chronicle* of 16 Oct. 1801.

      astonishing manner: Ibid.

      feast at the Greenhouse: The description of the party is based on an article in the *Shrewsbury Chronicle* of 13 Aug. 1802 and on the *Annual Register 1802,* p. 429.

Chapter 5 Sheringham Park

174   *It wants improvement, Ma'am:* Jane Austen, *Mansfield Park*, Penguin, London, 1996, (first publ. 1814), pp. 46–9.

177   *most favourite work:* Humphry Repton, Red Book for Sheringham, 1812.

178   *he had seen fine:* Joseph Farington recounting what Mrs Alnut said about Repton, 29 July 1810, *The Diary of Joseph Farington*, ed. Kathryne Cave, Kenneth Garlick and Angus MacIntyre, Yale, New Haven and London, Yale University Press, 1978–84, vol. 10, p. 3700. Uvedale Price criticised Repton for his mercenary attitude in a letter to Lady Margaret Beaumont of 10 Aug. 1820, quoted in Stephen Daniels, 'On the Road with Humphry Repton', in *Journal of Garden History*, vol. 16, no. 3 (autumn 1996), p. 174. When Repton visited Uppark in Aug. 1815 he wrote: 'this is the first visit I ever felt inclined to make independent of all professional pursuit', quoted in Margaret Meade-Fetherstonhaugh and Oliver Warner, *Uppark and Its People*, London, George Allen & Unwin, 1964, p. 87. *a thousand acres of rich arable:* Agreement between Cook Flower and Abbot Upcher, Norfolk Record Office, UPC 13/6, 10 Jul. 1811.
concentrate [his] property: Abbot Upcher, 'Sherringhamia', 1813–16, Norfolk Record Office, UPC 155, 641 x 8, entry for 11 Apr. 1815.

179   *a virtuous example:* Upcher's diary, 19 Jul. 1811, transcribed in Emma Pigott, *Memoirs of the Honourable Mrs Upcher of Sheringham*, London, Harrison & Sons, c. 1860, p. 36.
romantic: Ibid., 3 Jul. 1811, p. 35.
cruelly disappointed: Ibid., 30 Jun. 1811, p. 35.
quite at a loss: Ibid.
the society of those: Humphry Repton to Lord Sheffield, 22 Dec. 1805, quoted in Stephen Daniels, *Humphry Repton. Landscape Gardening and the Geography of Georgian England*, New Haven and London, Yale University Press, 1999, p. 150.
dazzling: Joseph Farington recounting what one Mrs Alnut thought of Repton, 29 July 1810, Cave et al. 1978–84, vol. 10, p. 3700.
everlasting talker: John Byng, 28 May 1792, *The Torrington Diaries*, ed. C. Bruyn Andrews, London, Eyre & Spottiswoode, 1936, vol. 3, p. 11.

181   *infectious vapours:* Jean-Jacques Rousseau, *The Confessions of J.-J. Rousseau: with the Reveries of the Solitary Walker*, J. Brew, London, 1783, vol. 2, 'Walk 7', p. 290.
Ambition, avarice, penury: Cowper, *The Task*, bk 3, l. 811, in *The Works of William Cowper*, ed. Robert Southey, London, Baldwin & Cradock, 1835–7, vol. 9, p. 158.
quit their healthy clean: Arthur Young, quoted in Raymond Williams, *The Country and the City*, London, Chatto & Windus, 1973, p. 146.
'humble' men: William Wordsworth, *Lyrical Ballads with Other Poems*, London, Longman, 1800, vol. 1, pp. xi–xii.

181   *Amongst them, on their:* Hannah More, quoted in Todd Gowan-Longstaffe, *The London Town Garden, 1740–1840*, New Haven and London, Yale University Press, 2001, p. 7.

182 *like Hydra's heads:* Upcher's diary, 31 Dec. 1811, transcribed in Pigott *c.* 1860, p. 40.

shepherds and shepherdesses: Gilbert White, *The Garden Kalendar 1751–1771*, facsimile of MS, London, Scolar Press, 1975, 28 Jul. 1763, f.155. Constable criticised this fashion in *John Constable's Discourses*, compiled and annotated by R. B. Beckett, Ipswich, Suffolk Record Office, 1970, vol. 14, p. 59.

milkmaids, ploughmen: William Gilpin in *Instructions for Examining Landscape*, quoted in Maggie Lane, *Jane Austen's England*, London, Robert Hale, 1986, p. 103.

moral duty: Nathaniel Kent, *Hints to Gentlemen of Landed Property*, London, G. Nicol, 1799, pp. 206–14, 276–8.

183 *You must not enquire:* Jane Austen, *Sense and Sensibility*, London, Penguin, 1995 (first publ. 1811), pp. 84–5.

domestic comfort and: Ibid., p. 13; and for Upcher, his diary, 19 Jul. 1811, and Upcher to Charlotte Upcher, June 1814, both transcribed in Pigott *c.* 1860, pp. 37, 67.

184 *a different species:* Repton, Red Book for Sheringham, 1812.

How do your weavers: Repton to William Repton, 21 Apr. 1812, Huntington Library, HM 40870.

'portentous' times: Ibid.

since the troubled days: *Leeds Mercury*, Dec. 1811, quoted in E. P. Thompson, *The Making of the English Working Class*, London, Penguin, 1980, p. 605.

trembled for the safety: Humphry Repton, Memoir (unpubl. MS), BL Add. 62112, p. 167.

London mob: Upcher's diary, Aug. 1811, transcribed in Pigott *c.* 1860, p. 38.

185 *tender and faithful:* Ibid., Apr. 1812, p. 43.

almost devoured: Ibid., 2 Jun. 1810 and 20 Jan. 1811, pp. 21, 24.

delightful evenings: Ibid., 26 Apr. 1812, p. 44.

shaven lawns: Richard Payne Knight, *The Landscape, a Didactic Poem in Three Books, Addressed to Uvedale Price*, London, W. Bulmer, 1794, bk 2, ll. 3–4.

The man of wealth: Oliver Goldsmith, 'The Deserted Village', 1770, in *The Poems*, London, Longman, 1969, ll. 275–80, p. 688.

186 *miserable huts:* Samuel Jackson Pratt, *Gleanings in England. Descriptive of the Countenance, Mind and Character of the Country*, London, A. Strahan, 1801, vol. 1, p. 431. More descriptions of Upper Sheringham: Edmund Bartell, *Observations upon the Town of Cromer, Considered as a Watering Place*, London and Cromer, John Parslee, 1800, pp. 74–6; and Repton's Red Book for Sheringham, 1812.

inconceivable expense: Upcher's diary, 10 Jun. 1811, transcribed in Pigott *c.*1860, p. 45.

much anxiety: Ibid.

never wrong: Byng, 28 May 1792, Andrews 1936, vol. 3, p. 9.

Nature's physician: Ibid., p. 10.

he will dolefully repent: Ibid., p. 11.

187 *The park was very large:* Jane Austen, *Pride and Prejudice*, London, Penguin, 1998 (first publ. 1813), p. 185.

188 *I must date it:* Ibid., pp. 286, 188.

    Seeing almost immediately: Repton, Memoir (unpubl. MS), p. 2.

    never cease to thank: Upcher, 'Sherringhamia', 11 Jun. 1812.

189 *grand beyond measure:* Upcher's diary, 23 Jun. 1812, transcribed in Pigott *c.* 1860, p. 46.

    made several arrangements: Ibid.

    Repton [was] hurt: Upcher's diary, 23 June 1812, transcribed in Pigott, *c.* 1860, p. 45.

    'intimacy' and *'confidence':* Repton, Red Book for Sheringham, 1812.

    Repton on nouveaux riches: Repton, Memoir (unpubl. MS), BL Add. 62112, pp. 169–74, 208–10; Humphry Repton, *Observations on the Theory and Practice of Landscape Gardening*, London, J. Taylor, 1803, p. 11; and Humphry Repton, *An Enquiry into the Changes of Taste in Landscape Gardening*, London, J. Taylor, 1806, p. 65.

190 *the prophetic eye of Taste:* Repton, Red Book for Sheringham, 1812.

    Walter Scott: George Carter, Patrick Goode and Kedrun Laurie, *Humphry Repton. Landscape Gardener, 1752–1818*, exhibition catalogue, Norwich, Sainsbury Centre for Visual Arts, 1982, p. 22.

    amus[ing] ourselves in looking: Joseph Farington at Home Park, 30 Oct. 1800, Cave *et al.*, 1978–84, vol. 4, p. 1447.

191 *Edmund Burke: The Correspondence of Edmund Burke*, ed. P. J. Marshall and J. A. Wood, Cambridge, Cambridge University Press, 1968; Carter et al. 1982, pp. 19–22.

    Feasibility: Repton, Red Book for Sheringham, 1812.

    perhaps too plain: Ibid.

    visitors to picnic: Ibid.

    <u>that</u> *almost forgotten Emblem:* Ibid.

192 *Sheringham Inclosure Act:* Printed extract from the Sheringham Inclosure Act, 26 Jul. 1811, Norfolk Record Office, UPC 56, 640 x 8, pp. 6–7; and Agreement between Flower and Upcher, 10 Jul. 1811, Norfolk Record Office, UPC 13/6.

    a mutual intercourse betwixt: Repton, Red Book for Sheringham, 1812; Upcher mentioned his passion for coursing many times in his diary.

193 *the occasional glitter:* Repton, Red Book for Sheringham, 1812.

    [Y]ou have presented me: Upcher, quoted in Ibid.

    They were viewing the country: Jane Austen, *Northanger Abbey*, London, John Murray, 1818, vol. 1, pp. 260, 263–4.

194 *become a mere jargon:* Austen 1995, p. 85.

195 *a Landscape of a Post:* Thomas Rowlandson and William Combe, *The Tour of Doctor Syntax in Search of the Picturesque*, London, Methuen Co., 1903 (first publ. 1812), p. 11.

    no scene in nature: Giardin, quoted in David Jacques, *Georgian Gardens. The Reign of Nature*, London, Batsford, 1993, p. 134.

196 *convenience:* Humphry Repton, *Sketches and Hints on Landscape Gardening*, London, W. Bulmer, 1794, p. 70, and Repton, Red Book for Sheringham, 1812.

196   *You are charmingly group'd:* Austen 1998, p. 39.

197   *had I a place:* Austen 1996b, pp. 46–9.

198   *£200 in a month*: Stephen Daniels, 'Cankerous Blossom. Troubles in the Later Career of Humphry Repton Documented in the Repton Correspondence in the Huntington Library', in *Journal of Garden History*, vol. 6, no. 2 (1986), p. 148.
      had gone mad: Repton to William Repton, 11 Dec. 1812 (letter included in a letter to Dorothy Adey), Huntington Library, HM 40837.

199   *nervous fever:* Upcher, 'Sherringhamia', 18 Oct. 1812.
      great depression: Repton to William Repton, 11 Dec. 1812.
      Nelson Trust: See letters between Repton and William Repton in Huntington Library: 5 Dec. 1808 HM 40853; 29 Dec. 1808 HM 40854; 21 Jan. 1809 HM 40857; and Daniels 1999, pp. 90–1.
      benefit from building: Repton to William Repton, 11 Dec. 1812.
      Consider on the Sale: Ibid.
      most striking views: Ibid.

200   *take very great pleasure:* Upcher, 'Sherringhamia', 12 Jan. 1812.
      [N]ear the house: Repton, Red Book for Sheringham, 1812.

202   *'theatrical' planting:* Mark Laird, *The Flowering of the Landscape Garden. English Pleasure Grounds, 1720–1800*, Philadelphia, University of Pennsylvania Press, 1999, pp. 331–76.
      Repton's recommendations: Mark Laird, 'Corbeille, Parterre and Treillage: The Case of Humphry Repton's Penchant for the French Style of Planting', in *Journal of Garden History*, vol. 16, no. 3 (1996), pp. 153–4; Carter et al. 1982, pp. 57–8; and Repton to Sir Harry Fetherstonhaugh, 8 Oct. 1815, quoted in Meade-Fetherstonhaugh 1964, p. 73.

203   *artificial screen:* Repton, Red Book for Sheringham, 1812.
      the happy medium: Repton 1794, p. 72.
      artificial object: And Repton's view on the ha-ha, Repton 1806, p. 10; and Humphry Repton, *Fragments on the Theory and Practice of Landscape Gardening*, London, T. Bensley, 1816, p. 7.
      houses should resemble Caves: Repton, Red Book for Sheringham, 1812.

204   *poor and needy:* Upcher's diary, 19 Jul. 1811, transcribed in Pigott *c.* 1860, p. 36.
      They were now approaching: Jane Austen, *Emma*, London, Penguin, 1996a (first publ. 1816), p. 75.

205   *rise at night to:* Repton, Red Book for Sheringham, 1812.
      tree-planting: Blanche Henrey, *British Botanical and Horticultural Literature before 1800*, London, Oxford University Press, 1975, vol. 2, p. 645; Tom Williamson, *Polite Landscapes. Gardens and Society in Eighteenth-century England*, Baltimore, Johns Hopkins University Press, 1995, p. 125.

206   *a nobler object than:* Alexander Pope in 1728, recounted by Joseph Spence in his *Observations, Anecdotes, and Characters of Books and Men*, ed. James M. Osborn, Oxford, Clarendon Press, 1966, vol. 1, p. 253.

206 *Repton on trees:* Repton was explicit about this in his Red Book for Beaudesert, 1814, Repton 1816, p. 46. For general information about Repton's opinion on trees, Stephen Daniels, 'The Political Iconography of Woodland in Later Georgian England', in *The Iconography of Landscape*, ed. Denis Cosgrove and Stephen Daniels, Cambridge, Cambridge University Press, 1988.

Banish the formal fir's: Payne Knight 1794, bk 3, l. 59.

Lord of the woods: Southey 1835–7, bk 1, l. 313.

the great oaks: Edmund Burke, quoted in Stephen Daniels, 'Landscape Design and the Idea of Improvement 1730–1900', in *Historical Geography of England and Wales*, ed. R.A. Dodgson and R. A. Butlin, London, Academic Press, 1990, p. 491.

While Oceans breath may: Repton, Red Book for Sheringham, 1812.

207 *The most obvious meaning:* Repton 1794, p. 49.

reoccurrence of the same: Repton 1806, pp. 21–2.

'nurses' for the trees: Ibid., p. 24; and Repton 1803, p. 49.

darken the Wood: Upcher, 'Sherringhamia', Mar. 1814.

Prayers, pruning in wood: Upcher's diary, 22 Feb. 1814, transcribed in Pigott *c.* 1860, p. 66.

208 *irresistibly compelled:* Upcher's diary, 13 Jul. 1814, transcribed in Pigott c. 1860, p. 66; and for description of London, *The Times*, 18 Jun. 1814, and Venetia Murray, *High Society in the Regency Period, 1788–1830*, Penguin, 1999, pp. 211–19.

Castle of Discord: For the party in London, *The Times*, 2 Aug. 1814.

Repton's 'masterpiece': Upcher, 'Sherringhamia', spring 1815.

a work of art: Repton, Red Book for Sheringham, 1812.

209 *the Agriculture of England:* Upcher's diary, 17 Mar. 1815, transcribed in Pigott *c.* 1860, p. 17.

Riots in Norfolk: Ibid., 17 Mar. 1815, p. 17, and Robert Hindry Mason, *History of Norfolk*, London, Wertheimer & Co., 1882–5, pp. 480–1.

This is a happy: Charlotte Upcher's commonplace book, 1815, after the battle of Waterloo, 18 Jun. 1815, in Pigott, *c.* 1860, p. 71.

angina pectoris: Repton to Fetherstonhaugh, Nov. 1814, quoted in Meade-Fetherstonhaugh 1964, p. 86.

kingdoms [were being] raised: Repton to Sir James Edward Smith, 9 Jul. 1815, Lady Smith, *Memoirs and Correspondence of Sir James Edward Smith*, London, Longman, 1832, vol. 2, p. 190.

210 *I should rejoice to:* Ibid.

of the first celebrity: Headlong Hall, in *The Novels of Thomas Love Peacock*, ed. David Garnett, London, Rupert Hart-Davis, 1948, p. 18; see also Edward Malins, *English Landscaping and Literature, 1660–1840*, London, Oxford University Press, 1966, pp. 127–9; and Elizabeth Wheeler Manwaring, *Italian Landscape in Eighteenth-century England*, London, Frank Cass, 1965, p. 221.

210   *are nothing but big:* Garnett 1948, p. 23.

211   *whole in mind:* Edmund Burke, quoted in Alistair Duckworth, *The Improvement of the Estate. A Study of Jane Austen's Novels*, Baltimore, Johns Hopkins University Press, 1974, pp. 46–7.

       coxcomb: Farington, 14 Feb. 1794, 29 Apr. 1794, Cave et al. 1978–84, vol. 1, pp. 163, 184; and Byng, 28 May 1792, Andrews 1936, vol. 3, p. 9.

       transient, as the snowflake: Upcher to Charlotte Upcher, 27 Nov. 1815, quoted in Pigott c. 1860, p. 70.

       like Gardens: Upcher, 'Sherringhamia', 5 Apr. 1815; for Holkham, see Edward Rigby, *Holkham, Its Agriculture*, Norwich, Burks & Kinnebrook, 1817, pp. 2–40, and Wade Martins 1980, pp. 49, 73–95.

       the regularity of cornfields: William Gilpin, *Observations on the Western Part of England, Relative Chiefly to Picturesque Beauty*, London, T. Cadell & W. Davies, 1798, p. 328.

212   *pig sty into the:* Repton 1803, p. 95.

       love-visit: Upcher, 'Sherringhamia', Jun. 1816.

213   *were indefatigable in their:* Ibid.

       beds, carpets, tables: Inventory, Sheringham (made after Upcher's death), Norfolk Record Office, UPC 233.

       violent inflammatory fever: Charlotte Upcher's commonplace book, quoted in Pigott c. 1860, p. 75.

       the most affectionate . . . that once happy paradise: Repton to Fetherstonhaugh, 1 May 1817, West Sussex Record Office, R18 (photocopy of the destroyed original), Uppark Papers.

       what to stop and what: Ibid.

       favourite & darling child: Ibid.

       her husband's will: The solicitor stayed at Sheringham from 13–14 Mar. 1817, Abbot Upcher's account with J. G. Fisher, Norfolk Record Office, UPC 225/3.

214   *united:* Pigott c.1860, pp. 80–1.

6 Chatsworth

216   *Paxton's first day:* Description based on Paxton's own account in W. G. S. Cavendish, 6th Duke of Devonshire, *Handbook of Chatsworth and Hardwick*, London, privately printed, 1845, pp. 111–12. The condition of the garden is also described in 'Paxton's Account of his Arrival at Chatsworth and the State of the Gardens to Answer the List of Questions to the Duke', Chatsworth, Paxton Group of Correspondence.

       looked around: Cavendish, 1845, p. 111.

217   *almost burn one end:* Paxton's description of the flues in the old hothouses at Chatsworth, *Horticultural Register*, vol. 1 (1831), p. 134.

       fell in love with: Cavendish 1845, p. 112.

219   *thriving condition:* George IV, speech of 1825, quoted in Asa Briggs, *The Age of*

Improvement, 1783–1867, London, Longman, 2000, p. 184.

219   *The 6th Duke's:* James Lees-Milne, *The Bachelor Duke. A Life of William Spencer 6th Duke of Devonshire, 1790–1858*, London, John Murray, 1998, pp. 17–42; David Cannadine, 'The Landowner as Millionaire: The Finances of the Dukes of Devonshire, *c.* 1800–1926, in *Agricultural History Review*, vol. 24, pt 2 (1976), p. 81.

220   *£4000 a year:* The Duke spent £54,753 on furniture between 1817 and 1829, Ibid.
       expenditure on gardens: Chatsworth Account Book 1826.
       £2000: Chatsworth Account Book 1829.

221   *Mechanical Age:* Thomas Carlyle, 'Signs of the Times,' in *Edinburgh Review*, 1829, quoted in Asa Briggs, *A Social History of England*, London, Penguin, 1999, p. 205.

222   *gas for heating: Magazine of Botany*, vol. 5 (1838), p. 81.

223   *increased garden budget:* Chatsworth Vouchers in Bundles, Plants and Gardens, 1827–8; Chatsworth Account Book 1830 (total for garden: £5277 7s 10d), Chatsworth Account Book 1831 (total for garden: £4687 3s 4d).
       Heating of hothouses: Magazine of Botany, vol. 2, pp. 103–4. Our descriptions of the construction of Paxton's hothouse are based largely on his many articles in the *Magazine of Botany* (e.g. vol. 1 (1834), vol. 2 (1835), vol. 5 (1838), vol. 8 (1841) and the *Horticultural Register* (e.g. vol. 1 (1831)).

224   *unsatisfactory place: Gardener's Magazine*, vol. 7 (1831), p. 395.
       pre-determination to find fault: Horticultural Register, vol. 1 (1831), p. 133.
       examples of the human: J. C. Loudon, *Remarks on the Construction of Hot-Houses*, London, 1817, p. 4.

225   *happy here:* Duke's diary, 15 and 19 Sept. 1832, and his passion for botany: Duke's diary, 23 Sept. 1833, and diary summary 1833.

226   *mysterious illness:* Lees-Milne 1998, p. 108, and Duke's diary entries.
       wheeled about in: Duke's diary, 12 Aug. 1833; for reference to Paxton and the garden, 23 Jan., 9 and 17 Aug., 23 Sept., 3 Oct. 1833.
       Dropmore: Ibid., 13 Feb. 1833; description of Dropmore based on *Gardener's Magazine*, vol. 3 (1828), pp. 257–63.

227   *[B]eauty in masses:* Ibid., p. 257.
       charmed by the flower: Duke's diary, 23 Jan. 1833, on the planned improvements; and for the description of the flower garden, *Horticultural Register*, vol. 4 (1835), pp. 57–8.

228   *Planting in masses: Magazine of Botany*, vol. 1 (1834), p. 154, and articles in vols 4 (1837), 5 (1838), 8 (1841), 9 (1842), 14 (1847); Brent Elliott, *Victorian Gardens*, London, Batsford, 1986.

229   *Paris:* Duke's diary, 21 Apr. 1834.
       Kew and Loddiges: Duke's diary, 24, 25 Nov. and 4 Dec. 1834. The flowers Paxton and the Duke bought are listed in the Account Book 1834.
       walked with Paxton . . . Chatsworthing: Duke's diary, 7 Sept. 1834 and 14 Nov. 1834.
       to find the pleasure ground: Duke to Paxton, 1 Jan. 1835.

229   *the arboretum:* Paxton's account, *Gardener's Magazine*, vol. 11 (1835), pp. 385–91.

transcendent: Duke's diary, 10 Sept. 1835.

You and Paxton, sitting: Lady Granville to the Duke, Apr. 1835, quoted in Lees-Milne 1998, p. 115.

230   *240 orchid species: Magazine of Botany*, vol. 1 (1834), p. 263.

Expenditure on hothouses: Chatsworth Account Books 1833, 1834.

231   *The orchid collection:* Kate Colquhoun, *A Thing in Disguise. The Visionary Life of Joseph Paxton*, London, Fourth Estate, 2003, p. 63, and letters between Paxton and the Duke, 12, 14, 16, 19, 23 Mar. 1835.

[O]ur Collection of orchideae: Paxton to Duke, 19 Mar. 1835.

twenty-five thousand: Eric Hansen, *Orchid Fever: A Horticultural Tale of Love, Lust and Luracy*, London, Methuen, 2001, p. 59.

mermaid's hand: Prudence Leith-Ross, *The John Tradescants. Gardeners to the Rose and Lily Queen*, London, Peter Owen, 1998, p. 153.

232   *botanic gardens in the growing Empire:* Donald P. McCracken, *Gardens of Empire. Botanical Institutions of the Victorian Empire*, London and Washington, Leicester University Press, 1997.

new type of packing case: John Gibson to Paxton, 12 Sept. 1835, Chatsworth India Correspondence.

Wardian cases: Nathaniel Bagshaw Ward, *On the Growth of Plants in Closely Glazed Cases*, London, 1852 (first publ. 1842), pp. 36–7.

235   *scale model of Great Stove:* Chatsworth Account Book, 1836.

Duke took the model to London: Duke's diary, 1, 2 Dec. 1835.

in imitation of Chatsworth: Paxton to Sarah Paxton, 26 Jan. 1836.

236   *clapping his hands like:* J. W. Masters (Wallich's assistant) to Paxton, 16 Mar. 1835, Chatsworth, India Correspondence.

237   *Indian savages would kill:* Miss Eden to Duke, 27 Sept. 1836, Ibid.

I wish they knew: Gibson to Nathaniel Wallich, 11 Oct. 1836, Ibid.

238   *drunk with Chatsworth:* Duke's diary, 2 Aug. 1836.

steam-driven machine: For the rationale behind Paxton's invention, his lecture at the Society of Arts, 13 Nov. 1850; *Illustrated London News*, 16 Nov. 1850, p. 385.

a rumbling noise: Paxton to Boulton & Watt, 20 Jul. 1836, quoted in Chadwick 1961a, p. 77.

foundation stone: 29 Sept. 1836, Chatsworth Garden Box Files, Garden Structures.

Description of Chatsworth: Gardener's Magazine, vol. 15 (1839), pp. 450–2.

239   *work of art:* Humphry Repton, Red Book for Sheringham, 1812.

calculated for displaying: J. C. Loudon quoted in Miles Hadfield, *A History of British Gardening*, John Murray, London, 1979, p. 258.

creation of art: Magazine of Botany, vol. 4 (1837), p. 257.

Astounding piece of folly: Duke's diary, 28 Oct. 1836.

240   *Asiatic:* Cavendish 1845, pp. 181, 173.

a continued trance: Wallich to Duke, 2 Nov. 1836, Chatsworth, India Correspondence.

gone wild: Gibson to Paxton, 9 Jan. 1837, Ibid.

most delightful letters: Duke's diary, 25 Jan. 1837.

enormous quantity: Gibson to Paxton, 5 Feb. 1837, Chatsworth, India Correspondence.

Gibson's cabin: Wallich to Duke, 3 Mar. 1837, Ibid.

of the three hundred exotics: Paxton to William Hooker, 26 Aug. and 9 Dec. 1837, Kew, DC vol. 9, English Letters 1837, ff.291–2.

241   *be good:* Queen Victoria's journal, quoted in Briggs 2000, p. 396.

perfectly ugly: The Duke, quoted in Lees-Milne 1998, p. 130.

economic crisis: Briggs 2000, p. 254.

Oliver Twist: Lord Melbourne to Queen Victoria, A. N. Wilson, *The Victorians*, London, Hutchinson, 2002, p. 28.

get Amherstia *down to:* Gibson to Paxton, 14 Jul. 1837, Chatsworth, India Correspondence.

in a grand fuss: Duke's diary, 17 Jul. 1837.

[T]here is not in England: Duke to Sir James B. Carnac, 19 Jul. 1837, Chatsworth, India Correspondence.

242   *to lavish [his] love:* Paxton to Sarah, 22 Jul. 1837.

Garden. Paxton. The Amherstia: Duke's diary, 4 Sept. 1837.

Natural habitat: Magazine of Botany, vol. 4 (1837), p. 82.

new adventure: Paxton calls for a subscription to the expedition, Kew, DC vol. 9, English Letters 1837, f.290; and Paxton to William Hooker, 9 Dec. 1837, Ibid., f.292.

243   *bears and women:* Agreement and contract of the expedition, and chronology of the journey, Violet Markham, *Paxton and the Bachelor Duke*, London, Hodder & Stoughton, 1935, p. 68.

obliged to drink: Quoted in Ibid., p. 81.

rejoiced at thoughts: Duke's diary, 21 Aug. 1838.

terrible stew: Paxton to Sarah, 2 Oct. 1838.

244   *grand leader of the band:* Ibid.

I am almost like: Ibid.

[a] little bored: Duke's diary, 12 Nov. 1838.

Progress update on the Great Conservatory: John Gregory to Paxton, 19 Oct. 1838.

warping the timber ribs: For the method of bending the timber, *Magazine of Botany,* vol. 8 (1841), pp. 255–6, and *Illustrated London News*, 16 Nov. 1850, p. 385. King's Cross Station: John Hix, *The Glasshouse*, London, Phaidon, 1996, p. 197; Brunel's viaduct: Colquhoun 2003, p. 72.

245   *Scaffolding accident:* Sarah to Paxton, 16 Dec. 1838.

Amherstia & daughter: Sarah to Paxton, 1 Jan. 1839.

[W]hat cannot be done: Paxton reporting to Sarah, 23 Feb. 1839.

own wretched unworthiness: Duke's diary, 17 and 18 Apr. 1839.

246   *saw a thousand beauties:* Paxton to Duke, 23 May 1839.

    glass panels: Ibid.

    decline the order: Paxton's lecture at the Society of Arts, *Illustrated London News*, 16 Nov. 1850, p. 385.

    cathedral: Gardener's Magazine, vol. 15 (1839), p. 450.

    a total failure: Paxton to Duke, 29 May 1839.

    gleaming like a silver: Gardeners' Chronicle, 8 Jan. 1842.

247   *really gigantic job:* Paxton to Sarah, 28 Aug. 1840.

    Horticultural community sceptical: Duke to Paxton, 27 Sept. 1840.

    tree transplantation: Henry Steuart, *The Planter's Guide*, London (first publ. 1827), William Blackwood & Sons, 1848, pp. 26–33.

    weeping ash: Leicester Journal, 26 Feb. 1836.

    palm trees: The description of the transportation of the palms is based on Paxton's accounts for 'Expenses Incurred in Conveying the Great Palms to Chatsworth', 1840, Chatsworth, uncatalogued material.

    transplanting machine: Chatsworth Account Book 1840.

248   *arrival of palm tree:* Chatsworth, unpublished notebook of James White (under-gardener), 24 Sept. 1840.

    bill for £726: 'Expenses Incurred in Conveying the Great Palms to Chatsworth', 1840, Chatsworth, uncatalogued material.

    plant orders: Chatsworth Account Books 1840–3.

    prevent deprivation: Chatsworth Account Book 1841.

    calico and fumigation machine: Chatsworth Account Books 1841, 1843.

    colour theories: Magazine of Botany, vol. 1 (1834), p. 154; vol. 14 (1847), pp. 160–1.

249   *Here is an event:* Duke to Paxton, Nov. 1843.

    presence would retard: George Ridgway (the steward) to Duke, 12 Nov. 1843.

    biggest event: The description of the party and the garden decorations is based on an article in the *Illustrated London News*, 9 Dec. 1843; Paxton's letters to Sarah, 15, 16 Nov. 1843; programmes of the queen's visit (Chatsworth Settlement Trust); *Annual Register 1843* and *Derby Mercury*, 23 Sept. 1840.

250   *free of irregularities: Magazine of Botany*, vol. 8 (1841), p. 136. On Paxton's advice for garden layouts, *Magazine of Botany*, vol. 8 (1841), p. 186; vol. 9 (1842), p. 181.

    Plants in the conservatory: Cavendish 1845, pp. 174–9; William Adam, *The Gem of the Peak, Or Matlock, Bath and Its Vicinity*, London, Longman (edns of 1838, 1843, 1845, 1851); Robert Aughtie's drawings, Bessie Harley and Jessie Harley, *A Gardener at Chatsworth: Three Years in the Life of Robert Aughtie, 1848–1851*, Self-Publishing Association, 1992; *Derby Mercury*, 23 Sept. 1840; catalogues: 'The Great Conservatory at Chatsworth', 1891, compared to 'Catalogue of Plants Grown at Chatsworth', c. 1840 (Chatsworth Settlement Trust). The birds and fish are mentioned in the *Illustrated London News*, 9 Dec. 1843; entries for 'bread for the monkeys' can be found in the Chatsworth

Account Books (e.g. 1840, 1842 and 1843).

250   *mountain[s] of light:* Cavendish 1845, p. 178.

251   *most stupendous and:* Queen Victoria's journal, 1 Dec. 1843, quoted in Deborah Duchess of Devonshire, *The Garden at Chatsworth*, London, Frances Lincoln, 1999, p. 69.
      Bengal lights: Harriet Mundy to Mary Frampton, 6 Dec. 1843, *The Journal of Mary Frampton: from the year 1779 until the year 1846*, ed. Harriet Mundy, London, Sampson Low & Co., 1885, pp. 421–2.

252   *two hundred men:* Charles Greville, 13 Dec. 1843, *The Greville Memoirs*, ed. Henry Reeve, London, Longmans, Green & Co., 1888, vol. 5, p. 220.
      I would like that: Duke of Wellington quoted in Lees-Milne 1998, p. 155.
      chemicals and manures: 'for chemical tests and apparatus' and 'for analysing soil', Chatsworth Account Book 1845.
      garden engines: Chatsworth Account Book 1848.
      three thousand pots: Gardener's Magazine, vol. 15 (1839), p. 452.

253   *gravity-fed fountain:* Description of the Emperor's Fountain based on Paxton's article in the *Magazine of Botany*, vol. 11 (1844), pp. 223–7.
      monster fountain: Ibid., p. 223.
      low and nervous: Duke's diary, 14 Jul. 1844.

254   *Duke's expenses:* Chadwick 1961a, p. 77.
      O Paxton!: Duke's diary, 15 Jul. 1844.
      It is well I follow: Duke to Paxton, 4 Sept. 1844.
      grandest triumph: Paxton to Sarah, 27 Aug. 1844.
      Rock Garden: Paxton published numerous articles about rock gardens, such as *Magazine of Botany*, vols 5 (1838), 8 (1841), 12 (1845). For rock gardens in general, Elliott 1986.

255   *Boulders from abandoned quarry:* Colquhoun 2003, p. 113.
      Art has been triumphant: S. C. Hall, 'A Day at Chatsworth', in *Art Journal*, 1851.
      The spirit of some: Cavendish 1845, p. 174.
      tree made of copper: George Hall, *The History of Chesterfield*, London, Whitaker & Co., 1839, p. 420.
      railway: Derrick Beckett, *Brunel's Britain*, Newton Abbot, David & Charles, 1980; L.T.C. Rolt, *Victorian Engineering*, London, Allen Lane, 1970.
      £35,000: Chadwick 1961b, p. 239.
      the command of every: Charles Dickens on Paxton, M. H. Spielmann, *The History of 'Punch'*, London, Paris and Melbourne, Cassell & Co., 1895, p. 84.

256   *two possible routes:* Tim Warner, 'The Railway that Never Was', in *Derbyshire Life and Countryside*, vol. 54 (Jan. 1989).
      Duke called for his gardener: Paxton to Sarah, 10 Apr. 1848.

257   *That's the way to:* Paxton to his friends at *Punch*, quoted in Colquhoun 2003, p. 149.
      I defy you to agitate: Quoted in Briggs 2000, p. 184.
      first train: Robert Aughtie, 4 Jun. 1849, transcribed in Harley and Harley 1992, p. 152.

257   *two thousand teetotallers:* Robert Aughtie, 26 Jun. 1849, Ibid., p. 155.

special permission: Adam 1843, p. 149, and for descriptions of parties in the garden, Robert Aughtie, 18, 20, 21, 24, 26, 27 Jun. 1849, transcribed in Harley and Harley 1992, pp. 110, 154–5.

258   *that the plant should:* Paxton to Hooker, 30 Jul. 1849, Kew DC vol. 28, English Letters K–Z 1849, f.149.

travel times: Robert Aughtie, 2 May 1850, transcribed in Harley and Harley 1992, p. 181.

259   *progress of Victoria regia:* Based on letters between Paxton and the Duke.

a large prickly bud appeared: Paxton to Duke, 2 Nov. 1849.

no words can describe: Ibid.

flowering of Victoria regia: W. Hooker and W. Fitch, *Victoria Regia, or Illustrations of the Royal Water Lily*, London, Reeve & Benham, 1851; Sir Robert Schomburgk's descriptions reprinted in Richard Mabey (ed.), *The Oxford Book of Nature Writing*, Oxford, Oxford University Press, 1995, pp. 110–12; *Illustrated London News*, 16 Nov. 1849.

the sight [. . . that] is: Paxton to Hooker, 11 Nov. 1849, Kew, DC vol. 28, English Letters K–Z, f.151.

260   *Annie on the leaf:* Paxton to Sarah, 25 Nov. 1849.

261   *not the production of:* Paxton's lecture at the Society of Arts, 13 Nov. 1850, in *Illustrated London News*, 16 Nov. 1850, p. 385.

beautiful example of natural: Paxton's lecture at the Society of Arts, 13 Nov. 1850, in *Transactions of the Society of Arts, Manufactures and Commerce*, vol. 57 (Dec. 1851), p. 6.

Lily House: The Gardeners' Chronicle, 31 Aug. 1850, pp. 548–9.

262   *Great Exhibition:* Gilbert Herbert, *Pioneers of Prefabrication. The British Contribution in the Nineteenth Century*, Baltimore, Johns Hopkins University Press, 1978; Hermione Hobhouse, *The Crystal Palace and the Great Exhibition*, London and New York, Athlone Press, 2002; Asa Briggs, *Iron Bridge to Crystal Palace. Impact and Images of the Industrial Revolution*, London, Thames & Hudson, 1979; John R. Davis, *The Great Exhibition*, Stroud, Sutton Publishing, 1999; Colquhoun 2003; letters between Paxton and the Duke, and between Paxton and Sarah.

very leisure would kill: Charles Dickens, 'The Private History of the Palace of Glass', in *Household Words*, vol. 43 (18 Jan. 1851), p. 387.

enchanted: Paxton to Sarah, 15 Jul. 1850.

the unaltered gardener: Duke's diary, 24 Jul. 1850.

263   *fostering hand:* Paxton to Duke, 13 Oct. 1850.

Opening of the Great Exhibition: Illustrated London News, 3, 10 May 1851.

264   *Look, look, there's:* Duke to Frederick Leveson Gower, transcribed in Frederick Leveson Gower, *Bygone Years*, London, John Murray, 1905, p. 43.

parade the architect about: Duke to Leveson Gower, Ibid.

Chapter 7 Hestercombe

266 *green and yellow Cadillac:* 'The Portmans and Hestercombe', unpubl. MS, Hestercombe.
very bad house: And for information regarding the house, Edwin Lutyens to Emily Lutyens, 16 Aug. 1903, RIBA, Lutyens Family Papers, LuE/6/5/1(i–v); and Lawrence Weaver, *Houses and Gardens by E. L. Lutyens*, London, Country Life, 1913, pp. 140–6.
seeking commissions: Jane Ridley, *Edwin Lutyens. His Life, His Wife, His Work*, London, Pimlico, 2003, p. 152.
ten thousand acres: Bailey's Magazine of Sports and Pastimes, vol. 73, no. 482 (Apr. 1900), p. 232.

267 *have more money:* Lutyens to Emily, 16 Aug. 1903.
real good sort: And for Portland's paternalism, Lutyens to Emily, 23 Apr. 1904, RIBA, Lutyens Family Papers, LuE/6/8/26(i–ii); T. W. Mayberry, *Orchard and the Portmans*, Taunton, T. W. Mayberry, 1986, pp. 43–4; *Bailey's Magazine of Sports and Pastimes*, vol. 73, no. 482 (Apr. 1900), pp. 231–2.
eating, hospitals and cattle: And following quotes, Lutyens to Emily, 23 Apr. 1904.

268 *little interest in politics: Somerset County Gazette*, 31 Jul. 1909.
a typical self satisfied: Lutyens to Emily, 23 Apr. 1904.
high game: Lutyens to Herbert Baker, 15 Feb. 1903, transcribed in *The Letters of Edwin Lutyens*, ed. Clare Percy and Jane Ridley, London, Collins, 1985, p. 104.

269 *curving and ever prancing:* Edwin Lutyens in his foreword to Francis Jekyll, *Gertrude Jekyll: A Memoir*, London, Jonathan Cape, 1934, p. 7.
voyages of discovery: Ibid., p. 8.
their modest methods: Ibid.

270 *Miss Jekyll has pretty:* Robert Lorimer, quoted in Ridley 2003, p. 124.
engines of warfare: Gertrude Jekyll, *Home and Garden*, London, Longmans, Green & Co., 1900, p. 17.
between quicksilver and suet: Emily to Lutyens, 12 Apr. 1901, RIBA, Lutyens Family Papers, LuE/4/10/7 (i).
best friend a man: Lutyens to Emily, 15 Apr. 1897, transcribed in Percy and Ridley 1985, p. 43.

271 *Lutyens' working practice:* Christopher Hussey, *The Life of Edwin Lutyens*, London, Country Life, 1950, p. 163; O. P. Milne, 'Reminiscences on Sir Edwin Lutyens', in *Architectural Association Journal*, vol. 74, no. 829 (Feb. 1959), p. 232.

272 *unrealistic designs:* An example of this can be seen in Repton's Red Book for Ashridge, where the available contemporary dwarf and climbing roses would not have achieved the effect Repton envisaged for the Rosarium. Richard Gorer, 'The Puzzle of Repton's Roses', *Country Life*, vol. 171i (11 Mar. 1982), p. 654–6.
[M]oney abounds: Lutyens to Emily, 16 Aug. 1903.
electric lighting in 1897: 'The Portmans and Hestercombe', unpubl. MS. By 1919 still only

6% of homes were equipped for electricity. Adrian Forty, *Objects of Desire: Design and Society since 1750*, London, Thames Hudson, 1995, p. 188.

273   *Lutyens' fees:* Based on what he normally charged. Percy and Ridley 1985, p. 44 n. 1.
rush and spend money: Lutyens to Emily, 16 Aug. 1903.

274   *didn't know how to:* Lutyens, quoted in Ridley 2003, p. 163.
has any influence: Lutyens to Emily, 19 Sept. 1899, transcribed in Percy and Ridley 1985, p. 80.
[T]o-day will prove: Lutyens to Emily, 16 Aug. 1903.
a wonderful way with: Milne 1959, p. 232.
nonsense games and comfy: Lutyens to Emily, 15 Apr. 1897, transcribed in Percy and Ridley 1985, p. 43.
[B]oth these crafts must: And Jekyll and Lutyens' work practice, Cherry Lewis (ed.), *Gertrude Jekyll. The Making of a Garden: An Anthology*, Woodbridge, Garden Art Press, 2000, p. 27; Jane Brown, *Gardens of a Golden Afternoon*, London, Allen Lane, 1982, pp. 102–5.
Everybody wants me: Lutyens to Emily, 13 Apr. 1904, RIBA, Lutyens Family Papers, LuE/6/8/14(i).

275   *Hudson and Lutyens:* Christopher Hussey, 'The Making of *Country Life*', in *Country Life*, vol. 141i (12 Jan. 1967), p. 54.
Hudson recommended Lutyens: Ridley 2003, p. 154; Keith Middlemas, *The Life and Times of Edward VII*, London, Weidenfeld & Nicolson, 1972, p. 43.
life in the country: Anne Helmreich, *The English Garden and National Identity*, Cambridge, Cambridge University Press, 2002, pp. 10–11; Jamie Camplin, *The Rise of the Plutocrats. Wealth and Power in Edwardian England*, London, Constable, 1978, pp. 92–5, 253; Martin Wiener, *English Culture and the Decline of the Industrial Spirit 1850–1980*, London, Penguin, 1981, p. 66.

276   *traditional craft techniques:* Mary Lutyens, 'Sir Edwin Lutyens', in *Lutyens: The Work of the English Architect Sir Edwin Lutyens*, exhibition catalogue, Hayward Gallery, London, Arts Council of Great Britain, 1981, p. 13.

277   *get Hestercombe done:* Lutyens to Emily, 18 Oct. 1904, RIBA Lutyens Family Papers, LuE/7/3/2(i).
redesign the large sunken plot: H. Avray Tipping, 'Hestercombe II – The Seat of the Hon. Edward W. Berkeley Portman', in *Country Life*, vol. 24, no. 615 (17 Oct. 1908), p. 526.
plant plans: Reef Point Collection, folder 77, file IV, item 9, Hestercombe, 'The Square Garden'.
fifteen-strong team: Photograph of the gardening staff in 1914, Somerset Record Office, C/FB/35.
batches of plants: Jekyll, notebook 9, 13 Dec. 1904, Godalming Museum.
My prices should not: Reef Point Collection, drawer 9, file 192, item 28; gardeners at

Munstead Wood, Sally Festing, *Gertrude Jekyll*, London, Viking, 1991, p. 248.

277   *pattern-books:* Reginald Blomfield, *The Formal Garden in England*, London, Macmillan & Co., 1892, pp. 44, 121, 129.

nothing to us: Ibid., pp. 235, 230.

279   *No artificial planting:* Gertrude Jekyll, *Wood and Garden*, London, Longmans, Green & Co., 1899, p. 156.

assembly of unfortunate beings: The Works of John Ruskin, ed. E. T. Cook and Alexander Wedderburn, London, G. Allen, 1902–12, vol. 1, p. 156.

to crude colour: William Robinson, *The English Flower*, London, Hamlyn Publishing, 1985 (first publ. 1883), p. 24.

blush with shame: William Morris, *Hopes and Fears for Art: Five Lectures Delivered in Birmingham, London and Nottingham, 1878–1881*, London, Ellis & White, 1882, p. 128.

280   *look happy:* Jekyll 1899, p. 2.

One cannot but: Gertrude Jekyll, 'The Garden: Changes of Fashion in Gardening', in *Nineteenth Century and After*, vol. 104, no. 618 (Aug. 1928), p. 198.

Kindly nature clothes: Gertrude Jekyll, 'Gardens and Gardens-Craft', in *Edinburgh Review*, vol. 377 (Jul. 1896), p. 165.

Princess Dolgorouki: Lutyens to Emily, 22 Jul. 1905, transcribed in Percy and Ridley 1985, p. 122.

presenting prizes: Somerset County Gazette, 24 Jun. 1905.

Wind in the Willows: First published in 1908; see also Peter Mandler, *The Fall and Rise of the Stately Home*, New Haven and London, Yale University Press, 1997, p. 180.

the garden is going: And party at Hestercombe, Lutyens to Emily, 31 Jul. 1905, RIBA, Lutyens Family Papers, LuE/7/7/9(i–ii).

282   *Lutyens' clothes:* Emily to Lutyens, 5 May 1906, transcribed in Percy and Ridley 1985, p. 130; Ridley 2003, p. 158.

possessed the faculty of: And Lutyens' shyness, Harold Nicolson, quoted in Lutyens 1981, p. 15; Ridley 2003, p. 131.

bubbling friendliness: And sketches, Harold Nicolson, quoted in Lutyens 1981, p. 15; Hussey 1950, pp. 155–6.

the paying Guest: Percy and Ridley 1985, p. 115, n. 1.

two motors and a: Lutyens to Emily, 15 Aug. 1905, transcribed in Ibid., p. 124.

ceased to be either: Oscar Wilde, *The Importance of Being Ernest*, in *Collins Complete Works of Oscar Wilde*, London, HarperCollins, 1999, (first performed 1895) p. 368.

283   *the birth of a new era:* Duke of Windsor, *A King's Story: The Memoirs of HRH the Duke of Windsor KG*, London, Cassell, 1951, p. 48; alterations at Balmoral, Camplin 1978, p. 104.

Plants for the Great Plat: Jekyll, notebook 9, Godalming Museum, Reef Point Collection, folder 77, file IV, item 12.

Some of the most: Jekyll 1899, p. 185.

284   *without learning or observing:* Ibid., p. 4.

    simple and tender charm: Ibid., p. 185.

    make our English waysides: Ibid., p. 4.

    [I]n looking on the yew: 'The Fine Arts Society's Gallery' (exhibition review), in *Illustrated London News*, 14 Mar. 1891, p. 350.

    The common flowers: J. D. Sedding quoted in Andrew Clayton-Payne and Brent Elliott, *Victorian Flower Gardens*, London, Weidenfeld & Nicolson, 1988, p. 45.

    In the older days: Gertrude Jekyll, *Old West Surrey*, London, Longmans, Green & Co., 1904, p. viii.

285   *It is impossible to:* Ibid.

    of our working folk: Ibid., p. 249.

286   *solid furniture of pure:* Ibid., p. viii.

    hybrids: Morris's opinion, Morris 1882, pp. 124–6.

    Thomas Hardy's early novels: Wiener 1981, pp. 52–3.

287   *Under its spell we: Daily News* quoted in Wiener 1981, pp. 49–50.

288   *out to the land:* George Cadbury quoted in J. Marsh, *Back to the Land. The Pastoral Impulse in England from 1880 to 1914*, London, Quartet Books, 1982, p. 222.

289   *town game:* Lutyens to Emily, 4 Aug. 1904, transcribed in Percy and Ridley 1985, p. 115.

    Jekyll's commissions: Michael Tooley's chronological list of Gertrude Jekyll's commissions specifies eleven for 1905. However, the list gives only a rough indication of the number of projects she was working on at any one time, as the dating of some commissions is not quite accurate (Hestercombe, e. g., is listed under 1908), and Jekyll may not have been working on all of the projects simultaneously. M. Tooley and P. Arnander, *Gertrude Jekyll: Essays on the Life of a Working Amateur*, Witton le Wear, Michaelmas Books, 1995, pp. 198–202.

    Jekyll at Munstead: Festing 1991, pp. 180, 204; Francis Jekyll 1934, p. 135.

    [P]ray that I may work: Luytens quoted in Hussey 1950, p. 146.

290   *I get so afraid lest we:* Emily to Lutyens, Jul. 1905, quoted in Ridley 2003, p. 159; for Lutyens' work practice, Milne 1959, pp. 232–3.

    hard at it eating: Lutyens to Emily, n.d., RIBA, Lutyens Family Papers, LuE/7/11/2(i). Although not dated, from its location in the archive the event may have occurred around Oct./Nov. 1905.

    Portman's grandfather: S. T. Moore, *History of Bryanston*, 1993, p. 173.

    make the land less: And the political situation, Henry Campbell-Bannerman quoted in David Cannadine, *The Decline and Fall of the British Aristocracy*, New Haven and London, Yale University Press, 1990, pp. 69, 452; and Camplin 1978, pp. 120–7, 128.

    unearned increments: Cannadine 1990, p. 61.

291   *Land gives so much:* Anthony Trollope, *The Last Chronicle of Barset*, London, Penguin Classics, 2002 (first publ. 1867), p. 605.

291   *I have to go to:* Lutyens to Emily, 25 Apr. 1906, RIBA, Lutyens Family Papers, LuE/8/1/24.

      cattle and sheep sale: Somerset County Ga*zette*, 7 Apr. 1906.

      Portman has accepted my: Lutyens to Emily, 5 May 1906, RIBA, Lutyens Family Papers, LuE/8/2/6(ii).

      Plan for east part of garden: Lutyens' Plan of the Gardens and Orangery, July 1906, Godalming Museum, Reef Point Collection, folder 77, file IV, item 7.

293   *Plans for front of Orangery:* Ibid., item 4; Jekyll, notebook 9, Godalming Museum.

      big trees in the grass: Jekyll, notebook 9, Godalming Museum.

      plans for the Dutch Garden: Gertrude Jekyll, Hestercombe, Planting Plan for Raised East Garden, Somerset Record Office, C/FB/18; in Jan. 1907 Jekyll sent plants for the buttress-wall flower border of the eastern section of the garden, Godalming Museum, Reef Point Collection, folder 77, file IV, item 5; and for the Pergola borders, Ibid., item 4.

295   *Pergola:* The planting of the Pergola is described in Tipping, 17 Oct. 1908, p. 530.

      not only as a distinctive: Gentrude Jekyll, *Garden Ornament*, Woodbridge, Antique Collectors' Club, 1982 (first publ. 1918), pp. 251, 293.

      Tennyson's celebrates: 'Song', ll. 9–12, *Alfred Tennyson: Poems*, ed. Lord Hallam Tennyson, London, Macmillan, 1907, vol. 1, p. 54.

      use the plants: Gertrude Jekyll, *Colour in the Flower Garden*, London, Country Life, 1908, pp. vi, 9.

296   *Merely having them:* Ibid., 1908, p. vi.

      in its best expression: Gertrude Jekyll in her preface to Francis King, *The Well Considered Garden*, New York, Charles Scribner's Sons, 1915, p. x.

      Colours and planting of borders: Mavis Batey, 'Gertrude Jekyll and the Arts and Crafts Movement', in Tooley and Arnander 1995, p. 70; Brent Elliott, *Victorian Gardens*, London, B. T. Batsford, 1986, pp. 206–7. For the planting of the borders: Gertrude Jekyll, Hestercombe, Planting Plans for Borders and Walls facing South, Somerset Record Office, C/FB/18; notebook 9 (accounts for borders 1, 2 and 3, and wall A), Godalming Museum; and Penelope Hobhouse, *Gertrude Jekyll on Gardening*, London, National Trust and William Collins, 1983, p. 145.

      difference between a garden: Gertrude Jekyll in preface to King 1915, p. x.

297   *Planting in the Rill Gardens:* Jekyll, notebook 9, Godalming Museum.

      The wide, paved ledges: Gertrude Jekyll, *Wall and Water Gardens*, London, Country Life, 1901, p. 176.

      Lutyens' client cancelled: Ridley 2003, p. 173.

298   *No one has any:* Lutyens to Emily, quoted in Ibid.

      I see there is going: Lutyens to Emily, 8 Aug. 1907, RIBA, Lutyens Family Papers, LuE/9/1/3.

298   *I have LOTS to do:* And following quotes, Lutyens to Emily, 16 Aug. 1907, ibid., LuE/9/1/14(i).

Don't forget Bumps: Lutyens to Emily, 26 Aug. 1907, Ibid., LuE/9/2/7(i).

Bumps [was] laden: Emily to Lutyens, 22 Aug. 1907, transcribed in Percy and Ridley 1985, p. 141.

party of suffragettes: Lutyens to Emily, 16 Aug. 1907.

pamphleteering on the beach: The title of the pamphlet was *Votes for Women*, Emily to Lutyens, 9 Aug. 1909, transcribed Percy and Ridley 1985, p. 173. For Emily's involvement in suffragette activity, see Ibid., pp. 105, 151, and Ridley 2003, p. 169.

299   *Jekyll's plants, February 1908:* Jekyll, notebook 36, Godalming Museum.

to improve my . . . speech: Lutyens to Emily, 6 Apr. 1908, RIBA, Lutyens Family Papers, LuE/9/6/2(i).

my hand shook: Lutyens to Emily, 9 Apr. 1908, Ibid., LuE/9/6/6(i).

300   *I am so sorry Asquith:* Lutyens to Emily, 6 Apr. 1908.

that damned Welsh attorney: Cannadine 1990, p. 227.

fine foliage of pretences: And following quotes, H. G. Wells, *Tono Bungay*, London, Macmillan & Co., 1912 (first publ. 1909), pp. 11–12, and Mandler 1997, p. 173.

301   *an architect can be:* Tipping 17 Oct. 1908, p. 530, and 10 Oct. 1908, p. 490.

stepping into another world: Francis Jekyll, and G. C. Taylor (ed.), *A Gardener's Testament. A Selection of Articles and Notes by Gertrude Jekyll*, London, Country Life, 1937, p. 44.

oppression of the antiquated: David Lloyd George quoted in Cannadine 1990, p. 69.

super-tax: Bruce K. Murray, *The People's Budget 1909/10: Lloyd George and Liberal Politics*, Oxford, Clarendon Press, 1980, pp. 136–7, 154–61.

302   *not a Budget but:* Lord Rosebery, quoted in John Grigg, *Lloyd George: The People's Champion, 1902–1911*, London, Eyre Methuen, 1978, p. 198.

an institution absolutely: Churchill's speech 'The Budget', 26 Jul. 1909, at the Budget League Meeting in Norwich, repr. in *Winston Churchill: His Complete Speeches, 1897–1963*, ed. Robert Rhodes James, New York and London, Chelsea House Publishers, 1974, vol. 2, p. 129.

Lutyens and Portman fishing: Lutyens to Emily, 25 Jul. 1909, RIBA, Lutyens Family Papers, LuE/10/4/5.

demonstration at Blandford: *Somerset County Gazette*, 31 Jul. 1909.

five hundred . . . ordinary men: Quoted in B. Gilbert, *Lloyd George. A Political Life*, London, Batsford, 1987, pp. 384–7, 395.

303   *that cad L. George:* Lutyens to Emily, 5 Aug. 1909, transcribed in Percy and Ridley 1985, p. 171.

Feudalism only fails: Lutyens to Emily, 9 Aug. 1909, transcribed in Ibid., p. 174.

man has distinctly asserted: Tipping 10 Oct. 1908, p. 494.

strangled the aristocracy: E. M. Forster quoted in Wiener 1981, p. 72

Index

Note: numbers in *italics* indicate illustrations